Stolen
from

Kent
Stevenson

299-7187

THE CANADIAN REVOLUTION

1985–1995

FROM DEFERENCE TO DEFIANCE

THE CANADIAN REVOLUTION

1985–1995

FROM DEFERENCE TO DEFIANCE

PETER C. NEWMAN

VIKING

Viking
Published by the Penguin Group
Penguin Books Canada Ltd, 10 Alcorn Avenue, Toronto, Ontario,
Canada M4V 3B2
Penguin Books Ltd, 27 Wrights Lane, London W8 5TZ, England
Viking Penguin, a division of Penguin Books U.S.A. Inc., 375 Hudson Street,
New York, New York 10014, U.S.A.
Penguin Books Australia Ltd, Ringwood, Victoria, Australia
Penguin Books (NZ) Ltd, 182-190 Wairau Road, Auckland 10, New Zealand
Penguin Books Ltd, Registered Offices: Harmondsworth, Middlesex, England

First published 1995
10 9 8 7 6 5 4 3 2 1

Copyright © Power Reporting Limited, 1995

Printed and bound in Canada on acid-free paper ∞

Canadian Cataloguing in Publication Data

Newman, Peter C., 1929-
   The Canadian revolution, 1985-1995

ISBN 0-670-86302-5

1. Canada—Politics and government—1984–1993.*
2. Canada—Politics and government—1993–   .*
3. Canada—Economic conditions—1971–1991.*
4. Canada—Economic conditions—1991–   .*
5. Canada—Social conditions—1971–   .* I. Title.

FC630.N48 1995   971.064'7   C95-930593-9
F1034.2.N48 1995

This book is dedicated to
STANLEY NEWCOMB KENTON,
in gratitude for his music, his integrity,
his time signatures, his friendship and his volume.
As with my other books, not a word
was written without his accompaniment
and the memory of his revolutionary spirit.

*"The meaning of a revolution
only becomes clear
after fifty years.
It is like a process of distillation.
The fumes evaporate, while
the essence of the brew
slowly gathers at the bottom."*

—ARTHUR KOESTLER

TABLE OF CONTENTS

PROLOGUE

The Canadian Revolution

*The Revolution that rocked Canada was
the greening of our discontent.*

T HE YEAR 1985 NOW SEEMS as distant as the Boer War. I remember flying to Ottawa from Cordova Bay, a tiny nick on the
southeast coast of Vancouver Island where I then lived. I watched
the runway markers of Victoria's antiquated airport fall away
beneath me. Radar had been installed in the flight tower only a
couple of years earlier; before that, worried air traffic controllers
would monitor incoming aircraft (which they referred to among
themselves as aeroplanes) with binoculars, trying to steady their
hands as they picked appropriate flight patterns.

It was a great time to be Canadian. Spiritual, extra-terrestrial and
royal personages had made neighbourhood rounds and we felt good
about ourselves and our country. We had waved a happy hello that
luminous season to Pope John Paul II, Marc Garneau (our very own
astronaut) and Queen Elizabeth II, whose only family "scandal" was
the benign divorce in 1978 of her sister, Margaret, from Lord
Snowdon. Allan Gregg, the Toronto pollster hired by *Maclean's* to test
the public mood, reported that three-quarters of Canadians had pronounced themselves wholly satisfied with their lot and that an even
larger percentage were optimistic about the future.

At Vancouver I changed planes to board Wardair, paying the fifty-dollar additional fee then charged for Business Class, and settled in for the trans-Canada journey. By that time it was dusk. As the serrated silhouette of the Rockies dropped away and we started to traverse the plains, I thought about my country. I recalled one July evening in 1968, being part of a group that was sitting around a pine table in a refurbished farmhouse near Ottawa, talking politics. Someone mentioned a French book he had been reading, *The Morning of the Magician*, and put forward the tentative notion that Trudeau was a political magician. Even though we were pretty deep into the Beaujolais, nobody hooted in derision. It didn't seem the least bit outrageous, then, to consider that the freshly minted prime minister might be the sorcerer we needed to transcend the complexities of the twentieth century. By the time he resigned sixteen years later, in June 1984, the morning of the magician was well and truly over. But that momentary illusion (or delusion) characterized the kind of time it was.

The great Pooh-Bahs of commerce—Robert Campeau, the Reichmanns and the Bronfman brothers—were flying high. Canada's dollar was strengthened by a booming economy. We believed our bankers knew what they were doing. The CBC-TV flagship current affairs program, "The Journal," hosted by the magnificent Barbara Frum, ruled the air waves. No one could predict that Canada's vaunted United Nations peacekeepers could ever murder a prisoner in cold blood, or that the Red Cross's carelessness could kill. Although they seldom ran on time, the passenger trains at least still ran. The Stanley Cup was not just a national institution, but *the* Canadian icon; the Grey Cup still pitted West against East in a much-loved rivalry. Immigrants and aboriginals "knew their place," and such phenomena as Ralph Klein, free trade, the Bernardo trial, Hibernia, rap music, the GST, Mike Harris, Internet, Lucien Bouchard, psychic hot lines, Kim Campbell, Forrest Gump, Meech Lake, John Wayne Bobbitt and Brian Tobin as turbot saviour had yet to be sprung on an innocent public.

Back in 1985, Canadians seemed so diffident about themselves that they behaved like strangers in their own land, while not feeling at home anywhere else. They neither proclaimed themselves nor the potential of their country and were happy in their ignorance. They had long before given up asserting their identities or challenging the righteous claw of authority. They remained deferential and blindly obedient to the powers-that-be. They fantasized about being Clark Kent instead of Superman.

Treading water became a national sport. You could easily spot the Canadians at any gathering: they were the ones who automatically chose to sit in the least comfortable chair. It was all part of a national affinity for discomfort and self-denial. Winners were frowned upon unless, like Terry Fox or Dr. Norman Bethune, they placed themselves in heroic circumstances that guaranteed their deaths. Winners in any endeavour found themselves having to mumble excuses about how winning had really been an accident that would—with any luck—never happen again. In few other countries would a rising tennis star (Marjorie Blackwood in 1980) firmly set her long-term sights on being among "the top forty tennis players," instead of going for gold. Quebec's Olympic champion speed skater Gaetan Boucher once explained why he competed in the American way: "Canadians come to me and say, 'So, you came in tenth, eh? Well, that's not too bad.' But it is. Compare that with the Americans. They do everything to win, not to finish tenth."

This national trait of becoming modesty had long been explained as the levelling influence on a country whose inhabitants had often been forced to organize and co-operate for survival. But with only the uninspiring imperative of outlasting a cold climate to spur them on, with no pretensions of manifest destiny in sight, Canadians huddled under the polar moon satisfied with their freedoms-from, instead of leaping to exploit freedoms-to. Becoming Canadian required no conversion to a new faith or even a salute, since the country lacked a distinctive flag for the first ninety-eight years of its existence. Founded on social compact rather than individual allegiance, Canadian nationhood proceeded so slowly that it took thirty-eight years after Confederation in 1867 for the other provinces to join—except Newfoundland, which waited another half-century, just to be sure.

Given the glacial nature of change in the Canadian political identity, my experience had left me unprepared for the events of the decade ahead as I flew across the land, that day in 1985. Counting

off the area-rugs of light that signified the great cities of the
Canadian plains, I could not begin to imagine how the next ten years
would transform my country. I could not know that blowing in the
wind was the start of a Revolution.

"When we're honest with ourselves," said Cesar Chavez, the
union leader who organized the Mexican grape pickers in California,
"we must admit that our lives are all that really belongs to us. So it
is how we use our lives that determines what kind of men we are."
The time was coming for Canadians to enrol in such a crusade. As
the shadows in a rock trigger a sculptor's skills and passions, so
what we sensed was wrong with Canada would determine what had
to be excised. Like the sculptor chiselling away at his rock,
Canadians would decide to discard anything or anyone who didn't fit
their vision of a more perfect and more equal society. If revolutions
are triggered by a people determined to upset the established order
of things, then what happened could only be described as
revolutionary.

Ottawa was then buzzing with the arrival in power of the *arriviste*
Boyo from Baie Comeau. His approval rating across the country
topped the charts at 54 per cent. His smiling *habitant* face decorated
the front pages and led the evening newscasts. I could not know, at
the time of my flight to Ottawa in the early winter of 1985, how
much Brian Mulroney—a Conservative, after all—would become
implicated in such revolutionary change.

Mulroney's most significant contribution may have been that he
politicized Canada to an unprecedented pitch. At times it seemed
that hatred of the prime minister was about the only emotion that
brought the country together. Old voting patterns disintegrated and
fresh voting alliances sprang up, as the desire to ensure his ouster
became a significant catalyst for change. Opinion polls in 1991 documented the astounding notion that 12 per cent of Canadians
believed Elvis Presley might be alive in a suburb of Memphis,
about the same number of decided Canadian voters who approved
of Mulroney's performance as prime minister. That free fall from
stratospheric approval ratings was based largely on public reaction
to his obsequious charm, evasive assurances and elastic treatment
of facts. He never told fibs exactly, but his pronouncements narrowed the isthmus between truth and expediency so that wish

became synonymous with action and reason became interchangeable with desire.

For a country that thrived on moderation, Mulroney proved to be
a personal and political extremist. On a personal level, his extravagant lifestyle offended the values of the middle class which had
warmly greeted him as a small-town boy made good. By severing
his working-class roots and opting instead for the conspicuous con-
sumption that became his and Mila's hallmark, he not only denied
his own identity but encouraged Canadians to do the same: abandon
their culture of prudence, civility and tolerance. His personal indul-
gences were paraded before a people who at the time were struggling to cope with falling pay and fewer jobs. This did nothing to
allay suspicions on the political playing field, where he was all Irish
bravado. "Brian cold-turkeyed on alcohol and cold-turkeyed on cigarettes," an exasperated Dalton Camp once advised. "Why can't he
cold-turkey on hyperbole?" But vanity was the one monkey he could
never shake off his back.

Though he was blamed for every sparrow that fell from the sky,
Mulroney was only the most visible agent of the convulsions that
transformed Canada during his regime. Something much more profound and permanent than the gutting of an opportunistic politician
was going on. As *Globe and Mail* columnist Jeffrey Simpson wrote
in his 1993 epic, *Faultlines: Struggling for a Canadian Vision:*
"Canada's traditional political culture cracked like river ice in the
spring." Angry and frustrated, lacking a framework to accommodate
their inexorable impulse for change, Canadians staged a bloodless
Revolution.

The fury that swept the land was visceral. Canadians felt its lash
not so much in the heart or the brain as deep inside the marrow.
Much of the anger had its roots in the recognition—vague, reluctant,
but there all the same—that the politicians whom Canadians had
come to loathe had been chosen, not by pod people or Trekkies, but
by themselves. In Brian Mulroney's case, he was confirmed in
power by popular mandate with two unprecedented majorities.
Mulroney was one of us; no better, no worse, just unlucky enough to
grab power at an impossible time and brave enough to attempt to do
something with it. The thoughtful contemporary political theorist,
J.D.B. Miller, observed that the contempt which people often

express for politicians is "the rage of Caliban at seeing himself in the glass."*

WHAT HAPPENED TO THE COUNTRY IN THE LONG AND TURBULENT season between 1985 and 1995 is the subject of this book. The story is as complicated as the individual and collective psyches of thirty million people, or as simple as a children's film. In Walt Disney's 1940 cartoon feature *Fantasia*, the sorcerer's apprentice is portrayed by a harried Mickey Mouse. In its initial segments, the animation shows a magician wearing a sparkling blue, conically shaped hat. He performs incredible tricks, changing the direction of the ocean's flow and bringing a series of amazing mirages to life. When the magician takes a nap, Mickey puts on his hat and tries to duplicate his tricks. At first all goes smoothly, but Mickey sets loose too many unpredictable forces, including a flood that at first appears to heed his commands but eventually drowns him.

The image doesn't really hold, because Pierre Trudeau was no more the all-knowing magician than Brian Mulroney was Mickey Mouse. But there is no doubt that in trying to govern Canada, the secret is knowing what not to touch, and that in an effort to ensure his place in history, Mulroney ventured so far beyond his mandate that he helped set off the Revolution which eventually overwhelmed him and permanently altered Canada.

At some point during the decisive decade 1985–1995, the country and its people changed. If the Renaissance was the green conclusion to civilization's hardest winter, the Revolution that rocked Canada was the greening of our discontent. There occurred a sudden bursting, like buds in springtime, of those barriers between thought and feeling that had kept Canadians from asserting their individual sovereignties and had left them indentured to authority far beyond its worth.

---

* The reference dates to one of the more influential, but obscure, political tracts of the modern period. French philosopher Ernest Renan, whose thought anticipated the existential anguish of the twentieth century, wrote the "philosophical drama" *Caliban* in 1877; in it, the aristocracy (Prospero and Ariel) lose to democracy (Caliban) because their alchemical spells (traditional sanctions) cannot work against a people infected with positivism. The tract defended republicanism against higher authority, such as the Church.

Deference to authority, the root attitude that separated Canadians from the earth's less timid mortals, had at long last come into open disrepute. As the Mulroney years rolled on and the attitude toward their namesake shifted from simple derision to blind hatred, Canadians set out to challenge that most painful of paradoxes: that in a functioning democracy like Canada, people get the politicians they deserve. By the early 1990s, this sentiment became too painful to endure.

Within a year of the decision to scuttle the Charlottetown Accord voters reduced the Conservatives, the country's founding political party which had provided Canada's alternate government for 55 of the past 126 years, to a pitiful, two-seat rump. The Tories no longer ranked as an official party in the Commons. Shortly afterwards their popular standing in the polls was reduced to 7 per cent, the political basement shared by such fringe movements as Rhinos and Levitators. As though they were slayers of a modern-day Dracula, Canada's voters drove a stake through the heart of Brian Mulroney's party to make sure he would never come back. At the same time, they decimated the New Democratic Party and expressed their regionalist disgust at the national parties by voting for two rogue political movements, the Reform Party of Canada and the Bloc Québécois. With one group advocating a Canada without side deals for Quebec and the other a Quebec without Canada, the stage was set for the 1995 referendum on separation.

The Revolution described in this book was social as much as it was political. The trend of independent thought and consent which began to set Canadians free had been foreshadowed by the feminist movement, one of the few political initiatives to survive the decade and the generation's most fundamental power shift. Feminism, whose language and organizing principles soon began to infiltrate all political dialogue, made possible a much wider assertion of individual autonomy, and thus, empowerment. Suddenly it was permissable to take "control" of one's own life, to not bother with "moderation" if it stood in the way of common sense or the pursuit of worthy goals.

It was only the beginning. The invisible hand of technology had provided citizens with the ammunition for their Revolution. The advent of saturation television coverage of real-time news events, such as the raw footage of the aboriginal standoff at Oka, Quebec, left politicians with no place to hide. The new rules expected open covenants be openly negotiated. But by the decade's end television, which had been the dominant technological force at the beginning of the decade, was being supplanted by the computer. A full-scale rout of authority was guaranteed with the advent of the power of the Internet. Unregulated access to unlimited, cheap information meant the computer channel that was signing up thousands of Canadian recruits daily had changed their world—and ours—by dramatically empowering its users. "If you are not comfortable with anarchy, you may not be comfortable here," warned Mark Skapinker, president of Toronto's Delrina Corp., a software company devoted to the Internet.

With the feeling of personal licence that flowed from their new-found militancy, the subjects of the once-peaceable kingdom became cranky, spiteful and troublesome to govern. The thrust of public anger was directed at the politicians but it extended to most of the country's sacrosanct institutions. "They're not only angry at themselves for having been too deferential for too many years," noted the pollster Allan Gregg in the fall of 1992, "they want to punish those people in power who stole their dreams."

A year later, when he climbed off Kim Campbell's express train to political oblivion, Gregg seemed much less sure of himself. "These days, you can't get 88 per cent of Canadians to agree that it's Friday," he complained. "I think I'll take some time off." The only comfort to be drawn from Gregg's confusion was that no one was exempt from it. No matter how many so-called experts paraded their instant wisdom across the nation's television screens, nobody knew what was really going on. No matter how authoritative the TV news anchors sounded, they were only as wise as their teleprompters. Unplugged, these glorified meat puppets would have nothing to say. The singular course of events had left them, like members of the Canadian Establishment, facing the world with the uncomprehending gaze of drowning guppies.

It was that kind of decade.

Canadians arrived at their private epiphanies in as many ways as there were people. The nation became theatre, performing a sub-Arctic update of Pirandello—thirty million characters in search of an author. The prerequisite for Canadian citizenship—inner silence, a form of emotional detachment so profound that nothing could

reach or touch it—was shattered. The move from deference to defiance was based not, like most revolutions, on a shock-troop of rebels
grabbing power from authority, but on the much more sensible
notion that men and women only lose their chance for freedom when
they abdicate its quest. The time had come to stop pretending that
being Canadian was some kind of inside joke dreamed up by a bored
God with a highly developed sense of the absurd.

The pages that follow trace the start and the course of that
Revolution and attempt to describe what happened and why. The
new Canada created by one of history's few bloodless revolts is still
in the process of defining itself. But whatever happens next, life in
these northern latitudes will never be the same. For it was a
Revolution of the spirit that Canadians launched in the mid-1980s
and, as Marcel Proust observed a long time ago: "The real voyage of
discovery consists not in seeing a new landscape, but in having
new eyes."

I THE CANADIAN REVOLUTION

ONE

THE GREENING
OF OUR
DISCONTENT

Counting the Ways

*"It's the first time in history that a government has
overthrown a country."*
FOLK SINGER BOB BOSSIN

ONCE OR TWICE A CENTURY, like a hurricane that eludes the
meteorologists' charts, the breezes of history unexpectedly
accelerate and blow away the touchstones by which a people live.
That was the painful, yet exhilarating process Canadians underwent
between 1985 and 1995.

It was a witch's brew of a decade. Instead of being able to apply
past experience to predict future trends, most Canadians at the close
of those turbulent years felt the continuity of their age being cut.
They knew only that what came later would be radically different
from that which had come before.

True to the post-modern character of the 1990s, authority was
deconstructed from institutions to individuals. Freed from official
restraint, people felt liberated enough to choose everything for
themselves, from their sexual orientation to their sense of nationhood. Deprived of their emotional moorings to the piers of authority,
a restless and militant population drifted off into a Revolution of no
mean proportions.

3

While it was still better to be Canadian than to be anything else and while Canada remained one of the most envied places on the planet, the country's operational code was thrown into question. The ingrained ethic that for more than a century had governed Canadians' collective behaviour and individual reactions—or lack of them—came unglued.

The nation's founding maxim of "peace, order and good government" no longer fit a people who felt their lives had become disorderly and anything but peaceful. The notion of government being good, let alone tolerable, was a dream.

Because he was prime minister for most of the revolutionary decade, Brian Mulroney bore the brunt of the public's disdain. "Give us twenty years, and you'll not recognize this country!" he pledged at the beginning of his stewardship. His words came true with a vengeance in less than half that time—but not in the way Mulroney had intended. The Progressive Conservative government risked unpopularity by sponsoring a series of measures required to modernize Canada's economy for the twenty-first century. That was as brave as it was necessary, but instead of being hailed as a radical reformer the prime minister aroused more fear and loathing than any previous Canadian head of government. Bob Bossin, the Gabriola, B.C. singer-satirist, spoke for most of his countryfolk when he described the situation as being unique. "It's the first time in history," he proclaimed, "that a government has overthrown a country."

National in scope and unforgiving in nature, the shared sense of affront moved far beyond the rational boundaries that had traditionally held Canadian tempers in check. If the country weren't so damn big and if the airlines had posted a seat sale for the occasion, Ottawa's parliament buildings would have been stormed in the style of a Latin American *coup d'état*. When Elijah Harper rejected the Meech Lake Accord—which, along with the sinking of the Charlottetown agreement, ranked among the decade's most significant acts of defiance—his weapon of choice was a feather. You can't get a Revolution more Canadian than that.

The absence of mayhem didn't mean that not much happened. What ultimately decides the authenticity of a revolution is not its acts of violence, social disruptions, mass demonstrations or other open challenges to established authority. To be authentic, a revolution doesn't require that blood be spilled (although in the colour-television age, blood-letting lends popular uprisings the required graphic legitimacy), but that at a given point in time, a society's animating ideas and most of the institutions which reflect them are weakened to the point of being discarded.

It was one of many steps but such a moment occurred on October 26, 1992, the day the energy of a whole generation reached its flashpoint of dissent. It was the day of the Great Referendum, when the majority of Canadians went against the advice of the country's élites by rejecting the Charlottetown compromises. Here was a proposition unanimously endorsed by the ruling classes, including the paladins of big business and leaders of every national political party, most unions, aboriginal organizations, mainstream journalists (including me), cultural groups and those observers who count themselves among the enlightened. Yet in the referendum that followed, the carefully crafted deal unravelled like a poorly knit sweater. Nearly eight million Canadians rose up and cried "No!" defiantly overturning the constitutional smorgasbord prepared by their best and their brightest. "The link between the Charlottetown Accord's defeat and our retreat from deference," says Michael Adams of Toronto's Environics Research Group, "was simply this: we asked ourselves, 'Why should we defer to our betters, when our betters aren't really better?'"

The political mainstream was reduced overnight to a muddy creek. The poet Karl Shapiro's passionate cry that "defiance of definition is the central meaning of the Jewish consciousness" applied equally to Canadians of the 1990s. Open defiance shouted down the stern warnings of an Establishment that had long demanded—and received—deferential acquiescence to its wishes. The Canadian Establishment's ability to have its way had traditionally depended on the diffidence of its subjects. The revolt that erupted across the once-dormant countryside thus drastically reduced the Establishment's reach and tempered its clout.

The combined defeat of the two constitutional accords turned out to be the Vietnam of the Canadian Establishment. It had been a long time coming, but the imperturbable possession of power that had characterized Canada's élites had finally been shattered.

The dirty little secret was out: the policies of the élites no longer reflected the public will. The verdict followed: the power of the élites failed to impose its political agenda. "When the Charlottetown Accord collapsed, the middle ground had been eroded," noted Peter

Leslie, a professor of political science at Queen's University. "We are now in a different game." Ken Battle, head of the Ottawa think-tank Caledon Institute of Social Policy, was more succinct: "The failure of Meech and Charlottetown has not gone away," he said, three years after both deals were dead. "It's still with us. The Con-federate Army is in Ottawa. It's called the Bloc Québécois."

Drastic measures would be required to rebuild the commonweal. The old Canada would have to die before a new nation, once again rel-evant to its citizens, could be born. It was chillingly reminiscent of the American artillery officer who, during the Vietnam War, explained away the saturation bombing of the once-idyllic settlement of Ben Tre: "It became necessary to destroy the village in order to save it."

Establishments die hard and with a vengeance. How an Establishment organizes itself determines how a nation pursues its objectives. For more than a century Canada had been run by a sur-prisingly compact, self-perpetuating *junta* numbering perhaps a thousand, linked more closely to each other than to their country. It didn't matter very much who was in office, since the Establishment placed its operatives within the hierarchies of both old-line parties which alternated in power. Members of this unchanging cluster constituted a self-selected extra-parliamentary government, whose members shared beliefs and values, habits of thought and action and, above all, common enemies. They may have been too busy, as one of them put it, "to kiss babies at summer picnics," but if they didn't run for public office they determined who did, or at least which set of political ideas carried the day. After the burial of the Charlottetown Accord, Canada's establishments—all of them—began to lose their authority and, of even greater importance, their self-confidence. It is a self-evident rule that any élite lacking in self-confidence no longer constitutes an élite. Gordon Cunningham, chairman of London Life, allowed that "a subtle but powerful shift took place in this country. Normally recalcitrant, quiet and uncom-mitted Canadians began to speak out."

They did indeed, in a transformation of such magnitude that it sig-nalled nothing less than a fundamental mutation in the national char-acter. Between 1985 and 1995, the dominant mood of Canadians had shifted from deference to defiance.

DEFERENCE TO AUTHORITY had been a gospel to live by for so many generations that rejecting it was a revolutionary act. That servile attitude dated back to the country's earliest commercial history, which in turn was influenced by the habits of its prey, those glorified water rats with the flat tails known as beavers.

The first Europeans into the wilderness were the Scots fur traders of the Hudson's Bay Company. From their landing points on the desolate shores of Hudson Bay and later, from their colonial head-quarters at Montreal, the Bay men were driven ever inland by the beaver because the furry critters were not nomadic animals. Beavers spend their lives in one lodge with one mate, building dams, grooming themselves, warning each other of danger with a tail that sounds like a snapped castanet and felling an annual average of 216 trees. Each time a beaver pond was fished out the Bay men had to move on, which was mainly how the country's western and northern frontiers were explored. The Hudson's Bay Company may have been history's ultimate absentee landlord, having sent its first ships into Hudson Bay in 1670, though none of its London-based governors bothered visiting the place until 264 years later, in 1934. But the British money men ran their outposts with an iron fist. They treated their North American holdings like a private hunting preserve until the huge territory, which at its apogee covered a twelfth of the earth's land surface, was sold at an enormous profit to the Canadian government in 1870.

The psychic legacy of that oppressive empire was enormous. The Hudson's Bay Company forts, which at various times numbered nearly a thousand, were operated like the company towns they were. The HBC owned and ran everything. To live and work in these bush settlements meant deferring to the HBC's rules and regulations, no questions asked. "Masters of the Company's posts is like kings," complained "Lame" Annie Redsky, a local cook who worked for the HBC at its York Factory post on Hudson Bay in 1912. "You can be birthed and died without their consent, but that's about all."

Because the nature of frontier development inordinately influences the character of the society it spawns, that early attitude of obedience and fear of distant authority was firmly implanted within the Canadian psyche. The tiny HBC forts were the ultimate expression of what the great literary critic Northrop Frye dubbed Canada's "garrison mentality." Frye described such communities as providing "all that their members have in the way of distinct human values . . . [they] are compelled to feel a great respect for the law and order that holds them together, yet confronted with a huge, unthinking, menacing and formidable physical setting."

That tendency to defer to the corporate authority within the garrison, and to nature beyond it, was one of the most significant differences between the Canadian and American frontiers. Lacking any corporate infrastructure, the American Wild West developed in exactly the opposite direction. There, rugged individualism became the way of life, enforced with the fabled six-shooter. Every man and woman was on his or her own, challenging or escaping authority, never catering to it.

America's early frontier was animated by professional gunfighters, crooked sheriffs, lynch mobs, galloping posses, high noon shoot-outs, saloon fights and Indian wars. "That we are a very violent people," wrote the American historian Barbara Tuchman, "is undeniable, and the reason for this goes back to the beginning. Conquest of the plains took fifty years of incessant warfare, including sixty-nine campaigns against the Indians which amounted to a form of genocide."

This was not the Canadian experience. The early fur traders did exploit the Indians and, later, the Inuit. They shattered their culture by turning them from hunting to trapping and disrupted their traditional way of life, while bestowing on them the white man's gifts of smallpox, syphilis and liquor. Despite such abuses, dealings between trader and aboriginal were based on a commercial relationship. The Indians killed or trapped the forest animals, skinned them and hauled in their pelts. Switching from suppliers to customers, they then exchanged their credit for blankets, copper pots, axes and other goods that made life in the wilderness more comfortable. "Never shoot your customers," went an early Hudson's Bay Company directive. It was mostly obeyed.

The curious case of Ta-tanga-I-yotank illustrates the early differences between the societies on either side of the forty-ninth parallel. Better known as Sitting Bull, the great Sioux chief had valiantly defended the land guaranteed to his people by the government in Washington after the U.S. cavalry attempted to recapture it for incoming gold prospectors. On June 25, 1876, Sitting Bull's warriors wiped out an invading troop of more than 200 mounted soldiers led by Lieutenant Colonel George Custer in the valley of Montana's

Little Bighorn River.* Tagged thereafter as "the most dangerous man in North America," Sitting Bull and about 5,000 of his supporters crossed the border at Wood Mountain into what is now southwestern Saskatchewan. They were met by Inspector James Morrow Walsh of the North-West Mounted Police, who rode alone into their war camp wearing his resplendent scarlet tunic, to stress his contrast with the dark blue uniforms of the U.S. cavalry. Walsh sternly explained that the Sioux could stay only if they obeyed Canadian laws. "They had been told by their grandfathers that they would find peace in the land of the British," he later reported to Ottawa. "They had not slept sound in years and were anxious to find a place where they could feel safe." Sitting Bull's people heeded Walsh's advice and lived peacefully on the Canadian side of the border for a half-decade. They returned to North Dakota in 1881, where the great Indian chief was gunned down by U.S. government agents nine years later.†

The corporate character of the Canadian frontier which offered such safe haven, if not much adventure, was perpetuated by each wave of newcomers. The Bay men were succeeded by agents of the Canadian Pacific Railway, built in the mid-1880s to link central Canada with the Pacific coast. That rapacious enterprise was immediately followed by the influx of that most quintessential of Canadian institutions, the bank branch, necessary to distribute the railway payrolls. The settlement process was policed every tidy step of the way by the North-West (later Royal Canadian) Mounted

---

* Custer never did make general, except in American legend. He served briefly as a brigadier in charge of a brigade of Michigan cavalry volunteers, but the U.S. Army listed his official rank as lieutenant-colonel.

† The contrast between the Canadian and American way of dealing with violence still holds. Witness the difference between the dramatic but peaceful standoff at Oka, Quebec, in the summer of 1990 when the Canadian military patiently waited out a band of militant Mohawks who had broken existing laws, and the storming of the Branch Davidian compound at Waco, Texas, which brought death and mayhem to participants on both sides. The comparison brings to mind a chestnut about the difference between the American prayer, *"God, I want patience— and I want it NOW!"* and its Canadian version, *"Dear Lord, please grant me patience...whenever you get around to it."*

Police, whose constables not only upheld the law but confiscated six-guns before anyone had much of a chance to draw. The Mounties enforced the law so emphatically that, during the wildest days of the Klondike Gold Rush in Dawson, you could get arrested for fishing on a Sunday.* The N.W.M.P. were succeeded by missionaries who used their positions to exercise divine authority through pursed lips and disapproving glances. By the time most of the settlers arrived, they found themselves in a field-office environment that demanded— and received—deference to tightly ensconced authority.

That incense of deference was to linger over Canada long after The Bay's decline into a K-Mart with a fancy crest. Even such a radical act as Pierre Trudeau's 1970 declaration of the War Measures Act to suppress the militant Front de libération du Québec (FLQ) was a reflection of Canada's deferential nature. There was no quarrel, even at the time, with the argument that the measures represented a massive show of force by the state, strip- ping citizens of their civil liberties and exposing identifiable groups—such as French-speaking academics, journalists and intel- lectuals—to arbitrary detention and punishment. The preservation of stability and order was placed above every other value, includ- ing individual rights. According to the polls, this turned out to be the single most popular measure ever taken by a Canadian govern- ment. Trudeau's approval rating shot up to 59 per cent—a jump of twenty-one points in one month.

Fearing disorder more than oppression, Canadians dribbled away their self-esteem in the risks they failed to take and the acts of daring they managed to avoid. This even applied to the simple act of speaking out. "Something deep in the Canadian spirit compels us to avoid direct statement, to skate around confrontation, and to choose comfortable decorum over uncomfortable truth," the author and journalist Robert Fulford told a University of Toronto convo- cation in the summer of 1994. The quintessential Canadian was probably William Lyon Mackenzie King, who ruled Canada with a few interruptions from 1921 to 1948, had the sex life of a gnat,

---

* The Mounties practised their own form of deference. The impulse to obey officers was so strong that constables on duty at Fort Walsh, deep in Blackfoot territory, were carried prone to the parade square in order to avoid reprimands for not having their trousers properly creased.

never took a political risk, and was so fastidious that on a 1949 New York trip to visit his mentor, John D. Rockefeller, Jr., he took along six spare shoelaces.

The national traits of self-effacement and self-denial, the syndrome of down-playing success earned and wealth gained, had to do with propitiating the Presbyterian deity that became the land's all-pervasive touchstone. That brooding, guilt-making presence was responsible for as much soul-destroying deference as the character of the Canadian frontier. Not only the HBC men and the Montreal tycoons who financed the railroads, but nearly all of the country's early authority figures outside of Quebec—bankers, clergy and politicians—were Scots. They were therefore Presbyterian, whichever church they attended, to the core of their pinched souls. Armed with the shorter catechism (and intestines armoured by all the oatmeal they could eat), these redoubtable creatures were close with their money and even more parsimonious with their emotions. They made up in loyalty and moral fibre what they lacked in creativity and exuberance. They believed, as if it were gospel, that a hard day's work well done was the only earthly path to salvation. It was a sombre code of behaviour which held that flashes of pleasure be barely endured and moments of splendour be made to appear accidental. Such theological hogwash held Canadians back from fulfilling themselves or taking the risks required to retain their splendid patrimony. The notion of following "the middle way" was not meant as a safe course between extremes. Instead, moderation became an end in itself—a secular mandate on how to conduct one's life. As such, it was an orthodoxy unworthy of the potential of its adherents. Presbyterian gloom was even more at odds with the acquisitive ethic of the 1980s, so that by the 1990s hard work for its own sake and obeying authority just because some misguided deity demanded it, had lost the ability to command.

EVERY COUNTRY IS A MYSTERY composed of the lives of strangers, men and women whose only legal link is a piece of paper proclaiming their vague allegiance to shared citizenship. Because Canada was born as an artificial political union in defiance of economic and geographic logic, it has been delicately poised on the edge of perpetual collapse ever since. A loose federation of wildly diverse regions on the margin of the civilized world, the country has always suffered from an inability to mobilize itself in times of internal crises (as opposed to European wars) because its people have shared few core values. At best, they were vague and indistinct: the qualities of tolerance and generosity, for instance, did much to foster an official stance of multiculturalism, but multiculturalism in turn triggered complaints that Canada was fostering values other than its own. The people of Quebec maintained a lively society of their own, but Canadians elsewhere achieved little more than a quiver of common intent that passed for patriotism. Even that sentiment, which coincided with playing host to a world fair or world series, expired as quickly as a twenty-four-hour flu.

In the past, nothing much disturbed the assumed legitimacy of national institutions and governments. Even the deepest shaking of events or a policy verging on cataclysm had hardly distracted Canada's governing classes from operating according to their usual mixture of creative fumbling and success by inadvertence. For lack of any clear mission save their own re-election, most Canadian politicians relied on the passivity—and bribability—of their subjects and paid only token attention to their demands.

The Canadian Revolution changed all that. Canadians came of age in a curiously uncharacteristic way. In uneven spurts between 1985 and 1995, they made the unruly passage from passive acceptance of closed-shop authority to open defiance of the established order. The burghers of a once-smug country staged a revolt against the notion of having their personal decisions made for them by self-selected hierarchies dedicated to their own perpetuation. This was true not only of governments but of every aspect of life and work, including businesses, unions, schools, universities and the family.

As the new populism took hold it remained a movement in search of a government. It spawned the Bloc Québécois and Reform to fill the political void, while Jean Chrétien's Liberals moved in as Ottawa's temporary custodians, their mandate conditional on being the best of a bad lot. As it turned out, the decline of faith in middle-of-the-road solutions did not signal a sharp turning to either the élitist right or populist left.

The Revolution also overthrew an ingrained bias on the part of the nation's intellectual leaders to support most liberal initiatives, including more government intervention in the economy and the

maintenance of social safety nets.* Conrad Black, the expatriate
Canadian media mogul who spent the decade favouring his home
country with poison darts disguised as shots of wisdom, had his
own theory why Canada was no longer a fit place to live for a
British Lord-In-Waiting like Himself: "When politicians try to
govern by raising a wet finger to the wind or on the basis of public
opinion polling," he declaimed, "the public gets to think that all
leaders are interchangeable, that the distinction between a Bob Rae
and a David Peterson is very subtle. It isn't. Rae was well to the
left of where Ontario wanted to be and Rae's followers were well
to the left of him. Perhaps all the accumulated chaos will rouse
Canadians out of their lassitude, as they realize that everything's
falling apart—that the country is on the verge of bankruptcy and
could crack up."

Such verbal thunderbolts aside, ordinary Canadians were confused
and troubled by their own audacity at having put the legitimacy of
their political leaders to the test. But they would not retreat from their
determination to pursue two bedrock objectives: first, that politicians
at all levels of government stop treating them as commodities to be
bought with their own money at quadrennial auctions called election
campaigns; and second, that some way be found to alleviate the
despair of the young, burdened by a shallow, antiquated education
system and diminished by a harshly narrowing job market.

As the decade under review ended, the Lenten tedium and
oppressive conformity of Canadian life had been lifted somewhat.
Canadians of all regions, occupations and economic circumstances
had spontaneously challenged the status quo and got away with it.
The breakdown of trust between the governors and the governed
was no longer limited to the radical poor or the discontented young.
Pent-up resentment of authority could be felt across the land, as
ordinarily placid middle-class citizens accused anyone in command
of lies and damned lies. "What the last ten years have done," the

---

* The best definition of a liberal was given by former U.S. Senator
Eugene McCarthy, who was a prime example of the species himself. "A
liberal," he explained, "is someone who throws a drowning man fifty
feet from shore a thirty-foot rope, while yelling: 'I've met you more
than half-way!' "

chair of Ottawa's National Forum on Family Security, David Ross, said in 1994, "has shaken us to our roots as a nation."

Unlike Pierre Trudeau, who spent his time in power levitating in a space all his own, Brian Mulroney worked around the clock digging into problems and turning over rocks that ought to have remained undisturbed. Despite a genuine desire to advance the country's cause in step with his own, he succeeded mainly in building himself a political tomb. His corporate agenda may have fit global economic realities, but domestically he managed mainly to radicalize the population against himself and his government. Never again would Canadians agree with the sour prescription of George Bernard Shaw's *Prefaces*: "If people cannot have what they believe in, they must believe in what they have."

Canadians being what they are, their Revolution waged no battles and took no prisoners. Laws continued to be obeyed. Most Canadians still murmured a self-conscious "thank you" to automated teller machines and refused to cross streets against the red lights, even at midnight with no car in sight. The exception was in not paying the GST. Here at last was the hot breath of revolution, Canadian-style. The taxes owing on an underground economy of $140 billion a year in goods and services, it was estimated by those who purported to know, vanished annually into the pockets of anyone fortunate enough to evade the tax. It was not much of a gesture as twentieth-century revolutions go, but for Canadians who seldom cheated on their taxes—and even when they did, made sure their fraudulent returns were filed on time—the boycott made a strong statement. Taxation without representation, after all, was how another revolution began.* Chrétien's finance minister, Paul Martin, had little doubt about the tax boycott's significance, interpreting it as "a withdrawal by Canadians of their consent to be governed."

By the mid-1990s Canada's most serious predicament—apart from such specific issues as the national debt and Quebec separatism—became the growing disbelief that anything very significant could be achieved through political action. The middle ground between smugness and despair had grown dangerously narrow.

---

* It would be nice to report that flying squads of Raging Grannies dumped tea into Victoria harbour to protest the GST, but this did not happen. At least not yet.

Individual and regional aspirations became more difficult to incorporate into a collective national will. The fun and social profit went out of politics. Jean Chrétien did his best to keep a lid on things, and for a time he succeeded.

But most Canadian voters were left sharing a sentiment expressed by Gene Hackman in an obscure but brilliant 1975 Arthur Penn movie called *Night Moves*. "Nobody wins," he mused. "One side just keeps losing slower than the other."

The losers were not only incumbent politicians but the system itself. Many once-powerful Old Boys (regardless of gender) found themselves powerless, or stuck in token roles as senators, honorary colonels of obscure regiments and judges at Grey Cup parades. Imperceptibly, a greater slice of decision-making was shifting directly to the people. Instead of curtsying before authority, Canadians wanted to exercise more power on their own behalf. This radical notion helped Preston Manning's Reform party to win fifty-two seats in the 1993 election. "We're reverting to a more active notion of citizenship than the purely electoral and representational theories encompass," noted Ralph Hedlin, the veteran Calgary journalist and energy commentator. "The Reform party seized on the idea of delegation because it has a strong resonance in western Canada. The co-operative movement provided a training ground for direct democracy and planted the will to define, determine and direct our own destinies. Ingrained in this determination was an anti-state bias and a commitment to decentralize decision-making to local control. In the Reform version of democracy the people, not Parliament, are supreme."

The Canadian political system was reformed not only by the public uprising against wasted patrimony and wanton patronage but by money. There wasn't any.* The old-line parties had run out of ammunition. They had to stop bribing voters, not because of any ethical conversion, but because the treasuries of all levels of

---

* Next to the constitution, the surest way to produced glazed looks among Canadians in the mid-1990s was to recite the country's national debt statistics. The anatomy of the problem was simple. In the sixteen years he held power from 1968 to 1984, Pierre Trudeau's wild spending habits moved the national debt from $17 billion to $200 billion. During the nine years Brian Mulroney ruled the roost, the debt ballooned to $465 billion.

government were beyond empty and dangerously in hock. It is hard to imagine, but politicians at the beginning of the revolutionary decade had faced an uphill struggle *convincing* Canadians that government debt was reaching a crisis point. By 1995, Canadian public indebtedness had become the source of such a chronic economic malaise that governments at all levels and of every political hue were reduced to a single policy option—debt reduction. No one was immune, and the decade closed with the incongruous sight of Paul Martin, Jr., the Liberal finance minister, presiding over the massive reorganization of a social policy network which had as its chief architect the late Paul Martin, Sr., his own father.

Was it possible to sustain the promise of democracy without the ability to pay those entitlements Canadian voters had come to regard as their due? How was it practical to govern when special interest groups agreed the federal deficit had to be drastically reduced—but only if not a penny came out of their stipends? The dilemma was described by David Frum, the conservative columnist for the *Financial Post*. "The old politics," he wrote, "the politics of 1945 to 1982, was a politics of easy choices. In those days, the way to get elected was to keep the market economy humming while cushioning people against its inevitable risks through ever more lavish social programs. In return, voters would reward politicians with incredibly long stretches in power. But beginning in the mid-1970s, Canada allowed its welfare state to grow too quickly. Since 1982, we have borrowed money to avoid facing this truth, but we cannot go on borrowing very much longer. So Canada must choose: preserve social programs or revive economic growth."

The realization that infinite demands had collided with finite resources slowly brought about the Canadian Revolution's second phase. Whether or not they agreed with the withdrawal of government, Canadians realized they were being thrown back on their own resources. No matter how worthy the cause or the recipient, the public money just wasn't there. That rude awakening amounted to another basic shift in the national character. Entitlements were so much a part of Canadian citizenship that it seemed the oath of citizenship had less to do with allegiance to the Queen than to the unemployment insurance fund. To contemplate the surrender of entitlements represented a significant breakthrough. The more thoughtful Canadians realized that it did no good any longer to childishly stamp their feet, demanding that the politicians "fix the bad." They could demand all they wanted, but governments no longer advertised a free lunch.

Two harsh truths cut to the quick in the mid-1990s. One was that any nation which had consumed more than it earned now had to earn more than it consumed. The other was that the entitlement culture was bound to break down once the attainment of social objectives became divorced from increased productivity. The bottom line (surely the most frightening phrase in the English language) was that by the fall of 1995, public-sector largesse had become more of a privilege than a right. The age of entitlement had come to an end.

THE UNIVERSAL IMPULSE THAT drove Canada's Revolution was the utopian notion that all Canadians are equal, or ought to be. That egalitarian ideal was beautifully captured by John Grierson, the brilliant Scottish-Canadian movie-maker who in 1939 created the National Film Board. Writing that no power clique, place or person should dominate another, he made the point that "every church, however local, is holy ground, and equally so." Taken to its logical conclusion, the notion of political equality grants everyone equal authority to represent themselves. Political parties would become obsolete because they would have nothing left to negotiate. At best, equality is a double-edged sword. It carries within it an inherent danger of turning a meritocracy into a mediocracy, a nation of Forrest Gumps. As the Vancouver literary critic Szuszi Gartner pointed out: "The notion of equality has been perverted from equality of opportunity and equality before the law to equality of outcome—we must all cross the finish line at the same time, otherwise life is patently unfair."

The scirocco winds of the turbulent decade left few touchstones intact. Establishments, political parties, authority and entitlement were all blown away, with only the tender sprig of equality left in their place. It was one thing to cast aside the symbols that had formerly tied the country together, it was quite another that few new ideals or institutions appeared to replace them. People—in particular Canadian people—need touchstones to live by, not because of their sanctity, but because of their security. A set of beliefs and their institutional response had provided a sense of safety and comfort. The Canadian Revolution had liberated individuals to an unprecedented degree, but at the cost of their collective security. It was a dubious exchange.

Two

GOD

Loss of Faith

*"Every day people are straying away from the church,
and going back to God."*
Lenny Bruce

Of the many institutional touchstones abandoned by Canadians during the past decade, no loss was more wrenching or more personal than the melting away of mainstream churches as a primary source of comfort and exultation. This was not merely a loss of faith in God, as expressed by declining attendance at places of worship, but a retreat from the Holy Spirit, as expressed by plummeting standards of personal integrity and a pronounced drop in the morality of the churches themselves.

Nobody knew what to believe in any more. At one time, the mainstream religions in all their diversity provided a common standard of public behaviour. Men and women of goodwill, regardless of their religious background, were presumed to share ecumenical values of piety, honour, duty, trust and just plain decency. But these bedrock values crumbled in the 1980s, eaten away by an epidemic the American philosopher William James once called "moral weightlessness." The disillusionment with organized religion was based not only on the sea-change of society in general—the retreat from the courtesies of deference to the furies of defiance—but on the fundamental switch from propriety to expediency that tainted nearly every field of human endeavour.

"The values of the marketplace have infiltrated every institution in Canada—the family, the church, the legal system," noted Arthur Schafer, head of the University of Manitoba's prestigious Centre for Professional and Applied Ethics. "Anti-human, commercial values are dominating every sphere of life. Now that we're coming into economic hard times, the sense of each man for himself—save your own skin, get whatever advantage you can—is going to sink public-spiritedness and make it much more difficult to preserve our sense of obligation to community."

There it was in stark summary—the move from the myth of community to the fact of solitude that so aptly characterized the decade. Entirely in keeping with the deregulation of the times, many Canadians opted for the ultimate act of privatization: the right to form their own religions, or at least to map out their individual spiritual journeys. When they could write their own tickets, why would they want to warm a pew while pretending to listen to a familiar stranger in the pulpit chew stale bon-bons of irrelevancy? The sense of personal quest which propelled the Canadian Revolution meant there was a clear distinction to be made between "religion"—which was unconnected, outdated and impersonal, and "spirituality"—which was relevant, timely and intimate.

"My sense is that in the past four or five years spirituality has ceased being a dirty word, it's even showing up in beer commercials," Douglas Todd, religion writer with *The Vancouver Sun,* said in a 1995 interview. "Still, I believe there's an incredible amount of confusion and a kind of inbred naïvete as people try to create their own belief systems. It's mainly the evangelicals who are still interested in the package deals that the authoritarian churches offer." The satirical comedian Lenny Bruce once put the distinction between church and the spirit succinctly: "Every day," he observed, "people are straying away from the church, and going back to God." Nowhere was this observation more fitting than in Canada. Near the end of the decade under review, a 1993 Environics poll showed 83 per cent of Canadians still believed in some form of deity while the remaining 3.4 million Canadians admitted to having no religious affiliation of any kind. But the same poll showed that an astonishing 70 per cent of respondents were devising "their own personal religion." Remi DeRoo of Victoria, the Roman Catholic bishop who has been at the forefront of Canada's religious evolution, caught this mood when he noted that: "While the physical membership of churches is collapsing all around us, that doesn't mean people are less religious. It's fascinating how words like 'values,' 'soul' and 'spirit' are coming back into ordinary discourse. People are as spiritually inclined as ever, in the sense that they still dream, they still have visions and aspirations for a better world, they still look for some kind of paradise."

As the mainstream religions lost their spiritual content, so too did they lose influence as one of the nation's animating institutions. Religious faith had been a key influence in settling the country, with black-robed missionaries hiking into the wilderness at the elbows of early explorers to bless their journeys to convert the "heathen." Until the 1960s, Quebec was the private preserve of the Roman Catholic Church, while Ontario belonged to the Orange Order.

Quebec's first twenty premiers followed the church's bidding as their Eleventh Commandment; it was not until Jean Lesage's Quiet Revolution that the Pope's battalions withdrew from running most of the province's schools and hospitals and stopped leasing its politicians. When Pierre Trudeau made headlines, as a brand-new minister of justice in 1967, by declaring that "the state has no place in the bedrooms of the nation," Quebeckers took the admonition one step further and rejected the Church as an unwanted presence under the bed covers. The province's birth rate dropped from the highest in the industrial world to the lowest within a decade.* Although nine out of ten Quebeckers were baptized Catholics, less than one-third still attended Mass. In parts of Montreal, the number of regular attenders is down to 7 per cent of the faithful. A 1995 Léger & Léger survey revealed that only 11 per cent of the province's Catholics still paid heed to statements made by the Pope or his cardinals. Montreal Cardinal Jean-Claude Turcotte declared, shortly after his elevation in the fall of 1994, that his church would not attempt to be all-powerful. Instead, it would "be at the service of society, operating on a spiritual basis where people are going to be looking for real values in life."

The Protestants who ruled English-speaking Canada from its beginnings—imposing their work ethic and the veneration of

---

* Johnny Carson has yet to be indicted for genocide.

Biblical truths on a God-fearing population—suffered a less precipitous decline. They dribbled away their Great Commission so slowly that the skeletal remains of their churches were still impressive. According to University of Lethbridge sociologist Reginald Bibby, even though eleven million Canadians listed themselves as Protestants in the 1991 census, less than 20 per cent of them exhibited any active church involvement. "Tragically," he reported in his controversial study, *Unknown Gods*, "religious groups are failing in what appear to be spiritually prosperous times. The churches are inept religious companies that cannot get the faith out of the warehouse . . . The news is that interest and intrigue persist, in spite of the problems of organized religion. The result may be a very sizable, ongoing spiritual vacuum."

The United Church, formed in 1925 through a union of Methodists, Presbyterians and Congregationalists, suffered the steepest decline. Three million Canadians declared their United Church affiliation to the latest census takers but less than 380,000 bothered going to church. Although the most liberal of the mainstream congregations, allowing for the ordination of gay priests and promoting the social gospel, the United Church found itself paradoxically unable to attract the young.* Beyond its hard-core membership of elderly faithful, the church discovered that younger converts were less interested in political messages than spiritual enlightenment. Accordingly, the church's fresh blood either hived off to more conservative Christian sects or inclined toward a self-defined spirituality. According to Bibby, United Church attendance rolls would be down to 50,000 within fifty years if present trends continue.

With 2.2 million census members and an active cadre of 784,000 adherents, Anglicans appeared at first sight to be a bit better off. Not so. As Archbishop Peter O'Driscoll warned the church's synod meeting in January 1994: "In the next ten to fifteen years the largest age group in the present Anglican Church of Canada will be dead. At the end of two generations, there won't be enough people to say that there's still an Anglican church alive in this country." An even

---

* An increasingly typical event was the closing, during the fall of 1994, of Chalmers United Church in downtown Vancouver. There wasn't a single member left on its congregational rolls who was less than eighty years old.

gloomier prediction was that of Edmonton Archdeacon Tom Maxwell, who foresaw the day when his church would be "reduced to a group of poor bishops holding together small congregations in local homes." That prophecy bothered the archdeacon not a whit. "We still have God's promise," he stoutly proclaimed, "that the gates of Hell will not prevail." Well, Amen to that.

The most visible sign of how seriously Protestantism had declined was to witness the puny remnant of the once-glorious July 12th Orange parades. Not that long ago thousands took part in the ritual, representing more than a hundred Orange lodges across the country. The marches celebrate the Battle of the Boyne in 1690, which delivered the British throne to Protestant kings and foiled a Papist restoration. The parades were once led by proud men on prancing white horses who elicited shouts from the crowds of: "God bless King Billy" and "To Hell with the Pope!" But that was in the age before political correctness, before official bilingualism, before French-speaking Catholics dared occupy the governor-general's mansion, and before Ontario premier Bill Davis, once an Orange hero, decided to fully fund Catholic schools. The Protestant hegemony faded and most people who caught glimpses of the surviving Orange Day celebrations-in-miniature probably associated the fuss with a Florida fruit promotion.

An exception to the downward trend was those faiths offering structure and orthodoxy in the midst of a society offering little of either. The 318,000 Canadian adherents of Judaism had not lost their fervour. Many Jewish-born men and women who gave up their active adherence after the forced worship of teenage years were returning to the fold, studying Hebrew texts, memorizing the Torah and finding unexpected solace in synagogues among their own. Between the 1981 and 1991 censuses, the Jewish population remained steady at about 1.2 per cent, but within the community there was an observed shift toward greater observation of tradition. Similarly, the dominant religions arising from Canada's Asian and African heritage—Buddhism, Hinduism, Sikhism and Islam—continued to enjoy unabated loyalty from the faithful and increased numbers of adherents, partly through immigration and partly through conversion. They remained small in number, however. While adherents of Islam more than doubled, from 98,000 in 1981 to 253,000 a decade later, Muslims still accounted for less than 1 per cent of the population. Within the Christian faith, the evangelicals and Pentecostals enjoyed the greatest growth in numbers. The Pentecostal church, for example, gained 100,000 new adherents in the census period and the Christian and Missionary Alliance doubled in size. But again, they remained small in relative terms; Pentecostals accounted for 1.6 per cent of the population and the Alliance churches claimed one in 500 Canadians as members. Along with older Canadians, they comprised the one-fifth who still attended church regularly.

But for most others, religious adherence was in steep decline. The Anglican church lost 250,000 members in the census period, the United Church shrank by 665,000 members, losses of nearly 10 and 20 per cent, respectively. Especially for "non-committed" Protestants, church became a court-of-last-resort, a fall-back position in case of illness or catastrophe. "Religion was insurance," the Canadian author Brian Moore, a questioning Catholic, explained in one of his novels. "It meant you get security afterwards. Just as long as you got an act of perfect contrition said before your last end, you'd be all set."

Although the clergy shared responsibility for the reduced role of the church, they also shared in its implications. Since 1985 an increasing number of preachers, especially members of the United Church, had banded together in quasi-unions called "professional associations" to protect their rights and seek decent wages and retirement benefits. A typical case of mistreatment was brought to light in July 1993 by Jack Kapica, religion reporter for *The Globe and Mail*. Captain Colin Lewery, in charge of the Salvation Army's Moncton citadel, had been fired in 1989 after his marriage ended. (Salvation Army commanding officers insist that Army ministers act as a married team.) Left to support four children, after twenty-one years of service he was given $1,440 in severance pay and ended up living in a rented van on a mall parking lot.

In a country where, not so long ago, being Protestant or Catholic was (after gender) a person's most significant defining characteristic, religious affiliation had virtually ceased to mean anything. With one exception, all of Canada's recent prime ministers (Trudeau, Clark, Turner, Mulroney and Chrétien)* have been Catholics. Their

---

* The exception was Kim Campbell. By her own definition a Yiddish-speaking Anglican raised as an anti-Papist, her spiritual c.v. was as dilettantish as her brief stab at the prime ministership.

religion never became a subject for debate, or even mention. Public life in Canada became exclusively secular and pluralist, routing religious conservatives who wanted Canada to remain a "Christian" nation. While the Canadian constitution, patriated at the beginning of the 1980s, recognized the supremacy of God, by the middle of the 1990s, daily prayers had been dropped from the House of Commons proceedings. When New Democrat MP Svend Robinson became the first parliamentarian to admit his homosexuality, he was met with understanding and acceptance, but when Liberal MP Roseanne Skoke opposed legal protection for homosexuals on the basis of her conservative Catholicism, she was rebuked by her party leader. In keeping with the revolutionary nature of the decade, this reflected a wholesale change in public morality from being based on Biblical principles to becoming based on individual choice.

AS THE MORAL BEACON OF THE CHURCH DIMMED, the process came close to being reversed: the gutter ethics of politics, and especially business, came to replace religion. As John Dalla Costa, of the Toronto firm Catalysis Communications Inc., said: "Advertising is probably a more pervasive influence on our culture than religion." At least for that period in the mid-1980s when human and spiritual values were broached by rampant and acquisitive materialism, he was right. A depiction of how loose these standards had become was portrayed in *Wall Street*, the film by Oliver Stone. Insider trading was accurately portrayed in the film not as a crime, but as a natural outcome of the value system at work. "Come on, who really gets hurt?" asked the film's anti-hero, an amoral and avaricious broker named Gordon Gekko. "It's ridiculous to have laws that regulate the free market, while muggers waste old ladies in the street. We can buy our freedom. There is justice higher than the law." This sense of frontier social justice—Adam Smith with a sheriff's badge—was embraced as the heroic aspiration of a decade that replaced God with Mammon. "Greed is good. Greed is right. Greed works," proclaimed the film's main protagonist, played by Michael Douglas. "Greed in all of its forms—greed for life, money, love, knowledge—has marked the upward surge of mankind." On October 19, 1987, just before the film was released, the real Wall Street suffered its most damaging crash since the Depression. The crash had been precipitated by an inability to distinguish the real worth of anything from the greed attached to possessing it. In one dramatic swoop, the limitations of greed as a replacement for spiritual principles had been exposed.

But the worship of Mammon continued to find a sympathetic echo within the Canadian Establishment. Conrad Black, who by the mid-1980s had become its undisputed dean, possessed the brash certainty all too common among the rich that they were exempt from the negative connotations of greed. This exhibited itself in his assumption that, since he already had so much, he should rightfully have it all. His belief system revealed itself in the ferocity with which he condemned his competitors, assuming that any corporate or private behaviour that ran counter to his convenience constituted wilful denial of his due. Within his imperious bearing there thrived a decided inclination to avarice. "Greed," he confessed to me in a 1982 interview, "has been severely underestimated and denigrated—unfairly so in my opinion. I mean, there is nothing wrong with avarice as a motive, as long as it doesn't lead to dishonest or anti-social conduct. I don't think greed, as such, is anything to be proud of, but a spirit of moderate acquisitiveness is not un-akin to a sense of self-preservation. It is a motive that has not failed to move me from time to time." An earlier entrepreneur might have thanked the bounties of a generous God; Black sent up incense to Acquisitive Capitalism. When he decided late in life to convert to Roman Catholicism, he made sure that God understood the power relationship. As he told author Ron Graham, in his book *God's Dominion,* "I didn't exactly go to them on my knees." He negotiated the Creed with Emmett Cardinal Carter, struck a deal and drank champagne—presumably to toast God's great fortune.

Conrad had nothing to do with it, but Pope John Paul II subsequently issued a revised Universal Catechism which updated the Ten Commandments to include such corporate ethical lapses as tax evasion, commercial fraud, speculation and environmental damage, which were classed as grievous sins worthy of burning in Hell.* The captains of capitalism merely bought more sunscreen.

---

* His Holiness was concerned not only with the spreading mercantile ethic but also with any New Age short cuts. The same catechism warned against astrology and the wearing of amulets or talismans.

THE SPIRITUAL EMPTINESS OF PUBLIC LIFE, whether in business or politics, made religion seem irrelevant to the economic and political
trends setting the national agenda. The churches decided to even the
odds by assaulting businessmen and politicians. Dozens of studies
and well-documented attacks on the downgrading of social programs were issued; the 1993 document of the Ecumenical Coalition
for Economic Justice, *Revamping Canada's Social Programs*, was
as devastating a study of the Mulroney government's failings as was
the parallel 1983 report by the Canadian Conference of Catholic
Bishops on the Trudeau government.

The unofficial leader of the move to politicize Canada's
churches was Bishop Remi DeRoo. Raised in Swan Lake,
Manitoba, DeRoo is a farm boy-turned-philosopher who earned
his doctorate in theology at the Angelicum University in Rome.
He gives the impression of preferring to devour Latin documents
in some dusty Vatican library to tending to his West Coast flock,
but his compassion is genuine; the sufferings of his congregation
are visibly etched into his wrinkles. "When I was a farm boy in
Manitoba," he recalls, "I remember the visit of the local archbishop, a wonderfully gracious man who would come to our little
parish church every five years or so. After church, he would greet
all the farmers by name. I wish I could do that now. The image I
had of the church as a boy and what I have experienced as a
bishop, particularly beginning with Vatican II, is that it's a totally
new world. The Roman Catholic Church has changed more in the
last thirty years than it had in the past three hundred. But for
people who are impatient, it's too little too late; it's never enough."

The author of a half-dozen tracts, DeRoo maintains that religion
has always been political. "We've become conscious, particularly in
the last ten years, of what I would call the cult of competivity," he
says. "Everyone seems to take it for granted that life is based on survival of the fittest. You have to fight. It's winners and losers. This
modern religion has absolutes: money, which is its ultimate value.
Everyone is rated by how many bucks they make. That's why we're
ready to excuse the multi-millionaires and billionaires who act
without a conscience, but we will jump immediately on the so-called
welfare bum who, in a moment of weakness or desperation, may
have stolen some baby food.

"The other absolute is productivity," he continues. "There is a wild chase after more and more production for its own sake. This masquerades as common sense and good business, but it's really an ideology, with its built-in redefinition of human beings as consumer/producers. Meanwhile, as one of my parishioners said, unemployment in our region is like a slow-moving genocide machine, with people being destroyed by the erosion of their security and self-worth."

Bishop DeRoo saw the worship of profit over human potential as a process aided and abetted by politicians, which helped explain why they became so discredited in the 1980s and early 1990s: "There's a pervasive sense that the politicians are becoming mouth-pieces for other forces justifying the status quo, rather than creative leaders inspiring us to take new approaches. This has been going on for some time, but I've become more conscious of it in the past ten years."

Unlike most other social activists, the bishop didn't blame Brian Mulroney for this trend. "He was a figurehead and naturally we tend to scapegoat the idol who was raised on a pedestal and is suddenly cast down. What has happened to this country is disastrous, but I'm not willing to personalize it." Other leaders of the mainstream churches were. Archbishop Michael Peers, Primate of the Anglican Church of Canada, a lanky and good-humoured intellectual, could hardly contain his anger. "I was Primate for seven of the Mulroney years, and all the church leaders together—all of us, Roman Catholic, United Church and Anglican, right across the spectrum— never got to see him once. Not ever. We saw Perrin Beatty when he was in Defence, because we may not have many divisions but we're well-connected around the world. And Tom Siddon in Indian Affairs, just after the Oka crisis when the government was really in the glue. Our record with the aboriginal isn't perfect, but it's long and committed, and they were desperate."

Political action didn't get the religious leaders far beyond a day's fuss in the press, but having caught the bug, they moved to direct action. Reviving their traditional function of feeding the poor, they opened their basements and turned them into food banks. That was a good move. Canadians may have lost a touchstone to nurture their souls, but those who needed it most found a compassionate source to fill their stomachs.

Perhaps it was also necessary for the church to rehabilitate itself. The Revolutionary Decade was, above all, a time when it was revealed that a great number of the black-robed men who were trusted with caring for the souls of children had instead been assaulting their bodies. More than a hundred anointed priests and pastors were jailed for raping children. Piety, honour, duty, trust and just plain goodness were debased by God's own princes and spear-carriers. The physical and mental damage inflicted on young lives by the 115 priests and pastors convicted of sexual abuse can never be calculated, never redeemed, never forgiven. Catholicism teaches that despair is the worst of all sins, but those who took advantage of the authority and trust bestowed on them, by wearing the habits of religious orders to sexually exploit the innocent, committed an act of depravity far beyond that—they were responsible not only for the lives they directly ruined but the despair they spread among the faithful. There is no description adequate to re-create the horror of those nocturnal gropings, no punishment adequate to expunge such evil. Hubert O'Connor, the Catholic bishop of Prince George, B.C., admitted to not only having sex with native girls in his spiritual and temporal care at residential schools, but also to disowning the baby he had with one of them. (O'Connor was not defrocked and his trial on rape charges was stayed after Crown prosecutors refused to hand over the psychiatric records of the women involved.) Father Leonard Buckley, the former principal of St. Mary's School at Cranbrook, B.C., confessed to molesting children more than 1,000 times. Father Richard Racine of Tamworth, Ontario, who admitted sodomizing a young boy from the age of eleven onwards, spent only five months in jail for it. The horrors of what happened inside Newfoundland's Mount Cashel Orphanage, St. Anne's in Fort Albany on James Bay, the Christian Brothers' training institutions at Alfred and Uxbridge, Ontario, and the many Indian residential schools (run by the Catholic, Anglican and United churches) have been all too well documented. In Quebec, 15,000 orphans who were victims of the abusive foster-care system took the province to court, demanding $1.5 billion in damages. Douglas Kenny, who ran Mount Cashel Orphanage in St. John's, Newfoundland, was sentenced to five years in prison for sexually preying on seven boys. There he joined eight other Christian Brothers previously convicted of physical and sexual abuse.

And so it went. Church leaders rushed in with lame excuses, while resolutely refusing to apply the same sort of soul-searching they demanded from their flocks. "Priests don't drop out of a cloud from heaven," Vancouver's Archbishop Adam Exner prissily explained. "They grow up. They have strengths and weaknesses like every other human being." Not once did any of these potentates pause to admit that the Pope's antediluvian insistence on celibacy might have something to do with the problem. The Church might have been in denial, but the public readily accepted that sexual assault from the pulpit was widespread. It was, after all, a willingness to lay complaints against these priests and pastors, a willingness for the police to investigate and a willingness for the courts to convict that led to their unmasking in the first place. This could only happen in a culture where people were ready to question authority; once the abuses were revealed, they became one more good reason to defy authority rather than defer to it.

Despite the efforts of the mainstream churches to become politically involved and relevant, their failures in moral and spiritual terms left Canadians with little choice. Many took the revolutionary step of finding God on their own.

I KNOW I DID. MY SPIRITUAL CONVERSION during the past decade, modest as it seems, was fairly typical of the times. I was raised a non-practising Jew back in my homeland of Czechoslovakia and while I survived the Holocaust, the Germans drove us out, confiscated everything my family owned and seized my father's factory. The Nazis gassed both sets of my grandparents and we were strafed by a Junkers 87 dive bomber as we lay huddled on a beach in Biarritz on our escape route out of Europe. The trauma of the Holocaust stripped my upbringing of any continual sense of community or worship, while at the same time fuelling a lifelong quest for stability. I needed something to believe in and looked for causes and heroes who would reduce my sense of vulnerability and validate my identity. This became the theme of my life's work. It is only in the last decade that I realized how fruitless it was to look for those things outside of myself, since if the comforts I sought were to be found anywhere, it would be within my own spirit.

In late 1940, when we settled on a small market-garden farm at Freeman, Ontario (north of Burlington and west of Hamilton), my main goal in life was to learn English. At the time few, if any, local institutions admitted immigrants and I was delighted when the fundamentalist sect that owned a nearby church hall allowed me to attend Sunday school. I didn't learn much about God, although when pressed at social occasions I can still belt out our class theme: "The Best Book To Read Is the Bible!" and can burlesque the hands-raised-in-rapture holy-roller gestures and impersonate that tell-tale lilt of the Saviour's name common to televangelists: "JAY-zus!" Having thus mastered fundamentalism, I settled into the comfortable groove now so familiar to Canadians of attending church or synagogue for weddings, baptisms and funerals. My backsliding ways were a source of irritating concern to me and I often thought that I really ought some day to do something about the dubious status of my soul. Like many Canadians, though, I soon grew comfortable with my infrequent pew.

It was only when I resigned as editor of *Maclean's* magazine in the spring of 1982 and moved to British Columbia that the spiritual stirrings began. It's not that geography defines spirituality, but there is a remote, surreal quality to the West Coast that prompts candour. The azure beauty of the sibilant rain, the trackless sea and the open skies tend to banish thoughts of alienation and encourage the spirit to soar. Before making the move to live aboard the sloop *Indra* in Tsehum Harbour on the rocky southeast coast of Vancouver Island, I had divided my professional pursuits among Toronto, Ottawa and Montreal. When I had time to think about life, which was not often, I found that the cosmopolitan cynicism of those places denied clear access to inner feelings. It seemed to me that the frantic treadmill of these metropolitan rat-cages left its inhabitants, myself among them, stretched to the point of nervous exhaustion and without emotional sanctuaries, a condition which made it difficult to be true to oneself. With their well-nourished grievances and corroded sensibilities on parade, the urban cowboys got through the days and nights by cultivating bullet-proof psyches and sporting a loose amiability to hide their wounds of loneliness.

In contrast, working and living on Canada's Pacific Coast encouraged a more sensible daily and seasonal rhythm. I found life on the continent's western margin to be full of thrust and sky. The days were not measured by the animal acts required to squeeze into the passing lanes of the Don Valley Parkway, but by the eternal faring of the tides and the flaming grace-notes of sunrise and sunset. Savouring the sights, the scents and the sounds of that intertidal existence created the allure of something that most disciples of the spiritual life claim as their quest. Despite the eyes rolled heaven-ward with which my Toronto visitors inevitably greeted any mention of the subject, there was nothing crazy about trying to become more spiritual—even if that graceful condition defied simple explanation or definition.

Still, there is an element of divine madness involved in the higher realm of the spirit that reminded me of a scene in *Don Quixote* by Miguel de Cervantes. In that timeless novel, the mad knight achieved one final moment of lucidity and realized how ridiculous he appeared. Instead of wallowing in self-pity he mischievously enquired whether any of the farmers poking fun at his costume and pretensions might like to join him in "casting off the melancholy burden of sanity." No one did.

Most of us would prefer to travel a less hazardous path to salva-tion than the *don*. In becoming spiritually awakened, which is all that I can claim to be, I have started along a path informed by an eclectic assortment of teachings, plus the lessons taught to me aboard my sailboat. At its core, my spirituality is concerned more with listening and learning than with preaching or competing. Its main tenet is to be open enough to new experiences so that, instead of planning a future in detail to be pursued at all costs, life is simply allowed to unfold.

The cathedral where I worship is the sky. Out in my boat, touring the serene ramparts of the British Columbia coast, I find sailing to be a proving ground of the soul. Sailing heals. It brings release from the *don*'s "melancholy burden." The wind is always on the nose, light-houses are never where they're supposed to be and the salt spray of the heaving ocean eats away the very fittings that hold the boat together. Yet there is magic in every landfall, which serves as a reminder of sailing's ultimate quest: the exhilaration of life's suffi-ciency and the joy of opening oneself to new experiences. This is the same sense of renewal that the mainstream religions once offered.

I am not alone in having discovered that the need for spiritual renewal is essential and that the device of mainstream religion as a means to get there is only one personal option. For many Canadians, the institution of religion has been reduced to a nuisance which gets in the way of their personal relationship with God.

After a few days at sea, a rhythm develops between the sailor and the craft, so that the slightest shift in wind or cloud, alteration in the state of the sea—even a flight of birds—take on definite meaning. Yet, drifting through a pod of Orcas is an unmatched experience. I once encountered a large number of these sacred creatures off Robson Bight, on the northern shore of Vancouver Island, and for the next half-hour none on board could speak above a whisper. There is nothing on God's earth that equals the excitement of sleigh-riding down the Pacific waves under a full moon. Nothing. I return from journeys like these with a heightened sensitivity and an ability to see the world freshly and vividly, as one would after a long spell of rainy days. If the spirit is what transcends the earth while embracing it, then these are my most spiritual moments.

THREE

KING

Royal Flush

It was a tad difficult to ask Canadian immigrants to swear allegiance to a foreign monarch who could literally no longer command the loyalty of a pack of Girl Guides.

ONCE UPON A TIME, LONG AGO, in a small town in southern Saskatchewan where the entire main street runs four blocks from Highway 18 to the CPR tracks, I witnessed what the British monarchy meant to Canada's hinterland. I experienced a tiny epiphany that day, in a part of the country then still recognized as keeper of the national soul. It helps to explain the impact of what happened many years later, when the connection with the Queen and her family had been shattered and neither royalty nor small towns in Saskatchewan mattered any longer.

The town was one of those dusty settlements that never made it into the history books, its name blown off the page by winds howling up from the great plains of North Dakota or down from Lac La Ronge. The farmers who arrived in their pick-up trucks to catch a passing glimpse of the Royal Personage walked with a decided starboard lean to compensate for that eternal wind, powerful enough to make little jib-sails out of the vents in their jackets. The women, dressed up in small crowns of afternoon hats, were nervous and watchful, uncertain whether they were suitably coiffed. I walked into the local beer parlour to hear the talk. As I watched the old-timers with their wind-red faces perched expectantly around the faded Formica tables, I could sense how important a day this was for them. Their excited chatter, the special looks they exchanged and the glasses of beer that grew flat between them (because they were too busy talking to drink much) attested to their sense of occasion. They held the visiting Royal in awe, as they would a creature from another planet, yet they felt genuine connection with the visitor, as though she were as much a part of their lives as an aunt living "the next farm over."

The connection, it seemed to me, was far less constitutional than spiritual. These originals knew that to be Canadian was to be a survivor—a knowledge gained not from reading Margaret Atwood's literary ruminations but from folk wisdom born of winters so severe that they couldn't see their own feet in snowstorms and land so tough that it yielded more rock than crop. To be a survivor in Canada's hinterland meant simply being there, feeling the quiet joy that flows from standing tall against the vastness of the land and sky. I've always thought it was the novelist Morley Callaghan, rather than Atwood, who caught the essence of this country. "Canada," he wrote, "is like a woman waiting in a window of an old house at a crossroads. She is an ageless, wild and hard beauty. Men riding by come to her in the night. They use her but never really possess her. They leave her and ride on, afraid of her fierce domination over them, knowing they can't handle her; she leaves them feeling small . . ."

That kind of spiritual loneliness demands emotional markers that give a larger purpose to life's struggles. For generations of Canadians, the monarchy was among the most significant of those touchstones. What I realized that dusty day in Saskatchewan was this: dreams can provide sustaining fantasies that lead not only to the belief in magic, but a reliance on it. Applied to the invisible but palpable bond between these people and the Royals, this involved an infinitely delicate balance of reciprocal illusions, a meshing so finely cogged that the slightest speck of dirt would hazard its continued functioning.

Those prairie folk demanded nothing of the monarchy but to keep the faith; expected nothing of the monarchy but to remain a symbol they could believe in. Instead, by the late 1980s the Royals had broken that faith and by the mid-1990s, they had irreparably shattered it. A Royal Personage bold enough to venture into Saskatchewan today could not, as the saying goes, draw flies to a mule.

NO OBJECT OF CANADIAN ADORATION, no institution that had once so nobly enshrined a people's ideals of dignity, rectitude and fidelity suffered a more brutal decline in prestige than the British monarchy. The cloying diffidence that still marked the 1984 Canadian tour of Elizabeth II had turned, a decade later, into not so much defiance as derision. When the Queen opened the Victoria Commonwealth Games in the summer of 1994, it was mostly pensioners and school children who turned out to wave the Union Jack. Nearly everyone else either shrugged or snickered at her troubles as the besieged head of the House of Windsor. The Royal presence, which had served generations of Canadians as an essential role-model, had ceased to charm or to excite.

Though she bore her private agonies with a stiff upper lip, the Queen had become the keeper of a house of horrors that made the Addams family values seem refreshing by comparison. One imagined Her Majesty rolling out of her canopied bed each morning, afraid to turn on the telly in case the BBC might be detailing some unspeakable act a family member had recently performed with a grouse. They'd done everything else, it seemed. The porn star Koo Stark, who briefly dated Prince Andrew, knew what she was doing when she blew off this dysfunctional tribe.

No wonder Her Majesty preferred to spend evenings in her private apartments, puzzling over *The Daily Telegraph* crossword, accompanied by only her pet corgis, while Philip was off on his own. The Duke of Edinburgh was reported to have enjoyed at least three lengthy affairs (with the Queen's first cousin Princess Alexandra of Kent, the actress Merle Oberon and the British society maven Katie Boyle) and is rumoured to have had numerous other dalliances. Charles, the Royal couple's eldest son, had meanwhile turned himself into a modern-day Guy Fawkes who planted verbal dynamite under the throne he longed to inherit. Expressing a desire to be reincarnated as the Tampax of one's mistress does little to advance royal decorum. It is not a good omen for the heir to a throne that carries the bold mandate that its occupant must act as Defender of the Faith.

Charles had been photographed in the buff. One of the Queen's daughters-in-law had been pictured topless, having her toes sucked by her Texan "financial adviser." The other royal daughter-in-law, the celebrated Diana, had made passionate love in just about every locale imaginable to the opportunistic cad who had become her riding instructor. (She even interrupted him while he was going to the bathroom at the Highgrove country house in Gloucestershire, where they trysted.) The Queen's daughter, Anne, had been no more successful in sustaining marriage as she traded in one feckless military officer for another. Only the Queen's youngest son, Edward, known around Buckingham Palace as "Barbara," was not suffering marital difficulties. This was because, as one royalty watcher so delicately put it, "nature has blessed him with a disinclination towards matrimony."

This sad tally* left out only the Queen Mother. At the age of ninety-five and in amazingly good fettle, she seemed to manage a fairly normal life amid her family's chaos by the understandable expedient of getting pickled. Her biographer, the Fleet Street journalist Michael De-la-Noy, tallied her average alcoholic intake at two glasses of wine during daily noon receptions, followed by two tumblers of white burgundy, a glass of claret and a flute of vintage champagne for lunch, with a similar liquid schedule at dinner. He confirmed the oft-told tale that, one midnight at Clarence House as she sat impatiently in her drawing room, she finally telephoned her butlers' pantry with the admonition: "I don't know what you old queens are doing down there, but this old Queen wants a drink."

Even such a brief summary revealed less a functioning royal dynasty than fodder for those supermarket tabloids that feature space aliens endorsing Newt Gingrich, two-headed babies who can sing *Sweet Georgia Brown* in harmony and a lucky woman who got pregnant by watching Elvis on television. The message was clear. Unlike most monarchies that have been displaced by republican

---

* The lengthy list of casualties from the fall of the House of Windsor includes the 1994 suicide of Lady Althea Saville, thirty-one, who had been engaged to James Gilbey, alleged to be the voice talking to the Princess of Wales on the notorious "Squidgygate" tapes; and the divorce of Camilla Parker Bowles, forty-seven, from her husband, Brig. Andrew Parker Bowles, fifty-five, ending their twenty-one-year marriage. She had been the open mistress of Charles while Brig. Bowles became known as the only Briton "willing to lay down his wife for his country."

fervour and overthrown by mobs storming their palaces, the British Crown—or at least the House of Windsor—had set itself afire, and no one could douse the flames.

The Royals were doomed by their inability to maintain the monarchy's essential mystique. "We must not let daylight in upon the magic," cautioned Walter Bagehot, the British essayist who defined the role of the modern Crown. It was only through their ability to perpetuate such a mystique that the Royals managed to convey the notion they were somehow elevated from the strivings and temptations of more ordinary mortals—and that, in turn, allowed them to exercise a degree of moral authority over their subjects.

That mystique and the authority it supported were shattered not so much by what the Royals did in bed, as what was published about what they did, and with whom or with what. The British monarchy has always housed more than its share of philanderers; it can get pretty boring being king in those drafty castles. King Henry I was known to have sired at least twenty children without benefit of clergy; Queen Caroline, the wife of George IV, pleasured a platoon or so of "special friends"; Edward VII even arranged for his mistress to have a special pew at his coronation.

But not until the 1980s did television and the press actually invade the royal enclosure with such abandon that nothing remained sacred or secret any longer. Privacy disappeared, a victim, along with civility, of the new climate of defiance. There were no social or cultural barriers left to shield the House of Windsor. It became an inbred family of promiscuous mediocrities, capable of capturing the public imagination only in death or scandal.

Another highly significant factor was the way royalty was spavined in the Canadian context. The monarchy's disappearance as a meaningful national institution was related, in part, to the erosion of its constitutional authority. Long before Elizabeth II graciously presided over the signing of a patriated constitution on Parliament Hill on April 17, 1982, the Crown had allowed Canadian sovereignty to become somewhat untouchable. It ultimately resided in an abstract concept—foreign, hierarchical and remote. But in 1982 the Queen signed away her country's last legal link with its former colony, proclaiming that the constitution "is Canadian at last." Interestingly enough, both Her Majesty and Prime Minister Pierre Elliott Trudeau recognized that they were taking part in a defiant act.

The Queen called it "a *defiant* challenge to history"; the prime minister described it as "an act of *defiance* against the history of mankind."

The shift, from the deference bestowed on the bearer of an overseas crown to the populist tiaras now proudly adorning the head of every citizen, was as much a part of the Canadian Revolution as it was the cause of it. Barbara Yaffe, a columnist in *The Vancouver Sun*, concluded after the 1994 Royal visit to the West Coast that the monarchy had become just another discredited Establishment institution. "In the media age the velvet curtain has been pulled back," she wrote, "and just as the Wizard was really no one but an old guy pulling levers to make all the fire and smoke in the land of Oz, so the Royals are just another, very rich, extremely dysfunctional family." *

Despite the Royals' fall from grace, Canada remained a constitutional monarchy. Its official head of state was still the United Kingdom's monarch, represented by a resident governor-general, an office that in recent years had seen its credibility eroded by the round of superannuated political hacks appointed to fill it. With an institution so terminally in disrepair, it was tempting to dismiss the monarchy altogether. Sentiment rose to be done with it and to elect in its place a Canadian president or a Beaver-in-Chief. "Canada no longer *has* a head of state," noted William Thorsell, editor-in-chief of *The Globe and Mail*, in 1994. "There is only a Governor-General representing an anachronism—a shadow representing a memory at the pinnacle of the nation."

Yet it was its downfall that made many Canadians realize how essential a touchstone the British Crown had once been—and how much they would miss it.

CANADIANS HAD IN THE PAST nurtured the idea of their political system culminating in some neutral and elegant figure who would personify the state in largely decorative functions, yet retain a role in

---

* Even on home turf, the Queen—forced to open her home to tourists—was having trouble maintaining dignity for the Crown, as illustrated by sweatshirts sold in London that showed the drawing of an elegant toilet under the slogan: "I've sat on the throne at Buckingham Palace."

constitutional crises, since this was an enlightened way they could differentiate themselves from the Americans. (In Washington, the president is both head of state and head of government, so that if the position comes to be occupied by a thug like Richard Nixon, the whole system is threatened.) As Gad Horowitz, the University of Toronto political scientist, wrote: "What is un-American about English Canada can be summed up in one word: *British.*"

The monarchy had always been the source of an all-pervasive anglophile sentiment in Canada. From the very beginning Canadians, at least those who lived outside Quebec, were raised in the comfort of believing the British monarch would in some indefinable way ultimately look after their interests. School kids followed the exploits of Nelson and Drake, not Radisson and Groseilliers; they read Byron and Dickens, not Layton and Richler. The two warm-weather holidays that counted, Victoria Day and Dominion Day, celebrated the British connection. So did the names of most main streets of most Canadian cities: King, Queen, Dorchester, Nelson, Wellington, Granville. The Royal Mail delivered the letters and the Dominion Bureau of Statistics kept track of trends. Somehow everything British seemed better, more civilized, more socially elevated. This was held to be true for objects, like teapots or tweed jackets. It was also held true for people, like the misfits holding Oxford degrees still smelling of Gestetner fluid, who sought economic exile in Canada. Their main qualification was the ability to look down their noses while speaking through them at the same time. Many Canadians were educated by visiting British matron-professors who taught badly, but applied their make-up with the steady hands of rhinoceros hunters.

This love of all things British stemmed from the post-exploration history of Canada, which had seen an accommodation of Quebeckers and the 50,000 United Empire Loyalists who left the thirteen colonies in 1783 after the Revolutionary War, opting for England and King George. It was the biggest-ever mass exodus from U.S. soil and helped shift the population balance from French to English. Though greatly outnumbered by succeeding waves of non-British immigrants, the Loyalists and their descendants set down a social environment that included faith in the British Crown and preference of evolution over revolution in all things.

For reasons unclear even in retrospect, Canadians over the next century subscribed enthusiastically to the idea of the British Empire rampant. Their faith seemed at times to be more theological than political. Upper Canada's Establishment felt no confusion about what to believe or how to behave. God, King, Flag and Family were the icons that mattered. The coveted virtues were honour, patriotism, discipline, frugality, chivalry, fair play and not being too bright or expert at any one thing—the cult of the all-rounder reigning supreme.

The wily Sir John A. Macdonald knew what he was doing in 1891 when he wrapped himself in the Union Jack and campaigned on the slogan: "THE OLD FLAG – THE OLD POLICY – THE OLD LEADER." He was seventy-six by then, looking not so much old as dead, the ravaged topography of his face resembling the weather side of the moon. He had made so many compromises that he could no longer be sure where he stood on any issue, but his instincts ran true. "My course is clear," he declared. "A British subject I was born—a British subject I will die." He did, only three months after the election, which he won with a thirty-one-seat margin.

Even Louis Riel, the quintessential rebel who led two uprisings and died prematurely on the gallows, found a good word to say about the British monarch of his day. Loyal to his Métis roots yet attracted to the Victorian ideal, he spent his life trying to overthrow an entrenched Anglo-Saxon ruling class in order, as he kept paradoxically insisting, "to gain our just rights as British subjects." In one moving address to his followers, Riel praised their wisdom for "having trust enough in the Crown of England to believe that ultimately they would obtain their rights"—even though the Queen's troops were, at that moment, marching west with orders to destroy him. Riel's sense of ambiguity even extended to his mode of dress. During the eight months he spent as president of the North-West Republic in what is now Winnipeg, Riel received visitors wearing hand-sewn buffalo-hunt moccasins and a formal Victorian frock coat.

By the time Queen Victoria celebrated her Jubilee in the shimmering summer of 1897, the Empire on which the sun dared not set encompassed more than a quarter of the world's land surface and 372 million people. The Jubilee was vintage light opera, with Edward Elgar writing the score and Rudyard Kipling supplying its libretto. Canadians found themselves caught up in the occasion, with floral arches thrown across main streets and patriotic events featured in nearly every community. One such moment was described by the writer June Callwood, who reconstructed the Jubilee festivities in London, Ontario: "As a warm darkness fell, fireworks spelling VICTORIA hung for a long, poignant moment in the black sky. People watched it sputter out and were transfixed. It seemed something important had happened to them, to the whole country. It felt like a flowering, a future greatness just opening to enfold them."

Lord Strathcona, who had started life as Donald Smith, a Labrador fur trader, had by then become Canadian High Commissioner to the United Kingdom. He laid on such sentiments with the thickest trowel of all. "I do not care to speak any longer of Canada and the other countries constituting the Empire as Colonies," he harrumphed at a ship-launching ceremony in 1898. "They are constituents of an Empire, one and indivisible. They are English quite as much as is Great Britain. To remain so for all time is the desire of Canada and all the other possessions of the Empire."

Today that kind of twaddle sounds hysterical if not comic, but Queen Victoria cast a strange spell over Canada and its early frontier. "Red Indians," as they were then called, swore oaths of loyalty to "The Great White Mother." In the La Ronge area of northern Saskatchewan an unruly character named Frank Russell, who had murdered a trapper, surrendered without a struggle when a local magistrate arrested him "in the name of Queen Victoria"—even though Her Majesty had by then been dead for three years. British fever came to a boil in the Canadian north with declaration of the First World War in 1914. Martha Black, wife of the Yukon commissioner, reported the reaction to the news of the audience at a Dawson theatre: "As though answering an overwhelming urge, they stood in unison and commenced to sing 'God Save the King.' The effect was electrical. With one move the audience was on its feet, and never in the world was our national anthem sung with greater fervour or more depth of feeling than in that moving picture house in that little town on the rim of the Arctic. Although 8,000 miles of mountain, land and sea separated us from London, heart of the Empire, yet England's King was our King, and England's Empire was our

Empire." Her husband, George, later commanded the 260 men of the 17th Machine Gun Company (attached to the Yukon Infantry) that had been donated to King and Country by the local gold-mining tycoon, "Klondike Joe" Boyle.*

Canada marched off to England's war, the infantry singing "It's a Long Way to Tipperary," the cavalry jangling behind, but the experience almost split the Empire asunder. Most of the British generals shamelessly used Canadian and Australian troops as cannon-fodder, allowing their home countries little decision-making authority. Lester Bowles Pearson, who spent time in a Canadian artillery unit before he joined the Royal Flying Corps, recalled that he had to get permission from the local English command post to shell the enemy. "After all, if we fired by ourselves, it might upset the Germans, to say nothing of the British." Prime Minister Robert Borden objected to the slaughter in the trenches, which prompted his appointment in 1916 to the Imperial War Cabinet in London. By war's end, Canada signed the Treaty of Versailles in her own name. Canadian nationalism asserted its grip in the postwar euphoria and the British Empire began its slow evolution into the token of Commonwealth, but Canada remained one of the few countries voluntarily swayed by British values and personalities, the monarchy chief among them. As late as 1936 Governor-General Lord Tweedsmuir told British Prime Minister Stanley Baldwin that "Canada is the most puritanical part of the Empire. It cherishes very much the Victorian standards in private life."

The most fervent admirers of the British connection were Canada's upper classes. Vincent Massey, scion of the agricultural implements firm, served as High Commissioner in London from 1935 to 1946. He took to wearing a handkerchief up his sleeve, referred to his native land as "Canader" and became so much more English than the

---

* The passion felt for Empire is hard to exaggerate. Typical was the saga of Warburton Pike, who had graduated from Rugby and Oxford but spent most of his adult life trapping, hunting and hiking in the Canadian wilderness. An Imperial adventurer to his core, he took countless risks exploring the outer edges of the northern tundra. At the outbreak of the First World War, when fifty-four years old, he went to London to enlist. When he was rejected because of his age, he hiked to Bournemouth, walked into the sea and plunged a knife into his heart.

English that Lord Cranborne, Lord Privy Seal in Sir Winston Churchill's cabinet, once observed with a perfectly straight face: "Fine fellow, Vincent—but he does make one feel a bit of a savage." *
To show off their sense of authority, Canadian business leaders after the Second World War tended to copy slavishly what they imagined to be the British way of doing things. They modelled their houses on Cotswold manor homes, not realizing that owners of the genuine article were furiously remodelling their surroundings to resemble suburbs of San Francisco. They furnished their offices to resemble partners' chambers in the merchant banks that lined Threadneedle Street, which was itself being vulgarized with electronic installations to compete with the likes of Merrill Lynch, then starting to invade the City. They trotted their children off to Oxford or Cambridge, affected mid-Atlantic accents and worshipped anything British. That meant taking (but not necessarily reading) *The Economist*, eating plum pudding, wearing Turnbull & Asser ties, praising nightingales. The most powerful of these tycoons sought British titles, following the earlier examples of Lord Beaverbrook (Max Aitken, third son of an Ontario preacher), Sir Harry Oakes and Sir James Dunn. Most notable among them was Roy Thomson, who managed to translate his string of rundown dailies in northern Ontario into ownership of *The Times* of London and control of Britain's most dynamic media empire. An incurable skinflint, Thomson celebrated his baronetcy by lining up at Burberry's and buying a new cashmere coat (reduced from seventy-four pounds sterling to forty) and having his official coat of arms (a beaver blowing an alpine horn under the motto: Never A Backward Step) carved on his office door. When a London dowager persisted in calling him "Mr. Thomson," he blew up. "Madam," he remonstrated, "I've paid enough for this god-damned title. You might have the good grace to use it." (His son, Kenneth, uses it only

---

* Massey's wartime stint was enlivened by having to be godfather to the thousands of Canadian servicemen and women posted to the British Isles. Not the least of his diplomatic legacies was his successful defusing of family situations, such as the one described in a letter to him from an English mother. "A Canadian soldier on leave has visited my house," she wrote. "As a result, both my daughter and I are pregnant. Not that we hold that against your soldier, but the last time he was here, he took my daughter's bicycle which she needs to go to work."

when he visits England and has never taken up his father's seat in the House of Lords.)

It could only happen in Canada, but the love of things British was even to be found in the bosom of French nationalists. This ambivalence was observed when James Cross, the British Trade Commissioner, was kidnapped by the radical FLQ in 1970. After he was released, Cross recalled a conversation with his captors. "What I don't understand about you chaps," he told them, "is that you always object that things are not being done in accordance with British justice and, at the same time, you keep attacking us British." Henri Bourassa, the leading Quebec nationalist of his day and founder of *Le Devoir*, told an appreciative House of Commons on March 12, 1901: "The more I analyze the vital parts and lusty members of the admirable political creation, the more my admiration for England has grown. I was always glad enough to be a British subject, but now I experience the full pride of my British citizenship." His heir, René Lévesque, was in opposition to constitutional measures introduced by Pierre Trudeau in the late 1970s which would have totally emasculated any Canadian role for the British Crown. The separatist leader felt that, as long as Quebec was part of Canada, its rights would be better protected with the monarchy in place. Speaking in his plummy Dickensian accent, Jacques Parizeau in 1993 allowed that his new Quebec Republic would, of course, remain a member in good standing of the British Commonwealth.

Constitutionally, Canada kept drifting ever farther from its British embrace. Mackenzie King won an election in 1926 by challenging the right of a British-appointed governor-general to intervene in the country's political process; Imperial Conferences held in 1926 and 1930 officially confined the monarchy's authority and the 1931 Statute of Westminster granted Canada full freedom in its international dealings. Eighteen years later, the judicial committee of London's Privy Council ceased being the final appeal from Canadian courts. The first domestic governor-general (Vincent Massey, masquerading as a Canadian) was appointed in 1952. A new flag that didn't incorporate the Union Jack was adopted in 1964. During the thirty-seven-day debate that raged in the Commons on the issue, both Prime Minister Lester Pearson and Opposition

Leader John Diefenbaker paraded their British connections. "Am I supposed to be forgetting my British past because I look forward to my Canadian future?" the Liberal leader demanded, while the Tory chieftain thundered that he wanted his country to be "all Canadian and all British."* Dominion Day became Canada Day and the national anthem was officially adopted a decade and a half later.

But old attachments do not die so much as transform themselves into nostalgic sentiment. The last gasp of Empire was probably Margaret Thatcher's defence of the Falklands in the spring of 1982. There was no doubt where Canada stood in that shoot-out. Canadians eagerly backed the trade embargoes against Argentina and all through that brittle conflict, every yacht club which carried the prefix "Royal" flew the Union Jack from its main flagstaff.

THE OFFICIAL TITLE OF THE QUEEN, who has been on the throne for forty-three of her sixty-nine years, is Elizabeth the Second, by the Grace of God of the United Kingdom of Great Britain and Northern Ireland and Her Other Realms and Territories Queen, Head of the Commonwealth, Defender of the Faith. † She is the richest woman on earth,

---

* One of the debate's stranger interjections came from F.J. Bigg, the Tory MP for the northern Alberta riding of Athabasca. "They took Joan of Arc's flag down," he explained, *a propos* of nothing much. "They put her lily banner in the dirt, and she was only a woman. But what a glorious woman she was. She put her lily banner out in front and never looked back, and with her small army swept the ranks clear. She put the rightful heir, I am led to believe, on the throne of France. Then the King of France ratted on her, and you know the rest. Now she's a saint. Which of those opposite, in their male pride, will stand up and say that they think the lily banner of France or the cross of St. George should be laid in the dirt?"

† Britain's Royal family changed its name to Windsor in 1917 when George V realized that the House of Saxe-Coburg and Gotha sounded too Germanic for wartime Britain. The House was founded by Edward VII and was named after his father, Prince Albert of Saxe-Coburg and Gotha, the Prince Consort to Queen Victoria. The name change prompted the Kaiser to enquire when he could attend the first performance of "The Merry Wives of Saxe-Coburg and Gotha."

presiding over a fortune estimated at seven billion pounds sterling. Although she handles cash only to buy sweets for her grandchildren at the village shop near Sandringham House or to play the horses at Ascot, she is known to be both penny-wise and pound-foolish. She really does turn out the lights when leaving her chambers and once objected to buying apples out of season for the fruit bowls at Buckingham Palace because they were too dear, yet she has been known to order the Royal Yacht *Britannia* back into port so she could post a letter.*

It is easy enough to criticize Her Majesty, as Lord Altrincham once did when he charged that "the personality conveyed by her utterances is that of a priggish schoolgirl, captain of the hockey team, a prefect and recent candidate for confirmation." But such criticism is hardly fair. The great strength of character Elizabeth II has demonstrated throughout her many ordeals flows from her view that her role is a covenant with God, which is why she will never abdicate. She finds herself caught in the dilemma of having a function rather than a responsibility. At the heart of that function is her determination to preserve an air of impenetrable intrigue. Her speeches convey not the slightest hint of what she thinks about anything. This has carried an emotional price.

The defining image of the Queen as mother was the occasion, forty-odd years ago, when she was shown arriving home from a foreign trip. She greeted her six-year-old son Prince Charles, who was so excited to see her that he was jumping up and down in glee, by shaking his hand. It takes several lifetimes to survive that kind of frigid upbringing.† That Charles hasn't found the inner fortitude of his mother is

---

* The royal yacht is due to be retired from service in 1997 and two years ago the Queen began to pay income tax. In line with her parsimony, the Calgary oil firm Canuck Explorations Limited received permission to drill for oil on the grounds of Windsor Castle when she is not in residence. Meanwhile, in a pathetic attempt to make himself useful, Prince Charles is marketing his line (Duchy Originals) of oat and ginger cookies, sold in Canada through Holt Renfrew at $6.50 a box.

† The monarchy's rigidity was demonstrated by the edict (in effect until Princess Margaret's divorce in 1978) that no divorced person be allowed into the Royal enclosure at Ascot.

hardly surprising. But his great failing as putative heir to the throne is not so much that he has strayed from his marital vows, but that he seems to understand nothing about maintaining the monarchy's essential mystique. He won't stop talking.

"Many a thing we know we'd like to tell him," the British commentator Julie Burchill has written about Charles, "many a thing he ought to understand. But how do you get him to shut the fuck up and listen to any voice save that of himself and his groupies? How can a man with such huge ears hear so very little?" He has lectured his audiences about the theatre, psychology, art, global warming, Shakespeare. A good example of his maladroitness was his 1984 pronouncement that modern architecture had done more damage to London's skyline than the Luftwaffe did during the Second World War. "Really?" asked Burchill. "How many children have London architects burned alive?"

"One has to say," wrote Andrew Wilson in his definitive *The Rise and Fall of the House of Windsor,* "that Prince Charles does not merely contribute to the difficulties of the royal house, he *is* the difficulty. The greatest problem faced by the House of Windsor is not Diana, it is her husband. And this would have been the case whether he would have married or not." Charles does occasionally make sense. He once declared that "the Catholic subjects of the sovereign are as important [as Protestants], not to mention the Islamic, Hindu and Zoroastrian."

The only aspect of Charles's public life more devastating than watching him on TV was to read his official biography by Jonathan Dimbleby, a volume aptly described by the British MP Edwina Currie as "the longest abdication note in history." He confessed the details of his quarter-century affair with Camilla Parker Bowles and portrayed himself in a Colombian bordello with a prostitute's hand on his thigh. He recalled being in Acapulco, where he was turned down for a dance at a waterfront disco and immediately lapsed "into a gin-and-tonic induced reverie." * It was as though Charles's only

---

* Camilla, known in Royal circles as The Rottweiler and to her partisans as "a woman with curves, not a bag of bones," was merely following a family tradition. She is the great-granddaughter of Alice Keppel, who was a mistress of Edward VII, Prince of Wales, the great-great-grandfather of Charles.

well-developed instinct was a death wish. Referring to his life, Charles lamented: "It has all the ingredients of a Greek tragedy. I never thought it would end up like this . . . How could I have got it all so wrong?"

One solution was available. Apart from his character flaws, Charles had a spectacularly rotten sense of public relations— especially when matched against his rival, the estranged wife, Diana. The Princess of Wales, her charm and beauty aside, understood that her power flowed not from her position or even her marriage but from her popularity. The image she managed to convey was that of an innocent maiden trapped in a loveless marriage by a dim-witted prince in love with another woman. As the sacrificial virgin and worshipped icon of the victimized, Diana became the most photographed individual since the invention of the camera. She played to the crowds at every occasion, developed her talents as a faith healer and became an all-around Fairy Princess. "Just because her altruism is so photogenic," professed a Royal watcher, "doesn't mean it was ever an act." Diana's activities did not meet universal approval. Some older, more conservative critics were convinced she had inflicted more harm to the British monarchy than anyone since Oliver Cromwell. British writer Auberon Waugh suggested the House of Windsor be "allowed to return to Germany with dignity and decorum, the plaudits of a grateful people ringing in their ears, and leave Princess Monster [Diana] behind on her own to receive the cheers of her adulatory fans, Madonna-like, until they grow bored and decide to tear her to pieces." None of it took. Even when that self-confessed bounder, Major James Hewitt, blew the whistle on his five-year affair with Diana, 65 per cent of Britons still wanted her as Queen—and 67 per cent of those polled blamed her affair with the former tank commander on Charles, for not giving her the love she needed. Hewitt hardly helped his cause by confessing that he had "known" at least fifty women in the preceding six years. "I'm very choosy," he confessed, reaching a new plateau of political incorrectness. "It's like looking for a good horse."

The Prince had pegged 1994 as his comeback year and even opened his own press office at Buckingham Palace. But he hired the wrong advisers and then helped them hurt his cause. The previous winter, he went skiing at Klosters in Switzerland with his good friend Peter Munk, the Toronto-based gold mining magnate who had previously helped finance the publication, in book form, of Prince Charles's quite respectable water-colours. Munk offered to help the Prince by paying for the services of David Wynne-Morgan, the distinguished head of Hill and Knowlton's European operations, who was among the United Kingdom's best P.R. consultants. Charles instead recruited his own dismal retinue, while Wynne-Morgan was hired as director of corporate communications for Munk's Barrick empire.* "Great was his responsibility, and grievous his failure," summed up London's *Daily Mail.* "Prince Charles is not a bad man. But he has been a bloody fool." His future appeared uncertain, particularly because the Church of England, which he heads, specifically forbids the remarriage of divorced persons. Still, there was hope. As Dan Wilson, a resident of Edenbridge, England, argued in a letter to *The Observer*, the standards for becoming King of England weren't really that high. "It is sufficient," he wrote, "if the monarch can stand upright, read a prompt card and not wet himself in public." Since he could no longer command respect on his native soil, it was inconceivable he could command the allegiance of Canadians.

The long descent in popular esteem left the British monarchy bereft of a meaningful following in Canada, which had so recently been one of its overseas anchors. The tradition of reverence Canadians paid to a long line of British kings and queens was dead; gone too was the comfort Canadians found in deference to a monarch. "What happened was a cumulative thing," speculated Rafe Mair, the opinion-making Vancouver radio talk-show host. "Suddenly the Royal Family were just like the rest of us, except a hell of a lot richer. It just occurred to me one day that I didn't give a

---

* There was a time when the Palace knew how to play the press perfectly. On the evening of January 20, 1936, when George V lay dying, his physician, Lord Dawson of Penn, realized that the monarch might linger into the following morning. This would have meant that his death would first be reported in the horrid afternoon tabloids, so he administered a lethal dose of chloroform to the ebbing monarch. Lord Dawson then joined Queen Mary and her children for dinner and, following a stiff brandy, announced the King's death to the editor of the morning *Times.*

damn any more and that if I were asked to defend the notion of a
Queen of Canada, I just couldn't do it. The mystique was gone." The
most humiliating moment came in June 1994 when the Girl Guides
of Canada decided to remove the pledge of allegiance to the Queen
as part of their induction ceremony. It was hardly surprising that Her
Majesty was dropped from a proposal for a new Citizenship Oath in
January 1995.* The new oath, written by a panel of Canadian fiction
authors, raised the expected objections. Calling it a "bureaucratic
conspiracy," Reformer Philip Mayfield, an MP representing the B.C.
interior, added: "The Queen is the head of our country. To exclude
her from the oath would reinforce the message that this government
is firmly on the path to erasing and denying us all our historical
foundations and connections." He might as well have shouted at the
tide to reverse its course. It was a tad difficult to ask Canadian immigrants to swear allegiance to a foreign monarch who could literally
no longer command the loyalty of a pack of Girl Guides.

The loss of the Canadian monarch, in spirit if not yet in fact, represented a fundamental shift in national attitudes. When lawyer
Susan Eng refused to include a loyalty oath to the Queen during her
swearing-in ceremony as a member of Toronto's police services
board in 1989, she immediately found herself facing the wrath of
Robertson Davies—a serious matter since no one had yet established whether the Caledon author looked like God or, as was more
likely, God looked like him. "The Crown is not a British possession," he thundered, "and the Queen is not, solely or even primarily,
that exemplary lady Elizabeth Windsor. The Crown and the Queen
are psychological realities, from which we derive a sense of order

---

* The old oath went: "I swear (or affirm) that I will be faithful and bear
true allegiance to Her Majesty Queen Elizabeth the Second, Queen of
Canada, her Heirs and Successors, and that I will faithfully observe
the laws of Canada and fulfil my duties as a Canadian citizen." The
proposed new oath read: "I am a citizen of Canada, and I make this
commitment: to uphold our laws and freedoms; to respect our people
in their diversity; to work for our common well-being; and to safe-
guard and honour this ancient, northern land."

and permanence. Monkeying with psychological realities is dangerous work for politicians and appointed persons. When they forget this or when we allow them to forget it, we are in danger."

Still, the decline of the monarchy was very much in keeping with Canadians' passage from deference to defiance, a psychological reality more immediate and real than their fading attachment to a tarnished Crown.

FOUR

COUNTRY

Derailing the National Dream

*It wasn't hard steel after all, but a thin umbilical cord of silk
and dreams and hands shaken on platforms.*

Having been conceived aboard the Orient Express, I've always had a special feeling about trains, even to this day. They are—or more accurately, in Canada's case, *were*—a singular way to travel. I was lucky enough to have been aboard for some of their last treks across Canada and fondly remember tossing in my berth, caught up in the hypnotic mantra of their noisy passage through the Prairie night—counterpointed by the clicks of wheels passing over rail joints: "I THINK I can; I THINK I can; I THOUGHT I could; I THOUGHT I could . . ."

About all that remains of those magnificent long-distance passenger trains is the jolt felt when driving over abandoned railway crossings on the edge of Canadian towns. But there was a time, not so long ago, when trains made this country what it was. "No nation owes more to the steel wheel on the steel rail," historian Donald MacKay has written, "though it is not always clear whether railways were built to unite Canada, or Canada was created to justify the railway-building."

The first paragraph of the 1871 pact which brought British Columbia into Confederation stated that the Pacific coast must, within ten years, be linked with Canada by a railroad. (The only passage over the Rockies at the time was a strenuous journey by pack-horse from Punch Bowl, near what is now Jasper.) Sir John A. Macdonald gambled his career on that railway. He knew that without it, most Canadian cities would become little more than dangling appendages of U.S. branch lines.

The CPR syndicate, which spent only $100 million of its own money on the rail line from North Bay, Ontario, to Port Moodie, B.C., was granted an astounding $206 million in cash subsidies by the Macdonald governments, plus twenty-five million acres of land along its route, which included some of the finest wheat-growing acreage on earth. Railway-building dominated Canada's fledgling parliament for its first thirty years and a CPR lobbyist once boasted that whenever the Speaker's bells rang for a division, there were more MPs in his lodgings swilling free booze than there were in the Commons.

By 1915, Canada had 40,000 miles of rail, built with government subsidies of $1.3 billion. Enough track had been set to traverse the longest span of Canadian territory east to west, from Cape Spear in Newfoundland to the Yukon-Alaska border, a dozen times over. The awe-inspiring proportions of the Canadian railway system made it the foremost engineering marvel of its time. Government subsidies *alone* spent on Canadian rail construction were nine times greater than the estimated cost of building the Panama Canal. The railway promoters became folk legends, reviled and envied at the same time. They inspected their empire of track and land from ornate private cars, some equipped with bathtubs that had fourteen-carat gold taps. CPR President Thomas Shaughnessy, who succeeded William Van Horne as Canada's leading railway baron, had a private rail car where he was dressed by a valet each morning, was fed by a private chef in a dining room of Honduran mahogany and took his brandy in an observation room of Circassian walnut. The rail barons gestured with fat cigars, felt they ruled the universe and rented the politicians they couldn't buy. Railway-building and politics became corresponding black arts, only marginally more ethical than piracy on the high seas.

But the railways did get built and there followed a golden age of steam that lasted from the 1890s to the 1950s. In 1913, when Canada's population was seven million, an astounding forty-six million passengers rode its rails. The ponderous locomotives were frightening to behold. Silhouetted against open boiler doors, engineers and firemen resembled demons. The smokestacks belched steam and fire, the whistles shrieked like curlews as the iron beasts squeaked away on six-foot driving wheels. "Hell in a harness," the American frontiersman Davy Crockett said, upon first sight of one of these monstrous machines.

But inside their carriages, the trains offered civilizing comforts. The plush green seats and mahogany panelling of the passenger cars, the rattle of crested china and silver-plated cutlery in the dining compartments and the excitement of sleeping in the swaying Pullmans while the panorama of nature unfolded through the window; all these turned train travel into a memorable experience. (You always remember a train ride; you try to forget a flight.) The conductors, in their navy blue uniforms with service bars, had the bearing and authority of ship captains. The big-city stations were not just functional depots but urban palaces of granite and fieldstone, as prominent as cathedrals and evoking the same sense of possibility and awe. Winnipeg's Union Station, built in 1911, was the most beautiful of them all.*

The unsophisticated steam train of the late 1880s physically and legally united this country, and its memory lingers still, symbolizing the open spaces it conquered and the simpler, less stressful times it represented. Although the last Canadian steam locomotive on a scheduled run pulled out of Winnipeg in the winter of 1960, passenger trains—the old-fashioned kind—remained an essential touchstone for succeeding generations of Canadians. Puffing their iron hearts out beyond the horizon somewhere, in Al Purdy's celebrated phrase, "north of summer," these trains became the country's domi-

---

* Canada's most romantic trains carried not passengers but silk. At the turn of the century, the CPR inaugurated express freight trains to whisk burlap bales of raw silk, off-loaded from freighters in Vancouver. Because it was a highly perishable commodity and market prices fluctuated daily, the silkers had priority over every other train, making the 2,749-mile dash to the National Silk Exchange in New York in as little as eighty-four hours, a day less than the fastest passenger trains. The silk was loaded into air-tight cars lined with varnished wood. The fourteen-car trains, with guards riding gunshot, hurled across the country at up to ninety miles per hour. Only four minutes was allowed at pit stops to change crews, check brakes, and refill water. The silkers were discontinued in the early 1930s with the advent of man-made fibres and efficient air transportation.

nant metaphor. While First Nations orators proscribed eternity by how long the rivers shall run, for Canadians of a certain vintage, the country seemed secure only as long as the trains ran—even if they never used them and even if they seldom ran on time. The railways were a silver cord that threaded its way through the farmland of the St. Lawrence, through the measureless plains and across the continental divide. Every small-town rail station was a link in a tangible chain that stretched *a mari usque ad mare*—from sea to (shining) sea. Because it gave form to a national dream; because a farm boy in Alberta could touch a rail and feel connected with the port of Montreal. Because it was unbroken steel, no one could imagine how fragile this link would become.

OF MY MANY TRAIN JOURNEYS, I remember most fondly the whistle-stop tours during John Diefenbaker's election campaigns of 1963 and 1965. The politician from Prince Albert, Saskatchewan, had been elected in 1958 with the largest mandate until then granted any Canadian prime minister. By the early 1960s he had exhausted the patience of just about every member of every élite in the country. An ardent populist with the countenance and speaking-style of an Old Testament prophet, his words sprang instinctively from him as he indulged in dreams and slogans that had only the vaguest connection with contemporary reality. As it became obvious that he was incapable of managing the daily business of government, he lost the trust and support of nearly everyone except small-town Canadians. In the face of such near-universal rejection, Diefenbaker retreated into a shell of his own. At the time, I wrote that like most self-made men, he began to worship his creator. By the mid-1960s, his most ardent disciples realized that he was a politician in the bleak evening of his career, to be used strictly for his symbolic value—just like the trains from which he insisted on campaigning.

During the first of those campaigns, on the run between Winnipeg and Saskatoon, his chartered train was supposed to stop only at Melville, Watrous and Semans, where local Tory organizers had promised to produce sizeable crowds. But that timetable had to be scrapped when word of his tour got out and people began to gather at nearly every whistle-stop. I remember watching the inhabitants of those flat, sad little towns turn out by the hundreds in the March chill to pay deference to their champion. He strode the station platforms, shaking hands and patting backs, a scramble of yelping dogs and children following his every move. He told a cluster of adoring supporters at Duck Lake, Saskatchewan: "They say I've made mistakes, you know. But they've been mistakes of the heart . . . The last time I flew over the people. This time I'm down on the ground with you. I'm not asking for support of the powerful, the strong and the mighty—but of the average Canadian, the group to which *I* belong." Diefenbaker lost office in the election that followed, but almost all of the ridings he had visited by train held fast.

Two years later, out of power and out of favour, Diefenbaker decided to campaign by private train not just across the Prairies, as he had done before, but across the entire country. His advisers had warned him that railway stations were no longer part of the active urban landscape and that few would turn out to see him. For the first leg of his journey it seemed they were right. I was on that train as it jolted out of Halifax. At Matapedia, Quebec, only five off-duty trainmen and three stray dogs greeted The Chief. At Amqui, Quebec, the local Tory candidate was one of a scattered half-dozen curiosity-seekers who turned up. The candidate introduced his son as *mon fils* (my son) to his party leader. In response, the least bilingual prime minister in Canadian history smiled and replied: "*Ah. Bonjour, Monsewer Monfils.*" It wasn't until we hit Saskatchewan and Alberta that the campaign got its kick-start. We puffed into the Prairie platforms at twenty-minute intervals, and John Diefenbaker moved like a legend over the land.

Everywhere the train stopped, people crowded about to catch a glimpse of him. The men, standing with their thumbs hooked into the front of notched belts, awkwardly raised their arms to wave at the former prime minister, while the women, wind fluttering their hair, executed rusty curtsies and shook his hand. Here, framed by the impatient train, was an instinctive communion that would never be repeated. Watching the scene from a polite distance, I realized the tableau was far more than a partisan political occasion. The locals who turned out at these soon-to-be abandoned railway stations were there not because they were Tories, but because the visitor reminded them of a time when they were at the forefront of Canadian civilization. Despite their impeccable manners, anger and resentment motivated their politics. They had turned the virgin sod into wheat fields and fought the good fight in two world wars, kept the faith and their part of the bargain. In return they had been pushed aside by a world they had seldom visited, and lost influence and their legacy to the moneyed navel-gazers of the urban East who had never served their harsh apprenticeship.

Clearing land in the plains meant tearing at the stubborn rock with bare arms and bent back. Displaced discs, strangulated hernias, strokes, frostbite and heart attacks were a daily hazard, not to mention dismemberment by machinery or death by influenza. These pioneers had learned the hard way that any battle against cold, wind and rock yields no victories, only the postponement of defeat. Two things sustained them in that great lone land—wishful thinking and the rail lines.

Like his people, John Diefenbaker had been written off as irrelevant. To make matters worse, he was literally falling apart. His jaw had collapsed around his shirt-collar like a Madame Tussaud wax figure in which the paraffin has run. Parkinson's disease caused him to shake uncontrollably, advanced years had weakened the once-powerful voice. Yet the mere presence of the man evoked the vanished virtues of a time when buffalo bones still littered the Prairies, Red River carts creaked along the Battleford Trail and people did a little business so they could socialize, instead of the other way round. Diefenbaker absorbed the fever of these events, which was like a hot swift fire that burned away the scrub of a hidebound life. At Melville, Saskatchewan, the Tory leader asked an old-timer when he had come West.

"Nineteen ought-three," was the laconic reply.

"But *which month*?" Diefenbaker persisted.

"September."

A gleeful Diefenbaker shot back: "We came in August!"

As the Diefenbaker train went tumbling through the nightside of its time, the press car echoed with the tapping of portable typewriters, the tinkling of glasses and the slap of cards on poker tables. At a whistle-stop in Richmond Hill, Ontario, a supporter had given Diefenbaker a chrome cage with a yellow canary. For some obscure reason the Tory leader, who rode in a private coach at the back of the train, decided that he would win the election only if the canary sang. The bird uttered nary a cheep, but on the morning of November 6, 1965, between Saskatoon and Prince Albert, the steward serving his car took pity on the old man. When Dief's back was turned, the steward whistled an acceptable canary imitation. Diefenbaker became very excited, generating the second wind he needed to finish the campaign.

The Prairies became a land to flee across; every town, village and whistle-stop, a destination. Just outside Stettler, Alberta, we passed a couple of ragged kids waving a hand-lettered sign with the hopeful spelling: "DEIF FOR CHEIF." At Morse, Saskatchewan, a clutch of local musicians serenaded Diefenbaker with a ragged version of "The Thunderer"; none of us journalists could file copy because the telegraph agent was the band's drummer. At every stop we were greeted by placards with the scribbled message: "HE CARED ENOUGH TO COME." At Swift Current, Saskatchewan, twenty-one ladies in blue gowns sang "Land of Hope and Glory" from the flatbed of a Mack truck. Diefenbaker lost the election, his last as P.C. leader, but he held every Western seat. And somewhere along that final train ride an old man sat by the tracks in the twilight, holding up a sign that read: "JOHN, YOU'LL NEVER DIE."

But he did (in 1979) and his trains vanished with him. I saw many of those Prairie whistle-stop inhabitants one more time two years later, on May 24, 1967, when angry farmers staged their last grand march on Ottawa. I mingled among them, saddened by the palpable sense they exuded of not only being dispossessed but forgotten. They stood on that spring afternoon in their ill-fitting suits on the manicured parliamentary lawns, making their claim to be heard, but nothing happened. Lester Pearson, who was then prime minister, did not deign to appear. The hapless minion sent out to appease the milling mob served only to enrage it. The decline of power among those who worked the land and the decline of the railway that crossed it were more than a mere coincidence of history. The one was very much implicated in the other, although Diefenbaker was the last politician who understood—and worked—the connection.*

---

* When he died in the summer of 1979, Diefenbaker willed that his remains be borne home to Saskatchewan aboard a special train, accompanied by his friends and former political associates. The cortège, placed in a remodelled baggage car, became the centre point of a cross-country wake, with many a toast offered to the old man. "He was always talking about the damn funeral train during his last years," reported Bunny Pound, who had been his secretary. "He would scream with laughter when he thought about it."

THE FIRST SERIOUS RAIL CUTS of the mid-1960s were followed in 1978 by the establishment of VIA Rail, a federal agency established to run what was left of the nation's passenger rail traffic. The Trudeau Liberals eliminated 20 per cent of its unprofitable services in 1981. The subsequent Tory government at first put in more funds, then in 1990 imposed the deepest cut of all. Half of VIA's remaining network was made redundant, including the CPR's historic *Canadian,* the train that followed the line's original route. By then, less than 10 per cent of Canadians had actually travelled by train. The populist protests against the rail cuts were as vicious as they were unexpected.

Effective January 15, 1990, the 3 per cent of Canadians who still regularly took the train found their VIA service had been cut in half. The federal government had sliced its operating subsidy from $800 million to $350 million a year. Gone were most regional services and the southern transcontinental route from Montreal to Vancouver, via Ottawa, Winnipeg, Regina and Calgary. It was still possible to cross the country by train, at a cost nearly double that of air travel, on the three days a week when the remaining northern route remained open.

At the level of pure logic, the rail cuts made sense. But logic had nothing to do with it and, in retrospect, there was no reason to think that it should. The great passenger trains were a national symbol—still are, years after their demise—and symbols do not operate on the level of logic, but of emotion. The nationalists who boarded the *Canadian* for its last journey, the poets, writers and journalists who joined them in spirit, the child who waved at a passing caboose before it, too, disappeared—all understood the train as a symbol that united a people with the great mystery of their land. It wasn't so much that they actually used the trains (I've only travelled on Canadian rail a half-dozen times since those Diefenbaker pantomimes), but they wanted to feel the trains were still there, rolling sentries on the land bridge that had given this country birth.

By killing the trains, Brian Mulroney was accused of killing the country. Stanley Hartt, the deputy minister of finance who would later become Mulroney's chief of staff, sat in on the cabinet committee meetings that decreed the depth of the VIA budget cuts. "You know what we should do?" he remembered suggesting, semi-seriously, to his colleagues. "We should buy a stereo amplifier company and install amplified speaker systems at every level crossing in the country that go, 'CHOO-CHOO' and reproduce the sound of train whistles. People will think that we still have trains. Since they don't ever use them anyway, they wouldn't realize the real trains were gone!"

The last *Canadian* crossed the country on January 17, 1990. The train crew wanted to mark the historic occasion by paying tribute to the CPR's beginnings. They asked to lay a wreath at the monument in Craigellachie, the whistle-stop near the Monashee Mountains where the last spike had been hammered in place by the railroad financier Donald Smith on November 7, 1885. Railway management withheld permission to make that sentimental stop, so the trainmen decided they would throw their wreath off the baggage car at the appropriate moment. But when the diesel engineer slowed down, he forgot to notify the crew. Nothing happened. So much for history. Yet if Paris was worth a Mass, surely Craigellachie was worth a stop.

Doug Young, transport minister in the Chrétien government, announced in the summer of 1994 that all rail subsidies would be eliminated by the year 2005. "The national dream of iron horses, steel rails and steam," he declared, "is dead. The national dream today is to try to protect the integrity of social programs such as the Canada Pension Plan and medicare. Railroads are just another way of moving people and goods. They don't get my heart going pitty-pat or anything like that." It was a frigid epitaph.

AT SOME POINT ON THE LAST of those evocative journeys with John Diefenbaker—and I still don't know if it was the result of having been aboard that train for most of a month or soaking in too much atmosphere at those Prairie way-stations—I began to understand why trains and the land they opened had become such essential elements in any debate about Canada's national identity.

I particularly remember one night when our iron horse was late leaving Fort Macleod. I went for a walk under the darkening sweep of the Prairie sky. What this elusive Canadianism of ours consisted of, I decided that evening—encouraged by the clarity of thought provided by a bottle of domestic *vin blanc de qualité*—was a kind of crazy pride that we had outlasted and outfoxed the elements. We may be a nation perpetually on the brink of breakup but damn it, we were still here. Despite our willingness to put ourselves down, our habit of avoiding the envy of others as a strategy for success, there was a certain valour in our humble stand against an impossible geography and a hopeless climate.

All men and women are sons and daughters of their geography, but nowhere is this more evident than in Canada, where the dominant gene of nationhood has been possession of the land itself. Canadians made their claim to citizenship by planting settlements on the shoulders of shores, the elbows of rivers and the laps of mountains. The main instrument in that process was the railway.

That connection between rail and land formed an early and essential image of ourselves as a people. Rail provided an imprint of the land upon the mind of a nation in its infancy. We subscribed to the *cri de coeur* of historian A.R.M. Lower of Queen's University: "From the land, must come the soul of Canada." Duddy Kravitz, the anti-hero created by author Mordecai Richler, expressed the same thought only not quite so nobly. "A man without land," he whined, "is a nobody." The concept of the land was as much an organizing principle of Canada as Roman Catholicism was to the Vatican. There really was no other legitimate reason for its being.

As the railways opened up more of the empty territories, place names began to indicate not just isolated whistle-stops of felled underbrush and a few root cellars but locations of noteworthy events. Still, it was less a tally of those events than the land itself that became the chronometer by which Canadians measured their lives. In many ways, their history was a series of plays performed on a vast stage—but the stage, and not the play, was the thing. It was a point of view that came from having tamed the largest national hunk of the earth's crust, connecting three great oceans. That undertaking became a magnificent obsession and it left Canadians magnificently obsessed with the land.

A place belongs to those who claim it the hardest, and Canadians—or at least that hardy generation that came out to greet John Diefenbaker—had claimed the land and, in turn, been claimed by it. Land-as-Identity became an accepted axiom, with territorial integrity becoming the country's strongest sustaining myth. Canada happily bargained away its energy resources to outside investors, sold ownership in its mines and oil wells at rock-bottom prices, spun off to strangers most of its manufacturing assets, relinquished to foreigners its capital, entrepreneurial skills and management class, allowed Hollywood and Madison Avenue to dictate its popular culture and voluntarily became a client state of the Pentagon. But let a foreigner sail through the North-West Passage, export a drop of its water or lay claim to a grain of its land and Canadians became fierce defenders of their patrimony.*

Part of the reason for Canadian land-mania was the country's outrageous size, stretching as it does across eighty-eight degrees of longitude and forty-two degrees of latitude, its six time zones spanning a quarter of the earth's day. Overlaid on a map of Europe, Canada would reach from the west coast of Ireland across the continent to the east of the Ural Mountains, deep in Asia. This vast landscape owed its predominant imagery to the Group of Seven, those magnificent visionaries of the 1920s who invented new techniques to capture the breathtaking magnitude of Canada's hinterland. "We came to know that it is only through the deep and vital experience of its total environment that a people identifies itself with its land and gradually a deep and satisfying awareness develops," reminisced Lawren Harris, the best of the Group of Seven painters, after one of his northern journeys. They, and the artists who followed, captured the essential hues of the Canadian landscape: the pewter-grey cliffs of Newfoundland, the scarlet slashes of Prince Edward Island's soil, the verdant farms of rural Ontario, the rich, mahogany loam of Alberta's eastern slopes and the moody blues of the Pacific Coast rain forests. Canadians have traditionally found spiritual sustenance in land and water, an inner solace that goes far beyond recharged brains or ventilated lungs. Marshall McLuhan postulated on the unique relationship of Canadians with nature. "We go outside to be alone," he proclaimed, "we go inside to be with people; a pattern that is antithetic not only to Europeans, but to all other cultures."

THE TROUBLE WITH HAVING A NATIONAL IDENTITY defined as an offshoot of nature is that it had so little to do with the Darwinian ethic of the 1980s. Once the passenger trains had stopped running, the romance went out of the land. For dwellers in the global village, circa 1995,

---

* The comedian Dave Broadfoot expressed Canada's territorial importance in his own way. "The world needs Canada," he explained, "because if Canada didn't exist, the Chinese could sail right across and invade Denmark."

the new frontier was the electronic territory known as cyberspace. Its landscapes were the virtual reality of the Internet. They could no more indulge themselves in the luxury of whimsical visions or put their trust in the land than a rail car could carry freight on the information highway. Canadians after the age of rail may have felt connected by cellular phones, they may in fact have been linked with blinding efficiency by fax machines, e-mail and satellite, but these were puny next to a line of shining rail that a farm boy could hobble along, and dream. The former passed through the ether and was without nation, the other bound the land.

The retreat from land-as-identity had, of course, started with plane travel. Flying at 30,000 feet over clouds or, on those rare flights when clear skies afford a spectacular view of the most magnificent landscape in creation, with blinds drawn to watch some third-rate Hollywood epic, was no way to touch the earth. During the decade covered by this book, the decade in which the country lost touch with itself and Canadians lost touch with their country, more Canadians travelled than ever before. More travelled within their own country. But the country, to them, was a string of dismal concrete airports and hotel chains. Besides that, air passengers and distance flown—both sensitive to recession—were about the same in the early 1990s as they were a decade earlier. Growth in telecommunications, meanwhile, had catapulted. Passenger rail revenues peaked at $546 million in 1981; they have since fallen to about one-quarter of that and most of it is travelled on short commuter runs. There were still, at decade's end, 70,000 commuters in Toronto and Montreal who rode the rails daily to work. But they were as disconnected from the land as any airplane passenger. During that same period, freight on the telephone lines doubled, from about $7 billion to $14 billion in revenues. There could be no denying that Canadians, in a very real way, were staying in touch with each other but they had lost touch with the land.

In a merciless global environment, land as a dominant theme of identity no longer filled the bill. In the new lexicon of values, land was just glorified dirt—and space, the air that filled the holes between places. If a suitable anthem for Canada before the 1980s was the haunting melody and lyric of Gilles Vigneault, *"Mon pays, ce n'est pas un pays, c'est l'hiver,"* (My country is not a country, it is winter), then Canada in the 1990s marched to Tom Cochrane's "Life is a highway." Canada's geography was still, and would always be, important. But instead of being the defining element of the country, land had become a mere backdrop to other events. Yet another once-reliable touchstone of the past had vanished.

Land had become increasingly abstract and unreal. There was no longer any attachment to territory, in the sense that no national politician would ever find it necessary to actually *cross* it, let alone dream of such a thing. With the trains gone, it could never happen again. It wasn't hard steel after all, but a thin umbilical cord of silk and dreams and hands shaken on platforms. It connected a people with the mother soil. When it was cut, it was cut forever.

FIVE

TOUCHSTONES

The End of Trust

He expired while begging for mercy in a gurgled whimper,
pleading for his life with the only English word he knew:
"Canada..."

THE CREDIBILITY OF THE SOOTHING INSTITUTIONAL IDEALS that had once tied Canada together had been forfeited by the mid-1990s. Like the broken pedestals of the toppled statues of Marx and Lenin in Berlin's *Alexander Platz*, only shattered remnants of the nation's once-holy icons remained. Instead of dutifully living out their destinies in the amiable latitudes north of the 49th parallel, Canadians were seized by a highly uncharacteristic sense of betrayal and distrust. Traditional values as expressed through their society's most significant institutions, which had guided Canada's leisurely gait from colony to nation, were being blatantly overturned by what was happening in peoples' own lives.

The nation's defining institutions first lost their credibility, then their authority and finally their followers. Nothing and no one was sacred any more. With few icons to command their loyalty or their service, Canadians abandoned their traditional sense of duty and feelings of trust.

Canadian soldiers, who once claimed their own beach in Normandy and treated their captured wounded as well as their own, now forced recruits to choke on their own faeces, paraded their bigotry before home video cameras and committed atrocities against the very people they were sworn to protect. They even propped up the heads of their lifeless victims for the cameras as though they had bagged an elk, not murdered a human being. Hockey and baseball stars became businessmen first, celebrities second and role models for a nation's youth hardly at all.* Priests lusted for choir boys' bodies instead of their souls; teachers sharpened their skills as trade unionists while their students struggled with maths and reading skills; Greenpeace activists turned into money-collectors;† politicians became a separate class that advanced its own interests, not those of the voters; auditors fixed books; experts turned out to be fools; lawyers went to jail; diplomats cheated; the Red Cross's carelessness killed. Small wonder that once-docile Canadians behaved like *Bounty* mutineers, casting the whole lot of them overboard.

Canadians wanted to rekindle their belief in institutions which could be depended upon to serve them, so that they in turn would have something to serve. They had tired of politicians who plundered the treasury for their own self-aggrandizement and institutions that served themselves, instead of the people who had elected, appointed or anointed them. What they got were Brian Mulroney's excesses of partisan largesse. They got an inept banking and business community that behaved with callous indifference as its own incompetence wiped out the life savings of many a pensioner. They got, above all, the message that the social contract was no longer valid and that everyone was on their own.

This breach of faith was the underpinning of the Revolution. Not that this was entirely a bad thing. "For me," concluded Bruce O'Hara, author and former employee-counsellor, "the most promising trend is that people no longer believe in experts for answers to

---

* At the same time, rural Canada lost its most essential touchstone: Canada Post closed 5,221 rural post offices, depriving small towns and villages of their natural meeting places and often the only Canadian flag flown in those communities.

† Captain Paul Watson, the rogue environmentalist who had been a founder of Greenpeace, complained that the once-militant outfit had deteriorated into "a bunch of Avon ladies"—a fund-raising operation with the majority of every dollar collected eaten up by commissions and administration.

anything, because they recognize that it was the same so-called experts who got us into this mess." The response was obvious: most Canadians turned for advice to the only experts they fully trusted— their own counsel.

The move to self-reliance was enhanced by the widespread use of technology. Suddenly everyone with a computer and modem *felt* connected; anyone who could watch CNN or CBC's Newsworld had access to real-time news events and newsmakers; anyone who could work a keyboard had access to a global data base. The yawning chasm between people's increased knowledge and their waning influence only served to deepen their resentment against authority. The Internet was exhilarating because it allowed users to bypass official information sources and thumb their noses at the media, which in the minds of most Canadians had long since stopped serving truth or community and had come to serve its inflated egos and the interests of advertisers.* Instead of defining themselves through the national identity (as interpreted by politics, business and culture) people began asserting their own identities. Instead of serving the national interest and feeling a sense of duty to national ideals, people felt a duty to pursue their own interest and serve their personal ambitions.

One of the side-effects of this power shift from community to self was a marked drop in civility in both political and social discourse. The taproot Canadian virtues of tolerance and respect had always been essential ingredients of the deference that typified the Canadian character. "We are in danger of losing our sense that civility matters," wrote Mark Kingwell, professor of philosophy at Toronto's Scarborough College, in the Winter 1994 issue of the *University of Toronto Magazine*. "Without it, social chaos and injus-

---

* The most popular Canadian Internet address in 1994 was "alt.pub-ban.homolka," which provided a forum for gruesome rumours of Karla Homolka's sex-torture-murder trial while a court ban prevented publication in Canada. The compilers were able to circumvent RCMP jamming efforts by running the Homolka file through an electronic labyrinth from a double-blind anonymous posting service based in Finland. The legal system to halt such exploitation was so antiquated in the cyberworld that it was rather like sending a detachment of Mounties on their Musical Ride ponies to do battle with the Green Berets.

tice are inevitable, if not imminent. A fashionable perception that hardball is the only game in town has led some people to believe that a little anger is good for Canadian politics, too long the preserve of bloodless elites and backroom consensus. The mistake here is to think that political passion cannot find expression in ongoing regular debate or to imagine that an appearance of fisticuffs at, say, a TV debate is a genuine mark of open democratic expression. Civility is not polite behaviour or good manners. It is much more the basic orientation to social interaction. Civility demands openness to the claims of others, combined with willing restraint of my own claims in the service of common social projects."

These qualities suffered a marked decline during the decade under review. Parliamentary debate reached such levels of disrespect for common decency that, when Tory MP William Kempling called then-Liberal backbencher Sheila Copps a "stupid slut," nobody got very excited and one MP was heard to mutter, "Well, she's not stupid . . ." The gossip sheet *Frank* magazine surpassed even its own allergy for decency and good taste when its editors launched a contest to see which young Tory could deflower the prime minister's daughter, Caroline, then sixteen years old. When her father complained that *Frank* had assaulted an innocent young woman's privacy for no other reason than to embarrass him—an observation that could hardly be denied, as Caroline held no public office—it served as fodder for the magazine to redouble its efforts.

The loss of civility was felt as sharply in the workplace as it was in politics. As unemployment in Canada created a horde of desperate jobless greater than the country's entire armed forces during the Second World War, violent protests and strikes grew commonplace. The most militant unions lost control of their rank and file. Instead of meekly following their leaders' instructions, the workers eyed their union bosses with the wariness of starving foxes. Cecil Taylor, the tough and dedicated president of the United Steelworkers' Union who had led a seven-week strike against Stelco Inc. which cost the company $70 million in lost profits, was shouted down at Hamilton's Ivor Wynne Stadium as he announced the victorious settlement he had reached on their behalf. When his members started setting the building on fire by lighting copies of the new contract, Taylor adjourned the meeting with the taunt: "If you want to light fires, I'll be at the union hall this afternoon. You can burn that down!" Canadian Labour Congress president Dennis McDermott led 100,000 unionist to Parliament Hill where they set bonfires while the labour leader threatened that next time his "guys" would forcibly take over Parliament itself.*

Violence became a habit. Vandalism was costing Toronto-area schools well over a million dollars a year; the murder rate in Halifax doubled while reported rapes were up 40 per cent.† A new lexicon entered the language, much of it imported from the United States but finding fertile ground in Canadian soil. Gang warfare, date rape, spousal abuse, sexual harassment, serial murders, bombings at abortion clinics and the P.E.I. legislature, drive-by shootings, all spoke to a weakening of respect for each other and a growing propensity for violence. While Canada had not been immune to crime in its past and its streets were still far safer than those to the south, the perceived rise in violent behaviour drove many to demand a tough law-and-order platform from their politicians. There was a corresponding rise in hostility in civil relations, as Canadians became ever more prone to litigate rather than negotiate, to point the finger rather than join hands for a shared solution. Pollster Allan Gregg documented the sullen turn in the Canadian character. "A pre-millennium anxiety has taken hold, shattering most of Canada's behavioural guidelines," he concluded.

Another reason Canadian society grew less pleasant was that so many sources of civility were silenced between 1985 and 1995. They included such distinguished writers and thinkers as Margaret Laurence, Morley Callaghan, Roger Lemelin, Arthur Lower, Hugh MacLennan, Northrop Frye, Bruce Hutchison, Marian Engel and Sandy Ross; Canadian illusionists *par excellence* A.J. Casson and Harold Town; parliamentary firebrand Eugene Forsey; those invaluable gurus of Canadian nationalism Walter Gordon and

---

* That fate was averted when Brian Mulroney disarmed and diverted McDermott by naming him Canadian Ambassador to Ireland, where politics was presumably conducted more to his liking.

† Toronto policemen went on wildcat strikes; Newfoundlanders captured and held a government ferry to protest schedule reductions; truckers jammed the highways to drive home their demands; Indians mounted roadblocks to protest a litany of issues.

George Grant; the enlightened chief justice Bora Laskin; social policy pioneers Tommy Douglas, Paul Martin and Pauline Jewett; comic Johnny Wayne; the incomparable Barbara Frum. While each of these remarkable men and women made their own contribution to the national character, they shared a sense of duty to their national *community*; one would not say of them, as could be said of many of the self-satisfied upstarts who replaced them, that they regarded Canada as a jumping-off point to a better career in a country that really mattered. Each served in their own way their nation, not their unwarrantedly inflated ego.*

IF PRINT JOURNALISM IN CANADA could boast of a dean and mentor, it had to be Bruce Hutchison, the crusty Victoria newspaperman who died in the fall of 1992 at the age of ninety-one. His 1952 biography of Prime Minister William Lyon Mackenzie King (*The Incredible Canadian*) and his continuing studies of political leaders remain watershed works, but his six decades of daily and weekly columns would be his most lasting monument. His talent was to draw large conclusions from small events and his graceful literary style helped obliterate the distance that usually separates journalist from subject.

"I write," he once told me, "because I may have learned something about the world and within it a Canada, now gone and quite unbelievable to most of its contemporary inhabitants, together with certain people who made it and unmade it." While he had an abiding faith in the reasonableness of ordinary citizens, Hutchison also believed that the assumption of power shuffled the elements in a person's character, so that the holder of high political office became

---

* More typical of the times than these gentle departed souls was the country's most outrageous redneck, Don Cherry, whose semi-literate tirades were watched by two million Canadians every "Hockey Night in Canada." Cherry, who looked down at the world from his starched collars and encouraged a generation of children to slash, pummel and slice each other to satisfy his blood-lust, tried so hard to be objectionable that even his on-air sidekick, Ron MacLean, couldn't understand the overstuffed blowhard's appeal. "People seem to enjoy it when he tells them off," he told Chris Cobb of the *Ottawa Citizen*. "He'll utter an obscenity to someone and they'll go away chuckling: 'Don Cherry told me to fuck off!'" So much for civility in the 1990s.

both a part of its mystique and a contributor to it. His most endearing quality was his affection for Canada, a passionate love affair that coloured everything he said and wrote. He was kind and generous to younger colleagues, lecturing them endlessly on the perfidy of those too shortsighted to share his vision of the country, but he never took himself as seriously as his quest. His passing diminished both his craft and his country.

Canada had a spiritual town crier of our aspirations and afflictions in Hugh MacLennan, the Montreal novelist, essayist and humanitarian who died in 1990 at the age of eighty-three. He was the author of six magnificent essay collections and seven major works of fiction, the most evocative of which, *The Watch That Ends the Night*, is my favourite Canadian novel. He was an ardent Canadian in his life and in his prose. To toughen himself to the country's harsh climate, he spent ten years of his youth living in a tent staked in the backyard of his parents' Halifax house. Despite international honours that included a Rhodes Scholarship, a Guggenheim Fellowship and a Ph.D. from Princeton, he never considered living or teaching anywhere but in Canada. His five Governor-General's Literary Awards notwithstanding, the nation never properly rewarded him for his loyalty. His best-known work, *Two Solitudes*, became the fountainhead for defining the shared loneliness that is at the heart of the Canadian experience. It brought him an initial royalty cheque of only $4,500. Worse, although he had taught English literature with distinction at McGill University in Montreal for more than three decades and had inspired generations of young writers, in 1985 he was unceremoniously booted out of his modest office space that had previously been promised to him as a writing refuge in his old age.

Released from the novelist's bonds of plot and characterization, his essays succeeded in portraying what the American literary critic Edmund Wilson called "a point of view surprisingly and agreeably different from anything else I knew in English: a Canadian way of looking at things." His best-selling book was the nonfiction *The Colour of Canada*. It warned against Canada's absorption by the Americans and advised Canadians to act "in the spirit of a girl in the backseat of a taxi, with one eye on the meter and the other on the profile of the determined man who took her out that night." Equally scornful of anything British or American, MacLennan jealously guarded his Celtic heritage and credited his Highland roots for the sensitivity of his perceptions. "A Celt," he once confided to me, "hears a dog-whistle sound that an Anglo-Saxon simply doesn't get." He was contemptuous of academic aesthetes and believed that a writer must be engaged with the issues of his time, echoing D.H. Lawrence's dictum that "the novel treats the point at which the soul meets history."

He was obsessed by Pierre Trudeau. "The light in his eyes has a subtle and curious Giaconda-like intensity. I doubt if even the painter of Mona Lisa herself could capture it," he wrote me, and then blasted Trudeau for being a cheapskate. "He once invited us to a conference in the Laurentians and put [renowned lawyer and poet] Frank Scott and me up in a clip joint. Another time, he invited Margaret Atwood and me to 24 Sussex for lunch, at the end of which he departed in his limousine, and it took us an hour to get a taxi to the airport." MacLennan's last years were filled with suffering. After he was expelled from his McGill office, his apartment was threatened with conversion to a condominium. His second wife, Frances (his first wife, Dorothy Duncan, died in 1957), was struck by lightning and suffered brain damage, while he was afflicted with a rare form of MSG food poisoning. "The symptoms are preposterous," he wrote me. "One wakes up and believes one is dead."

He most assuredly was not. None of his mishaps diluted his passion for life or for his country. He complained that Canadian politics were at least forty years behind the times and that Quebec had gone crazy as never before. Unlike Hutchison, who played at being the eternal optimist, MacLennan felt not at all certain that Canada would amount to anything. "Some fibre went out of us," he complained. But no fibre ever went out of Hugh MacLennan. He was a fine man and a great writer, and the Canada he left behind was made poorer by his passing.

The absence of both these writers underscored and symbolized something that was lost in this country during the decade. It was a quality that defined them as much as it defined their country, and once it was lost, it could not be replaced. It was the sense of completion to be found in a decent life spent in dutiful service.

CANADA LOST THESE VOICES at the same time as the deadliest recession since the Dirty Thirties shook people's faith in an economic system that only two decades earlier had provided Canadians with the world's highest standard of living. Canadians had raised their kids to believe that the world would improve with each new generation. Instead, some of the bushy-tailed youngsters that the junior chambers of commerce used to salute as "young leaders of tomorrow" found themselves slinging hash at fast-food joints. In a country which once prided itself on being classless, two distinct Canadian classes emerged: the first was the thin crust of computer-literate, superbly educated, mentally flexible young men and women who could master the radical workplace changes of the electronic society; the second, road kill on the information highway.

About the only safe profession to follow, it seemed, was the law. Even though a disproportionately high number of lawyers spent parts of the decade in jail for fiddling with their clients' funds, their income levels rose with each turn of the Revolution, which they were willing to serve, on whichever side posted the highest legal fees. The worst example of the breed was Julius Melnitzer, the London, Ontario, attorney who cheated Canadian banks out of $43 million through a complicated share certificate forgery scam. Sentenced to nine years, he only served three, then wrote a self-congratulary book to cash in on his crimes. The Montreal-born, U.S. real-estate and publishing mogul Morty Zuckerman made the wisest comment on the practice of law. When he abandoned his legal studies while still in college, he explained that being a lawyer was "the exact opposite of sex—even when it's good, it's lousy."*

The decline in civility was measured by the brutally high legal levy added to just about every personal and corporate move. This transactional-cost burden made Canada, the world's most over-lawyered country, considerably less competitive. The descent into legal bickering became so widespread that Dr. Pat McGeer, a leading Vancouver brain researcher and former B.C. science minister, once half-seriously advocated that the only solution was to sign a free trade pact with Japan. It would have only one clause: for every engineer the Japanese sent to Canada, we would send them fifty lawyers.

The tendency for once-cooperative Canadians to use lawyers as

---

* To the curious who wondered why talented feminist Gloria Steinem had a lengthy live-in affair with Zuckerman, she explained: "He was miserable, and I found a man who said he was miserable irresistible."

hired assassins was so great that some assignments proved too tough even for the most heartless of these legal eagles. When the Toronto-based CTV Television Network was trying to sort out details of its corporate ownership, the firm's legal counsel gave up. CTV President John Cassaday assigned the job to Roger Fisher from Cambridge, Massachusetts, then the western world's toughest conflict resolution specialist. Fisher had previously shepherded the entente that resulted in the 1978 Camp David Accord between Israel and Egypt and had more recently mediated between the South African government and the African National Congress. Doug Bassett, the most significant and most argumentative player in the CTV imbroglio, when asked at a CRTC hearing to define a network, replied, "It's a group of people quarrelling." Despite Fisher's best efforts, the dispute remained unresolved.

Canada's 40,000 accountants and auditors proved as diligent in their application of sound accounting practices as its lawyers had been in seeking the resolution of disputes. Members of both groups had forgotten their prime function of adhering to professional standards. None of Canada's top eight accounting firms escaped court action against their audits. In the spring of 1991, for example, Peat Marwick Thorne, the country's biggest accounting firm, paid $240,000 in damages for negligence in auditing a Montreal conveyor-belt distributor. That firm, along with Toronto's prestigious Ernst & Young, paid a large but undisclosed out-of-court settlement for allowing Edmonton's failed Canadian Commercial Bank to operate two years after it was technically insolvent. The same two firms were penalized $43 million for their careless auditing methods in the 1985 collapse of Alberta's Northland Bank.* Coopers & Lybrand piled up lawsuits worth more than $800 million for its audit of the bankrupt Castor Group in Montreal. When Peter Earle, of Price Waterhouse, audited Calgroup Graphics Corp., a resource-company-turned-movie-distributor, he assessed the company's film collection as being worth $15 million, though a later settlement established its accounting value to be $32. (The Institute of Chartered Accountants of Ontario heard the

---

* Lowenthol & Horwath, the seventh-largest American accounting firm, was forced to file for bankruptcy in 1991 after losing several malpractice suits, and U.S. regulators also filed claims of negligence worth $560 million against Ernst & Young.

case but took no disciplinary action.) A 1988 review by the Ontario Securities Commission discovered that fully a quarter of the financial reports filed that year contained serious accounting errors. "The large C.A. firms now appear to have as their chief concern international competitiveness," observed Henry E. McCandless, a principal in the Office of the Auditor General in Ottawa, "not leadership in their respective countries serving public accountability. The great firm of Clarkson Gordon under the guidance of the Gordons and J.R.M. Wilson viewed serving public accountability as a duty of the profession. We don't have that kind of leadership today, either with its successor firm or the senior partners of other firms."*

While lawyers and accountants lost some of their sense of duty to the public, Canada's diplomatic corps was busy diluting its sense of duty to the country. Becoming a Canadian diplomat was once considered to be Canada's highest calling, with fierce competition among the country's best and brightest to write the exams that determined who would get one of the few available slots. Cultivated, clever and cordial, most Canadian diplomats made up for their lack of ideology and passion by being trustworthy and hard-working representatives of their country abroad; theirs was a service that had never been sullied by financial scandal and they were proud of it. But in 1992, a routine audit at External Affairs revealed that nearly 12 per cent of Canada's diplomatic corps—300 members including several ambassadors—had been cheating on their expense accounts to the tune of $567,200. The RCMP investigation that followed found plenty of evidence to lay charges but no one was prosecuted or discharged.† Meanwhile, those diplomats

---

* After these revelations a Bay Street joke went the rounds about how chief executive officers pick their corporate auditors:
  The CEO asks each canadidate: "What's two plus two?"
  The first applicant answers: "Four."
  The next one hedges his bets: "Five?"
  The auditor who gets the job replies: "What would you like it to be?"

† In typically Canadian (but hardly revolutionary) fashion, the External Affairs Department dealt with the cheaters by making the fraudulent legal. By handing diplomats the cash equivalent of full-fare tickets and demanding no receipts in exchange, fraud could not be documented ever again.

who worked at the department's Ottawa head office pursued more mundane swindles. In the eighteen months ending in the summer of 1992, they stole 2,998 teaspoons, 2,218 forks, 1,438 knives and 1,349 dessert spoons from External's cafeteria. Vending machines were jammed with Danish kroners, Belgian francs and Italian lire by diplomats trying to save a few pennies on Bar-B-Q Chips and undrinkable instant coffee.*

"WE ATTACK AT DAWN," ran the sarcastic toast in Canadian military messes. "That way if things don't work out, we won't have wasted the whole day."

That bitter little witticism accurately caught the stereotype of Canada's armed forces. Most citizens tended to think of their military men and women—if they thought of them at all—as short-haired amateurs, misfits who couldn't make it in civilian life, but who weren't particularly warlike about their profession. The late Hal Lawrence, one of Canada's genuine war heroes (he was awarded the Distinguished Service Cross for sinking a German U-boat by jumping on the submarine's conning tower and lobbing down a grenade) summed up this attitude in a letter to me:

> After Admiral H.T.W. Grant had retired as Chief of Naval Staff I was at his home one evening and asked him: "Why is it, sir, that when I'm in the United Kingdom and someone asks me what I do and I say I'm a Lieutenant in the Royal Canadian Navy, he says, 'Oh, really, jolly good. You must come down to the country for a weekend.' And when I'm asked the same question in the States and give a similar reply, I'm told, 'Oh yeah? Why don't you come over to the house and meet the family?' But when the

---

* Coincidentally, the diplomats of other countries stationed in Canada were caught abusing their tax-free cigarette privileges. By 1991, the relatively small (10,000 members including families and clerical workers) diplomatic community in Canada was buying an annual 111 million tax-free cigarettes and selling them for a $1 billion profit. Even after allocations were reduced in 1992, foreign diplomats still bought enough cigarettes that if they were consumed as they claimed, for their own use, each embassy member would have had to smoke twenty packs a day.

same question and answer are exchanged in Canada, there's an awkward pause while everyone thinks: 'Poor guy. Probably didn't do well in Grade 12.' "

"My dear Lawrence," the Admiral replied, "it has always been thus. In the U.K. everyone knows the Navy and that it has kept them free for centuries; it doesn't matter if it's true or not. In the U.S. the military threw off the oppression of a distant tyrant and sailors have kept the tyrant out ever since. Again, it's not as simple as that, but that's what they believe. In Canada, on the other hand, we've always fought distant wars: in Egypt in the last century, in South Africa at the turn of the century, in Europe in 1914–18, North Africa, Europe and the Far East in 1939–45. So, have another glass of port and calm down."

Lawrence's complaint was fair ball, but it applied less to his wartime incarnation than the off-duty years that followed. Canada's contribution in the two world wars was stunning—1.5 million men and women performing gallantly under arms, plus the sacrifices of civilians at home which contributed millions of dollars' worth of goods and services shipped to Britain and other Allies. Out of the blood and mud of the 1917 trenches came the first stirring of Canadian nationalism. Capturing Vimy Ridge when no one else could meant we were capable of running our own affairs; out of the Second World War came an industrial machine and a self-confident labour force to run it. Still, the notion that Canada could produce effective fighting men and women ran counter to the image we preferred of ourselves as citizens of a "peaceable kingdom." Canada had fought no wars of independence; its home-grown rebellions, at Red River and Batoche, ranked as minor skirmishes; its assault on the Spanish fleet to protect turbot stocks was a victory of sorts, promptly followed by a diplomatic defeat. "Canada is an unmilitary community," wrote the historian C.P. Stacey. "Warlike her people have often been forced to be, military they have never been."

That the armed forces lost their context and relevance in peacetime was not surprising in a country that prided itself on being a cultural free port with designs to conquer no one. Members of the peacetime Canadian military thus found themselves divorced from Canadian society. They rarely possessed any clout in Cabinet and except for a general feeling of pride in their past achievements, celebrated during one minute of silence every November 11, few cared what happened to them. They were a bit like a third-string hockey team perpetually on the road, with nowhere to call home ice. They had lived on the hockey bus so long, playing games that so few watched and fewer remembered, that team members kept what remained of their sanity by inventing complex myths, private rules, obscure initiation rituals and their own *patois*. A strictly hierarchical society committed to a way of life outside the Canadian mainstream, the men (and odd woman) who commanded Canada's armed forces studied thick volumes of intelligence reports and understood what was happening in every country but their own. They knew every chapter and verse of the officer's manual, but they were baffled by the contents of the morning newspaper.

The ultimate expression of the Canadian military mentality was the National Defence Headquarters building in Ottawa, a monstrosity originally designed for the Ministry of Transport. An airless concrete block filled with paper battalions and occupants who had acronyms instead of names, the building itself represented the Canadian preference of hiding its military under a rock. Canada's attitude toward the military was best gauged by the quality of their peacetime equipment. When NATO still had a functioning navy, three of the destroyers assigned to the Alliance as part of Canada's official fleet were permanently docked in Halifax and Esquimalt so they could be cannibalized for parts to keep the other ships afloat. When a New Brunswick army reserve unit ran out of weapons, the troop marched to manoeuvres carrying broomsticks. The incident culminated in a remarkable exchange between two recruits who confronted one another:

"You've had it, man," one of them yelled, pointing his broom. "I shot you with this rifle."

"No you didn't," came the calm reply, "I'm a tank."

In the summer of 1990, when the navy was asked to contribute two warships to the United Nations flotilla trying to blockade Saddam Hussein's military ambitions, the commanding officers of the only two hulls available for the mission—HMCS *Athabasca* and HMCS *Terra Nova*—were seriously worried that the Iraqi dictator might bomb them with turpentine, since the ships—the elder of the two destroyers dated back to 1959—were literally held together by countless coats of grey paint.

UNABLE TO FIGURE OUT WHETHER THEIR COUNTRY was the least of the great nations or the greatest of the small powers, Canadians decided in the smug afterglow of the Second World War to become something Lester B. Pearson dubbed a "middle power." Then the secretary of state for external affairs, Pearson concocted the idea of a United Nations Expeditionary Force to maintain peace between the belligerents in the Suez Crisis of 1956 and he later won a Nobel Peace Prize for his efforts. It served as the model for sending Canadian soldiers to calm the world's trouble spots. They could be shot at, mauled and manhandled but were seldom permitted to return fire or retaliate in any way. It was perfect casting for a nation that had turned deference into its state religion. For the first time we could project our capacity for diffidence to a grateful world; the troops of no other country had been raised at their mothers' knees to become experts at being hit without hitting back.

Being a Canadian abroad took on a whole new meaning with the success of each peacekeeping assignment. We were the perfect buffer. Wearing the blue beret meant being pure of heart and noble of purpose. Canadian passports became an invaluable commodity; having one immediately identified its bearer as harmless. A generation of youths (some were even Canadians) hitchhiked through Europe with the Maple Leaf sewn on their backpacks as a talisman against misfortune. Several of the most senior Soviet spy masters (including such major players as Robert Soblen, Colonel Rudolph Abel and Gordon Lonsdale, who obtained the plans of Britain's nuclear submarines) operated on Canadian identity papers. Olaf Rankis, executive vice-president for security and intelligence at Gordon Liddy & Associates, the Miami firm that supplies mercenaries to various industrial groups, confessed that he always travelled "wearing a red maple leaf pin in my lapel. Nobody hates the Canadians." A senior American diplomat in Ghana once revealed to Michael Valpy of *The Globe and Mail* that U.S. State Department personal security courses advise anyone due for a hazardous posting not to look too obviously American. "They tell us to try to look Canadian," he admitted. "We're supposed to fade into the background and say *oot* and *aboot*."

In the past three decades, more than 80,000 Canadian soldiers were part of peacekeeping operations in Laos, Vietnam, the Dominican Republic, Nigeria, Syria, Afghanistan, Yemen and Cyprus. They were not altogether peaceful assignments, with Canadian forces suffering ninety fatal casualties and many more wounded. (The casualties would have been much higher but for the fact that these postings usually pitted Canadians against belligerents even more poorly equipped than themselves.) By the early 1990s Canada was contributing 10 per cent of the United Nations' total peacekeeping force, even though the country's population represented only 1 per cent of UN membership. The Canadian military had found its home-ice advantage at last, even if it was in someone else's home. So long as they remained abroad and didn't hurt anyone, peacekeepers were a source of Canadian pride. The soldiers who served in UN forces were aware of this and behaved accordingly; Canada earned a well-deserved reputation as no-nonsense but fair intermediaries.

Armed forces mirror the character of the societies on whose behalf they are pledged to fight. If the ultimate purpose of Canada's military force was hard to pin down, it was because Canadians as a people lacked any definable creed or even a set of common beliefs. Even the least xenophobic citizen realized that survival on this delicate planet depended on the will Canadians could muster to protect their institutions—and that, in turn, depended on how much they valued them. But since Canada was indefensible in any event, maintaining peace at the world's flashpoints seemed like the armed force's perfect assignment. It finally provided the armed forces with a reason for being. From being a fringe institution Canada's military came into its own, particularly after Major General Lewis MacKenzie took over as chief of staff for the 14,000-member UN Protection Force in Yugoslavia. One of those natural-born leaders who inspire confidence by his belief in the soldiers under his command, "Lew" MacKenzie gave Canadian peacekeeping its first public face and articulate voice. His thirty-two years with the Canadian army had included UN experience dating back to a 1963 stint on the Gaza strip; he later served as a peacekeeper in Cyprus and was a team commander with the International Commission for Control and Supervision in Vietnam. His Yugoslavia assignment turned out to be less peacekeeping than peace*making*. ("Peace enforcement is an oxymoron," former UN officer Lieutenant Colonel J.C. Berezowski pointed out. "Its synonym is war.") Most of MacKenzie's front-line equipment had been painted white and shipped to Yugoslavia from Canada's NATO division in Lahr, after the West German base was closed. MacKenzie's "peace enforcers" won world recognition when they captured and held control of the embattled Sarajevo airport, allowing fearless Canadian pilots of C-130 Hercules transports to deliver much-needed food and medicine amid a hail of ground fire.

Despite MacKenzie's proud record, Canada's reputation as a compassionate peacekeeper died shortly after his Yugoslav assignment expired. In a hot, dry slice of East Africa known as Somalia, a fatal blow was delivered not just to peacekeeping but to a military reputation intact for half a century and more. On March 4, 1993, soldiers from the élite Canadian Airborne Regiment serving on a UN intervention force shot two Somali youths trying to infiltrate their base camp at Belet Huen. Twelve days later the Canadians captured a young local Somali, Shidane Abukar Arone, trying to sneak into their compound. He claimed to be looking for a lost child, though he might have been hoping to do a little pilfering. The sixteen-year-old youth, as it later turned out, not only owned a camel and his own herd of goats, but he had a wife (Haliomo Abdi Ali) and a dwelling that could be collapsed on the back of the camel so the couple could follow rain patterns and keep their animals alive. For reasons that never became clear, even during the half-dozen court martials that followed, the soldiers beat and tortured the youth to death. They took photographs of his agony and even posed with his battered body for trophy-shots, propping his bloodied head up for the camera with a broomstick. More than fifteen members of the Airborne, including officers, heard his screams and did nothing. He died after suffering three hours of brutal indignities. He expired while begging for mercy in a gurgled whimper, pleading for his life with the only English word he knew: "Canada..."

Canadians were astonished and disgusted by the televised photo images of the grisly incident, plus a video depicting members of the Airborne making ugly sexist and racist jokes about Somalis. Canadians had naïvely imagined that peacekeepers had something to do with benevolence and goodwill. Of the six Airborne charged, only Private Elvin Kyle Brown received a serious sentence (five years for manslaughter), while Master Corporal Clayton Matchee tried to hang himself after being arrested, suffering brain damage that rendered him unfit to stand trial. Arone's father was paid $20,000, representing what the Canadian army claimed to be the customary compensation, equivalent to the cost of a hundred camels. The family insisted that even by that standard they were owed twice as much. That incident was followed by another amateur video shown on Canadian television of the Airborne's hazing rituals. They included young soldiers eating their own vomit and excrement, urinating on bread they fed to each other, forcing a black soldier to crawl on his knees with "I love the Ku Klux Klan" scrawled in excrement on his back and other obscenities too disgusting to mention. The official military explanation that this was a necessary part of the bonding process impressed no one, least of all Liberal Defence Minister David Collenette, who promptly disbanded the Airborne Regiment. The decision hit military morale hard, as did the ensuing one-third cut in the defence budget. But public opinion was hurt even more acutely. The notion was unacceptable that Canadian peacekeepers, even as an isolated incident, could torture and kill the very people they were sent to protect. One more institutional touchstone and the values it represented had been lost, the notion of duty at arms.

NO SENSE OF BETRAYAL hit the average Canadian quite so hard as the scandal involving the Red Cross. No routine cluster of do-gooders, the Red Cross was an organization that, until the contaminated blood scandal of the 1990s, touched the lives of Canadians only in the kindest and most compassionate of ways. Red Cross first-aid courses and water-safety programs were part of every Canadian's upbringing; elderly relatives were cared for by Red Cross home-care workers; the victims of any disaster looked to the Red Cross for succour, clothing, temporary shelter and hot food—and they were never disappointed.

The international organization's Canadian branch had been founded by Dr. George Sterling Ryerson, medical officer of the army troop despatched from Ottawa in 1885 to quell the Riel Rebellion at Batoche, Saskatchewan. To distinguish his little field hospital, he made a rough flag by cutting sheets of red cloth into a cross and stitching them over a cotton sheet. He flew the hand-made banner from his horse-drawn ambulance, parked next to his makeshift operating room.* The Red Cross was active in helping Canadian soldiers during the Boer War and several other smaller conflicts, but it really came into its own during the two world wars. Between 1914 and 1918 the Canadian Red Cross shipped $35 million worth of relief supplies overseas and operated a half-dozen hospitals in England and France, providing recreational huts and ambulance convoys as well. The Second World War saw those efforts multiplied many times over, to be followed by years of service to veterans and caring for refugees and children orphaned by the war. In 1947, the organization took over the country's blood transfusion service and quickly attracted a million donors a year. The Red Cross was one of those seminal Canadian institutions like winter, the St. Lawrence River or spring's maple syrup run-off. It was beyond attack or even comment. Canadians took it as an article of faith that they provided for each other in a time of crisis with "the gift of life." It was one more thing that distinguished us from the Americans, who were less altruistic and paid their blood donors. Canadians believed that in a crisis the blood being pumped into their veins likely came from a healthy, bright-eyed volunteer, unlike the United States, where it might have sprung from the collapsed veins of a drug addict desperate for a fix.

Then came the 1994 commission of enquiry into Red Cross operations by Ontario Court of Appeal Judge Horace Krever. Overnight the sanctity of its reputation turned into a tragic sham. There were almost daily revelations of how this supposedly compassionate organization had not only distributed blood contaminated with the HIV virus that leads to AIDS, but in many cases had done so knowingly and a time when it had safe blood in its own storage vaults. At least 1,440 Canadians innocently exposed to these transfusions acquired the syndrome and more than half have already died, though the count will never be complete since some may have unknowingly infected their sexual partners and others. At least 12,000 more were

---

* The original Red Cross Society was founded by a Swiss humanitarian named Jean-Henri Dunant under similar circumstances at the 1859 Battle of Solferino. The design he chose for the organization's emblem—meant to guarantee the safety of relief workers—was the reverse of the national flag of Switzerland.

infected with preventable Hepatitis C, a viral infection that can lead to fatal liver cancer. The inhuman carelessness of the Red Cross decimated Canada's haemophiliacs, who depended on clean blood transfusions to live. From symbolizing angels of mercy, the Red Cross had overnight come to be represented as the sickle of death.

The most bizarre revelation to come to light was that while these transgressions were mostly committed in the 1980s, even as the Krever Commission was hearing witnesses and tallying up the horror stories, the Red Cross still hadn't cleaned up its act. As recently as September 1994, a U.S. inspection team had found nineteen serious deficiencies at the main Toronto blood collection depot and halted any shipments of Canadian plasma into the United States. It was the ultimate insult to Canadian pride: our blood was no longer good enough for the U.S. market. Ottawa health regulators had meanwhile closed Red Cross distribution centres in Montreal, London, Regina and Saskatoon.

All this happened even though AIDS, first diagnosed in 1981, had become the most publicized disease in medical history. Neither was there any reason for the Canadian Red Cross to have distributed the bad blood, except for the accepted ethic of the day—deference to authority. Here it was in its most evil incarnation—the idea that one could avoid the moral consequences of one's actions when obeying the authority of superiors. Several doctors operating regional labs and distribution depots in the 1980s wanted to destroy the tainted blood, but instead of acting on their impulses, they bowed before the tunnel-visioned authority of their head office. They did nothing and later defended their crimes of omission by pleading the Nuremberg defence. It was difficult to believe these death-dealing decisions were made not by some minimum-wage automatons but by medical doctors pledged to relieve human suffering.

This dereliction of duty was made all the more obscene by the knowledge that in several cases the difference between distributing safe plasma and knowingly sending out tainted blood was a matter of hours. On June 30, 1985, Dr. John MacKay, who was then and remains medical director for the Red Cross in New Brunswick, sent out four vials of HIV-tainted blood products for use by haemophiliacs at a Saint John hospital. At that very moment his own office had on hand 843 vials of safe heat-treated plasma, scheduled to replace the unsafe product the next morning. An incredulous Kathryn

Podrebarac, legal counsel for the Canadian Haemophilia Society at the Krever enquiry, asked: "Is it so important to follow instructions that at the point when you know that the heat-treated product is coming the next day, to be issuing product that you knew to be unsafe?" Dr. MacKay's answer was brief and to the point: "We follow guidelines." Good Canadians following orders meant that New Brunswick suffered the highest per-capita rate of HIV infections among the country's haemophiliacs; more than fifty, including many children, died from the bad blood.

In Montreal, Red Cross officials admitted that in the mid-1980s their downtown clinic at the Berri-de-Montigny subway station was collecting fifty times more HIV-contaminated blood than any other collection point in the country. This was hardly surprising, since the Berri station, straddling the city's red light district, held its largest concentration of intravenous drug users and was next to Montreal's main gay bar scene and inside the Haitian enclave—all groups identified with a high risk of AIDS infection. This clinic was operated for most of eight years even though the Red Cross lawyer Michael Worsoff advised the Society at the time that it had a "moral and legal obligation to assure the safety of the blood it accepts." Randy Connors of Halifax, himself dying of AIDS from a blood transfusion in the early 1980s, led the fight for government compensation to victims of the Red Cross's carelessness. He spoke with understandable bitterness but no exaggeration when he declared: "It's just plain murder what they did, giving out a product that they know is going to kill you." The tragedy's most poignant twist came with the Red Cross admission that they drew up priority rosters of which patients would receive good blood (mostly what they called "virgin haemophiliacs" who had not already been exposed to contaminated product) and which would be given the bad, untreated plasma. These Schindler's lists determined who would live and who would die.*

There was no way to encompass—emotionally or rationally—how the Red Cross, an institution whose only purpose was to bring comfort and help to those who needed it most, could excuse its

---

* As late as March of 1995, after a year of the Krever hearings, the Red Cross still hadn't cleaned up its act. The Society found itself having to suspend Dr. Michel Hébert, its Quebec City medical director, because his blood collection centre had failed a flash Health Canada inspection.

own behaviour. Given the chance to at least apologize for what had happened, its secretary-general took a pass.* Addressing the Toronto chapter of the Canadian Club after most of his Society's death-dealing ways had been exposed, Douglas Lindores said: "To the extent that any institutional or human failing of the Red Cross has contributed to the increased suffering of even one Canadian, I express our deepest, profoundest regrets." A Canadian Press reporter asked Lindores whether he was, in effect, extending an apology. "No," replied the head of Canada's erstwhile humanitarian organization, that by then was indirectly responsible for the deaths of more than a thousand innocents, "I wouldn't use that word." Others might have.

THE DECADE THAT WITNESSED Canada's transition from deference to defiance was neatly bracketed by two events that expressed both of these polarized emotions. The defiance at the end of the decade was symbolized by Brian Tobin's piratical stance on behalf of the turbot fishery off Newfoundland in March of 1995. But it had been preceded a decade earlier by the defining expression of deference, which was Brian Mulroney's visit to the Economic Club of New York on December 10, 1984. His trip turned out to be the prologue to the momentous Free Trade Agreement—the most fundamental change to the country's economy, society and culture that occurred during the Canadian Revolution.

Drifting around the private receptions before the New York meeting, I found it difficult to name any Canadian power brokers who hadn't turned out for the prime minister's American debut. More remarkable was the appearance of the 1,400 big hitters representing the U.S. banking and investment community. Many of their spouses were also there, attracted by the reputation of Mila and Brian as North America's most glamorous power couple. "Listen, Janina," I overheard one "wife of" breathlessly briefing another, "this is really a big deal. That guy with the hair is the president of Canada!"

---

* Despite the strong evidence, no member of the Canadian Red Cross was charged with anything. In France, even those who were indirectly responsible for the distribution of tainted blood were indicted—such as French President Laurent Fabius and his chief of staff, Louis Schweitzer.

Mulroney understood that the illustrious sharks who thronged the Grand Ballroom of Rockefeller Center's Hilton Hotel wanted to be loved even more than they craved fat bottom lines. Third World politicians could get elected by depicting Ronald Reagan as a senile Dr. Strangelove and then demanding U.S. aid—not Mulroney. The Hilton's men and women chomping their *filet mignon* ached for outsiders to bless their righteousness and recognize what was left of the American century. Mulroney's message, delivered in his best Kirk Douglas whisper, was pointed and friendly: send us your cash and we'll be your friends. "To all who seek a definition of peaceful association between nations, I say look no farther," he advised them. "It is unlikely you shall find a better illustration than the simple story of friendship and prosperity that has marked the evolution of our two countries over the years."

These merchant adventurers were not frightened off by investment risks and had never been bothered by Pierre Trudeau's closet anti-Americanism or René Lévesque's separatist dreams. What they could not tolerate were any politicians who changed "the rules of the game" under which funds had originally been invested. They interrupted Mulroney with applause eleven times, but the loudest ovation of the evening greeted his declaration: "Canada is open for business!"

His audience correctly interpreted that statement as meaning that Canada was for sale—lock, stock and oil barrel. Chief executive officers of the Fortune 500 seldom bothered with policy declarations issued by foreign governments, or even the "situationals" prepared by their own research departments. They preferred to get the news directly from the guy who was running the country. Mulroney repudiated Ottawa's made-in-Canada measures by promising to kill the National Energy Program and neuter the Foreign Investment Review Agency. He reversed its mandate, so that instead of restricting foreign investment, FIRA would be charged with attracting it.

Mulroney played his audience as masterfully as a Johnny Carson. When he interrupted himself to ruminate on the undefended border between the two countries, he ad-libbed: "There hasn't been a shot fired in anger between us since 1812. That wasn't much of a war. We captured Detroit, took one look around and gave it back." It was a good speech, savoured by his audience. Even the book-end Mounties guarding the dais managed to stay awake. As the crowd dispersed, the faces of the Economic Club members relaxed into a post-coital glow:

Canada was A-OK. The guy with the hair was user-friendly. As they climbed back into the limos, they reverted to type.

"Hey, Virgil," somebody yelled across the street, "what's the world's fastest animal?"

"Beats me."

"A chicken—in Ethiopia!"

THE FREE TRADE PACT had many proponents, but the most influential of them was Paul Robinson, a former U.S. naval officer and Chicago insurance broker who took Ottawa by storm and the country to the cleaners. Appointed the U.S. ambassador to Canada by Ronald Reagan (in return for raising $700,000 for Reagan's election campaign), he exercised extraordinary influence in both national capitals. For example, in a briefing before Reagan and Mulroney were due to begin their 1985 Shamrock Summit on St. Patrick's Day in Quebec City, U.S. Secretary of State George Shultz was having a problem communicating with Erik Nielsen, the deputy prime minister and minister of national defence. Nielsen, who had used up his weekly quota of 100 words, was living up to his reputation as the most tight-mouthed Canadian not inhabiting a monastery. Finally, Shultz leaned across the table and said to Robinson: "This fellow doesn't say much." To which Canada's deputy prime minister deadpanned: "I only talk to Paul."*

That brief exchange neatly summed up the impact of the U.S. ambassador who had wormed himself into the confidence of three Ottawa administrations since his arrival in July of 1981, acting less like a diplomat than a crusader for Manifest Destiny. Unlike most ambassadors, who boast an unlimited tolerance for ambiguity, Robinson operated in only one gear: full speed ahead. (A super-patriot, he would not allow any letters to leave his office postmarked

---

* At one hush-hush Ottawa conference on Canada's patrol frigates, Robinson became so vehement on the subject of Canada's maritime vulnerability that a senior civil servant jokingly suggested that one of the new ships ought to be christened the HMCS *Robinson*. The U.S. ambassador thought this would be a grand idea. Realizing to his horror that he might have been taken seriously, the bureaucrat quickly pointed out that all the vessels were being named after Canadian cities. Even that didn't faze the envoy. "Hell," he said, not missing a beat, "you could always rename one of your cities."

December 7, the anniversary of the Japanese attack on Pearl Harbor.)
He always said exactly what he thought. He attacked the Foreign
Investment Review Agency and the National Energy Program as if
they were satanic conspiracies and treated the eternal quest for the
Canadian identity as a joke: "Well, I suppose it's all right to keep
debating that stuff, as long as you don't take it too seriously."

Robinson never tried to hide his partisan roots and Canadian politicians took full advantage of them, none more so than Mulroney, who
worked the Robinson connection to nail down White House invita-
tions before and after becoming prime minister. Robinson took much
delight in the Mulroney-Reagan entente because he choreographed
much of it himself. "Those two got on like long-lost fraternity brothers," he bragged. "I attended maybe eight meetings between Reagan
and Trudeau, and there was a charged atmosphere because their aides
got into sharp discussions. But at Quebec City, the two men themselves did all the talking, and that's the way it should be. I sat on the
president's left with two briefing papers and I didn't once have to pull
out a page to reinforce anything the president was saying. We all just
sat there listening.

"Their styles are similar. Brian has no fear of America gobbling up
Canada. He sees our closeness as an asset, and he's right—who
wouldn't like to be anchored next to the world's biggest market?" The
Robinson formula for Canada-U.S. relations was nothing if not
simple: "If it's good for one, it's got to be good for the other."

The potential mutual benefits were led by free trade. Out of
Robinson's simplistic ruminations an embassy task force evolved
which worked with Tom d'Aquino of Canada's Business Council on
National Issues to push for a free trade agreement with Washington.
Knowing it was a sensitive Canadian issue, the planning documents
referred only to "freer trade."

The idea was moved to centre stage in September of 1985 by the
report of the Macdonald Royal Commission on Canada's economic
prospects, which recommended free trade as a desirable "leap of
faith." With Ronald Reagan pledged to his "North American
Accord," it seemed like a good moment for Mulroney—to mix a
metaphor—to take that leap of faith through a window of opportunity. The issue had been, for all intents and purposes, sealed when
Brian, Mila, Nancy and Ron linked hands to croon "When Irish Eyes
Are Smiling" at the Shamrock Summit gala—even if Canada's

prime minister sounded flat on the high-note solo, which was supposed to be an A in the key of C.

According to their pre-revolutionary, self-deprecating sentiment, Canadians worshipped all things American. The only meaningful validation of Canadian accomplishment was success in the United States. Canadians were country cousins awed by the American Empire and anyone who studied at Harvard, bought a dress on Fifth Avenue, wrote a book praised by *The New Yorker*, beat the tables at Las Vegas, got a tan at Palm Beach or a hysterectomy at the Mayo Clinic were well ahead of the game. This mood dissipated as Canadians began to judge themselves by their own, instead of imported, values and as they became alienated by the Vietnam War and the scrap-iron presidents thrown up by U.S. voters. It was a straight line from "tricky Dick" Nixon to "Slick Willie" Clinton, interrupted by the curious reigns of Gerald Ford, Ronald Reagan and George Bush. Reagan tried to run the world with the macho mentality of John Wayne and, among other heresies, genuinely believed (having read something about the interaction between leaves and atmospheric vapours) that "trees cause more pollution than automobiles."* It's not easy to pick George Bush's most inane statement, but a strong contender was his defence of an Alaska pipeline project against environmentalists who claimed it would interfere with caribou migrations. "The caribou love it," enthused Bush. "They rub up against it and have babies. That's why there are more caribou in Alaska than you can shake a stick at."

Free trade was aimed at getting rid of tariffs between the two countries, under the firm guidance of a powerful binational tribunal, and at eliminating the countervail that allowed the U.S. to levy administrative charges whenever Canadian goods threatened one of their markets. The original idea was for Canadian companies to get unrestricted access to a huge market. The tariffs were eliminated, but the tribunal was diluted to a review panel with no executive powers and the countervail wasn't really touched. Neither was there any definitive agreement on the all-important concept of government subsidies. Instead of selling Canadian goods in the U.S., many Canadian companies moved their plants south, while most of the U.S. branch plants

---

* Students at a California college took advantage of the Gipper's expertise on the subject by hanging a banner from a large oak tree on his cavalcade route that read: "CHOP ME DOWN—BEFORE I KILL AGAIN!"

in Canada were turned into warehouses. Canada became a northern extension of the American sales territory.

Canada-U.S. trade did multiply, but as Ho Chi Minh wisely observed about the French Revolution, it was still too early to say what the ultimate benefits of the free trade agreement will turn out to be. It did reorient the country, whose East-West axis had been set in place for more than a century, in a North-South direction. For Mulroney, the greatest fringe benefit of free trade was his re-election. His 1984 coalition held together on the issue four years later, with Quebec and the plains—especially Alberta—hanging in to achieve what they believed would be unimpeded access to U.S. markets. The deal's worst feature was what U.S. trade representative Clayton Yeutter rightly called "the jewel of the agreement," a clause that granted the Americans unimpeded access to Canadian energy sources.* Even when Canada starts to run out of its oil and gas reserves, under the terms of the treaty, Ottawa has to provide Washington with "proportional access to the diminished supply" with no price discrimination. The definitive comment on this bizarre arrangement was the quip by Ramon Hnatyshyn, when he was energy minister in the short-lived Clark administration: "Free trade in energy with the Americans is like wife-swapping with a bachelor."†

Simon Reisman, Canada's chief free trade negotiator, was asked just how strongly he felt about his mission. "I'm putting my life on the line for free trade," he declared. Unfortunately, he never made good on the offer. The deal he structured left the country vulnerable to the Darwinian ethic of unfettered competition, where survival of the fittest and the fastest was all that counted. Most significantly, it left Canada vulnerable to cultural genocide. The problem was that "culture" takes on very different meanings in Canada and the United

---

* Yeutter also best summarized free trade's impact. "The Canadians," he said, "do not understand what they have signed. In twenty years, they will be sucked into the U.S. economy."

† Free trade's harshest critic was the Liberal's Sheila Copps, who contended that its chief victims would be the unborn. Once the agreement was signed, she shrilled, U.S. lawyers would pour across the border in search of surrogate mothers' wombs to rent for their childless clients—presumably because the process would be cheaper under Medicare.

States. To the Americans, it is their most successful commercial export; to Canadians, it is their most fragile of domestic commodities. Though maturing, Canada remains a putty culture—penetrable and unshaped. The problem with the U.S. is that its imperialistic writ spans the world, persuasively setting the global cultural agenda.

But the cultural conquest of any nation takes place not on battle-fields or in boardrooms, but within the soul of its people and the minds of their leaders. The choice between surrender and resistance is dictated by the admission that something is lacking that the conqueror might supply. In Canada's case, that lacking element had always been nerve, the political will and individual determination to dig in and say, "This far, and no farther." It remained to be seen whether the shift from deference to defiance would supply such resolve.

BY THE MID-1990s, Canada was moving into the post-national world. Even if nobody could agree on exactly what that meant, the death of Canadian nationalism was as good a definition as any. There was no shortage of signals. Chrétien's heritage minister, Michel Dupuy, the accident that walked like a man, announced that domestic ownership restrictions for broadcasting and cable companies would soon be lifted; government support continued to be slashed, not only for the CBC but an extra $676 million in the Heritage Department's budget, so that the nation's already vulnerable cultural industries had to be placed on life-support systems. Even before the reduced budgets for Canadian content, foreign fare was being shown on 97 per cent of cinema screens across the country; three-quarters of books sold were imported; all but 10 per cent of television and record revenues came from outside sources. Yet the preservation of culture, as former TV Ontario chairman Bernard Ostry had pointed out, was essential: "It is central to everything we do and think. It is our environment and the patterns of our adaption to it. It is the way we know ourselves and each other, it is our web of personal relationships, it is the images and abstractions that allow us to live together in communities and nations. It is the element in which we live."

Despite its anti-cultural bias, the Chrétien government kept scaling ever higher peaks on the public approval meter, a measure of the low support for nationalism. This played directly into the hands of American cultural entrepreneurs, who regarded Canada as nothing more than an extension of their northern sales districts. To them, the U.S.-Canada border was just an imaginary line on maps, like the equator. Val Ross wrote in *The Globe and Mail* that these global info-jockeys regarded culture "simply as product, to be copyrighted and sold, the value-neutral stuff that hums through satellites and wires and screens. Given that definition, it makes no sense when other countries insist on treating culture differently than pig iron."

Canada had further slipped into post-national status by the appointment of non-Canadians to the head of many of the country's important institutions. More offensive than their lack of citizenship was their lack of a basic rapport with the country, with what being Canadian meant or why it was important in terms of the institutions they were being asked to lead. Roger Parkinson, who hailed from New York State and had served as a first lieutenant with the Green Berets in Vietnam, was placed in charge of Canada's national newspaper, *The Globe and Mail*. Hollis Harris, a Georgia good ol' boy who still commuted to his family home in Atlanta, was placed at the head of Canada's national airline, Air Canada. Briton Colin Bailey, who confessed that his knowledge of Canadian art was limited to "a few early twentieth-century landscapes" he'd glimpsed while senior curator at the Kimbell Art Museum in Dallas, was made the new curator of the National Gallery. My argument with these appointments is not that only the Canadian-born should lead essential Canadian agencies—otherwise, having been born in Austria, I could never have been editor of *Maclean's*. My contention is that those who are appointed ought to have some basic knowledge and appreciation of the country they presume to serve.

The message was clear: to run Canadian cultural institutions properly no longer required a knowledge of the country or its people, just an appreciation of the bottom line. The trends had started in the 1980s, when Brian Mulroney heaped rhetorical scorn on what remained of Canadian nationalism, neutered its few remaining means of enforcement (such as the Foreign Investment Review Agency) and threw open the doors to foreign takeovers. The national economy was suborned to the global economy, which in practical terms meant that the Americans took over most of the profitable corporate assets. This invitation to take over applied equally to sovereignty, especially in the North. The Mulroney government broke its pledge to build a polar icebreaker and instead Bill McKnight, then the defence minister, admitted that "defending Canada's Arctic waters will have to be left to the United States."

None of these disparate trends, which were strengthened under the Chrétien government, meant the end of Canada. But nationalism—the idea of protecting key sectors for Canadians—had, at least temporarily, been shelved.

There were many manifestations of this harsh reality, few more poignant than the disappearance of the Grey Cup and the Canadian Broadcasting Corporation as once-essential elements in holding the country together. The Grey Cup was significant among Canada's lost touchstones, an annual reminder to Canadians that they were part of something bigger than themselves. That was also true for the CBC.

"BLESSED WITH MONEY but deprived of community," wrote sports historians Randy Roberts and James Olson in *Winning Is the Only Thing*, describing how rumbles in the commercial jungle had transformed North American sport. The idea of sports as an essential touchstone of the Canadian identity didn't come easily. Baseball remained the quintessential U.S. pastime, although Canada had two major league teams and had beaten the Yanks at their own game; professional hockey knew no borders since the NHL expanded to Boston in 1924; professional basketball had only recently found an audience in Canada.

But Canadian football was different from the start. The Canadian game, featuring a longer and wider field and three downs instead of four, dated back to 1861. After 1874, when Harvard played McGill in Boston, the two national leagues had evolved independently and Canada's first Grey Cup (Toronto Parkdale against the University of Toronto) was played fifty-eight years before the first Super Bowl. Back in the heyday of the Canadian Football League, no matter what was happening politically in the country at large, Confederation worked one day a year—the afternoon of the Grey Cup.

There really were white horses that Stampeders fans would ride into the lobby of Toronto's Royal York Hotel to prove nobody knew what—except that it was proven exuberantly loud and clear. That was the real significance of the Grey Cup—an expression of civic and regional pride. East played against West and each side had a hidden agenda that had nothing to do with the sport. "If you grew up in the East," wrote columnist Jamie Lamb in *The Vancouver Sun*, "the Grey Cup meant a war that pitted civilization against the barbarian hordes. Here you were, trying to achieve equal status with the likes of London or New York and Paris, and suddenly the sports pages and TV screens were filled with yokels in funny cowboy hats, cooking up breakfast pancakes and riding horses into hotels, reeking of frontier whisky and roll-your-own smokes. You had to support your eastern team so that it might put down this uprising of jumped-up Sweeneys and boors . . . From the western point of view, the Grey Cup was doing battle with the effete East, that place that forever looked down its nose at you, was happy to take your labour and resources and send back cars at jacked-up prices, that place where bankers wouldn't approve your loans because they assumed you were one step removed from the peasant steppe. The Grey Cup meant a chance to cock your snoot at these snobs . . . That's what the Grey Cup was about: fostering togetherness through divisiveness, a Canadian trait if there ever was one."

The games were held on cool weekend afternoons in late autumn, the annual harbinger of winter. "I remember the bright chill Grey Cup day when Montreal played Edmonton at Varsity Stadium in Toronto," the pundit Dalton Camp reminisced, "and before the game, a crowd was sitting in the rooftop bar at the Park Plaza Hotel on the other side of Bloor Street, stoking the fires of chauvinism and taking on fuel against the afternoon cold. In those days, the guys wore camel-hair coats, the women fur and they carried Hudson's Bay blankets. It was a great game played before a full house and if there was any better football anywhere else in the world, no one in the crowd had seen it."

In the mid-1970s, the Grey Cup was consecrated by Parliament not merely as a sports event, but as the official repository of Canadian patriotism. The Commons debated a bill banning the entry of the World Football League into Canada, because it would cut into the Canadian Football League's home market. "My government is widely prepared to do what it can to preserve the CFL as a Canadian entity and the Grey Cup as an instrument for national unity," declared John Munro, sports minister in the Trudeau government.

But by the fall of 1994, the game had unalterably changed. The Grey Cup was set in Vancouver, but instead of playing a team from eastern Canada, the Lions were matched against a generic squad from Baltimore. The short odds were that this would be one of the last Grey Cups played on Canadian Astroturf. To make the league profitable, the league had recruited such decidedly un-Canadian teams as the Memphis Mad Dogs, Birmingham Barracudas, Shreveport Pirates and Las Vegas Posse (who rode out of town after one dismal season).

It wasn't the end of the Canadian sport, because the new teams had to abide by CFL rules, but in terms of expressing national unity or acting as the national safety valve, the game was history. The CFL officially decided to realign playoff schedules in 1995 so that the final game each season would match the champion teams of the North (Canada) against the South (U.S.) divisions. "It was part of the inevitability of things being organized on a North-South basis, instead of the former East-West direction," explained CFL chairman John Tory. "But I think people will look at it [as] Americans playing the Canadian game, as opposed to feeling that it's the end of the Canadian game. I make the point that I didn't see anybody in Canada offering to send back the World Series trophy when the Blue Jays won it; nobody was saying, 'Well, it's their game, we should send it back.' So if an American team wins the Grey Cup, I say that's fine—they've played our game really well and next year we'll win it back."

A LONG DECADE AGO, I was among the media groupies who founded and later nurtured an organization known as Friends of Public Broadcasting. The idea was to provide the CBC, which seemed always to be under budgetary pressure, a constituency outside itself. We set ourselves up as defenders of the faith that a national, publicly supported broadcasting system was essential to linking this country from ocean to ocean to ocean through lively and relevant programming. At first, we enjoyed some minor successes, even beat back a budget cut or two, and ten years later we still counted 40,000 Canadians as members. But gradually our self-imposed assignment went sour, or at least it did for me. The CBC we were trying to defend turned out to be the memory of a formerly great network. From helping tie the country together by airing some stellar Canadian TV series, the CBC had become a bad joke. Having managed against all odds to establish "The Journal," for example, as a world-class public affairs program that found emotional resonance with its viewers, management killed it and substituted a news show at nine o'clock, when every remote control in the country was scanning the top-rated U.S. sitcoms. Then, having managed to lose their audience, the CBC's programmers returned to the sensible time slot they had abandoned—then promptly fired their best and brightest interviewer, Pamela Wallin.

Except for the occasional blockbuster like "The Boys of St. Vincent" or "Anne of Green Gables," CBC's television fare (unlike

CBC Radio, which had never been better) deteriorated into a spend-thrift, semi-commercial network that specialized in mediocre variety shows. Watching laundry spin itself dry was more fascinating than viewing most CBC television fare. The CBC's English-language televi-sion network's cultural offerings had been hived off to the self-indul-gent preserve of Adrienne Clarkson, who had yet to disprove Double Exposure's satirical sketch of her show's introduction: "Hello. I'm Adrienne Clarkson . . . *and you're not!*" The investigative public affairs programs that once decorated the CBC schedule were reduced to earnest young reporters with low hairlines asking imponderable questions of talking heads who pretended to know the secrets of the universe.

Although it had once given voice to the nation's soul by judicially fair reporting of news and comments, by the 1990s these standards had been abandoned. An example of such distortion was cited by Elly Alboim, the network's political editor and Ottawa bureau chief at the time of the Meech Lake debates. (He later became an Ottawa lobby-ist.) Speaking to a conference of Calgary academics seven months after the original accord was signed, Alboim tarred the proposed agreement as having been "a highly political and cynical exercise that had very, very little to do with the reconstitutionalizing of Canada. Brian Mulroney needed, for his own purposes, to establish that he could do in Quebec what Pierre Trudeau could not. That was, to my mind, the sole motivation for the federal initiative. I think we were engaged in a highly political and partisan exercise by the Prime Minister." Alboim then attacked the provincial premiers, claiming that they went along "determined to capture as much as they could in exchange for their acceptance" and concluded: "This wasn't a nation-building exercise." Noting that the Mulroney government's popularity was then in a free-fall, Alboim pointed out that some Canadian media felt they were in a situation similar to the U.S. media in the early days of Watergate. "We were focused on the extraordinary story of what appeared to be the collapse of the government with the largest mandate in Canadian history," he explained. "When confronted with that sort of reality, plus a clear understanding of the fragility of the deal and the rush to text and passage, we began a search for dissent. We went to Chrétien, we went to Romanow. We looked for constitu-tional experts. I looked around the country, searching for people who were going to say in the first week or two, 'Boy, there's something wrong here.' The Trudeau watch started. Every day we sent a reporter down to Trudeau's office."

"To have assumed that the government was driven solely by one motive and one man," commented John Meisel, the Queen's University political scientist, "to have been implacably convinced that the motives of Brian Mulroney were merely some petty, peevish rivalry with Pierre Trudeau, to have convinced himself and then to have devised a strategy reporting the ongoing events accordingly, revealed, to my mind, not only extremely questionable judgement, but also constituted a quite inexcusable attempt by a key media player to engage in the political process. Convinced that the party opposition to what he saw as a cynical and dangerous government initiative was inadequate, Alboim proceeded to do what he could to provide an alternative." Meisel's accusations were all the more serious because Mulroney's position was not in fact partisan, since it was supported by Liberal Leader John Turner, NDP Leader Audrey McLaughlin and most of their elected members, plus the ten premiers. Certainly, Alboim's preconceived notions made a powerful difference in the outcome of the debate, because Canadians who tuned in to the CBC's initial Meech Lake coverage presumed they were watching balanced programming.

Lack of funds was blamed for the sad plight of the CBC; lack of inspired leadership was the real problem. Patrick Watson, who ought to have applied his once-sacrosanct sense of integrity and his know-how to improving the corporation he so badly wanted to head, occupied the chairman's office for five years without leaving a single creative imprint. "The CBC," claimed Daryl Duke, who had been one of the network's best creative directors, "compromised its moral integrity when it voluntarily abandoned local broadcasting on December 15, 1990. That's where new people get trained; that's where the public goes into the studios to debate and have town meetings; that's where community documentaries get done; that's where each national issue finds its initial resonance. The CBC pretends it eradicated regional broadcasting for budgetary reasons. It was done for reasons of control. Toronto wanted to spend all the dollars."

On programming, Duke was most concerned about the fact that CBC offered so little in ballet, opera and concerts. "How dare they say that people who live in Prince George or North Bay, and can't travel to Massey Hall or the Orpheum Theatre, shouldn't see any live performances?" he demanded. "And I'm not being élitist. Culture is all of us. We're only as good as our past. If we destroy our cultural and institutional memories, we'll just be another Idaho." Laurier LaPierre, once the CBC's star interviewer, heartily supported this view. "The CBC/SRC have lost the loyalty of Canadians and *Canadiens*," he said. "That has nothing to do with the 500-channel universe. It has much to do with being unable to be present where the people of Canada live: at local and regional levels. The whole world cannot be encompassed from Toronto and Montreal."

With the demise of nationalism and the CBC that had once been its house organ, Canada would have to find a different set of sustaining mythologies. In the post-national world, Canadian identity no longer begged definition. It mattered only *that* we were, not *who* we were. Our mythology would have to tap alternative sources. It was time to abandon the quest for the Canadian identity, time to treat the subject with the light-hearted circumspection advocated by Charles-Louis Montesquieu. The eighteenth-century savant had observed that Frenchmen almost never discuss their wives, in case the listener knows more about the subject than they do.

During the decade under review, Canadians individually and collectively lost common cause with their institutions. Divorced from their sense of God, King and Country—thus separated from their sense of religion, monarchy and land—Canadians carried their own Cross, wore their own Crown and held their own Orb. As more and more citizens perceived they were not being dealt with honestly, not just by politicians but by those in authority everywhere, benign social attitudes turned to acts of anger and thoughts of Revolution.

II THE ECONOMIC REVOLUTION

SIX

TORONTO

The Centre That Didn't Hold

"Money has no heart, no soul, no conscience, no homeland."
MAGNA INTERNATIONAL CHAIRMAN
FRANK STRONACH

E very nation's character is disproportionately affected by its largest metropolitan centre. Whether London, Paris, Rome, New York or Tokyo, the big city is where money, politics and culture meld to determine economic priorities and popular tastes. Defining the kind of society it occupies, the big city rules the roost.

As Canada's metropolis, Toronto historically spread its arrogance across the country, dispensing omniscience, alienation, notoriety and destiny. At the same time, it drained the nation of its talent, its energies and its capital because it was the national vortex for success. Once you made it at King and Bay, your dues were paid up everywhere.

Being a Torontonian, in those smug times, did not convey membership in some readily definable sociological or regional sub-set of Canadian society. It carried instead the presumption that Toronto was the centre of the Canadian Universe, and that the decisions made by its various élites set the national agenda. While Ottawa exercised political authority, Toronto ran everything else—including Ottawa. Loved or hated, Toronto was a national touchstone. Montreal may have been more cultured, Calgary potentially richer,

Vancouver much more liveable—and they somehow managed to survive even in Winnipeg—but if you wanted to get serious about anything important, you had to be in Toronto. No matter what the issue or trend, Toronto was Canada's role-model and its decision-makers were the nation's authority figures.

What Toronto chose to publish or broadcast was what the rest of the country read, heard and saw. What Toronto chose to invest in was what the rest of the country would build. Once vetoed by Toronto's money-movers, most mines, factories, oil refineries, strip malls, pulp mills, motels and housing developments had a slim chance of being erected anywhere in the country.

It was a perverse reality of Canada's structure that despite this kind of cultural and economic clout, Toronto was never able to artic-ulate any sustaining myths to the country at large that would provide English Canada with some sense of nationhood. By virtue of its indolence and wealth, Toronto was a city without a soul. (That it defined the soul of the nation was part of the Canadian paradox.)

"When the French Canadians say, emotionally, we are *a nation*," noted the Quebec author Mordecai Richler, writing in Britain's *New Statesman,* "all Toronto can muster by way of reply is a troubled and rational but uninspired plea—yes, yes possibly, but the business of government, the gross national product, the CPR and the CBC, work better this way. But so does IBM." Edward Brados, an Alberta-born teacher who later moved to Ottawa, put it even more strongly: "Like the sibling who inherits the family fortune but has no idea who he is, Toronto lacks the self-acceptance of less favoured siblings who have had to struggle. The city is largely unable to search within itself and discover something that is worthwhile and joyful. Scratch the American glitz of Toronto and you'll draw cold water, not warm blood."

While most Canadians deeply mistrusted Toronto's influence over their lives, the city's inhabitants could never understand what all the fuss was about. Why couldn't the rest of the country be just like Mississauga—on the unruffled margin of things, quietly manufac-turing Jolly Jumpers and barbecue gloves (or whatever it was they did out there)—not bothering anyone about anything important, taking their lead and inspiration from the country's epicentre? Torontonians saw themselves as the natural custodians of Canada's colonies (the land beyond the Humber River) and guardians of the

Upper Canadian Ethic. That belief system held life's main purpose to be the accretion of as many dollars as possible; life's main genius as being smarter than the next fellow and faster on both feet; and life's animating philosophy as the idea that motion represents progress. Any upstarts who dared question the proposition that Bay Street ran the country were treated with barely suppressed condescension and summarily dismissed. They were considered fortunate they weren't stripped of their VISA cards.

To farmers, trade unionists, Social Crediters, Communists, stake-hungry prospectors and hard-shell Baptists—not to mention ordinary Canadians—Bay Street had been a synonym for greed and damnation throughout modern Canadian history. But it was always less a place than it was a symbol, particularly since that December day in 1982 when the Toronto Stock Exchange closed its doors on Bay Street and moved around the corner to a Reichmann-owned building on King Street. Yet myths die hard, and it was still something of a shock to discover that just up the street from the legendary brokerage address were a Bargain! Shop and Regin's (More Than A Drug Store).

What allowed Toronto to maintain such fiscal pre-eminence into the 1980s was its financial infrastructure, which could be reproduced in miniature but not completely duplicated in any other Canadian city. Even though the 4.2 million citizens in the Toronto commuter shed occupied an area of 5,600 square kilometres, the city's decision district was crammed into a dozen downtown blocks. Five different-coloured skyscrapers, owned by Canada's five largest banks, dominated the skyline. It was the fountainhead of investment funds that financed everything from pipelines across the plains to a vaguely legal screech distillery in St. John's. It was where the prestigious auditing firms did their painful things. It was where legal factories like Blake Cassels or Goodman, Phillips & Vineberg could, in one shirt-sleeved weekend, put together a shopping mall in Red Deer or an offshore bank in the Bahamas. Anything was possible. It was the grand scale of its fiscal transactions—about $2 billion a day—that gave the city its national clout. At the height of its influence in the mid-1980s, Toronto was many times more dominant in relation to its hinterland than was New York. The U.S. wealth capital was home to one-tenth of the Fortune 500, while Toronto housed nearly half of Canada's top half-thousand corporations.

In the devastating recession of the early 1990s, the city's real-estate values collapsed like papier mâché houses in a Biblical flood epic. Toronto's self-assured invincibility was permanently altered. As Canadians across the country began to examine the city's influence set against its new, impecunious circumstances, Toronto ceased to be an object of reverence, envy or even much hatred. Toronto came to be viewed by the rest of the country for what it was: Canada's largest city. Period.

IT WAS AN UNPRECEDENTED TWIST in Canada's social and economic geography. With the traditional deference reluctantly ceded to the Empire City a tarnished commodity, Outer Canadians set about defying a metropolis that had lost its authority to rule their tastes, their decisions and their future. This was a good thing, everyone (outside of Toronto) agreed, but it did leave a temporary gap. Without Toronto as an all-purpose Canadian scapegoat, hinterlanders had to become masters of their own fates. This was not entirely reassuring. Toronto may have driven the rest of the country to distraction with its benign indifference, but at least it was *benign* indifference. In a global village gone berserk, where new employment opportunities were created only in low-cost locales, the smaller market capitals of Vancouver, Montreal and Calgary found themselves melancholic with the oxen's yearning for the yoke.

But that was only part of the Toronto story. Like most Empire cities abandoned by their colonies (London, Vienna, Paris, Lisbon) Toronto took on a brand-new and in some ways revolutionary function of its own. Having ruled in idleness for so many generations, Toronto's establishments did not regret for a second the fact that they had lost their ability to command the quiescent heartland. They did not try to recapture their historic dominance, they simply switched locales. Led by Conrad Black's example, some of their best and brightest moved away; not only to London, New York, Nassau, Bermuda and the Caymans but also to Vancouver, Calgary and even Victoria, where the weather was grand and where fax machines and modems could keep the info flowing. Toronto's diaspora developed fresh sensibilities and new loyalties, limiting their visits home to family occasions on alternate leap years.

More significant was the invisible export of talent and energies as those who remained behind diverted their attention outside of

the country. By the mid-1990s they had turned Toronto into the world's seventh-largest financial centre. In high-rise offices, behind doors decorated with galloping cadences of names stretching toward the ultimate ampersand, lawyers were still running the same factory practices, but they were charged with out-of-country mandates. In addition, accountants, marketers, engineers, architects and financiers of a similar mind became more familiar with the flight schedules to Heathrow, O'Hare, Orly and Narita and the hotels of Frankfurt am Main, Buenos Aires and Hong Kong than they were with the shuttle to Montreal or the discounts available at Winnipeg's Fort Garry Hotel. While this was evidently not true of the vast majority of business people—since Canadians continued to conduct most of their trade among themselves, followed by trade with the United States—it was more true for Toronto's new corporate élite.

The advent of the global players replaced an Old Boys' Network that had been in charge before the Revolution began. Its members were no longer at the leading edge of the action, but they provided legitimacy for those who were. Their hallmark was that they lived their lives as a series of throw-away gestures, so that all achievements and pleasures were made to seem effortless rather than planned, ordinary instead of ostentatious. The easy grace of their limb movements and casual slurring of vowels betrayed their Upper Canada College (or Ridley or UTS) backgrounds; they were possessed by that indefinable confidence of the well-born that allowed them to be waved through passport line-ups while wearing what appeared to be cast-off clothes. They eschewed personal publicity with the ferocity of werewolves avoiding the dawn, and couldn't quite figure out why people to whom they had never been introduced—and to whom they would not want to be introduced—suddenly seemed to be running their city. But life went on.

By their own definitions, these paladins of a vanishing breed didn't spend their fortunes recklessly or conspicuously. The mansions in Forest Hill and Rosedale and the condominiums in Florida or the Bahamas were appreciating investments; the Land Rovers and the Mercedeses, safely locked in garages with strategically mounted motion detectors, were sensible transport; the children's tuitions at the international schools of Gstaad, Geneva and Brussels were essential, given the state of public schools; the fortunes set aside for comfortable pensions and respectable inheritances were their right and due. They smelled faintly of mothballs and their influence was on the wane, but there was one remaining function which the Old Toronto Establishment dared not miss: the Garden Show that takes place just before the Royal Winter Fair, held every November on the Canadian National Exhibition grounds.

They continued to behave like the well-connected patricians they were, glued together by money and class, a pseudo-aristocracy which refused to circulate at parties but was egalitarian enough to allow others to approach them. They still had power, lots of it, but they were vulnerable to changing fashions in finance and cruelly innocent in their knowledge of global business techniques. Soon, their names would disappear from contention and their telephones would stop ringing. It had already happened to their forebears, known as the FOOFs (Fine Old Ontario Families), and no one had really missed them or remembered their names.

MANY A FAMILY COMPANY DIDN'T SURVIVE the 1990s. Among them were such bedrock Toronto institutions as the Gersteins' Peoples Credit Jewellers and the Hermants' Imperial Optical.

Imperial Optical had over-expanded in the 1980s and had backed nearly all of its bank loans with commercial real estate, whose values plummeted out of sight in the 1990s land crash. Even though Sydney Hermant had been a director of the Canadian Imperial Bank of Commerce and its predecessor, the Imperial Bank of Canada, from 1960 to 1983 (he was the first Jew appointed to any Canadian bank board and was, for a time, its largest share-holder), it was the CIBC that foreclosed on his company. Family members in private were deeply resentful of the speed and manner with which the Commerce had moved. They felt that things could have been worked out, and that it was the Commerce's massive blunders with its over-lending to the Reichmann family that had caused the bank to act so harshly with some of its smaller accounts. "The generous and pleasant people you see originally when you're borrowing the money from the bank," complained one of the Hermants, "are not the same hard cases you have to deal with when you're in trouble." Three of the four sons had struck out on their own: Andy ran a recording company; Adam was with a safety equipment firm; John was looking after his own investments. Peter,

who had been brought in by his father to run Imperial in 1962, had
the most difficult time deciding how to spend the rest of his life.
"The receivers had a hard time trying to find the yachts and racing
horses," observed Peter's wife, Katie. "We never lived that kind
of life."

The Hermants were as closely knit a family as existed among
Canada's business élite. Sydney took over the company from his
father, Percy, who had founded Imperial in 1900. In the mid-1970s
he divided the company's assets among his sons, who each drew
the same salary. What was unusual about the Hermant approach
was that even if all the shares were held by family members, they
acted like a public company, with the accountability and cost
control that implied. Well, not quite. "A bottom-line philosophy,
pure and simple, is highly destructive to building loyalty and
morale over a long period," the elder Hermant explained. "I'm not
saying that we're necessarily right in taking the long-term view,
because nobody can predict the future. But we indulge ourselves in
the occasional luxury." He was referring to two Imperial employees who worked in an office next to his, both in their eighties, who
came in to work every day because they couldn't stand staying at
home. "We once had a salesman," Hermant recalled, "who until his
early nineties came in about ten o'clock every morning and did
nothing but talk to his old cronies. Until the very day he died, he
thought he was running the business. He kept dictating letters to
some imaginary customer whenever he got upset, but none of them
were ever transcribed and he could never remember if he was
expecting an answer." Just before it went into receivership,
Imperial had 250 employees who had been on the payroll for more
than twenty-five years.

Because the business was highly profitable until the 1991 recession, Hermant had plenty of buy-out offers. The American big-
game hunters would arrive and promise to make him a director of
some huge multinational, offer a generous purchase price and the
use of their corporate jets. With the contented air of a man puffing
an imaginary cigar, Hermant would explain that there was no price
high enough for him to surrender his freedom. "Nobody," he would
boast, "tells me when to be in New York or Chicago or somewhere
else at any given moment." A few weeks later a higher-ranking
raider would arrive with a fatter bid, and when that was summarily

turned down he too would leave, shaking his head, puzzled by the stubborn Canadian.*

On December 23, 1992, on the day his company went into receivership and four days short of his eightieth birthday, Sydney Hermant died of a broken heart. At the memorial service, a veteran employee came up to one of his sons and said: "You know, your family's problem was that you were far too generous with everybody."

A similar fate to the downfall of the Hermants was suffered by the Gerstein family, which became yet another victim of the riptide of foolishness that replaced common business sense in the 1980s. Irving Gerstein, the third-generation Toronto jeweller who led his family into the fiasco, had a dream of becoming the world's largest jeweller. For a while, he was. When that vision turned into a nightmare, it not only ended his business career but destroyed the family dynasty. In 1986, together with a Swiss-Austrian partner, Gerstein purchased the Dallas-based Zale Corp., the world's largest jeweller. His management style and the recession eventually drove it into bankruptcy, dragging down with it Peoples Jewellers Ltd., one of the country's finest and most venerable family firms.

Gerstein was a handsome, fun-loving entrepreneur who believed in himself with unbridled gusto. Even under the most trying of circumstances, he demonstrated a grace under pressure rare for his class. A graduate of the University of Pennsylvania's prestigious Wharton School of Finance, he sat on the boards of a dozen important Canadian companies and was a past governor of such bedrock Toronto institutions as the Albany Club, Upper Canada College and Bishop Strachan School. He lived well, maintaining a Swedish-built Swan 50 sailboat, one of the world's most luxurious yachts, at the

---

* Away from the office, the Hermant boys amused themselves by putting together a band to serenade the neighbours—a muscular combination of banjos, gut bucket and guitars. They lived within a mile of each other in Toronto's luxurious Rosedale district and once even took the band overseas to play at Adam's wedding. To get the gut bucket past customs, they declared it as a farm implement. On the Saturday before the ceremony, the Hermant boys played the only unscheduled concert performed in the Pinafore Room of London's Savoy Hotel.

ready for quick getaways to Antigua or the Mediterranean; his home was one of the most luxurious mansions on Toronto's Bridle Path.

When he first took over Zale in the spring of 1987, Gerstein was mightily impressed by having captured control of a company eleven times the size of his own. "We had a net worth of $50 million and Zale was worth about $550 million," he boasted. "It seemed unthinkable that we could take it over, but a change had taken place in the financial markets that allowed some unthinkable things to come about." That change was the introduction of junk bonds, and no one was more enthusiastic about that dubious invention than Gerstein. He relied on junk bonds to engineer the $750-million leveraged buy-out of Zale; three years later, long before the Zale deal was fully assimilated, he went back to the financial trough for another $375 million to buy out Gordon Jewelry Corp., the second-largest jewellery chain in the United States. By the end of the decade, Gerstein had consolidated his dream of becoming the world's largest jeweller. But Zale had amassed $1.62 billion in debt.

Peoples had been managed with loving care and creative conservatism from the day in 1919 when Gerstein's grandfather started selling silver flatware door-to-door for fifty cents down and fifty cents a week. It had already tried to penetrate the U.S. market in 1978 with the purchase of the fourteen-outlet White jewellery chain of Salt Lake City. But the investment turned sour almost immediately and the family switched its attention to Zale in 1980. It took six years for the Gersteins to capture control, and they ended up paying $65 a share—twice Zale's book value. Even at the time of purchase, analysts claimed that the Dallas company was not throwing off enough cash to pay the interest on Gerstein's extravagant financing package. The leveraged buy-out was bound to fail. Several Canadian banks backed out of the financing at the last minute, having noted that unlike most jewellery retailers, Zale rented its stores, so that there was no real-estate value to back up its cyclical retail revenues. "I don't understand the deal. I don't know what Gerstein has in mind," Arthur Lichtendorf, an authoritative retail analyst with E.F. Hutton in New York City, commented at the time. Nothing in the historical performance of Zale justified the price Gerstein had paid; nothing but greed explained it.

Among the incentives for Zale's acceptance of the Canadian takeover were the generous golden parachutes Gerstein offered Zale executives. Some were paid as much as $2,600 an hour as consultants; others received stock options worth $29 million. At first, the U.S. expansion seemed to be working; as late as 1990, Zale and Peoples were still in the black. But the extra cost of the Gordon acquisition had added so much debt to an already awesome overload of obligations that the ratings services placed the operation under credit surveillance. By mid-1989, Zale's debt ratio was approaching 72 per cent of its capital structure and Peoples couldn't meet the accelerating interest payments on its junk bonds. Zale's suppliers were owed $100 million and even an injection of $45 million by Zale employees failed to halt the slide. Eventually the whole structure collapsed under its own weight and the Gerstein family vanished from contention.*

The kinder, gentler fortunes of previous generations had become as rare as humidors and spats. The Massey house on Jarvis Street had been converted to a restaurant, hordes of students from Etobicoke pounded through Falconer Hall, the Gooderham mansion had been turned into a private club, a developer lived in Lady Eaton's former house on Old Forest Hill Road and no one cared any longer who belonged to the Rosedale Golf Club.† One of the last reminders of their epoch was provided by elegant society spender Nancy Phillips, who lent new meaning to the term "social merry-go-round" when she purchased a decrepit, thirty-two–seat carousel, had it repaired and placed it in her garden. Guests swore there was nothing quite like sitting astride one of her wooden horses, sipping champagne and dreaming to the tinkling sounds of the calliope. "It's a lot more fun than a swimming pool," she explained. "Derek, my husband, called it middle-age madness, but I call it the Best Folly in the World."

Despite the appearance of a new generation, Toronto was still a

---

* The fates of other, much larger, Toronto-based business empires that collapsed between 1985 and 1995 are described in Chapter Seven and Chapter Eight.

† Some of the more interesting curmudgeons went in style. When Charles Slater, a distinguished Bay Street legal counsel who had also served as vice-chairman of the Ontario Securities Commission, realized that he was terminally ill with cancer, he walked into the A.W. Miles Funeral Home on Bayview and told the manager: "My name's Slater. I'm dying. Let's talk price."

place where the power élites could get through a whole day of business deals without ever mentioning anyone's last name. They knew who was meant by *Matt* (Barrett), *Doug* (Bassett), *Tom, Sonja* or *Tom, Jr.* (Bata), *Conrad* (Black), *John* (Cleghorn), *Jack* (Cockwell), *Eddie* (Cogan), *Mickey* (Cohen), *Jimmy* (Connacher), *Garth* (Drabinsky), *Fred, Thor* or *John Craig* (Eaton), *Trevor* (Eyton), *Tony* (Fell), *Al* (Flood), *Diane* (Francis), *Hal* (Jackman), *Tom* (Kierans), *Robert* (Lantos), *Alan* (Lenczner), *Michael* (Levine), *Jean* (Monty), *Peter* (Munk), *Gordon* (Osler), *Alf* (Powis), *Rob* (Pritchard), *Ted* (Rogers), *Joe* (Rotman), *Andy* (Sarlos), *Sam* (Slutsky), *Brian* (Steck), *Maurice* (Strong), *Dick* or *Ken* (Thomson), *Galen* and *Hilary* (Weston), *Bill* (Wilder), *Red* (Wilson).

The "Wives Of" these Establishment cohorts tended toward wispy women who punctuated their husband's conversation with supportive little cries. Sought out for their private thoughts and passions, they complained guiltily about their daughter's interest in a Kenyan musician ("I'm not prejudiced, but a *musician!*") and detailed their Arizona spa treatments at Main Chance. Their fingers and necklines were heavily adorned with the square-cut and pear-shaped reminders of their many marriage anniversaries, which they wore like military long-service medals. Money, gobs of it, was carelessly evident in the cut of their Chanel suits, the glitter of their Cartier jewellery and the elegance of their Via Spiga shoes.* As they grew older, these Rosedale mavens stopped using standard cosmetics and instead went somewhere to get iced, like birthday cakes. The effect was not always aesthetically pleasing. The result often made them squint like debauched gazelles whose eyelids didn't quite close.

They similarly tended to approach social gatherings in the way gazelles approach watering holes—with their eyes in constant, wary motion. Their friendships, which were defined in terms of social

---

* In the winter of 1991, when Patricia Appleton, an influential Toronto socialite, was dying of scleroderma—a disease that eventually cut off her breathing—her friends Cathie Bratty and Susan Davidson paid thousands of dollars for a Chanel bag to hide the mobile oxygen tank she had to carry around with her in order to attend their gatherings. Appleton told another society friend, Anne Delicaet, that "These people are my life and my breath; I'd rather be with them than breathe."

advancement, allowed them to join protective ranks where they could keep a collective eye on their husbands, who were occasionally to be found in thrall of some legs-to-belly-button nymphet who giggled provocatively at anything they said—while auditing the room for richer game.

During the 1980s a new breed of Fast Money entrepreneurs appeared on the scene. They were usually men (although, as "reconstructed" men, they invariably hired fashionable women as their personal assistants and then tried hard not to call them "my gal Friday,") sporting year-round bronzed faces and dyed chest hair. They leafed through sheaves of documents by wetting their thumbs and nursed the platitudes they offered the way a golfer holds his driving wood in mid-air after a successful follow-through. Their body language was spastic with insecurity and they seemed to be constantly in emotional traction, feeling highly uncomfortable in their own skins. Their motto was Frank Stronach's dictum: "Money has no heart, no soul, no conscience, no homeland."

It wasn't so much that they didn't have souls as that they didn't know where to find them. Being enthralled by materialism, many were sent searching under the hoods of their Porsches, beguiled by the manufacturer's advertising copy: "Within the Carrera 911 resides something rare among modern sports cars: a soul." (Materialism was, after all, their *deus ex machina*.) The divine right of *things* took over their lives. Even pleasure became not a moment for illumination, self-discovery or joy—but a distraction from the numbness of their being. Observing these strange, materialistically driven creatures, the Toronto-born novelist and philosopher Scott Symons decreed: "We have moved from an age of public decorum and civility to one of candy-coated debacle. We've seen the end of the Methodist–United Church society that shaped this country for most of its history, with its folk yeomen tradition of probity and loyalties. This country now runs on greed." He was right. Anything that could be possessed, counted or evaluated was measured by how it ranked on the scale of life's diminishing certainties. They traded in their wives the way they traded in their cars, searching for emotional satisfaction in big-game trophies with manes of shampoo-ad hair and bodies as thin as their Patek Philippe wristwatches. Establishing a category of her own was Marilyn Lastman (born Myriam Bornstein), who complained to former *Globe and Mail* society columnist Rosemary Sexton that her hus-

band, Mel (a former appliance discount dealer who became the popular mayor of North York), was the only guy she knew "who showers,
shaves, takes his hair off and comes to bed in his shorts. I would prefer it if he would take his shorts off and leave on his hair." She also
was a black-belt shopper. "There's a fine line between crass and class,
but I know how to draw it," she insists. "When Mel was making money
hand-over-fist, I held up the economy single-handed. I was definitely
an acquirer. I love expensive possessions."

Unlike the Establishment paladins who preceded them, these
opportunists were made-to-measure catalysts of the Canadian
Revolution. Almost effortlessly, they gave a bad name to a free-
enterprise system which, despite its faults and abuses, had driven the
Canadian economy from its inception.

The end of their era was recorded by the precipitous drop in real-
estate values, which presaged doom for the *arrivistes* in the same
way a comet's tail foretold the end of the dinosaurs. By the fall of
1991, office vacancy rates in Toronto had hit a high of 21 per cent
and land values were down by 50 per cent. The real-estate collapse
struck at the core of the fast-money fortunes, built on leveraged
finances against developments which turned out to be built as solidly
as a house of damp cards. The unfinished foundation of the
mammoth Bay–Adelaide Centre, the hollow core of a planned but
never built fifty-seven–storey office tower, became a symbol of the
period—the tomb of the unknown developer.* Although their afflu-
ence was illusory, the consequences of their imprudence were real.
During the 1990-92 recession, a brutal one-third of the half million
jobs lost in the country were lost in Toronto. Brian O'Malley, president of Standard Trustco, spoke for his peers in 1987 when he rhap-
sodized: "Heaven is Ontario in 1987." Four years later, Toronto's
economy was *in extremis* and Standard Trustco in bankruptcy.

Except for a few belligerent die-hards, the real-estate meltdown of
the early 1990s decimated the racy speculators and toned down considerably the few who made it through. By the post-recession period,
Toronto had firmly become an international city and the people who
mattered were those who had mastered the new rules of global trade,

---

* Toronto even lost the rationale for its nickname. The Ontario Stock
  Yards at Keele and St. Clair, which had once handled a million animals
  a year, were closed in 1993. Hogtown was no more.

borderless capital and a lightning-fast business environment, the inevitable consequences of the new communications technology. Having direct access to a satellite became the new status symbol. Instead of being a target for the country's envy or malevolence, Toronto found itself becoming a model for its post-revolutionary future.

Because they were forced to constantly weigh the cost/benefit ratio of time versus money, the post-recession types aimed to live out their dreams of meaningful achievement. They remained ultra-ambitious and while their goals included power and money, they felt more than a little world-weary and in private would readily confess that their yearning for prime relaxation time was at the top of their agendas. If they felt any overwhelming loyalty, it was to their vitamin regimes and jogging paths. They were influenced in large measure by the growing numbers of women who had crawled up the same corporate ladder, only to find disappointment in the hollowness of life at, or near, the top. In a much-copied cartoon of the day, one such woman says with a start: "Ohmigosh, I forgot to have kids." It struck a chord among many women regretting not only the lack of children, but the elements of a balanced life. A newer generation was determined to sidestep burn-out by mastering the arts of harmony and pacing. They became compulsive in their moderation.

One of the realities of the information age was that money was no longer tied to property. Instead of a factory, money could be made from home; instead of investment funds, the new entrepreneur relied on speed, wits and desire. In a reversal of Marxist theory, it was the liberation of everything but labour, with the result that the restless impatience that during the 1960s would have been called rebellion was being harnessed in the 1990s into a personal revolution.

The new breed of financial animators quickly amassed considerable wealth, had self-confidence to burn and defined success in their own way. "It used to be that the measure of business success was a membership in the Toronto Club and a salary equivalent of one of our largest companies," noted Gordon Sharwood, who had left behind his earlier incarnation of heir-apparent to the presidency of the Canadian Imperial Bank of Commerce to become a Toronto private investment banker. "Most of these new-style entrepreneurs couldn't care less about the Toronto Club, don't even know where it is. About the only place they come together is the Jockey Club, which is a much more casual environment for the monied set. I tried to get some of them involved with the C.D. Howe Institute and public policy options. They attended a couple of meetings but they came to me and said, 'Ah Gord, it's such a waste of time, it's so boring sitting there listening to old professors going on about the Gross National Product. I'd rather be out on my Chris-Craft.'"

Most significant of all, the well-connected in post-apocalyptic Toronto emphatically crossed gender lines. The New Women of the Revolutionary Nineties were not preoccupied with museum-quality furnishings or souvenir collectibles; they lived clean, spare lives and collected memories. Instead of exercise limited to walking their Lhasa Apsos through Yorkville (a breed of dog which appeared calm and collected next to its keeper) and shying away from physical exertion, they were energetic, gregarious, ambitious and tough. "I've seen a very definite new trend developing in the last couple of years," said Sally Armstrong, editor of *Homemaker's* magazine, "and that is lunches or dinners held to honour women in the business and entertainment worlds. They're movers and shakers, but they aren't moving and shaking because of their husbands or family money. They're truly incredible women doing incredible things."*

If they didn't actually go into business, they became effective social animators and fund-raisers—but they were unwilling to confine their political action to safe causes intended to assuage their bourgeois guilt. Instead of putting the touch on friends for orphanages, they were more likely to be found agitating governments for social change. They tended to be suavely international, but the self-indulgence of the jet set bored them—instead they dabbled in exotic cultures and adventures. They pursued creative

---

* In addition to Armstrong herself, this group included Heather Reid (public relations); Her Honour Madame Justice Gloria Epstein; Shirley Dawe, Director of the National Bank and Moore Corp.; Rona Maynard, editor of *Chatelaine*; Mildred Istona, vice-president of Maclean Hunter; Martha Durdin, vice-president of the Bank of Montreal; Sue Bochner, on the advisory board of Altamira; Bonnie Brooks, editor of *Flare*; Sheryl Black, senior vice-president of Estée Lauder; Nancy Birnbaum, managing director of Young & Rubicam; Audrey Loeb, condominium law book author; Ann Boden, president of McKim Media Group; Marilyn Brooks, fashion *doyenne*; Margaret Wente, editor of the *Report on Business* magazine; and Carolyn Keystone, president of Tsumura Canada.

relationships with men while determined to find fulfilment in their own lives. As such, they no longer found it necessary to get married in order to have children, such as the recent issue to former film-festival diva Helga Stephenson and Bay Street whiz kid Gerry Sheff. Neither did they find it necessary to turn to crochet after menopause, as the latest trend among these 1990s women was to take younger lovers.* Catherine Nugent first came into prominence in the 1980s, but had since become an acknowledged star of Toronto society. The Brazilian-born Nugent had enough clout that when she decided to attend a function, others went just to be near her. When the glamorous Rosemary "Posy" Chisolm Feick organized a grand ball in Rome during the spring of 1995 in aid of the Peggy Guggenheim Collection in Venice, Nugent's decision to attend prompted other Torontonians to make the journey, including Carole and Jerry Grafstein, Cathie and Rudy Bratty, Harriet Bunting Weld, Mary Carr-Harris and decorator Michel Tashereau; Peter and Melanie Munk sent a cheque for $10,000 but didn't attend. The Brazilian Ball each February, founded by Anna Maria de Souza, remained *the* Toronto social event. The annual feeding frenzy for the status-conscious, in 1994 its net proceeds (donated to Wellesley Hospital) passed the $1 million mark. But even such society mavens as Nugent found the glitter had dulled somewhat. "We don't socialize as much as we used to," she confessed. "I mean, we used to go to the opening of an envelope, but now we have other interests. The 1990s are totally different. It's as if everybody woke up at the end of the 1980s and the world had changed. For one thing, hardly anyone is wearing conspicuous jewellery any more. I was in St. Moritz recently and the people spending all the money were members of the Russian mafia." The undisputed leader of Toronto society was Liz Tory, whose husband, John, ran the Thomson communications empire. She was the new breed of socialite, in the sense that her power was based on her innate wisdom and moral authority rather

---

* Overheard at Prego's was this priceless bit of advice from one attractive older woman to another: "Don't sit on top of him, Linda. He'll notice how much your boobs sag."

than the number of parties she attended. She had been at the centre
of things for so long and knew so much of what was going on,
that she was as often consulted by corporate hitters trying to out-
manoeuvre one another, as by apprentice glitterati trying to fill
their social calendars.

By the mid-1990s, business in Toronto had turned into networking. The depth and spread of a player's network determined the
place of precedence on the *infobahn*. The old contacts of school and
family were unchanging, but the networks flipped as quickly and as
constantly as an electronic relay. Day and night they buzzed with
anyone who had a deal or wanted one. The connections were not
made over brandy snifters while dozing in ox-blood armchairs in
some archaic club, but through cellular phones while munching
penne puttanesca at Prego's. The most successful of the breed,
among these new 1990s types, were the so-called "export nationalists" who created major Toronto-based entertainment conglomerates
and swept the world with their products. Chief among them were
Garth Drabinsky, whose mega-success with *The Phantom of the
Opera* was the catalyst of his surging Livent empire; Robert Lantos,
the Hungarian-born producer whose Alliance Communications
Corp. had put together some of Canada's most profitable movie
deals; Allen Karp of the Bronfman-controlled Cineplex, who assembled North America's largest movie-theatre chain; and film direc-
tor/producers Jon Slan of Paragon, Michael MacMillan of Atlantis
and Michael Hirsh of Nelvana.

TORONTO'S BUSINESS COMMUNITY was united during the first half of the
1990s by its fear of the Bobarian at the gate. After the NDP government of Bob Rae moved into Queen's Park on September 6, 1990, a
favourite tale among the business community was to quote from a
CITY-TV broadcast. Political commentator Colin Vaughan had asked
Ontario Treasurer Floyd Laughren: "When did your government
lose its grip on reality?"

Laughren thought for a minute and replied: "It's hard to pin down
precise dates on these things."

Establishment Toronto hadn't been so upset since Pierre Trudeau
admitted he'd once paddled a canoe to Cuba for a visit with Fidel
Castro. It was one thing to have a stylish leftie ensconced in Ottawa,
but for a socialist to storm Queen's Park with a political cadre whose

supporters sported spiked hair and body rings—just a dozen blocks north-west of King and Bay—well, that was more than any right-thinking Bay Street capitalist could tolerate. When Liberal or Conservative governments had taken turns running the heartland province, their administrators were typically recruited from a revolving door to Bay Street. There was unimpeded contact—and often blurred distinctions—between business and government. Historically, Toronto business élites enjoyed easy access to power. At least one Bay Street lawyer, Richard Rohmer, had a direct line to a red telephone on the desk of then-Premier John Robarts. But when Bay Street called Bob Rae, it didn't get the requested favours. That state of affairs left the Toronto power brokers feeling impotent and angry.* Business objected to an agenda for Ontario that was driven by socialist ideals instead of the market. But Rae had been elected to be different; even had he wanted to, he could not behave like a pink clone of the government parties that had ruled the province in the past. However justified his approach, it seriously reduced the province's credit rating and stalled Ontario's industrial expansion. One major Toronto machine manufacturer, who decided to build his plant extension in Texas, was asked why he didn't recommend a Toronto site to his board of directors. He replied: "Actually, I did. First they sat there with their mouths hanging open. Then they burst out laughing. As long as Bob Rae is around, nobody in their right senses would build anything of consequence in this province."

That was a harsh judgement, in no way justified by Rae's words or actions. And yet it was a reaction universal enough that Canada's two other notionally socialist premiers in office at the time—Roy Romanow of Saskatchewan and Mike Harcourt of British Columbia—rushed to distance themselves from their Ontario colleague. When the

---

* According to a joke so often told that it had retreads, three Bay Street cronies were bitching about how impossible it was to get a hearing at Queen's Park. One tentatively suggested that he might know just the right contact to get them a hearing. "Listen," he said, "my wife once had her picture taken with a guy who knew a guy now working at Queen's Park." It wasn't promising, so the second suggested: "I once went to a summer camp with somebody who cuts Rae's hair. Maybe we could use him." Again, there was a general shaking of heads. "Oh hell," the third shrugged, "let's use my cleaning lady. She's in the Cabinet!"

Rae government's 1991 budget deficit tripled to nearly $10 billion, Romanow told the Albany Club, where Toronto Tories go to die, that he would never follow the example of the Ontario NDP's grand-scale deficit financing, while Harcourt confided to another audience that "deficits of that size are foreign to my thinking."

Rae never did comprehend the business mentality even after he was beaten by Mike Harris. In office, he was preoccupied with issues of social justice, which left no common ground with the Bay Street Gang who regarded social justice as an unaffordable luxury and were primarily concerned with the creation of wealth, not its distribution. It never occurred to either side that you couldn't have one without the other.

NO DEMARCATION LINE EXISTED between pre- and post-revolutionary Toronto, but the closing of several of the city's most treasured social institutions helped define that great divide. The most telling sign of the 1990s was the change in Toronto shopping habits. Hazelton Lanes and Yorkville, which fed the feverish consumerism of the 1980s, turned into commercial graveyards. The only games left in town were Holt Renfrew, Chez Catherine and Ira-Berg. The bankruptcy of Creed's in 1990 was certainly a body blow, as Allan Fotheringham noted: "This was somewhat like the Vatican going bust. Matrons from Rosedale to Forest Hill raced for the smelling salts. There is nothing sacred left in the world that bears thinking about if Creed's has gone boobs up." Other Toronto institutions bit the dust, including Fenton's, the *nouvelle cuisine* fern bar which always included among its luncheon guests a scattering of married men and women—few of them to each other—being primed for a nooner.* Fenton's opening in 1976 had driven Joanne Kates, the

---

* One of Toronto's most legendary courtships took place behind a Fenton's fern in the fall of 1986. David Nugent, the scion of a well-connected British family who had served with the S.A.S. in the Suez, Malaysia, Lebanon and Cyprus, had spotted Catherine Leggett (then married to Crown Attorney Stephen Leggett) at an Italian restaurant the previous evening. He found himself enchanted by her beauty and the spirited light in her eyes. He invited her for lunch at Fenton's the next day and an hour after she had joined him he asked her to marry him; seven hours later he took her home. He became a perfume tycoon and the two are still happy and still married.

usually gloomy *Globe and Mail* restaurant critic, into spasms of oral rapture. "My taste buds are jumping for joy; my sensibilities have been coddled to the point of ecstasy . . ." Evidently the restaurant's reputation as a trysting spot had affected the reviewer, but it did not prevent the restaurant from closing. This was followed on December 14, 1991, by the bankruptcy of the $45 million King Ranch health spa, a magnificent seventy-one–hectare palace of joy put up with funds provided by Murray Koffler, founder of Shoppers Drug Mart. There weren't enough customers to pay the $2,500-per-week tab it cost to be pummelled and starved.

But none of those sad occasions compared to the closing, on May 5, 1992, of Winston's. The Toronto red-plush equivalent of the Savoy Grill in London, Harry's Bar in Venice or the Polo Lounge in Beverly Hills, Winston's had been home to the city's Establishment for a quarter-century. Diners there compared fiscal exploits over soup, shared confidences over Chateaubriand and made the arrangements that would spread their cash and their self-assurance across the country over cognac. Winston's twenty-three–table seating arrangement was choreographed with the exquisite care of a Sadler's Wells ballet by owner Johnny Arena. "I assign certain tables for very specific reasons," Arena explained. "There are people who come here and wish to be seen, while others desire maximum privacy."* The power-lunchers arriving for their standard Winston's two-hour lunch sought a fix of blood-rare steak and even bloodier gossip. Nodding their heads like wise turtles (they never moved below the neck), they sipped their Meursault smug in the assumption of unending fame and fortune. The restaurant was as much a private club as a metaphor for the calm possession of power that counted in the Toronto universe. John Napier "Chick" Turner hung out at Winston's, pursuing the only career he was ever much good at,

---

* Only two clients were actually barred from Winston's. Duncan Macpherson, the *Toronto Star* cartoonist, got the bum's rush for starting a fistfight in the place. (He also enjoyed the distinction of having been barred for life from the Toronto Press Club three times.) A Toronto investment broker who had stolen the restaurant's silver cigar clipper was caught by Arena in the act. After Arena removed the instrument from the broker's pocket, the man wrote a letter profusely apologizing for his kleptomania. Allowed back in, he promptly swiped it again.

that of prime-minister-in-waiting. Turner's table had one of two private telephone lines in the place (the other was a floater), and the menu listed a John Turner Salad (sliced tomatoes with chopped onions). His legal clients were sprinkled throughout the room, and Larry, his favourite waiter, hovered nearby waiting to light his post-coffee Montecristo cigars. "Arena is very astute and certainly takes good care of his clients if he's of the view that they have some prominence," observed Conrad Black, who held a dinner at Winston's the evening prior to his first wedding. "One evening I took the Duke of Wellington there and even though he had very little notice, Arena was at the door to greet us. His every third word was, 'Your Grace.' Wine was served in decanters by him personally. I have to hand it to the guy." The restaurant, evidently, served the best plate of servility in town.

By the spring of 1990, with Toronto's economy in free-fall, the Winston's crowd dispersed to more affordable locations and Arena decided to sell what was left of his assets. That called for a farewell party. Seventy-four Establishment survivors spent the evening of May 5 saluting their favourite day-care centre. The menu was unusually unpretentious: smoked salmon, lamb and cheese. The party was blessed by the presence of His Eminence G. Emmett Cardinal Carter, who had himself been a Winston's regular, while Bishop Arthur Durrant Brown held up the Anglican end of the affair.* John Turner provided a moving address, it being difficult, in retrospect, to know whether free trade with the U.S. or the closure of Winston's meant the end of Canada as he knew it. The drollest speech was that of Doug Creighton, the red-faced (even when sober) publisher of *The Toronto Sun.* "John Arena is a true gourmet," he told his fellow diners, "but not always... Shortly after he arrived in this country, a customer asked John how the escargot was that night. John made a face and replied: 'I was looking at the dirty little things in the kitchen and before I'd touch escargot, I'd eat snails.'"

Then Creighton became serious: "I've been coming to Winston's for over twenty years. Many of you, longer than that. The food and the service was great, and John Arena was always at the door. Now, he's walked outside instead of in, and it won't be the same again."

---

* For a list of those in attendance, see Appendix 1: The Last Supper.

During the evening a fake front page of *The Toronto Sun* was distributed with the headline: "THE END OF AN ERA." It was indeed. But little did those on the fabled guest list realize that the era drawing to a close was not that of a high-priced beanery, but the end of their own *belle epoque*.

SEVEN

THE ECONOMICS
OF DESPAIR

Ethical Endgame

*Once men and women equated their net worth with their
self-worth, the social contract exploded.*

POLITICS WAS WHAT PEOPLE ARGUED ABOUT; religion defined how
they felt about the universe; love measured their passion and commitment beyond themselves. But work was where they lived. "And
what do you do?" was the dominant personal identification code.

The most dramatic measure of how profoundly the Canadian
Revolution altered people's lives was found in how the answer
changed over the decade. Back in the mid-1980s, the reply would
probably have been: climbing the corporate ladder at one of the
large manufacturing, service or resource companies. By 1995, the
answer was more likely to be: ask me tomorrow.

As jobs disappeared along with many of the companies that had
once provided them, the very idea of having steady, paid work within
an organization suddenly seemed risky, if not obsolete. "That much
sought after, much maligned social entity, a job, is vanishing like a
species that has outlived its evolutionary time," wrote William
Bridges in *Fortune* magazine. "The modern world is on the verge of
another huge leap in creativity and productivity, but the job is not
going to be part of tomorrow's economic reality. There still is, and will
always be, enormous amounts of work to do, but it is not going to be

contained in the familiar envelopes we call jobs. In fact, many organizations are today well along the path toward being 'de-jobbed.'"

That observation didn't apply to lifetime jobs with fringe benefits and a gold watch at age sixty-five, as those had vanished long before. Nor was it a function of geography, confirming that jobs had become as impossible to find in Cape Breton or Yukon, as careers in Hamilton steel mills or Newfoundland canneries. Neither did it cover the obvious warnings about living in an information age and how those who remained computer-challenged would spend their lives dishing out Big Macs.

This was a phenomenon that ran much deeper, a mutation fully as significant as the Industrial Revolution that had pushed an agrarian, craftwork society into the machine age, forcing people to seek jobs instead of exploiting their individual talents. Artisans eventually became assembly-line drones, but there was a trade-off: those who sold their labour and performed effectively could expect regular earnings, paid holidays, a lengthening list of fringe benefits and long-term employment. They had *jobs*.

Civilization is the history of social organization. Jobs had emerged as a way of managing the mass efforts of people working in factories, mines and bureaucracies. Prior to the Industrial Revolution, work was organized around individual projects, so that masons, glaziers, roofers and bell-founders might, for example, worked on a cathedral, but they were not cathedral-builders. Each task required a different combination of crafts; people had skills, not jobs. That changed with mass production and the expansion of small firms into industrial giants. Henry Ford's chain-driven assembly line didn't kick into life until 1913, so that the idea of having a "job" was a relatively recent phenomenon. With globalization, computers, robotics, product customization and the growing inefficiencies of large-scale organizations, the trend reversed itself by the mid-1990s. The great multi- and trans-national corporations were in a race to "outsource" and "unbundle." Instead of maintaining their bloated payrolls, they farmed out many of their tasks to independent contractors who often worked from their homes—just as the artisans had done before the Industrial Revolution.

"Filling a profitable niche" became the path to glory. By mid-1994, nearly four million Canadians were working, part and full time, out of their homes. Even if they didn't have a spare minute to think about it,

they were in the vanguard of a Revolution in the sense that they felt
entirely responsible for their livelihood for the first time in their professional lives. This implied zero-tolerance accountability—to themselves—and the liberating sense of being in charge of their own
fortunes. There was no boss to blame, no corporate culture to foster
alienation, no feeling of impotent rage (or bovine contentment) at having to perform repetitive tasks for a fixed income. Employers became
"customers" and individual security became rooted in people's own
skills, their willingness for self-renewal and their adroitness at luring
business their way. That meant not having to depend on governments
which had run out of money or corporate honchos who were themselves terrified of losing their positions and privileges. "The marriage
between people and companies has been broken," maintained Richard
Earle, president of the Canadian Institute of Stress. This was a divorce
of life-altering significance, he added, "because most of us are more
married to our work than to our spouses."

As more Canadians assumed an independent way of work, they
typically discovered that they were labouring twice as hard as when
they had held down regular jobs. Yet, those who took time to look
around to see how others who were less well educated, less aware of
modern technologies or just less lucky were doing, they knew that
they belonged to a fortunate, if stressed-out, minority. "I run into a
lot of 'refrigerator-chart people,'" explained Bruce O'Hara, a
British Columbia therapist, "who are so busy they have to orches-
trate their time really tightly—who's going to pick up the kids,
who's going to get dinner at the deli and so on. If one thing goes
wrong, the whole day is screwed up. I remember counselling this
fairly high-profile couple. They were young, articulate, verbal, intelligent and successful. When I asked if they'd had any problems, they
both giggled and said no, they hadn't, not recently. Then they confessed that the hour they were about to spend with me was the only
time they'd seen one another in the past three days."

Home as an income-earning base, with all its perks and problems,
was one ascending arc of the work revolution. The other was how
employees in large organizations were learning to cope with the
New Economy. Many didn't get the chance. Industrial giants such as
Eastman Kodak, IBM, General Motors, Stelco, Proctor & Gamble,
Canadian National and Dofasco closed plants and brutally cut payrolls. "A world-wide job crisis threatens not only global economic

growth but the capitalist system itself," wrote Richard Barnet in *Global Dreams*.

The progressive companies that continued to prosper, particularly in such burgeoning fields as computers, telecommunications, environmental monitoring and biological engineering, chose new work routines designed to eliminate the traditional notion of jobs. Instead of filling slots in organizational charts, valued employees were being assigned to task forces and becoming flexible in their attitudes and routine. They became more attached to specific projects than to overall corporate objectives, acting as if they were self-employed or at least had an equity stake in the project. Such groups still required bosses, but they didn't fit the pattern of the old top-down hierarchies. Some task leaders were technical gurus, organizing knowledge that advanced project definitions and outcomes. Others provided the emotional and spiritual coherence that inspires any great team to make the intuitive leaps required to stay ahead of competitors. Team leaders earned their authority. Tom Peters, the management consultant who helped pioneer the new approach, was told by some of its more enthusiastic adherents: "We report to each other."

That trend and the rapidly growing "outsourcing" of jobs to independent operators were the twin pressures displacing the standard notions of work. Some companies spent fortunes eliminating jobs. *The Vancouver Sun*, for example, paid up to $200,000 each to buy out 900 of its 1,300 employees. At a Heinz cannery in Leamington, Ontario, workers took a $4-million voluntary pay cut just to keep their plant from shutting down. Meanwhile, the organizations dedicated to protecting workers—the unions—seemed to be the last group in society to realize that the traditional workplace was vanishing. Most rank-and-file refused to share the remaining jobs while the termination of one Canadian Auto Workers' strike was delayed because some members had not returned from their fishing trips. In the spring of 1992, the same union rejected GM demands that Oshawa members work an extra hour of overtime. Despite organized labour's ostrich-like defence of the status quo, "de-jobbing" became the buzz-word of the decade.

It was not for everyone. Only those workers with special skills and self-starting natures could earn their living as freelance contractors. The workplace was bisected into two classes: the overworked and the under-employed—and there were many more of the latter than of the former. Some people were working sixty hours a week, others hardly at all.

Canadians had in the past prided themselves on living in a classless society. In fact it was not classless at all—there was no similarity of fortunes between the son of a Rosedale dynasty and the daughter of East Asian immigrants—but there was class mobility and the levelling reality that most families did belong, as George Orwell said of his own, to the "upper lower middle class." This had originally fostered an egalitarian impulse in the new nation forged across the attic of North America. But with the advent of the New Economy, class barriers appeared where none had existed before. Those who faced vocational extinction for themselves or shrinking opportunities for their children felt betrayed by circumstances over which they had no control. They grew angry and rebellious. One of the decade's defining moments occurred on January 9, 1995, when a line of 26,000 shivering applicants snaked around a convention-centre parking lot at Pickering, Ontario. The job-seekers stomped the snow, waiting to be interviewed by General Motors of Canada recruiters for $22-an-hour assembly-line jobs—which did not exist. GMC president Maureen Kempston Darkes later explained the company's aim had been merely "to create a pool of workers who could fill in for normal attrition some time in the future." But the image of desperate people waiting forty-eight hours to claim positions which might some day materialize dramatically illustrated how the nature and availability of jobs had changed. It had become tough to get a job in a society that had operated not too long ago on the principle that those willing to work would be rewarded. That's how revolutions start. In Kitchener, Ontario, 290 people applied for one $6.50-an-hour restaurant counter job; in Montreal, 34,000 applicants turned up for 135 jobs with the provincial auto insurance corporation.

No matter what else happened in the country between 1985 and 1995—a decade when Canada went to war, put down an insurrection, wrestled with its constitution and confronted a secessionist movement—it was unemployment that consistently topped the social and economic agendas. To work was to live. Had Brian Mulroney only kept one of his many promises—that he would provide "JOBS! JOBS! JOBS!"—he might still be in office. Instead, his tenure became identified with the eternal recession that blighted the latter half of the decade. This was despite the fact that between

1983 and 1988, Canada enjoyed the second-highest (after Japan) growth among the world's industrialized nations and the fastest rate of job creation anywhere. But in the long and gloomy periods bracketing those good years, the economy went comatose. Milton Friedman, the economist and Nobel laureate who became the darling of Canada's right-wingers, concluded that there were no economic cycles, only ups and downs.* But the ups were a lot less frequent than the downs. The Eternal Recession officially began in April 1990, and never seemed to go away. People and companies felt as if they were going broke and many actually did.

Instead of being regarded as financial lepers, those who got rid of creditors by going bankrupt were hailed as being wise. Personal bankruptcies, which were less than 20,000 in 1985, had more than tripled by 1992. The most imaginative bankrupt was Raymond Malenfant, a Montreal entrepreneur with the self-confidence of a high-wire acrobat, whose chain of a dozen hotels (including the Fort Garry in Winnipeg and the Manoir Richelieu at Pointe-au-Pic, Quebec) owed creditors more than $150 million. He attempted more than 300 separate legal manoeuvres to stave off bankruptcy. To maintain his image, he had his chefs carve larger-than-life busts of himself in lard as hotel lobby displays and at one point invited creditors to stay free in his hotels, but nobody took him up on the offer.

Everyone felt threatened. Many of those who escaped bankruptcy had to cancel their credit cards, cash in their RRSPs, remortgage their homes. Even the rich were humbled.† Profits in every

---

* John Kenneth Galbraith, the Canadian-born economist and a fervent critic of Friedman, was telephoned a few years ago at 3:00 a.m. by an Israeli journalist seeking his reaction to Friedman's appointment as an adviser to the Israeli cabinet. "With Milton Friedman as your adviser, you have nothing to worry about from a few hundred million hostile Arabs," Galbraith proclaimed, and went back to sleep.

† The Recession produced its own brand of dark humour, including one story about the wealthy occupant of a Palm Beach mansion who came down to breakfast one morning and said to his wife: "Erika, I've been thinking. This damn recession is getting even to us; we've got to economize. Why don't you learn to cook, so we can fire the chef?" The wife's reply was immediate and to the point: "Sure, Harry but why don't you learn to make love, so we can fire the chauffeur?"

industry dropped to survival levels—or below, if the company happened to own commercial real estate. Consumers curtailed their spending and travel. Shopping malls turned into killing fields for traumatized merchants with long-term leases. Between 1990 and 1992, the world's airlines lost an astounding $15.7 billion—more than the total profit earned by the aviation industry since the Wright brothers first sputtered into the air at Kitty Hawk, North Carolina, in 1903.

AN APOCRYPHAL STORY MADE THE ROUNDS during the darkest days of the Cold War, when the Soviet Union would show off its latest means of mass destruction every May Day during an elaborate military parade past the Kremlin. The country's leaders would take the salute from a concrete balcony, figuratively thumbing their noses at what was then a nervous Western coalition. On one of those occasions, after the rows of tanks and newest missiles had rumbled past the reviewing stand, an old car brought up the rear of the parade. It was occupied by two middle-aged men in untidy suits, waving to the crowds. Leonid Brezhnev turned to an aide and furiously demanded what the jalopy was doing in a military parade. "But they are our most damaging weapon, Mr. Chairman," came the explanation. "They're economists!"

In Canada's case, professional economists spread needless confusion and alarm. They demonstrated not the vaguest idea why the Recession was so deep or when it would stop, but pretended to know the solution. Despite their inherent caution and stubborn assurances that Canada was not, technically, in a Depression, economists did recognize some striking similarities to the Dirty Thirties. Both decades followed orgies of irresponsible spending and borrowing. In the 1920s, gullible investors bought swampy real estate in rural Florida; in the 1980s, even more gullible investors purchased highly leveraged office buildings in downtown Toronto. Both periods were populated by high-stakes gamblers who masqueraded as conservative businessmen. The 1920s had Ivar Kreuger, the crooked match king who committed suicide when his empire collapsed; the 1990s had Bob Campeau and Paul Reichmann, whose greed turned fiscal manipulations into an abstract art form. Their demise, like the millionaires who bit the dust in the 1930s, hurt many innocents, not to mention the bankers (a separate category from the innocent) who discovered that some of their prized collateral was worthless.

One reason economists had so much trouble predicting the impact of the Great Recession of the 1990s was that it broke the pattern of the seven other economic slow-downs (lasting an average of 11.8 months each) that Canada had experienced since 1945. The 1990 slump had been partly triggered by the inability of Canadians—as a nation, as corporations and as individuals—to service the debt they had accumulated. While it was valid to argue whether or not the size of the debt ought to have made any real difference to the country's economic performance, there was no doubt that it presented a psychological barrier to growth. Canada's national debt had exceeded $500 billion and become unmanageable. Canada was experiencing what economists called a "self-feeding liquidity crisis," which in plain English meant that the country was awash with unsecured debt. "To claim that this is not a Depression because the statistics are not as horrendous as in the 1930s misses the point," insisted Dominik Dlouhy, a Montreal-based investment strategist. "At that time the public sector was very small, whereas now governments have captured a large and growing percentage of the GDP, financed by ever-higher taxes and borrowing. To claim that this is not a Depression because unemployment and human suffering are not as severe as in the 1930s is like saying that the Persian Gulf War was not a war because millions weren't killed in the trenches as they had been in the First World War." Just as none of the hundreds of thousand Iraqi soldiers who served in the desert trenches would doubt for a moment that it was a real war, neither would any of the unemployed confuse their unremitting joblessness with an economic "cycle" or necessary "correction." Dlouhy and others pointed out that the number of working-age jobless in the 1990s was about the same as it had been in the Depression. Unemployment insurance and welfare payments made their plight slightly more bearable. But to the jobless and working poor the soup lines, unseen during the prosperous postwar decades, looked and felt exactly the same as in the 1930s.

Apart from the 1930s, Canada had only one full-fledged Depression, between 1873 and 1879. Similar jobs in similar numbers had appeared again once those economies recovered; the difference in

the 1990s was that many of the jobs were gone for good. In the
past, the revival of retail sales reduced inventories, allowing
manufacturers to return to full production. But that could only
happen when consumers began to feel confident about their future,
which in turn required a sharp reduction in unemployment and
fear of unemployment. Exactly the opposite was happening in
the 1990s.

Large-scale industrial layoffs were commonplace, reflecting
the changing nature of work. Industry was no longer the engine of
job creation, so the old reliance on consumer confidence to stimulate
manufacturing and spark economic recovery no longer had much
meaning. Unemployment rates seemed unaffected by economic
growth, floating between 8 and 11 per cent for most of the decade.
The traditional bonds between economic performance and job
creation had been severed. In 1988, when Canada's strongest economic performance of the decade resulted in a 5 per cent growth in
GDP, unemployment was at 7.8 per cent; two years later economic
output actually declined slightly, but unemployment remained
steady at 8 per cent. By 1993, the economy had made a lame recovery and was growing by 2.2 per cent a year, but unemployment had
increased to more than 11 per cent. With job creation moving from
the industrial to the post-industrial sectors, consumers could no
longer equate their personal job security with the general health of
the economy.

Consumer spending in North America ground to a halt. General
Motors, the world's largest manufacturing company, laid off 79,500
people. IBM—the company which had trumpeted its place at the
leading edge of modern technology—was planning to lay off 20,000
employees. Here was Big Blue, a corporation with $76 billion in
annual revenues operating in 137 countries, admitting that its corporate culture was kaput. IBM's iron-fisted corporate ethic amounted
almost to a religion and had forced its bushy-tailed staffers to spend
their lives in blue suits and white shirts (and the female equivalents).
Better they should have worn loafers and sweatshirts and at least
have been comfortable.

NO WONDER THAT SURVEY AFTER SURVEY showed more than half of
employed Canadians ranked the loss of their jobs as their chief

worry.* Most of the traditional sources of work had dried up. Manufacturing accounted for 15 per cent of available jobs; resource industries, the historical backbone of the Canadian economy, by the autumn of 1993 accounted for only 3 per cent of the labour force; agriculture ranked a puny 1 per cent. The economy's commodity base was vanishing, in part because of technological developments. Copper in telecommunications lines was being replaced by fibre optics, aluminum was taking the place of steel in automobiles, electrolytic galvanizing had reduced the amount of zinc needed to galvanize steel.

Bank of Canada Governor John Crow's obsession with inflation, probably more than any other single factor, helped scuttle hopes for the economy's recovery. While price stability was desirable, Crow's anti-inflation policies† exacted too high a price. Ever since his "zero inflation" crusade began in the winter of 1988, Crow had kept such a tight grip on the economy that factories began to close and unemployment increased to an agonizing 1.6 million people. While it was difficult to calculate the extent of human suffering Crow's stubbornness inflicted, the best estimate (from former T-D Bank economist Doug Peters, who later became a minister in the Chrétien government) was that by reducing inflation from 5 per cent to 2 per cent between 1990 and 1992, Crow had bled $104 billion in lost production from the economy, which both triggered and prolonged the Recession. Peters also calculated that in 1992 alone, lower interest

---

* This infused such tension in relationships, especially among double-income couples, that Toronto sex therapist Sue Johanson claimed her polls had shown they were making love only once a week, usually on Saturday nights or Sunday mornings, down from their previous 2.2 weekly average. To help divert that North American trend, or at least to *appear* to be turning the other cheek, Roger Libby, the head of the Atlanta, Georgia, organization, the National Organization of Sexual Enthusiasts (NOSE), gave out instructions on how women could more credibly fake orgasms. Everybody wanted to be Meg Ryan.

† Crow seemed to regard inflation as a disease, like the bubonic plague, that had to be eradicated at all costs. In the winter of 1989, he was so furious about a report urging the Bank of Canada to boost employment by lowering its interest rates that he demanded an immediate audience with its authors, including John Fryer, head of the

rates might have allowed another million Canadians to be employed, which aside from its human benefits would have lowered unemployment insurance costs by $15 billion and generated an extra $7 billion in tax revenues. In response to Peters's attacks, a confidential Bank of Canada memo noted that "reducing this [1.6 million unemployed] by one million would take us well below the natural rate of unemployment." That heartless view revealed more about Crow's tunnel vision than a hundred of his after-dinner speeches or policy declarations. Crow's anti-inflation mania was based on the premise that rising prices created economic inefficiency and social inequalities. That was true enough, but his black-and-white edict of striving for *zero* inflation turned an economic proposition into a religious crusade. Crow also seemed to believe that sustained economic growth would automatically follow once inflation was erased, yet there was no evidence to support this theory. Another policy error was that between 1989 and 1991, Crow kept the value of the Canadian dollar artificially high. This wiped out any advantages Canada might have gained from its free trade agreement with the U.S. At the same time, he kept Canadian interest rates up to five percentage points above those in the U.S., further devastating the country's economic prospects.

One of the many peculiarities of Crow's stormy stewardship at the Bank of Canada was that he seldom practised what he preached. Constantly spreading his dogma that no single element in his battle

---

National Union of Provincial Government Employees. According to *Pillars: The Coming Crisis in Canada's Financial Industry,* by Michael Babad and Catherine Mulroney, Crow lectured the group for forty-five minutes, insulting their knowledge of both economics and the English language. Fryer finally attacked Crow for having a closed mind. "There's a different way of looking at this," he said. "There are a lot of people out there who are paying the price for this policy. You should look at some of the people who are the victims." Crow, enraged, began to shout: "Ah! I've heard this class nonsense before. I'm from London." Fryer shot back: "I grew up in London as well and you know how we settle things there. Perhaps we should settle this matter outside." The two men lunged at each other, fists at the ready, but the presiding chairman calmed them down. Crow gave another twenty minutes of speech, still propounding his inhumane view of the world.

against inflation was more essential than lower labour costs, he urged unions and management alike to accept lower wage offers. Yet, while preaching the virtues of poverty for the great unwashed, he accepted annual pay raises for himself of up to 21 per cent. Crow added $103,000 to his annual salary—raising it from a maximum of $150,000 to a maximum of $253,200. (The precise dollar figure cannot be given as the stratospheric salaries of senior mandarins, in order to protect the guilty, were published as ballpark ranges.) Crow's predecessor, Gerald Bouey, who had run the Bank of Canada from 1973 to 1986, refused to accept raises when interest rates were high and former Federal Reserve Board Chairman Paul Volcker, who held the equivalent job in Washington, took a salary cut from $116,000 to $60,000 under similar circumstances. When Crow was forced out of the Bank by Liberal Finance Minister Paul Martin, he was handed a $250,000 gratuity and given a $30,000 farewell party. Getting rid of him would have been cheap at double the price.

IN A COUNTRY BUILT ON THE PROTESTANT ETHIC, work had become a privilege. Statistics Canada reported a million Canadians were being permanently laid off from their jobs annually, even in such boom years as 1988. By mid-1993, the government agency claimed that an astounding 7.4 million Canadians aged fifteen years and older were not looking for work, though some of that number were living in normal, if under-capitalized, retirement. In the same year, with the economy pulling out of the Recession, nearly half a million economically disenfranchised people joined the 4.3 million Canadians who had already fallen below the poverty line; a quarter of a million were homeless and forced to eke sustenance from food banks. Compassion was spread very thin. The deadliest downturn since the Depression shook the people's faith in an economic system that, only two decades before, had provided them with the world's highest living standard. Canada was not alone in its misery. Western Europe was in disarray, with 18 million unemployed. The Japanese economy, the supposed epitome of capitalist efficiency, broke into such panic that Tokyo stockbrokers spent more time praying at Shinto temples than trading shares. Sweden, once Canada's model, became a muddle; in the Soviet Union, the only remaining growth industries were protest marches and crime.

For young Canadians, higher education no longer guaranteed work, but the lack of it guaranteed the minimum wage. Half the jobs created in the 1990s required more than sixteen years of schooling, twice the number of a decade earlier. By December of 1994, the rate of unemployment in the age group between fifteen and twenty-four was 28.5 per cent among those with eight years or less of schooling. The young, who had once been promised that their lives would be better and richer than those of their elders, found that they would almost certainly be worse. "Party hearty and die young," became their motto.

During most of the decade under review, Canada made the worst of both worlds by exporting yesterday's raw goods and importing tomorrow's finished products. Research and development spending by all sectors of the economy, including the universities, totalled a pitiful 1.3 per cent of the gross domestic product—less than half of other industrialized nations. "The cost of doing nothing is not zero," warned Ottawa economist Michael McCracken. The few exceptions were such enlightened companies as Nortel Inc. (the former Northern Telecom, which spent $1.3 billion a year, or more than 13 per cent of its total revenues, on research and development) and some smaller high-tech firms which were in business largely to do research. Still, the decade was also characterized by the emergence of computer software programmers who beat the world. SoftKey Software Products Inc. of Mississauga, Ontario, for example, was Canada's fastest-growing company in 1992, with a revenue increase of a hundred-fold since 1986.

The march of technology gained an unprecedented haste. It's likely that patents have not yet been taken out on inventions we will be using in the year 2000. The vacuum tube had given way to the transistor, which in turn had been replaced by integrated circuits and transformed by the microchip. The great breakthroughs promised for the last half of the 1990s were not so much in computer capabilities—though those electronic brains were beginning to exercise their own intelligences and were able to follow voice commands and even hand gestures—but in the processing speed and the networks connecting them. Utilizing new laser-based breakthroughs in fibre optics, keystrokes traversed the earth in microseconds; boosting one currency or wiping out another, exposing national priorities to global realities. "Digital networks will provide a new central nervous system for the world economy," predicted George Gilder, the guru of digital technologies. Although such predictions sometimes smacked of the unwarranted boosterism of *Popular Mechanics* covers from the 1950s, where a helicopter was parked on top of every garage, the pace of change introduced by computers made them appear plausible. They were also far more revolutionary in their implications. Gilder went on: "Transformed by convergence and computerization, television will burst forth in a new flowering of choice and empowerment. Great cities will give up their current role as hives of industry and emerge as havens of social activity and entertainment. Productive citizens will retreat to rural redoubts and reach out to global markets and communities. Throughout all these changes one theme will triumph: the empowerment of individual families and customers against remote and irresponsible organizations. In essence, people will no longer settle for whatever or whoever is playing on the tube or at the mall or in the local corporate centre. Instead, they will seek out and command their first choices in jobs, culture, entertainment and religion."

THE TIMES THEY WERE A-CHANGING, as was the nature of Canada's economic system. Although the political Revolution captured most of the headlines, Canada's economic transformation was equally significant and much more traumatic.

Canadian society is usually examined in terms of its identity crises, its bilingual agonies or its cultural struggles set against the temptations of the American empire. Curiously, Canada is rarely viewed through the prism of its indisputable status as one of the world's most successful mixed economies. The capitalist catechism holds that society is a commercial transaction. Faith in the self-regulating mechanism of supply and demand dated back to Adam Smith's "invisible hand" of free markets as the best means of allocating the most productive uses of labour, capital and resources. Disciples of this harsh orthodoxy—who tended also to favour Darwin and Hobbes as mentors on charity and social planning—conveniently forgot that Smith had authored a companion volume (*The Theory of Moral Sentiments*), in which he advocated that proper regard for others was the basis of civilized society. The impact of Smith's bottom-line ethic had been diluted in Canada by federal governments that had used intervention, regulation, moral suasion and an intricate system of income redistribution to foster equality of compassion and opportunity, if not equality in the absolute. Even if it was capitalism, it was capitalism with a human face. Canada's mixed economy aimed for the economic benefits of capitalism with the human and organizational benefits of socialism. It was a blend uniquely suited to Canada, as the country's forbidding geography and absence of large-scale economies had, for instance, prompted governments to create 464 state enterprises with assets worth $84 billion, in charge of everything from the national airline to the national broadcaster.

Then came the Mulroney years. In part because he was a Conservative with a caucus and a party that had Neanderthal traditions to uphold, but mostly because Pierre Trudeau had left behind a bare treasury, the value systems of the private sector came to dominate public-sector decision-making. Canadian capitalism dropped its human face and people found themselves, naked and alone, in a Darwinian jungle neither of their making nor to their liking. Mulroney privatized two dozen Crown corporations, deregulated financial services and energy exports, dismantled the Foreign Investment Review Agency and removed the universality of Canada's social security net. The public response took on the characteristics of class warfare, with the concerned and the comfortable battling it out for the nation's soul. "The overarching message of the Mulroney Tories was that solid communities are built by individuals taking responsibility for themselves," observed David Ross, executive director of the Ottawa-based Canadian Council on Social Development. "It was a system based on individualism and greed, in the sense that it presumes if everybody's looking after themselves, then society will look after itself. There was a moment in his second mandate when Mulroney set out his aims for free trade and said, 'We have to be competitive, we have to hone our human resources, we have to cut and thrust...' and I thought, my God, that's not a mission statement for a country, that's the mission statement for the Iron Ore Company of Canada.'" Despite wearing his social conscience on his sleeve, Mulroney's actions were clearly intended to replace the collective security of Canadian society with a national creed of individual self-reliance.

The Mulroney approach was the antithesis of the loose-jointed, play-it-by-ear, help-the-underprivileged attitudes that had distinguished previous postwar governments. It certainly bore the fingerprints of Tom d'Aquino, president of the Business Council on National Issues, the lobby group which spoke for Canada's top 150 corporations. D'Aquino drew the appropriate image when he explained that he wasn't a bit sensitive about being called a lobbyist: "After all, the Pope is a lobbyist." Brian Cardinal Mulroney made no effort to hide his faith. "We're going to re-energize the private sector in this country because that is the way new jobs are created," he told the House of Commons in his maiden speech as prime minister on November 7, 1984. "The private sector must be free to do what it does best—the generation of jobs and opportunities and wealth for all Canadians." It was not a gospel to feed the soul, in fact its God had been killed by post-industrial economics, but Mulroney had no other faith available to him. Had he wished to lavish Canadians with every form of government support imaginable, the money simply wasn't there.

"The Mulroney government's record was a fundamental attempt to change the way Canadians think and act," declared Anglican Archbishop Michael Peers. "They wanted to make us selfish and they achieved that by pushing us to look only to ourselves for solutions. But they also made us cynical and angry. And we will not soon pull out of that."

Just as the public sector underwent a metamorphosis, the private world of Canada's business Establishment moved through its own Revolution.

THE PASSING OF THE OLD GENERATION of business élites was symbolized in 1989 by the death of Edward Plunkett Taylor, eighty-eight, in Nassau. He had long since vanished from contention, having departed Canada's shores for the Caribbean in 1970. But in the struggle between the haves and the have-nots, he had once stood out as the epitome of riches gained and power wielded. He was condemned by socialists as "the crushing Croesus of Big Business," by communists as "E(xcess) P(rofits) Taylor—the mad miser of millions" and by prohibitionists as the Beer Baron personally responsible for the plight of every Canadian alcoholic. With good reason, Canadians felt that no matter where they spent their money, they would inevitably enrich this top-hatted eminence who was often to be found in the horse-racing tabloids, binoculars perched on portly stomach, blandly accepting the latest trophy.

His influence grew exponentially through the 1950s and 1960s; by 1964, a random sampling of trades on the Toronto Stock Exchange would show fully 10 per cent of any day's transactions

were in companies that he controlled. Prevailing myths to the contrary, Taylor was neither the richest Canadian of his day (that honour
was shared by Sam Bronfman and John David Eaton), nor did he
inherit wealth. His father, who had served as a sharpshooter in the
Riel Rebellion of 1885, was financially comfortable but left his son
exactly $12,225. Young Eddie attended Ottawa's Ashbury College,
graduated as a mechanical engineer from McGill in Montreal, then
moved back to the nation's capital, where his first ventures were Red
Line Taxi and the Yellow Bus Co. (He did some of the driving
himself.) Taylor eventually acquired from his grandfather a tiny
local brewery, Brading's. Over the next decade, speeding across the
countryside in a black Packard sedan outfitted as a mobile office, he
acquired thirty breweries across Canada and the United States and
turned them into Canadian Breweries Ltd., then the world's largest
malt shop, selling suds worth $1 million a day.

Taylor spent the Second World War in unpaid government
service, mostly as head of the Washington-based War Supplies Ltd.,
which co-ordinated U.S. and Canadian arms purchases. He was later
appointed by Winston Churchill to run the British Supply Council,
which managed the United Kingdom's North American war require-
ments, but resigned from the war in 1944, declaring, "by then, I
knew which side would win." He subsequently captured control of
Dominion Stores, the St. Lawrence Corp., Dominion Tar &
Chemical, Victory Mills Ltd., B.C. Forest Products, Massey-Harris
and, briefly, Peruvian International Airways. Massey's international
operations were the centrepiece of his empire, but in 1957 Taylor
abruptly fired James Duncan, the tractor company's chairman with
forty-six years' seniority. Accused of being ruthless, Taylor replied
in feigned indignation: "Me, ruthless? Certainly not. But when I'm
right and management's wrong, of course I get rid of management."
Despite his despotic corporate behaviour, there was a charming side
to Taylor, his cherry-cheerful face grooved by laughter lines as he
began each phone conversation with a chuckled, "This is Eddie . . ."
His mind worked like a telephone exchange, enabling him to switch
from one set of numbers to another without missing a beat. "Eddie
can read a balance sheet like a poem and tell you where it doesn't
scan," went the Bay Street buzz. Even his main relaxation turned
profitable, as his horses won the Queen's Plate ten times and his
Northern Dancer captured the Kentucky Derby.

Taylor spent most of his life in the fast lane. "The worst days are Saturdays and Sundays," he told me on his seventy-fourth birthday, "because I'm the only one who wants to work." He flew restlessly between board meetings in his Hawker Siddeley jet, painted in his racing colours of turquoise and gold. He sold Canadian Breweries for a $117.7-million profit in 1969 and moved to Lyford Cay on New Providence Island in the Bahamas. There he built a private club where millionaires could sun themselves in an atmosphere made surprisingly tranquil by the absence of such dubious refinements of civilization as personal income tax and death duties. He became a Bahamian citizen in 1977 and gradually phased himself out of any Canadian involvement. The last time I saw him, Taylor had just signed a deal with Daniel Ludwig, then the world's richest man, to build assembly-line housing for the Third World and was actively negotiating with the Shah of Iran and the president of Indonesia.

Taylor was the last and most successful of his breed: a genuine robber baron who didn't pretend to have a conscience, who bested nearly all his competitors and lived to enjoy the spoils. If there was one prize that eluded Eddie, it was his childlike longing for a British title. He was made a Companion of the Order of St. Michael and St. George (a colonial order ranking beneath those of the Garter, the Thistle, St. Patrick and the Bath), but even though he had bought the appropriate manor house (Birch Hall in Windlesham, Surrey) to enjoy it, the cherished knighthood never came.

In sharp contrast, the new breed of business leaders who took over most of Canada's private sector in the 1980s had few social pretensions and knew that the kind of authority and influence that counted had to be earned, hard step by hard step. Business became a contact sport. Having the right connections was no longer merely useful, it meant everything. As they careered down an information highway that was anti-hierarchical by its very nature, they didn't even need a fixed address—just as long as they were in the loop, were bankable and had an *infobahn* address. The connection made, the adrenalin would start to flow. They were a bit like jazz musicians, these networkers, picking up spontaneous clues from one another, improvising, getting into a mutual groove, bringing it all home.

TYPICAL OF THIS STRANGE BREED was Peter Thomas, a Vancouver entrepreneur so diligent at networking that he even took his cellular phone to bed at night. "It's my sword," he claimed. "The voice calls now available are fabulous. I have conversations all the time with people I've never met. They leave a message on my voice mail and I leave a message on theirs." I had first met Thomas at the launch of *The Acquisitors*, the second volume of my *Canadian Establishment* series, which was held at Hy Aisenstat's Mansion restaurant in downtown Vancouver.* The business scene in Vancouver was very different then, dominated mainly by real-estate flippers who favoured Jordache jeans and Porsche aviator sunglasses. (They were convinced beyond redemption that some women and some driving machines were more ultimate than others and traded up in both categories.)

As the Acquisitors who had been the subject of my book—Peter Brown, Sam Belzberg, Herb Capozzi, Jack Poole, Nelson Skalbania, Neil Cook, Geoffrey Lau, Edgar Kaiser and Jimmy Pattison, among others—began to arrive at the Mansion, Jack McClelland, my Toronto publisher, confessed to feeling shaky. "My God," he whispered, "these guys are for real. I thought you'd made them up." That they really existed hit home when Peter Thomas waltzed in. I had described him in my book as "wearing links of heavy silver chain, jangling like Indian spirit shields on his hairy chest, framed by an open-to-the-navel sweatshirt." The description seemed to fit, but the moment he spotted me, Thomas steamed over to complain: "You lied! You said I wore silver chains around my neck, jangling like Indian spirit shields on my hairy chest. Not true." He pulled a couple of examples from the thicket of his neckline and wiggled them at me. "Lookit. They're *gold*!" McClelland was never quite the same after that. He didn't say much, but seemed in a particular haste to scurry back to Toronto, where men of substance spent the currency of their lives with orderly,

---

* Hy's place was still swanky then, though Hy himself was going through a bad time because his Calgary steak house had just burned down and the local fire chief couldn't figure out why. "I know what happened," Hy confided to me as we were setting up the dinner seating plan. "It was either a tri-lite on the second floor or an Israelite in the basement."

pre-ordained decorum—and the kind of *joie de vivre* on display at the Mansion only happened to people one didn't really know.

When I next saw him in the fall of 1994, Thomas had become a bit of an icon. Except for Peter Brown and Jimmy Pattison, who had become corporate CEOs, he was the last of the Acquisitors still flipping real estate and still collecting toys for big boys. But the chains were gone. Instead, his muscular, 165-pound frame was encased in a navy blue suit, white shirt and a restrained banker's tie.

"My God," I exclaimed in mock horror, when I saw his work uniform. "A *white shirt*? You've gone too far."

"I know," he confessed. "I'm just losing it all."

During the thirteen years since that party at the Mansion, Thomas had nearly gone bankrupt, executed the Canadian real-estate deal of the century, and had acquired four million shares of Samoth (Thomas spelled backwards) Capital Corporation, a merchant bank he controlled that specialized in "vulture" real-estate deals—swooping in to take advantage of undervalued or bankrupt situations. Samoth was both lean and mean, its payroll limited to eight workaholics with a floating cadre of a dozen consultants hired on an individual contract basis. "I'm a risk manager, not an asset manager," Thomas explained. "One of the reasons we've been so successful is that we've learned to quantify real-estate risks, something the oil industry has done forever. You've got to limit your exposure so that, for example, you option land, zone it and sell out, instead of staying with a property the whole nine years it takes to put up a building for which there may or may not be a market. That's like playing cards in Vegas and continuing to bet. You're bound to lose. The house always wins."

His original aim was to achieve a personal net worth of $100 million before he reached fifty years of age. He didn't make it, probably because he grew too careful. "You can never be too cautious," insisted the semi-reformed Acquisitor. "Deals are like trains. Every ten minutes a new one comes along. I don't fall in love with my investments. Going into a deal, I always have an exit strategy. I structure the business as if I intended to go bankrupt in ninety days, with firewalls built around subsidiaries, family trusts in place and each operation hived off into a separate limited-liability company." His first big business deal was his 1975 acquisition of the Century 21 franchise for Canada. Until the 1982 Recession he was flying high with 326 branches and annual gross revenues of $3 billion. His toys included a $120,000 Clenet convertible ("Number 234 out of only 250 made"), a seventy-two-foot Stephens yacht, a 1,200-cc Harley-Davidson motorcycle and a Piper Cheyenne turbo-prop airplane. He lived with his family in a private suite on the twelfth floor of Victoria's Harbour Towers Hotel that featured early-Nevada casino decor complete with thick blue carpeting which crawled up the walls and a matching Himalayan cat.

What brought him to ground was a joint venture with Nelson Skalbania (the poor man's Peter Thomas) that cost him most of his toys and $30 million. "We were victims of the King Arthur disease," he later lamented. "In those days, when somebody came to you with a deal, you'd tell your wife, your lawyer and your accountant about it and half the time they'd try to talk you out of it. But you did the deal anyway and made money. So after a while you didn't consult anybody. You got too embarrassed to tell them about the crazy deals you were doing. I was once in Eugene, Oregon, because my daughter was attending a gymnastics meet. I had nothing to do, so I bought this building called the Atrium for $1.4 million, and sold it a few days later for $2.4 million without hardly taking a good look at it. That's how you catch King Arthur's disease."

After an abortive bid for Jim Bakker's PTL Heritage U.S.A. Theme Park (he wanted to make it less spiritual), he sold Century 21 to his partner, Gary Charlwood. That deal, which was consummated at the very peak of the 1980s property market, yielded Thomas a $26-million profit. "Money is a curse," he quipped. "If you were broke, you wouldn't have to spend so much time looking after it."*

---

* Time was the only problem Thomas acknowledged. To manage his crowded schedule he devised what he called his "executive toolbox," a leather-bound loose-leaf collection of facts, admonitions, homilies and epiphanies that guided his life. "Total Freedom is Total Discipline!" and "Freedom is the Absence of Necessity!" were some of the slogans that decorated his personal Bible in bold, theatrical type. It set out his Ten Commandments (including "Walk whenever possible," "Don't show explosive anger to anyone," "Eat only salad for lunch" and "Don't be concerned about spoiling myself"). His travel plans were detailed twelve months ahead of time ("Attend Cannes Film Festival," "Go to Wales to hear its great singers"). "I can give you my schedule for March 1999 right now," he enthused. The book was divided into three sections: Health, Happiness and Freedom.

Which left unanswered the question why he would spend so much naked energy in pursuing it. His blessings he listed as those moments in his life that gave him a "high," like flying across the Atlantic in a Concorde jet, buying his "ultimate dream machine" (a 1973 Daytona Spider Ferrari) or celebrating his birthday by scuba-diving after turtles in Maui, when he decided to ask Rita Morrice, his companion of the previous seven years, to become his second wife. "The idea," he enthused, "is to create your own future and not have it shaped by circumstance. You have to keep your thoughts positive because your thoughts become your words. And you have to keep your words positive because your words become your actions. And you have to keep your actions positive because your actions become your values. And you have to keep your values positive because your values become your destiny." Such men are capable of anything.*

Thomas moved to Phoenix in 1994 to concentrate on real-estate investments in the American south-west. "I'm a doubting Thomas," he explained, "and I go where the investments are most attractive." His departure was typical of the restructuring of the Canadian economy. The mobility of people and money, the shift away from traditional sources of activity, the effects of globalization and the rise of information technologies were eroding borders faster than any formal free trade arrangement. It also showed how great was the 1980s lure of the fortunes that could be made through specula-tive investments, which were by their very nature the earning of a profit from the application of nothing. It was money earned in complete detachment from the intrinsic value of things, and the

---

* To keep boredom at bay, Thomas indulged in two leisure pursuits: rare cars and country music. He owned, among others, the first Lamborghini and the first Audi ever built, a Bentley turbo and a half-dozen Ferraris, including the 1965 Ferrari 308 GTS that Enzio Ferrari hand-built for his son, Dino. (At one country-and-western–motif birthday party for his three hundred closest friends, Thomas had four red Ferraris tied to a hitching post outside his front door.) He also had a $40,000 Boss Hoss, a brute of a motorcycle powered by a Corvette V8 engine that could accelerate from zero to sixty miles per hour in 1.4 seconds flat. His country-and-western label, Savannah Records, had signed such Canadian stars as Michelle Wright, the Good Brothers and Gary Fjellgaard.

ease with which it could lead to massive fortunes spawned a cult of speculation that came to infest the most venerable of Canadian institutions.

THAT WAS DISRUPTIVE ENOUGH, but at another level, the ethical endgame played by business during the decade provided ammunition galore for the Canadian Revolution. While most business proprietors and executives remained honest, the exceptions were so spectacular that they cast a shadow on the entire private sector. "Immoral behaviour is bad for business," wrote David Olive in *Ju$t Rewards*. "Like an infectious disease, it starts small and spreads until the contagion either is destroyed or has undermined whole companies and entire industries . . . The preoccupation with getting ahead while paying little heed to the consequences is jeopardizing the health of business and of the society in which it operates." Michael Millken, the junk-bond king who had earned $700 million a year in commissions—edging out the profits of all but sixty-four of North America's largest corporations—became a role model for the new profiteers, even after he was found guilty in 1990 of securities fraud and fined $1.1 billion.* His operational code was described by author Connie Bruck in *The Predator's Ball*: "Morality and legality became mere conventions—accepted modes of conduct for the less creative, the less aggressive, the less visionary. Millken's firm was the brass-knuckles, threatening, market-manipulating Cosa Nostra of the securities world."

   Money and morality have seldom been a good mix. As Lewis H. Lapham, the editor of *Harper's*, has pointed out: "Like the rain, money confers its blessings on the just and unjust, on the criminal and the saint; it can commission Michelangelo's Sistine ceiling or underwrite the architecture of Auschwitz." Looking around the

---

* Millken claimed in court that he could not recall many details of his trading activities because he carried on several conversations at once. "I would say that I listened to no more than 25 per cent of the conversation I would have during any trading day," he testified. "I would come in and out, buy and sell securities during any conversation." That may even have been true. During an interview with the *San Francisco Chronicle*, Millken couldn't recall the name of the best man at his wedding or his wife's middle name.

wreckage of corporate Canada at the dawn of the 1990s, most people could only agree.

The ethical endgame of business in the Revolutionary Decade had many players. Canada's milling industry, which seldom made news, was charged in the winter of 1990 with a scam that defied morality at any level. Asked to fill a $500-million government contract to deliver milled grain to Ethiopia, Chad, the Sudan and other famine-stricken countries of Africa, the main Canadian mills (Ogilvie, Maple Leaf and Robin Hood) rigged their bids to keep prices artificially high. How many starving people were thus denied nutrition couldn't be calculated, but the millers pleaded guilty and were fined $1 million each. Another case that set new limits to the profit motive came to light in the late summer of 1994. Imperial Tobacco, it was revealed, had commissioned a study by Professor Jean-Pierre Vidal to prove that smoking was good for the Canadian economy, despite its $9.7 billion annual health bill. The good professor's logic was impeccable. "Anti-smoking groups," he concluded, "rarely consider the reduction in health costs resulting from the premature deaths of certain smokers." No quarrel there; they certainly did die young. "A person who dies of lung cancer at age seventy," he went on, "will not be hospitalized later with another disease." But of course. Silly *moi* to disregard the economies of dying. Smoking killed more Canadians each year than traffic accidents, suicide, AIDS and murder combined, which only proved what generous benefactors the folks at Imperial Tobacco really were. According to their line of reasoning, the Holocaust had been a great money-saver and the Great Flood a financial bonanza. Any government running a Medicare deficit could simply infect the water supply with the Ebola virus and prevent hospitalization for some silly reason, like natural death. "Imperial Tobacco's new brand of logic," noted columnist Allan Fotheringham, "is the type of innovation that has made capitalism so popular since the days when its advocates put children in the mines—so as to keep them off the streets."

Another sign of the decade's decadence was the lengths to which some of its most successful practitioners went to avoid taxes. Although the exact amount was cloaked in the family's traditional secrecy, there was no doubt that the largest estate executed in 1993 was that left by New Brunswick billionaire K.C. Irving, who had luxuriated in his Bermuda tax haven since 1972. A tearless Presbyterian who didn't drink, smoke or swear, Irving was ruthless and unfeeling in pursuit of the Almighty (dollar) to the point of denying farmers the right to salvage firewood from the loose logs left at a river's edge after the spring log drives of his forestry companies. His corporate structure was so complicated that when the mariners aboard one of his tankers, *Irving Ours Polaire*, sought union certification, they literally couldn't find out the name of the subsidiary that owned their vessel. When he died, Irving willed the bulk of his wealth, estimated at $7 billion, to a Bermuda-based trust. He left instructions that it be jointly administered by his three sons, but there was a catch: they could only claim the fortune if they became non-residents of Canada, to ensure that Ottawa never receive a penny in tax revenues. Such was the gratitude shown by a family that had made the bulk of its corporate profits from the $9.3-billion contract to build a dozen patrol frigates for Canada's navy. "That Irving empire," Charlie McElman, a Liberal senator from New Brunswick, accurately observed, "operates with the power of a lion, the appetite of a vulture, the grace of an elephant, the instincts of a barracuda and the principles of an alley cat." Fashions change; the Irvings never did.

When western Canada's leading department-store chain, Woodward's Ltd., closed its doors in the spring of 1993, long-term employees and suppliers received only thirty-seven cents on the dollar of the money owed to them. But the company's nine senior executives, who had run the stores into the ground, shared $6.6 million in severance, retirement pay and something called "special restructuring bonuses." That kind of self-imposed generosity by the very people who had deprived a company and its workers of their livelihood was a moral abomination, but it was typical of the times. Paul Stern, who had single-handedly almost destroyed Northern Telecom's corporate culture and moved its balance sheet dangerously into the red, was compensated with a package worth $8.5 million, just so he would wave goodbye. Top CPR executives negotiated a farewell bonus for themselves worth $30 million. The most valuable corporate parachute was that awarded in 1987 to Bernard Isautier when Polysar Energy & Chemical, the company he headed, was taken over by Bob Blair's Nova Corp. As well as a bonus of $2 million on top of his hefty salary, Isautier received stock options worth $20 million.

Foundering companies, big and small, became notorious for cheating their suppliers, creditors, shareholders and employees. When Chicken Chicken Inc., an Ontario-based fast-food franchiser, went bankrupt in the spring of 1991, company chairman John Gillespie attended the creditors' meeting where the company was officially dissolved and never said a word. No matter what information the hapless shareholders and franchisees demanded, no matter how often he was criticized or insulted, Gillespie just sat there, silent and unmoving, as if he were hatching an egg. Peter Menoutis, one of the failed franchise holders, complained afterwards: "He's the head chicken, and he's flown the coop!"

Another instructional episode in corporate ethics was the saga of Michael DeGroote, the former controlling shareholder of the Ontario-based waste management firm Laidlaw Inc. Although he never specifically denied the allegation by the Ontario Securities Commission that he had made a $17-million profit short-selling Laidlaw stock after learning privately that some of its dump sites were about to be declared toxic, DeGroote claimed he had done nothing wrong. He proved his innocence in a strange way. He agreed to pay a $23-million fine, one of the largest ever levied by the O.S.C., for contravening its provisions against insider trading, but his lawyer insisted that the transaction had been an "honest mistake." As an oxymoron, that ranked with jumbo shrimp, Ottawa nightlife and uncontested divorce.

The prize exhibit in the gallery of lapsed ethics had to be Donald Cormie, the Edmonton financier whose web of financial companies collapsed on August 10, 1987, incurring the loss of up to $492 million by his 67,233 investors. The collapse was doubly bitter because most of them were middle-aged men and women looking for a safe way to protect their nest eggs. "All your money is kept in a vault, like a bag with your name on it," had been the Cormie sales pitch, delivered with broad, if false, hints that investments made in his firms were covered by Ottawa's deposit insurance plan. An official enquiry by Calgary lawyer William Code had found Cormie "both dishonest and fraudulent." Cormie pleaded guilty to conspiracy to defraud and paid what to him was a token fine of $500,000. There was never any question about his guilt, but there remained the issue of motive. There was no need for him to cheat, no need for the stupid tax dodges like paying his daughter, Allison, $288,000 to "study the weather," his wife, Eivor, $275,000 to "attend Edmonton social functions" and God-knows-how-much for God-knows-what to his great, good friend, Christa "Cupcakes" Petracca (who ain't telling). He was such a wealthy and very careful man. At his 18,000-acre ranch, he had raised 2,000 head of purebred Hereford, Charolais and Simmenthal cattle, monitoring each of the animals through a computer in his office so that he could tell, for example, that a mightily exhausted Swiss-born bull named Signal had produced semen worth $2,348,000.

Cormie was driven by monumental greed and the need of a never-ending shopping spree (at the end of his run, he owned six large houses kept ready at all times for his personal use). The collapse cost ordinary people their pride and their savings, while Cormie escaped with enough assets to continue leading the comfortable life. He kept five of his houses, a $600,000 motor yacht at a marina in Sidney, British Columbia, and several other cattle ranches. As his empire was collapsing he had transferred large amounts of cash to banks in New York and Europe; his secretary, Diane Stefanski, testified that he had drained as much as $66.6 million out of his empire, through sweetheart "loans" to himself, family members and Cupcakes.

With swindles of that magnitude in the air it was hard to get excited about executive salaries, yet the corporate culture that produced the obscenely swollen pay-packages for CEOs in the 1990s became an instrument of revolutionary intent. While blue- and white-collar workers were being asked to forego raises or to cut back their incomes, their bosses kept raking in monumental pay-packets that had little connection with the success or failure of their enterprises. That created tremendous resentment and weakened the people's faith in the system. Apart from the dismal ethics of this charade, the fact that compensation was unrelated to profit meant there was little incentive for higher productivity and no motivation for many of Canada's industrial leaders to try harder. Almost the opposite was true: no Canadian company suffered a more humiliating meltdown than Royal Trust, which went from a top-rated financial institution to virtual bankruptcy in twenty months. Although Royal Trust's fifty top executives had boasted in the good years that their compensation was tied directly to their sterling performances, when they had run their once-great enterprise into the ground, they were forgiven the loans they had taken out to finance their share purchases and lost none of their bonuses.

Stupidity became its own reward. The rocket scientists who operated Hamilton's Dofasco Inc., once the pride of the Steel City, decided in 1988 to purchase Sault Ste. Marie's debt-ridden Algoma Steel Corp. The move cost Dofasco an out-of-pocket $713 million in cash. Two years later, Dofasco had lost every blessed penny of its investment and the value of its equity had been cut in half. Instead of committing hara-kiri, or at least voicing some excuse or apology, Chairman Paul Phoenix and President William Wallace accepted $1.6 million in executive bonuses on top of their $4.3-million salaries. Being rewarded for losing that much money was particularly reprehensible because at the same time, Dofasco was laying off its mill workers and other employees as part of its so-called "urgency economy measures."

At Canadian Pacific, which laid off 37,000 employees during the decade, Chairman and CEO Bill Stinson raked in extra hay based on the flimsy premise that while CP's balance sheets continued to gush red ink, its losses were getting smaller. In 1993, Stinson received a $619,866 bonus on top of his $905,000 salary (up by $31,300 from the year before) for a total of $1.5 million in compensation—just for reducing the annual losses—caused by his own decisions—from a disgraceful $478 million to a merely shameful $190 million. Bank of Nova Scotia Chairman Peter Godsoe was handed a 131 per cent compensation increase for 1994, a year when his institution performed the worst of the Big Five banks and profits dropped by one-third.* Gerry Pencer, whose dubious background raised many doubts, milked Cott Corp., the private-label beverage company he headed, for stock options that he sold for $41 million and he still retained options worth $65 million. Stephen Banner, who joined Seagram's as an executive vice-president, was paid a signing bonus of $4 million plus 50,000 Seagram shares, on top of a salary of $7.4 million for the seven months he put in between June and December of 1992. Stephen Bachand, recruited by Canadian Tire in the same year, was handed a starting bonus of $3.9 million (plus his $1.2-million salary), not to mention a $1-million interest-free loan to purchase a home and stock options worth $2.1 million. The biggest salary hike of 1994 was the 1,035 per cent increase (to $13 million) granted Brian Hannan, the CEO of Methanex Corp., the Vancouver-based refiner of methanol, a gasoline additive.

---

* The ethics of the day are best understood by placing Godsoe's $1.9-million salary and bonuses next to the $960,000 the company saved by cancelling the annual Christmas bonus for its retired employees. About 3,200 of the bank's pensioners had received the $300 bonus since 1983, but the bonus was cancelled as a savings measure the same year the bank reported its fattest quarterly profit in its history—$211 million, or 82 cents a share.

The money earned by the best executives—often proprietors and minority shareholders—was easier to excuse. Perhaps Frank Stronach wasn't worth the $41 million he paid himself in 1994 but without him, Magna International would never have existed. Peter Munk's $32-million stock-option package in 1991 seemed like a fair return for the founder and operating genius behind Barrick Gold Corporation, which within a decade he had turned into the world's third-largest gold producer. Between 1983 and 1995, Barrick stock had gone up 2,900 per cent. Less understandable was the fifteen-fold raise (to $3.8 million) Peter Allen awarded himself in 1988 as head of Lac Minerals, which he ran with no imagination and little energy. In contrast Paul Desmarais, Montreal-based chairman of the aptly named Power Corp. of Canada, paid himself a relatively modest $1.66 million although his firm's net earnings were a healthy $200 million. A case history worth noting was that of Marvin Marshall, the Texas buccaneer brought in to save Bramalea Inc., once Canada's premier house builder, which also owned and managed thirty-six million square feet of commercial real estate. On December 23, 1992, when Bramalea and its thirty-seven subsidiaries filed for bankruptcy court protection, Marshall couldn't be bothered to interrupt his ski holiday in Colorado. He addressed a Toronto news conference by speaker phone, even though it was the second-largest bankruptcy in Canadian corporate history, with creditors owed $5 billion. More to the point, Marshall was the only Bramalea employee not to suffer from the company's demise. When his company lost a howling $90 million in 1993, he was paid $971,225. When Bramalea was finally wound down in March 1995 and shareholders lost everything, Marshall was still collecting his $1 million a year salary.*

---

* In the days Bramalea's stock dropped from a high of $24 to 13 cents a share, Marshall complained that it took six shares to buy a cup of coffee and that he couldn't find a restaurant to accept them. Despite his company's troubles and eventual bankruptcy, Marshall's office surroundings were more suitable to Versailles. He worked at a $6,000 rosewood desk, met his board around a $50,000 walnut table, enjoyed snacks from Wedgwood china and a custom-made Leif Jacobsen dining set, and soothed his nerves by listening to an $18,000 sound system. Head-office furnishings worth $4 million were auctioned off, including a $20,000 print of Bramalea's palatial head-office building, commissioned six weeks before the company went belly-up.

Apart from their generous pay-packets, chief executive officers received fringe benefits that recognized few limits. Rad Latimer, a former president of the CNR who was hired to run TransCanada Pipe Lines in 1979, was a gross example of a life enjoyed beyond the fringe. His corporate culture was more American than Canadian and many of the more conservative TCPL executives questioned his free-flowing expense accounts, including the unlimited use of the company's two executive jets for personal trips.*

Latimer and his wife, Jacquie, appropriately nicknamed "The Velvet Barracuda," often jetted off to their winter lodge at Mont Tremblant, Quebec, or on European shopping trips. He had his office decorated in bordello-red velvet, had the company buy him a Jaguar Sovereign and used company employees to cater his parties and paint his house. There were no problems as long as TransCanada was controlled by Dome Petroleum, but when Bell Canada Enterprises obtained control in late 1983, Latimer's stewardship was abruptly terminated. The story of his departure was worth repeating because there existed so few documented accounts of CEOs being dismissed over their abuse of personal expenses. His unmasking began with an anonymous letter outlining his transgressions which was circulated to TCPL executives, with an indication that a copy had been sent to Ottawa's tax assessors. As soon as Gordon Osler, then TCPL's chairman, read the document, he phoned John Clarry, a partner at the law firm McCarthy & McCarthy and TCPL's legal adviser. He suggested the issue be turned over to the board's audit committee. "We then had to go over to the Petroleum Club where there was a reception which we were hosting," Osler recalled. "I drifted around and spoke to each member of the audit committee and asked them to come to my room after dinner. When they arrived, I gave them each a copy of the letter and said, 'It's your problem.' They appointed a lawyer and he worked with the auditors to produce a report which was discussed at some length, and we later had a board meeting at McCarthy & McCarthy's office in Toronto not attended by Latimer. Jack Gallagher, who was still a director, kept

---

* The fleet included a $9-million Gulfstream II, popular among corporate executives "cuz you can stand up in the potty." Its twenty-passenger configuration had been reduced to ten luxurious reclining sofa-seats for added comfort.

coming into the room saying, 'Can't we save this fellow? Can't we somehow get around it?' And I said, 'No, we can't.' Jean de Grandpré, representing Bell's controlling interest, also said, 'No, we can't.' It was finally agreed that I would have to do the deed. It wasn't fun. Latimer had to go; his style was not the TransCanada style." On September 4, 1985, Latimer was dismissed with a golden parachute worth $3.8 million, an annual pension of $291,200—plus the Jaguar. Latimer was never charged with any criminal offence, but his fellow CEOs noted his fate carefully. The 1990s brought with them a revulsion with excessive spending, a rebellion against the 1980s ethic that more is better, that efficiency and monetary gain ought to be the ultimate goals of human activity. No more free houses at Palm Springs or Palm Beach, no more monogrammed golf balls, no more bodyguards, no more Mont Blanc pens, no more weekends with Henry Kissinger.* If the slogan of the 1980s was, "He Who Dies with the Most Toys Wins," the motto for the 1990s was more likely to be, "He Who Dies with the Most Toys—Dies Anyway."

Meanwhile no corporate empire was safe from the ravages of the Recession, not even Ma Bell, which had for generations been Canada's safest and most dependable investment. Bell never lost money, always increased dividends and never laid off employees. During the 1990s it reversed all three of these tenets. In 1993, Bell finally closed the books on $350 million in real-estate losses (which followed $940 million in write-offs and unrecovered loans since 1989) and sold Montreal Trust for $292 million after having paid $875 million for the company in 1989 and investing in it another $175 million. BCE reported a 1993 loss of $750 million, the first in its history. Bell quickly cleaned up its act when Lynton "Red" Wilson was brought in as chairman in April of 1993.

Once a major industrial player, Montreal's diversified paper company Domtar Inc. spent the decade barely solvent, laying off 4,000 employees and recording losses totalling more than $600 million. One of the chief architects of its downfall was Jean

---

* The real status symbol of the 1980s was to have an executive phone rigged with a breath-monitoring device that could indicate if the calling party was unusually tense and presumably lying. It was said to be a good test to differentiate wives from mistresses.

Campeau, the former head of the Quebec nationalist *Caisse de dépôt et placement du Québec*, who later became Jacques Parizeau's minister of finance. As Domtar's chairman, he took several lengthy leaves of absence to work for Quebec separatism. When Campeau formally resigned to go full-time into politics, Domtar's board of directors rewarded the departing chairman with a bonus of $450,000, leaving unanswered how much Campeau would have been paid if the company had actually made a few dollars during his tenure. Incidentally, this had not been a case of a Montreal company favouring a powerful separatist with an overly generous payoff. Before Campeau arrived on the scene, Domtar lost $294 million in 1990 and had written down the value of nearly all its assets. The company that had formerly consisted of twenty-five profitable forest-products companies suffered major layoffs at its twelve surviving businesses; one-quarter of its salaried employees were let go. Most of Domtar's troubles flowed from its ill-conceived and badly managed diversification policy of the mid-1980s, which had been masterminded by Chairman James Smith and Chief Operating Officer Raymond Pinard. They bought Genstar Gypsum Products and its five U.S. wallboard plants in 1987 for $314 million. None of those divisions ever turned a profit. For almost destroying what had once been a jewel of a company, the duo was rewarded with nearly $2 million in salaries, bonuses and special payments. On top of that, by the simple act of leaving, Smith kicked in an astonishing pension plan designed to pay him $430,766 a year for life, while Pinard had to scrape along on an annual pension of only $327,804.

The reputation of Quebec's business class, worshipped as the knighted heroes of the Quiet Revolution, was put at risk during the decade. They turned out to be just as vulnerable to economic pratfalls as their counterparts in English Canada, but there was an important difference. The legions of English-Canadian CEOs pleading receivership were regarded merely as the victims of a dismal economy or their own incompetence. In French Canada, because they had become such admired role models, their failure caused a severe shock. Among the most spectacular of these debacles was Claude Castonguay's unrealized dream of building his Laurentian Group of more than one hundred companies into a world-class financial institution. Minister of social welfare in Robert Bourassa's first Liberal administration in 1970, father of the province's health-care system and later a Conservative senator (appointed by Mulroney), Castonguay was foremost among the Montreal business élite. Widely regarded as a man of ability and conscience who would weld together a huge one-stop money machine under the Laurentian umbrella, his group generated annual revenues of nearly $3 billion. But the conglomerate's real-estate investments proved to be disastrous, as did its insurance operation. There were so many internal write-downs that Laurentian was eventually folded into the Desjardins Group, the mammoth credit union based in Montreal. Only a month earlier, there occurred the spectacular fall from grace of Bertin Nadeau, the elegant and outspoken chairman of Unigesco Inc., the management company whose asset base he had built from $15 million in 1966 into Canada's seventh-largest company, with annual revenues of $7 billion. Nadeau operated at the very centre of Montreal's business Establishment, not only occupying some of its most important directorships but using his own boards to bring together many of its most important players. Decked out in his Armani suits, Nadeau had cut a dashing silhouette speaking out for free trade, federalism and any other issue that struck his fancy. But in the process of building up his empire, he had accrued overwhelming debts, including a $115-million junk-bond issue that he couldn't honour. Steinberg's, once Montreal's most profitable grocery chain, became history after shipping tycoon Michel Gaucher took over the firm (aided by Quebec government money to keep it out of English hands) and ran it into the ground. Leopold Property Consultants, the city's liveliest real-estate firm, went belly-up; even the Ritz-Carlton, for heaven's sake, had to be rescued by a German hotel chain.

But the most significant bankruptcy occurred in the summer of 1991 when Bernard Lamarre's $1.2-billion Group Lavalin Ltée bit the sawdust. A vain peacock of a man, Lamarre boasted of getting Third World contracts by bribing officials. I recall interviewing him while he was seated in front of Guy Montpetit's *Sex Machine*, a garish painting that he hung in his office. Lamarre explained that whenever he did business in the Third World he never handed out bribes without first demanding a receipt. "I make sure we get a signed invoice," he said, warming up to his subject. "And payment is always in the form of a cheque, not cash, so we can claim it on our income tax. Of course, we have an advantage over the

Americans, as they're forbidden by law to pay out such 'agents' commissions.'" In the process of expanding his business, Lamarre became more of a politician than an engineer, lobbying for contracts as he worked the tables of Montreal's Beaver Club. He developed intimate links in Ottawa and Quebec City and employed several prominent former politicians, notably Marcel Masse and Pierre Trudeau, who were placed on retainers by Lamarre to wheedle contracts out of the Soviet Union and lesser customers. Lamarre built up his aggregation of seventy technical companies into the country's largest engineering firm, completing 600 projects in 112 countries. For a time, he was the New Quebec's most idolized and most envied business leader. Attendance was *de rigueur* at his corporate Christmas parties, where guests were met by a receiving line of one: Lamarre. But his ambitions were too big for his britches and, despite a last-minute Quebec government loan of $55 million, his firm filed for bankruptcy, leaving $860 million in unpaid debts.

OF THE MANY EXECUTIVES WHO GAVE CAPITALISM A BAD NAME in the decade under review, one name stood out above all: Victor Rice. The head of Canada's most renowned manufacturing company, Massey-Harris, he persuaded Ottawa to finance its resurrection and as soon it had recovered, moved the company to the United States. Adding insult to insult, he chose Buffalo as its operating headquarters.

During almost two decades as head of Massey, Rice expended most of his energies reducing its size and its debts, causing great havoc in the process. Looking back on that experience, he made a point of recalling the opening day of the 1986 Blue Jays season, when he walked into Toronto's Exhibition Stadium, looked around at the 52,000 spectators and told a friend: "I suddenly for one fleeting second had this unhappy thought that everyone in the stadium worked for us . . . We just that morning had laid off our 52,000th employee."

The unwritten rules that have traditionally held in check even the most avaricious of business leaders were broken in the convulsions that shook Massey and finally saw it depart from the country. Rice's actions seemed so reprehensible partly because of Massey's long history in Canada. Founded in 1847 by Daniel Massey in Newcastle, Ontario, it had originally supplied the farmers of Durham County with sap-boiling kettles. The company had grown rapidly from its start as a small machine-shop operation. After amalgamating with A. Harris, Son & Co. in 1891, Massey burgeoned into a major conglomerate, turning out bicycles, windmills, home freezers, milking machines, stoves, kerosene engines and washers, plus its line of agricultural machines of a quality unsurpassed anywhere in the world. During the opening of the Canadian West, a Massey marching band would lead parades of newly delivered tractors and harvesters down the main streets of local communities. The company treated its beaming customers to dinner and a free concert.* Massey's reputation spread overseas when its harvester won a grand prize at the 1867 Paris International Exposition. Operations were extended into the United States with the purchase of the Johnston Harvester Company of Batavia, New York, in 1910. The introduction of the self-propelled combine, developed mainly at its Argentina branch, revolutionized harvesting methods. Sir Edmund Hillary used its tractors on his historic overland expedition to the South Pole and Massey purchased the prestigious F. Perkins Ltd. of Peterborough, England, the world's largest manufacturer of diesel engines. At its height, the company employed 65,000 people in 120 countries.

After the Second World War, Massey slipped under the effective control of Argus Corp., the Toronto capital pool first headed by E.P. Taylor and later by Bud McDougald. It endowed the Argus partners with the international prestige and aristocratic connections they so craved. Massey's London office overlooked the exclusive Claridge's Hotel, where the firm maintained an ostentatious permanent suite for its chairman; nearby was a carpeted garage housing the two Rolls-Royces and a Daimler, maintained by Massey for its visitors from Canada. (The larger of the Rolls was decorated in royal colours and, to McDougald's panting delight, was borrowed by the Queen for ceremonial occasions.)

Massey's management had grown slack by the mid-1970s, having been taken over by Al Thornbrough, an American lightweight who commuted to Toronto for three days a week from his beach home in Boca Raton, Florida, yet claimed Canada's highest corporate salary.

---

* Nowadays, a farmer purchasing a combine harvester is tossed a baseball cap and a keychain advertising the company logo.

The company's problems were both in structure and management. Its growth and diversification had been grounded in opportunism, rather than long-range planning and development. When Massey moved into the United States it lost the Canadian market, without ever winning over much new American territory; that would have required development of a 100-horsepower tractor, which the company bungled. With the notable exception of the self-propelled combine, Massey had never really been an innovator, due to lack of research and the inability to meet the customer's needs. The crisis first came to the public's attention on March 10, 1978, when Thornbrough announced to the company's annual meeting a first-quarter loss of $38.8 million, temporary plant shut-downs and the liquidation of several manufacturing facilities. Argus had been taken over by Conrad Black, who moved into Massey on August 16, 1978, settled into the chairman's quarters and proclaimed: "Logically, Massey should probably have gone bust years before, but some things defy all laws of economics and nature—like bumble-bees." Within weeks of Black's take-over, Massey announced the largest annual loss suffered by any Canadian corporation up to that point: $257 million in U.S. dollars. Black kicked Thornbrough upstairs and named his friend, the aforementioned Victor Rice, as president. The son of a London chimney sweep, Rice was an impatient man who made quick rabbit-like gestures with his hands and his nose. He seemed so bent on his own path that he appeared to seldom consider how his actions might ruin the lives of others. He replaced fifteen of Massey's twenty-one vice-presidents, closed seven plants and even saved $30,000 through banning inter-office memos with executives' names printed on them. Black and Rice enjoyed teasing Massey's surviving vice-presidents about their grandiloquent titles, especially such geographical designations as Vice-President in Charge of Africa, and so on. At one point, Rice proclaimed himself President of the World, and the only way Black could top him was by anointing himself Interplanetary Chairman. Rice canvassed international lending institutions and eventually produced new loans of $580 million from 212 banks, but nothing worked. The cost of servicing Massey's swollen bank debts increased beyond endurance. At the time, the Canadian Imperial Bank of Commerce's Massey obligation was the largest unsecured commercial loan in the world and the bank eventually had to take a $100-million write-off.

Less than two months after his resignation as Massey chairman, Black quietly wrote down the value of Argus's investment in Massey to zero (which at its height had been worth $32 million) and later donated the all-but-worthless stock to Massey's pension fund. "I am amazed," he declared, "by the number of so-called financial experts who are luxuriating in the view that I am some sort of punch-drunk prizefighter on the ropes. Well, screw them." By the end of 1982, Massey was reporting a $413-million loss, its Australian operation was in receivership and most of its dealerships were in trouble.* Meanwhile, Rice had mounted a $715-million refinancing effort, which wasn't quite enough to shore up the company. By Rice's own often repeated admission, the move that really saved the firm was a bank guarantee of $200 million issued by the Ontario and federal governments.

In May of 1986, Rice divided Massey into two new companies: Varity, which took over the healthy operating assets; and Massey Combines Corporation, into which he folded ownership of the money-losing manufacturing operation at Brantford, Ontario, that employed 1,500 people, a $200-million corporate loan, as well as the responsibility for pension and medical benefits of 5,000 of Massey's laid-off and retired workers. With such heavy burdens, the Combines company inevitably went bankrupt and Rice walked away from the firm's obligations, including $27 million owed to 3,000 pensioners who had spent their lives working for the original Massey. That same month, Varity reported profits of $50 million. To twist the knife, Rice bid on the machinery at the bankruptcy auction of the Combines' plant equipment, purchased it for next to nothing and had it shipped off to Varity's American plant at Des Moines, Iowa. "It's the crookedest deal ever perpetrated on the Canadian public," proclaimed a story in *The Financial Times of Canada*. Court appeals later forced Varity to partially restore some of its obligations.

The arrangement also broke the terms of Rice's agreement for government aid, which had obliged him to maintain manufacturing

---

* Not to worry, that disastrous year Rice arranged for a pay-packet of $554,000—a 40 per cent boost from the year before, when Massey had lost only $240 million.

facilities in Canada and to export the company's technology and machinery out of the country only with Ottawa's approval. The one cloud remaining in Rice's life was the high taxes he had to pay out of his huge pay-packet. At last count, he was being paid $1.2 million annually and held stock options worth more than $4 million, as well as a golden parachute that would pay out at least $5 million. But, as he told *Financial Post* editor Diane Francis, "when marginal rates hit fifty per cent, something happens in a country. It's at that point that a person begins to cheat." Rice's reaction was to move the whole company, which at that point had sales of $3.5 billion, into the United States. He chose as its state of incorporation the tax haven of Delaware, and located its operating headquarters inside a luxurious mansion in Buffalo. The Canadian government's conditions for having saved Massey had been violated once again, but when a justifiably disgruntled shareholder at the company's 1990 annual meeting asked Rice whether he felt any moral obligation to keep Massey in Canada, the answer was a blunt: "Not at all."*

Rice's snorty presumption that he could do anything he wanted, even when dealing with money that belonged to Canadian taxpayers or Massey pensioners, went beyond acceptable levels of corporate arrogance. Canada's fairly aggressive brand of capitalism doesn't forbid very much, but it does demand that the private sector follow common legalities and the market-place. According to that standard, Massey should have either made it on its own or been forced into receivership. Instead, Victor Rice used a dubious ploy to get his company into the black, thumbed his nose at his benefactors and jumped ship. But then, not everybody gets to lay off 52,000 workers and to skip out on a $200-million obligation. At least he felt kind of queasy about it, if only for a ghostly moment one day at the ballpark.

A VERY DIFFERENT INCARNATION OF CAPITALISM under siege was the chronicle of Ted Rogers, arguably his generation's most successful entrepreneur and undoubtedly a man who felt the chill and the clout

---

* Only two Massey directors, Hal Jackman, who later became lieutenant-governor of Ontario, and Lynton "Red" Wilson, the BCE Inc. chairman, resigned from the Massey board in protest. Ironically, the patriotic Wilson was eventually replaced on the Varity board by Robert Gates, the former head of the Central Intelligence Agency.

of the Canadian Revolution and its shift from deference to defiance.

The defining anecdote about Rogers, the cable king who became a multi-media mogul when he swallowed Maclean Hunter in the spring of 1994, dated back to the time when he was a Big Tory on Campus—which, at the age of sixty-two, he still resembled. In 1961, Ted was a law student at Toronto's Osgoode Hall and hyperactive in campus Conservative politics. He needed to see the party leader, John Diefenbaker, on a policy issue. He was granted precisely five minutes in the great man's office, but Diefenbaker spent half the allotted time telling him a political joke. Then he excused himself to use an adjoining bathroom. Rogers knew exactly what to do. Realizing that his time was just about up, he barged into the toilet and made his case standing next to the startled but temporarily immobilized prime minister. That kind of aggressive, won't-take-no-for-an-answer attitude marked Rogers's amazing rise through the corporate world ever since. He successfully lived out the dictum advanced by his late mother, Velma: "Don't bang your head against a brick wall. Go over it, under it or around it—anything but through it."

In his flashy career, Ted Rogers occasionally slowed down enough to be called a workaholic, but most of the time he made that category seem comically inadequate to describe his daily grind, which more closely resembled the schedule of a donkey chained to the water pump in a tropical penal colony. "My idea of slowing down is putting a fax in my car," he once told me. He perked up when I mentioned that new fax machines for use on pleasure boats would soon be available. Rogers promptly mounted a fax aboard his yacht, a brand new thirty-five-metre, $5-million power boat, *Loretta Anne*. Constantly in motion, he went from being the proud owner of Canada's first FM radio station, CHFI-Toronto, when he was still a university law student, to the harassed choreographer of corporate assets worth more than $5 billion. His customary state of barely suppressed dementia had a purpose. Never satisfied with merely making his own companies grow, he was always trying to advance the cause of Canada and its technology. He hoped to instil in others the thrill he felt in discovering new ways of doing things, anxious to perpetuate his corporate vision of the world. He was, no doubt about it, a driven man. Robin Korthals, the former president of the Toronto-Dominion Bank, where Rogers did most of his banking, once confessed that the cable king had burned out at least fourteen credit officers in the past twenty years. (Rogers finally had to spread his business around several banks when his line of credit—not just its administrators—came dangerously close to burning out.)

Rogers's desperation to succeed was based on his fear of dying before he could do more than his father never had the lifespan to complete. He lived in order to outdo his father. It was Mission Impossible, not only because he had already done so, many times over, but because his tally of achievements was measured not in dollars but under the "I'll-show-them" column. This meant he would never be satisfied as long as there were doubters who had yet to be convinced he could actually do the impossible—like taking over a profitable $3-billion publishing house that had at least twice his credit lines available for self-defence but failed to use them.*

Although it was his father, Edward Samuel Rogers, who got most of the attention, his other ancestors were equally interesting and just as rebellious. John Rogers, a canon of Old St. Paul's in London, was burned at the stake in 1555, thus becoming England's first Protestant martyr of Queen Mary's reign. Seventy years later, Thomas Rogers, in another bid for religious freedom, left for the New World aboard the *Mayflower*. In the Seven Years' War, Robert Rogers led the storied band of irregulars known as Rogers' Rangers, the subject of several novels and films. It wasn't until 1801 that Timothy Rogers, a Quaker seeking greater religious freedom, came to Canada and settled in York County, now Toronto. Rogers's father, born in 1900, was the first amateur radio operator in Canada to successfully transmit a signal across the Atlantic and inventor of the radio tube that made it possible to build AC receiving sets, doing away with bulky, leaky and expensive batteries. He founded Rogers Majestic Corp. in the mid-1920s to manufacture the new design and eventually upgraded his ham operation into a commercial station with the call letters CFRB (Canada's First Rogers Batteryless), which grew to command Canada's largest radio audience. As early as 1931, the elder Rogers was granted the first licence to broadcast experimental

---

* The Ted Rogers/Maclean Hunter stand-off that preceded his takeover was described as the Riverboat Gambler facing off against the Village Parson. "I guess that's true," quipped Rogers at the time, "but I don't know why they keep referring to me as a Village Parson."

television, but he died eight years later from overwork (and a bleeding ulcer) at the age of thirty-eight, when Ted was only five. Ted
subsequently attended Upper Canada College, being chauffeured to
school each morning while his sports car was brought around during
the day so he could drive himself home. In 1963, he married Loretta
Anne Robinson, daughter of Lord Martonmere, a former British MP
who had served as governor of Bermuda. Three years earlier, Rogers
had bought for $85,000 all the shares in CHFI, a tiny 940-watt
Toronto radio station that pioneered the new frequency modulation
sounds at a time when only 5 per cent of Toronto homes had FM
receivers. By 1967, he was in the cable television business, rapidly
expanding beyond his original Toronto system. Within a dozen years
he became the world's largest cable operator, with more than two
million subscribers. Each of Rogers's business expansions had been
buoyed by a new technological "wave," right up to cellular telephones. He plunged into Cantel so far ahead of its time that at first
his own board of directors refused to accept the idea; more recently,
he claimed ownership of Canada's section of the information super-
highway.

A disturbing part of Rogers's personal philosophy was that he
treated his frequent illnesses not as warning signs to slow down but
as annoying distractions. When he underwent cataract surgery in the
early 1980s, his pal and chief adviser, Phil Lind, recalled seeing a
group of company executives gathered around Rogers's bed, deep in
discussion on a future cable project, while their boss still had his
eyes bandaged. (The vision in his right eye remained at only about
10 per cent of normal.) When Rogers suffered a coronary aneurysm
several years later, he was back at work long before doctors thought
it wise. His 1992 quadruple bypass surgery drove the medical staff
at the Mayo Clinic in Boston to distraction. He was dictating letters
before the anaesthetic had properly worn off. Rogers's firm turned a
handsome $79-million profit on the Maclean Hunter deal, all from
the stock he had bought just before making the buy-out offer, and his
company later purchased Ted's preferred shares in Rogers
Communications for a cash pay-out of $125 million. His style of
living matched his income. A few years ago, when Rogers decided
that he wanted a tennis court near his stone mansion on posh
Frybrook Road in Toronto's exclusive Forest Hill district, he purchased the house next door (belonging to Neil McKinnon, former

chairman of the Canadian Imperial Bank of Commerce) and tore most of it down to make room for the courts. "My God," went the neighbourhood rumble. "What if Ted decides to take up golf?"

If he was a true visionary, as his boosters claimed, it was partly because Rogers wouldn't allow financial constraints to trim his ambitions. For a while, cable TV was such a hot business that the word on Bay Street was, "Even Ted can't lose money on this one." But he did, always reinvesting in ever-riskier ventures, trading equity for debt, expanding assets instead of dividends. He would gleefully point out that the price of his shares had moved from seventy cents to twenty dollars since Rogers had gone public in 1979—despite the fact that his company had yet to post a profit or pay a dividend. "All we have to do to make money is stop growing," he explained.

And then it happened. Rogers had successfully turned cable television into a perpetual money machine; every year or so, he would increase the number of channels available over his system and raise his monthly fees. No one objected for the very good reason that Rogers's operations enjoyed monopolies. The only way to receive a clear TV picture and multiple channels was to pay his mounting fees. Rogers's revenues from this lucrative source exceeded $2 million a day. Then, in early 1995, Rogers offered its usual negative-option marketing ploy, charging an extra $2.65 a month for five new Canadian channels. The whole spectrum of the service was altered so that some popular channels vanished unless the option were added and subscribers had to specifically reject the new arrangement or they were automatically billed for it. There was nothing new or startling about that; Rogers subscribers had meekly accepted many similar deals in the past, as had subscribers to just about every book, video and record club extant.

Ted Rogers hadn't realized there was a Revolution going on. His company's move triggered the country's first cable-TV rebellion. Subscribers cancelled his service and took him to small-claims court. His offices were picketed; politicians were cheered for proposing laws that would turn negative-option marketing into a crime; newspaper editorialists lashed out at "government-sponsored, élitist arrogance"; the country went berserk. Vancouver playwright John Gray was moved to comment that normally docile Canadians, "faced with declining medical services, separatists in Quebec, high unemployment, a seventy-cent dollar and the loss of the cod fishery, stood up, dug in their heels and drew their line in the sand—over their right to receive CNN and The Sports Network on their basic cable.

"Predictably," Gray went on, "the media portrayed this as a 'consumer revolt.' But what I find interesting about the protest was that these expressions of collective rage are usually reserved for *governments*. In a way, the tone of the protests revealed that to many people, the cable television monopolies have become a kind of *government*. In a way, the protests over cable television resembled the squawk of broiler chickens who discover that somebody up there has been meddling with their feed. But these demonstrations were an admission on the part of consumers that somebody up there *could* meddle with their feed. If they didn't like what was offered, all they could do was squawk."

The fury of the cable protest, wrote *Maclean's* editor Robert Lewis, "serves as a warning for establishments everywhere, whether corporate or political. The people of Canada have been in a grumpy mood, starting with the rejection of the Charlottetown Accord in the 1992 referendum. The same volatility was evident in the rout of the Conservative Government in 1993 and the reaction to the cable companies. It is an era when people do not trust their leaders or, generally, the country's élite."

"I was stunned," Rogers confessed, when it was all over. "Now I know how those turbot must have felt, swimming toward the Spanish fish boats. From now on, our customers will determine what level of service each one of them will get."

It was a small skirmish in a long war, but there was little doubt who had won.

THE REVOLUTIONARY DECADE WAS MARKED by the disintegration of some of the country's largest business empires. In each case their animators, among them Robert Campeau, Paul Reichmann, Bernard Lamarre and Reuben Cohen, went against the Canadian grain by dreaming too big and thinking too small. They established world-class business empires on shifting foundations of high risk and leveraged debt and came to grief, corporately and personally, retiring from the field as case histories of rise, decline and fall. In the process they not only damaged themselves, but cost their employees a livelihood and devastated their shareholders and suppliers. Their ego-driven extravagances dramatically validated the revolutionary loss of faith in capitalism. Instead of countering the market theory that high risk carried high rewards, the lesson of their performance was that the greater an entrepreneur's ambition and flamboyance, the greater the chances of failure.

The most openly grasping and ostentatious of these high-flyers was Robert Campeau, the one-time Sudbury house builder who wangled about $11 billion in loans from Wall Street's astute merchant bankers to purchase two of America's largest department-store chains, Allied and Federated. It was an astronomical sum, but then Campeau seldom used cash or collateral of his own when he could get the money on spit and a promise. Neither was Campeau's ambition deterred by the thought of borrowing far more than he could ever repay; Campeau wanted to make deals that would go down in history.

They did. He presided over North America's largest and most sensational retail bankruptcy and had the distinction of becoming a symbol of the stock market crash of October 13, 1987. Most post-mortems agreed that Campeau's erratic behaviour had been a chief trigger of the crash. Campeau's inability to meet his debt obligations created a climate of doubt in the junk-bond market that detonated the most serious share-price correction since the Great Crash of 1929. As *The Wall Street Journal* noted: "The shaky junk-bond market received its biggest jolt from Campeau Corp., which created its U.S. retailing empire with junk financing. Campeau developed a cash squeeze that caused him to be tardy on his interest payments and to put the prestigious Bloomingdale's department-store chain up for sale."

The jitters set off by the collapse of Campeau's securities, described by the *Financial Post* as "the junkiest of junk," set off a panic about the debt load threatening to sink Campeau's entire empire. Many national treasuries can barely afford to carry debt burdens of Campeau's size. If he had been a country, he would have qualified for Third World developing-nation status, which in the prevailing climate might have prompted the World Bank to come calling with debt forgiveness and the offer of emergency loans. Instead, Campeau watched helplessly as the value of his company's stock, four decades in the making, plummeted from a high of $30.38 a share to 22 cents. "Thus did an age of excess unravel," wrote Carol Loomis in *Fortune* magazine, "with Robert Campeau as the catalyst and also the symbol of excess carried to its dumbest, most egregious limits. The Campeau drama had no rival for absurdity as it proceeded and for shattering effects as it ended. The overarching wonder of this affair is that so many supposedly shrewd lenders forked over so much money to a man whose instability would probably keep him from being hired as a Bloomingdale's sales clerk."

It was unlikely that anyone with Campeau's psychological profile and financial record could in fact have been hired to perform any job, however menial, if it required even the most rudimentary stability. Prior to his berserk shopping spree for U.S. department stores, Campeau had suffered three major nervous breakdowns: one during most of 1970, after he temporarily lost control of his company to Paul Desmarais; a second in 1980, when he was prevented from taking over Royal Trust; and a third in 1985, when he grew so depressed over his business dealings that he could not force himself to get up in the morning. He was able to work regularly only by appointing his psychiatrist, Dr. Alan Mann, to the Campeau Corp. board of directors, where the therapist could look after his star patient firsthand. Any brief encounter with the man would quickly inform the most casual visitor that Campeau's great mind for business and quick wit had been borrowed against the faculties of self-possession, judgement and prudence.

Even in those moments when he was suspended in mid-arc between mania and melancholy, he hardly qualified as an average, clean-cut, board of trade "leader of tomorrow." The private devils haunting him may well have made Campeau one of the most competitive humans ever to stalk the planet. On a holiday jaunt one summer to a private fishing camp in northern Ontario with a few friends and his son Robert, Jr., the group made a fun wager to see who could snag the longest fish. When they compared their catches at the end of the day, Robert, Jr. had won. Not for long. His father stomped on his fish until it was longer, albeit grotesquely squashed, to claim victory. He refused even to lose his race with age. He had regular injections of sheep-brains, supposed to guarantee eternal youth; Campeau at first wore a toupee, then had a follicle-by-follicle hair transplant; his teeth were capped; his face had been lifted so often his beard had curly hairs and his neck-skin had been stretched tight as a tenor timpani; he went through painful Rolfing rituals and swam daily in the private pools attached to his three residences, but not in the usual chlorine-treated water. The pools were equipped with special ozone systems to eliminate impurities; the water was drinkable.

His family quarrels became legendary. When Campeau, then a millionaire many times over, sold his Ottawa house to his daughter, the transfer was held up for months because he insisted the basement washer and dryer hadn't been part of the deal. Campeau's family troubles became public when he sued his son Jacques and his daughter Rachelle to retain voting rights over the family trust he had set up in 1961 as a tax-avoidance measure. Father and son did not talk for seven years and Campeau refused to meet Jacques's wife or visit his granddaughter. He was still married to his childhood sweetheart, Clauda Leroux, when he set up a separate residence with Ilse Luebbert, his German-born mistress, who bore him three children and later became his second wife. "A great woman," a friend described her, "provided, of course, you're into Valkyries."

ROBERT CAMPEAU'S ORIGINAL CLIMB had been as legendary as his eventual fall. One of fourteen children of a Sudbury blacksmith and auto mechanic, Campeau quit school in grade eight and, finding himself too young to get work, used his dead brother's baptismal papers to falsify his age and get a job at Inco. He built houses in his spare time, married his childhood sweetheart and moved to Ottawa, where he became a successful developer. Campeau's most spectacular brush with the Canadian Establishment had been his aborted 1980 attempt to buy control of Royal Trust, then run by a crusty Montreal-based Anglo retainer who went under the humble monicker, Lieutenant-Colonel (Ret.) Kenneth Alan White, C.D. "You may think that money talks," White warned Campeau, "but I don't like you, and I'm going to call up my friends and lock up 50 per cent of the stock before you can turn around." In an unprecedented show of solidarity the mavens of Canada's Establishment, led by Toronto-Dominion Bank Chairman Dick Thomson, Noranda President Alf Powis and the Reichmann family, slapped together an overnight syndicate that bought $200 million of Royal Trust shares at $4 *below* the Campeau offer—enough to hold the intruder at bay. The movement to save Royal Trust, which was based on a personal dislike of Campeau rather than his fiscal weakness, grew so strong that being part of it became a status symbol. Don Love, a millionaire

Edmonton developer, for example, counted his entry into the Establishment's inner core from the day he was invited to participate in the anti-Campeau crusade. For their shoddy tactics, White and John Scholes, one of his senior executives, had their trading privileges revoked by the Ontario Securities Commission. No matter: the Sudbury interloper had been routed. Campeau went back to real-estate promotions, but he neither forgot nor forgave the massive slight he had suffered. "If the Royal Trust tactics had been used in the United States," Campeau blustered, "those people who breached security laws would have gone to jail and the others would have paid large fines." The man's obsessive desire to grasp legitimacy from the business élite he envied prompted him to take on the entire Canadian Establishment. Typically, he refused to play by their rules. "They're stodgy, ridiculous and anyway, their power is dwindling," he once told me. Consumed with proving himself in their jaundiced eyes, he transferred his acquisitive itch to larger targets south of the border, just to show them he could play in the big leagues.

Campeau's first major thrust into the United States was his $4.9-billion takeover in 1986 of Allied Stores, America's fourth-largest department-store chain. Its outlets included such well-known units as Bonwit Teller and its revenues, at an annual $5.7 billion, were twenty-seven times larger than Campeau Corp.'s. He paid (or rather, borrowed) $2.4 billion for the initial key block of Allied shares that he purchased from the Los Angeles brokerage firm, Jeffries & Co., until then the largest single block ever sold on any U.S. stock exchange. Campeau and his company contributed a measly 4 per cent holding in Allied, which also had been purchased for borrowed money. That amazing deal created so much debt that Campeau had to jettison some of Allied's best assets, including the fashionable Ann Taylor division and Brooks Brothers, the respected New York City menswear store, which he sold to Britain's Marks & Spencer for $925 million. Still, had he held on to Allied's remaining assets and managed them carefully, the purchase would have been a brilliant move, yielding him a potential net profit of $500 million.

Instead, Campeau plunged into even deeper undertows of debt. Seventeen months later, he paid an inflated $8.2 billion for Federated, the country's oldest chain of department stores that included such giants as Bloomingdale's, Abraham & Strauss, Berdines, Sterns, Jordan Marsh and The Bon. He grossly overpaid for the bragging rights. Campeau's original offer of $59.70 per share (a total $5.4 billion, closer to Federated's real value) was run up to $90.70 per share when management enlisted competing bidders to stave off the Campeau terror. Not only did Campeau pay too much, he had to mortgage most of his valuable real estate to meet interest payments that came close to $1 billion a year. He tried his old trick of hiving off Federated's money-making assets to keep ahead of the bailiffs and even put Bloomingdale's, that day-care centre for the New York rich, on the block. "It took the special genius of Robert Campeau to figure out how to bankrupt more than 250 profitable department stores," sniffed *The New York Times*. The more earthy *Daily News* attacked him for devaluing his investments so quickly that no buyer stepped forward to claim Bloomingdale's. "Bloomie's woes," the tabloid editorialized, "are as if Kim Basinger had announced she needed a date and no one responded."

As a result of Campeau's wild gambles, the bonds of both Federated and Allied were placed on Moody's B-3 category—which was just one step above their "anticipating bankruptcy" rating. The two companies lost $367.5 million in the first six months of 1989 and by January of 1990, the Allied-Federated combo was forced to seek Chapter 11 protection under the U.S. bankruptcy code. Campeau had promised Allied bond-holders that he would not use junk financing for the Federated purchase. But his word had been as good as his bonds.

His endless asset shuffles, his sleight-of-hand borrowing from one source against another and his inability to settle in and actually operate any one of the many companies he acquired—or at least to put competent managers in place and not interfere with their decisions—shook the foundations of the junk-bond market. That was no mean feat in a market populated almost entirely by corporate vultures feeding on paper carrion.

After all that sweat and tension, after mortgaging his soul to prove to Canada's élite that he could slap a bigger deal on the table than they could even imagine, Campeau enjoyed only one moment of triumph. That was his house-warming of September 1984, or to be more precise, his mansion-warming. Campeau invited the glitterati of Toronto's Establishment to his new $8 million house at 64 The Bridle Path, in the city's fashionable northern reaches. He and Ilse had designed the 25,000-square-foot home in mock French *château* style, complete with a burled wood-panelled library that boasted the complete leather-bound works of Honoré de Balzac. The entrance hall, which was three storeys tall, was roomy enough to contain a standard suburban bungalow. It featured floors of Italian marble and a glass dome from which was suspended a tiered crystal chandelier, suitable for swinging from. The house had an expansive granite patio that concealed a roomy shockproof bunker stocked with canned food and its own forty-five-day air supply, designed to serve as a sanctuary from terrorist or nuclear attack. "It could resist a bad whack and radiation," claimed the mansion's architect. Its indoor swimming pool was covered by a retractable floor and could, at the touch of a button, be transformed from spa to ballroom.

The luminaries who attended the Campeau party included the ubiquitous Conrad Black,* Fred Eaton (Eaton's), Bill Mulholland (Bank of Montreal), Don Fullerton (Canadian Imperial Bank of Commerce), Ced Ritchie (Bank of Nova Scotia), Murray and Barbara Frum, Trevor Eyton (Brascan), Leo Kolber (Liberal bagman and powerful Senator), Pierre Trudeau (recently retired as prime minister), Bill Davis (then premier of Ontario) and Emmett Cardinal Carter, who formally blessed the greystone edifice. Terminally gauche, even in this moment of triumph, Campeau and Ilse insisted on holding court in the hangar-like reception hall, directing the guests firmly back out into the garden before food was served. This created at least one practical problem, resolved by allowing women visitors to use a downstairs hall bathroom. But the men, including Campeau's bankers, found themselves using a device few had ever christened before—the porta-potties scattered about Campeau's lawn—an experience which couldn't have escaped their memories when reviewing their host's credit rating.

The guests had come not out of respect or even amiability, but out of curiosity. Campeau's Gonzo tactics made them shiver with scarcely disguised disgust, but they also knew that Bob and Ilse and their Versailles-on-the-Don had to be seen to be believed. They were treated accordingly. Apart from the fact that they had been shunted

---

* Black was the only member of the Toronto business élite who paid serious attention to Campeau—apart from some bankers who nervously held his paper—by appointing him to the board of his main holding company, Hollinger Inc.

into the garden, their discomfort increased when they saw the place cards on the wooden tables where dinner was to be served. It was as if someone had deliberately set out to embarrass each guest, placing him or her next to the invitee they liked the least or were suing the most.* As the guests munched wild mushrooms dipped in raspberry vinegar, followed by roast suckling pig with avocado paste, they were serenaded by Paul Anka, "a close personal friend" of Campeau's paid handsomely for the appearance, who just happened to drop in with his entire Las Vegas show band. He sang—what else?—"My Way." In Anka's version, the last verse went:

> All Canada loves Bob Campeau,
> This Taj Mahal he calls a chateau,
> Is he extraordinaire? Bet your derrière,
> But he did it . . . HIS WAAAAY!

THERE WAS A BITTER-SWEET quality about Robert Campeau's demise, a fall not from grace, because he had so little, but from contention as a serious player, which was the worst punishment of all. It was the classic tragedy of self-delusion surpassing reach; his career became a metaphor for the excesses of the 1980s. "Even though he cannot escape responsibility for the wreckage he left behind," wrote Arthur Johnson, in a devastating profile of Campeau in *The Globe and Mail Report on Business*, "Campeau was also a product of the times. Never before and perhaps never again, will the ambitions of a Robert Campeau coincide with the flood tides of such easy money on Wall Street. It wasn't just a flawed character that brought him down. It was a flawed system."

It was indeed. What made Campeau's gamble possible was the fact that by the mid-1980s, Wall Street had turned into a casino using

---

* Campeau had asked Rosemary "Posy" Chisolm Feick, the doyenne of Toronto's beautiful people, to help him with the guest list and seating arrangements. The mischievous "Posy" knew a potentially dull party when she smelled one, so she thought it might be fun to generate a little excitement—and perhaps even a little reconciliation—by placing the worst of friends at the same tables. At first, the gambit fizzled and the dinner conversation was as glum and terse as the chatter at a Benedictine monastery; later, they all began to talk and settled many old scores.

junk bonds for chips, and the "house" always won the richest pots. High-powered lawyers, bankers, consultants and money-letter writers pocketed $250 million in fees for assembling the Frankenstein's monster of Campeau's deals. If even one of them had possessed the decency to reject his fat fees and explain to him why the properties he was buying could never carry the gargantuan debt load they accumulated, he might have saved himself. But Campeau was flying so high at the time that he would have been impervious to advice, however sensible and well-meant.

Edward De Bartolo, an American shopping-centre tycoon out of Youngstown, Ohio, and Paul Reichmann moved in to rescue his tottering empire, but their price was high. De Bartolo snagged some of Federated's best shopping-centre properties and the Reichmann loans totalled $510 million, secured by drastically reducing Campeau's ownership of his own firm. (Being "saved" by a Reichmann was a bit like being rescued from a stranded isle by Captain Blackbeard.) In the process, Campeau lost control of Toronto's Scotia Plaza, his most valuable remaining asset. Meanwhile, Montreal's *Banque Nationale* came looking for repayment of the $150-million loan it had foolishly made to Campeau to buy shares in his own company—the shares themselves, which were rapidly becoming worthless, being the loan's main collateral.*

Saddled with the burden of having to pay the cost of their own acquisitions, Allied and Federated declared bankruptcy in January of 1990. Campeau found himself facing claims of $8.2 billion, including settlement packages for 6,500 laid-off Federated employees, as well as threats from an angry horde of 50,000 suppliers short-changed on delivered goods and banks screaming to get their loans repaid. That chaotic scene was followed by three consecutive blows to his ego: he learned that Campeau Corp. was about to be drastically restructured, leaving him without any corporate assets; the Bank of Montreal suddenly called an outstanding $30-million

---

* Campeau's lead banker was Cedric Ritchie of Scotia Bank, whose 1993 pay-packet totalled $2.6 million, the year's highest compensation for any Canadian bank chairman. Presumably the bank's investment in its top executive had been justified by Ritchie's ability to size up a good credit risk, which meant that the abstracted department-chain buyer with a debt ratio similar to postwar Bosnia had met Ritchie's standards.

personal loan; and asked to testify before a U.S. bond-holders' committee in New York, Campeau was deterred by forty-three lawyers ready to challenge his every word. Instead of facing them he sent a doctor's certificate, pleading yet another nervous breakdown.

He made one last curtain call at Campeau Corp.'s annual meeting on July 30, 1990, where he announced that he was discharging his bankruptcy and everything was looking up. This must have seemed dubious even to the most optimistic shareholders, since the company's stock price had dropped in the previous year from $22.25 to 85 cents a share and it had reported a loss of $1.74 billion (the second-highest in Canadian history). The loss included a $958-million write-down, the amount Campeau had overpaid for control of Federated. He told the shareholders whose investments he had ruined that he shared their pain. "My family and I understand how you feel," he lamented, waved a V-for-victory sign at the cameras and was gone.

But not forgotten—and not really gone, either. Campeau had moved large quantities of cash to the tax haven of Liechtenstein in central Europe, and used it to build a $10-million castle on the southern shore of Lake Attersee, at St. Gilgen, near Salzburg, Austria. The cost of the magnificent structure escalated many times over because of Campeau's insistence that an Olympic-size swimming pool be built on its enclosed roof, so he could enjoy a scenic view through cathedral windows while taking his morning dip. This latest extravagance was unwittingly financed by Campeau's ill-starred shareholders, since most of the money had come from a Campeau Corp. loan backed by the Bank of Nova Scotia. It seemed the ultimate insult.

Stanley Hartt, Ottawa's former deputy minister of finance who became one of the private sector's most imaginative and most intelligent animators, took over the pitiful remains of the Campeau empire in the fall of 1990 and nursed the much-reduced company into the black. He sued Campeau to recover $10 million in wages and another $1.3 million to have returned corporate artwork, cars and a communications system still in his possession. Another suit, undertaken in Liechtenstein, demanded the payback of $4.6 million that Campeau had used to acquire the 15.5 acres of land upon which he built his storybook castle. The case was lost because it turned out that Campeau had not bought the land outright, but instead had acquired it through a trust arrangement known as a *stiftung*, which owned the property. (A *stiftung* is an investment vehicle used mainly by those who want to hide the source of their funds. It cannot be touched under Liechtenstein's strict secrecy laws.) Campeau promptly counter-sued his former company for $100 million, claiming damages for the "high-handed and callous way" he had been treated and other such mischievous nonsense.

Like a latter-day Samson in his own Biblical epic, Robert Campeau tried to pull everything and everyone down around him. But he no longer had the power to hurt anyone except himself. I have often thought about Campeau after his tumultuous demise, but my impressions have faded with time. I am left with a mental image of him astride the ramparts of his Austrian castle, his Valkyrian consort, armed with shield and spear, at his side. Campeau seems to be bellowing something. But nobody is listening.

REVOLUTIONS ARE POLITICAL but their roots are economic. The Mulroney government shifted the responsibility for the economic well-being of Canada from the public to the private sectors, which turned out to be a calamity for its victims and a disaster for its agents. Enough members of Canada's business community spent the 1980s destroying people's faith in capitalism that by the end of the decade, they had come dangerously close to succeeding. (Capitalism is a bit like Winston Churchill's description of democracy as "the worst form of government, except for all those other forms that have been tried from time to time.") The shift in public opinion was registered by Angus Reid. "Canadians really did look at big business as the solution for a whole series of problems," he reported after repeated polling on the issue. "But by the end of the decade, a sense of cynicism had set in, especially about the extent to which companies were really concerned about the welfare of their employees."

Different from the more introspective entrepreneurs who followed them in the 1990s and the genuine Establishment paladins who had preceded them, the professional opportunists of the 1980s were made-to-measure catalysts of the Canadian Revolution. They gave capitalism a bad name without really trying, just by blatantly doing their own thing, because greed was their animating juice. It was the great truism of the period that once men and women equated their net worth with their self-worth, the social contract exploded.

EIGHT

BANKERS

Bonkers in Their Bunkers

*"If I owe a million dollars, I am lost. But if I owe $50 billion,
the banks are lost."*
INTERNATIONAL FINANCIER CELSO MING

A S THE INSTITUTIONAL TOUCHSTONES that had once been the
nation's Pole Star fell away, Canadians began automatically
to distrust anyone who exercised authority over their lives. That this
should have included the country's Big Five chartered banks
(Canadian Imperial Bank of Commerce, Toronto-Dominion Bank,
Bank of Montreal, Royal Bank and Bank of Nova Scotia) was astonishing, since bankers had been, if not exactly friends, then certainly
trusted. Canadian bankers had traditionally been safe, middle-class
men who represented safe, middle-class values and could be
counted on for their prudence, integrity and, occasionally, help.
They occupied a place in the community somewhere between familiarity and contempt, in the same block as the clerics. "We're like
priests in a confessional," said John Coleman, a former deputy
chairman of the Royal Bank. "We have to keep everything we hear
in confidence, even when we're in on both sides of a deal."

Fitted for their high calling (for that was how they viewed it)
more by temperament than by family background or education,
Canada's bankers had moved softly and talked things over in voices
sounding as dry and determined as elders at a Presbyterian synod.

They were seldom impatient, never pushy, always careful, gracious, smug in the knowledge that they were God's own gardeners tending the delicate flowers of commerce. Scottish in their deportment and parsimony (even if they were born in Moncton and wouldn't know whether to carve the bagpipes or play the haggis), they lived a muted existence, feigning pious amusement at the ostentations of their clients while remaining content to quietly exercise their undoubted veto. Since they controlled who got credit and who didn't, they regarded themselves as chief operating officers of the free-enterprise system. They believed that they were exercising not power, but responsibility. If they were not the high priests of capitalism, they were its guardians of the temple.

The quaint trait shared by all these old-style bankers was their passion for certainty. Loans seldom went sour because risks were only allowed to disrupt dealings by accident. In this Jurassic period of Canadian banking, which ended abruptly in the mid-1980s, the decision to lend serious money carried with it not only cash but an imprimatur. The bankers were in fact remarkably sage, if far too conservative, and the country's banking system was the envy of the Western world. It also ranked first in profits, well above the runners-up of Japan and Great Britain. Canadian bankers usually remained with one institution for life, content to occupy their assigned place in the hierarchical pyramid. Only two misdeeds were serious enough to warrant dismissal: embezzlement or organizing a tellers' union.

THEN CANADA'S BANKERS went bonkers in their bunkers. It was difficult to keep track of every dollar, or in truth every billion, but between 1985 and 1995 Canada's chartered banks wrote off bad loans in the interstellar ballpark of $30 billion. These loans were not granted by officers under the influence of mass hysteria or transmissions from outer space, they were the result of their best, presumably rational, considerations. The most astounding aspect was how bankers reeled from financing one disaster to the next—Dome Petroleum, Third World debt, leveraged buy-outs, Robert Campeau, Bramalea, Central Guaranty Trust, the Reichmanns—without ever learning to be more circumspect. The ghosts of yesterday seldom haunted the nightmare decisions of today. (These were, by and large, the same cadre of administrative officers who by 1995 had placed much of their customers' funds deep into the dangerous waters of high-risk

derivatives, clearly a disaster waiting to happen.)* In the process
they abandoned their mandate, freely granted by Canadians, to be
responsible and vouch for the stability of their institutions. As
blunder tripped upon blunder, bankers were transformed from being
regarded with awe to being recognized as just another bunch of
addle-brained professionals. Instead of protecting Canadians against
the Revolution, they became one of its instigators. Canadians realized, with a shudder, that the only people who could resolve the
country's financial mess were the same ones who had underwritten
it. Worse, ordinary citizens came to the devastating conclusion
that bankers ran banks with the same foresight and skill most Canadians brought to their personal finances. Panic City. An editorial
cartoon by the Montreal *Gazette*'s talented Aislin (a.k.a. Terry
Mosher) captured the hysteria of the moment. A typical couch potato
was depicted watching the CBC evening news. "I don't know
anything about finances," he said, "but when I see Der Hoi Yin
on *The National* three nights in a row, it's time to stuff the cash in
the mattress."

Canadian banks, at least the Big Five, continued to dispense safe
and efficient services, but they no longer provided a credible unify-
ing force for the country. "What their record shows is not only not
good banking," declared Senator Michael Pitfield, the former clerk
of the Privy Council, "but a violation of the fundamental principles
of the system which they are paid to administer and protect." Allen
Lambert, a former chairman of the Toronto-Dominion, happened to
run into Page Wadsworth, a former chairman of the Commerce, on
the manicured front lawn of Toronto's Royal Canadian Yacht Club
in August of 1992. Both men had been great bankers in their time. In
the summer of the Reichmann loan debacle, they briefly compared
notes and Lambert remarked to Wadsworth's nodding approval:
"There isn't enough money made or printed to get me back into
banking. It's become quite a dangerous profession."

Canadian bankers hadn't stopped being honest or middle-class,
they had just got out of touch. They exercised a bunker mentality,
leading insulated lives, demanding grovelling deference from their
staff and seldom leaving their hushed, carpeted corner suites to

---

* Sure enough, by the first quarter of 1995 the Commerce had lost $43
  million on derivatives—and counting.

taste the real world. No wonder they were duped so easily by such street-smart operators as Paul Reichmann, Brazil, Jack Gallagher and Bob Campeau. This insular mentality was magnified by the fact that no matter how many loans went toxic, their institutions were so rich and so large that they could write off each calamity, regroup and sail self-confidently to the next one. Having little choice, Canadians continued to support their banks and to use their increasingly automated and impersonal services. But there was an undercurrent in public attitudes that had never been there before. "Some of the first people to feel the problem were the farmers in Ontario's Bruce and Grey counties," reported Michael Peers, the Anglican Archbishop of Canada. "In the late 1980s, when free trade trashed fruit sales, the banks foreclosed many of their farms. The bankers, who later had no trouble absorbing the billion-dollar losses of the Reichmanns, couldn't tolerate an apple orchard going under. So the bank managers in these little towns became villains, even though previously they had been a local force for the good. What happened of course was that the branch managers were paying the price for policy decisions reached sixty storeys above reality in downtown Toronto and in truth, they had no more control of the situation than the apple farmers.* What that said to Canadians was that the big structures couldn't be trusted, that no matter what we do, no matter what we say, no matter what we think, no matter—and this is where people really had a lot of trouble—no matter how hard *I work*—the system is not going to produce for me. So people reacted by telling themselves, 'Well, then, the values I need to survive, they have to be *mine*.' And that was how we moved from collectivism to a kind of personalism that maintained: 'Whatever I find, I'm going have to find myself. Government's not going to do it. The banks aren't going to do it. Education isn't going to do it. Organized religion's not going do it. Trade unions aren't going to do it. Nobody's going to do it.' As a result, there was this great withdrawal into private searching."

Allan Taylor (the most compassionate of the chairmen, who headed the Royal from 1983 to 1995 and doubled its assets) caught

---

* It was no coincidence that hooded and armed farmers, infuriated by the banks' actions and prevailing high interest rates, set fire to a local branch of the Commerce at about this time.

this questioning mood when he quipped, while speaking to a home-coming celebration at the Saskatchewan Centre for the Arts: "Bankers are so unpopular these days, that in response to complaints from the animal rights people the University of Regina has decided to use bank executives instead of white rats in all future biological experiments. There are three reasons for this new policy: there is an unlimited supply of bank executives; the researchers don't get attached to them; and there are some things a rat just won't do." Speaking at about the same time, Matthew Barrett, chairman of the Montreal, wisely conceded that times had changed by pointing out that "the days when bank chairmen ruled the world like imperial warlords is over. They were fine for their time, but for me at least, I find the world too complex and too fast-changing to have the arrogance that I alone can dictate every right move." Annual meetings, where bank shareholders once vied with each other to demonstrate their fawning approval, took the chairmen to task for collecting such high salaries in the face of disastrous results. "You people run the largest bank in Canada and you're supposed to know what you're doing!" shouted shareholder Joseph Haziza, when Taylor reported 1992 profits had dropped by $876 million and loan losses for the year came in at more than $2 billion. "How could you have made so many bad loans and why did you get involved in the Olympia & York real-estate disaster?" At the Toronto-Dominion meeting, Bob Verdun of Elmira, Ontario, wanted to know why the bank's performance had been so bad: "Where is the leadership?" he demanded. Chairman Dick Thomson tried to calm him down, but Verdun persisted: "That's the Canadian way. Americans would have had you out of your job for this poor performance!" Disillusioned with how tight credit checks had become for small and medium businesses, while the Reichmanns and others walked away with billions they never had to repay, many businesses—especially in the start-up mode—began bypassing the banks and raising their own funds. There were countless examples of this trend, especially in the high-tech field. Turned down by the banks, friends and associates raised the $350,000 seed money for Montreal's SOFTIMAGE Inc., whose animation techniques were featured in the film *Jurassic Park*. When the company was taken over by Microsoft in 1994, an original investment of $5,000 had become worth $1.5 million.

In a way, the most frightening revelation of the period was that Julius Melnitzer, the renegade London, Ontario, lawyer who later went to jail for his massive frauds, was able to steal millions from Canadian bankers before they even noticed. "One can't help admiring Melnitzer's skill and sheer nerve in persuading the banks to do exactly what he wanted—how he knew which button to push, how to play on his value to them as a client and on their rivalry with each other," commented Catherine Kentridge, executive editor of *Canadian Lawyer.* It became astonishingly easy to steal from the banks without wearing a balaclava, as frightening tales of bank fraud spoke volumes about lax internal controls. Long before a young trader combined with an even-younger trading instrument known as derivatives to sink Barings Bank, a middle-level bank manager in Canada gambled—literally—with huge amounts of depositors' funds. Brian Molony, an assistant manager of the Bay and Richmond branch of the Commerce in Toronto, was convicted of embezzling $18 million through fictitious loans—$10.2 million was missing at the time of his conviction—which he intended to repay through his gambling addiction in Las Vegas and Atlantic City. The amounts missing were a fraction of the amounts gambled by Molony with funds raised through extending customers' lines of credits and approving fictitious loan applications. In *Stung,* his brilliant book on the case, author Gary Ross demonstrated that in the first four months of 1982, Molony—who was picked up by private jet and whisked to the gambling resorts—had won $450 million at the gambling tables and lost $457 million. No one noticed the missing amounts; Molony survived a comprehensive audit of the branch and was discovered quite by accident.[*]

But Molony's high-stakes gambling was nothing next to that of the banks, which took breathtaking chances without a backward or forward glance. At one point the Nova Scotia, once the most staid of the Big Five, was exposed to shaky American commercial real estate (including the hallucinations of Robert Campeau) to an amount that equalled the entire shareholder equity in the bank. The defining

---

[*] Pulled over by police for driving thirty kilometres an hour in a twenty-kilometre zone, Molony was carrying the detritus of his life as a gambler, including receipts for millions of dollars from casinos and $30,000 in cash.

image of how the banks operated was a scene in the Robert Collison documentary, *Prisoners of Debt*, aired on the CBC. Showing bankers at work, the film demonstrated how their sense of responsibility had been diluted by the careless mismanagement of credit policies. Edward Mercaldo, the Montreal's vice-president of international banking who broke records accruing Latin American debt, spoke in the film to one of his superiors about a client:

"He said forty million would be fine, but he'd really like fifty."

"Well, we'll try and get him as much as we can."

"He doesn't want as much as we can. He wants *fifty*."

"Well, that's probably a bit more than we can..."

"I told him he hadn't seen anything yet!"

It turned out the client was Brazil, which was suffering from 127 per cent inflation and was on the point of disowning most of its foreign debt.

That Mercaldo's kinetic energy and disregard for proper collateral protection could be tolerated revealed a lot about how the banks were changing. Canadian companies went on an unprecedented acquisitions and mergers binge while inflation made it far cheaper to buy assets than to build them. High profits during the 1980s had made most dominant Canadian corporations cash-rich, while a dormant stock market had left many controlling blocs of shares undervalued. Instead of pioneering new techniques or building new facilities, companies rushed to "rationalize"—a buzzword for increasing efficiency through buying out a larger company's assets—then spinning some of them off to pay for the purchase. This required a new style of bank credit. Loans were no longer based on realizable collaterals or projected future earnings. They became as speculative as the investments themselves and were secured by character judgements, or more likely, the realization that if one bank didn't approve a loan, a rival would. Keeping up with the Reichmanns, the Bronfmans and all the others who had moved into the financial stratosphere became a status symbol. No wonder that a relief map of Canada's corporate world no longer consisted of a series of plateaus with the occasional bulge; the relevant image was a few steep mountain ranges that gave the whole economy its essential contours. The dominant families who squatted atop those half-dozen peaks controlled more than 1,000 companies among them. According to the Ontario Securities Commission study, 80 per cent of the Toronto Stock Exchange's Composite 300 Index were owned by these family compacts. All but thirty-two of the *Financial Post's* top 500 Canadian corporations were controlled by single shareholders, compared with 410 of the firms on the comparable U.S. list, *Standard & Poor's 500*, which had no shareholder controlling more than 10 per cent of company stock. Corporate concentration had turned into corporate gridlock. "It's sick," complained Bill Mulholland, chairman of the Montreal, at the time. "People are finding that it's cheaper to make money with money than to make better goods or new products or bring in new resources." The Mulroney government had encouraged the trend with special concessions to some of the largest deal-makers. Ottawa facilitated the purchase of Gulf Canada by the Reichmanns in 1985, for example, by foregoing at least $750 million in tax revenues and forcing Petro-Canada to buy the company's downstream assets.

The once-orderly world of finance became a circus. The new buzzwords appropriately described the process: there were bear hugs, poison pills, Pac-Man defences, golden parachutes, greenmail and all those wonderful bafflegab phrases to describe companies going through "negative growth," forming "strategic alliances" and making "negative contributions to profit" because of "volume variances from plan." Imperial Oil lost money for the first time in its history; Bell's diversification program was an unqualified disaster; Royal Trust's shares plummeted from $19.38 to 39 cents;* thirteen trust companies and nine mortgage companies went bust. Canadian

---

* Royal Trust's fall from the country's richest and most credit-worthy trust company was due mainly to the antics of its Bronfman-appointed chief executive officer, Michael Adriaan Cornelissen. He not only went on wild buying sprees in the United Kingdom and the United States, paying millions for dubiously priced financial institutions just before the real-estate crash, but behaved personally in a way that made him unique among Canada's corporate presidents even in the 1980s. He appeared at a 1992 Christmas staff party wearing a brassiere stuffed with rubber imitation breasts, spent most of a Royal Trust executive meeting trying to put a condom over his head and was asked to leave the grounds of the Royal Canadian Yacht Club for streaking and excessive drinking. He was nevertheless retired with honour and a highly favourable financial settlement.

Pacific, once the pride of Canada's corporate world, reported losses of close to $1 billion.*

Making errors in judgement seemed only to advance the bankers' careers. A case in point was the meteoric rise of Al Flood, who became chairman of the Commerce on June 7, 1992. There was no easier way of tracing his bank's major loan losses than to follow his career. He had been area executive and then general manager for Latin America, making most of the loans on which the bank eventually lost $1.7 billion; he was then transferred to its U.S. division just in time to take part in the leveraged buy-out craze on which the Commerce lost buckets; that was followed by his promotion to head the corporate banking division, where he was the point man in some of the dream-machine loans to the Reichmanns that cost the bank $1.3 billion. When he was rewarded for his circumspection by being moved into the chairman's office, one of Flood's first directives was that the bank immediately form a special "risk management" group to tackle "the CIBC's credit-quality" problems. Obviously, the right man for the job.

Despite their miserable record, the power of Canada's banks grew exponentially during the decade. They absorbed nearly every big brokerage house in the country and all but one of the major trust companies (Canada Trust). The Big Five, plus *Banque Nationale du Canada*, controlled $739.7 billion of the total domestic Canadian banking assets of $740.4 billion. Now, that's concentration.† At last

---

* The only good news some companies received was the departure of a CEO. The shares of Deprenyl Research Ltd., for example, jumped 54 per cent in the summer of 1993 when Morty Shulman, its motor-mouth chairman, resigned. It was a tough choice, but at the top of my list of Canadian executives who had an ethical by-pass at birth was Harold Ballard, the piratical CEO and controlling shareholder of Toronto's Maple Leaf Gardens. After his death in 1990, an audit revealed that the multimillionaire Ballard had been secretly pocketing the proceeds from scalping season tickets to his own arena and selling broken hockey sticks to teenage fans that were falsely purported to have been used by his star players.

† The only foreign bank to make significant inroads at the retail level was the Hong Kong Bank of Canada which, under the inspired presidencies of James Cleave and Bill Dalton, not only pioneered some imaginative customer services but consistently earned higher returns than any domestically owned institution.

count, there were more bank branches (8,836) than taverns in the country, but the four pillars (banking, insurance, trust companies and investment houses) that had once characterized Canada's financial sector had vanished. William Dimma, president of Royal LePage and chairman of Ottawa's advisory committee on financial institutions, voiced his concern about "an expansion of the role and clout of the larger chartered banks in relation to the other members of the financial service industry." He pointed out that the country's largest chartered banks were capable of devouring the entire insurance and trust brokerage industries without a burp—which, of course, was exactly what began to happen. Bob MacIntosh, the Cambridge-trained economist who then headed the Canadian Bankers' Association, insisted that the banks only wanted "to maintain the concept of the level playing field, so that all those who provide a given financial service to the public be subject to more or less the same set of rules." To which Hal Jackman, chairman of Empire Life and a longtime critic of the banks, shot back: "When the banks talk of a level playing field, they mean a hippo in a sand box with three mice."

The point was that through the 1980s, the banks multiplied a veto power which had already been immense. Anyone requiring senior financing suddenly had no alternative source for funds. To make matters worse, eight banks disappeared during the decade (*Banque Provinciale*, Mercantile, Unity, Bank of British Columbia, Northland, Morguard, Continental and Canadian Commercial Bank), leaving the Big Five and Quebec's *Banque Nationale* holding all the marbles. Of the bank failures, the collapse of the Canadian Commercial Bank was the most fascinating and the least necessary. It was difficult to comprehend the sequence of errors that took place and why they were condoned. In one way at least, the CCB was bound to fail. I still vividly recall visiting Howard Eaton in early 1981, when he was riding high as chairman of the Edmonton-based bank which had just hit an asset base of $1.4 billion. Perched on the corner of his fancy glass desk and dressed in slacks and a loud sports jacket, he boasted how he was the only bank chairman in the country who drove himself to work: "In my *red* Porsche 911E!" he added for emphasis, and I knew right then that he was done for. Even in the crazy 1980s, Canadian bankers remained careful not to display too much cuff and none of them expected to get into banker heaven in a red sports car. Still, Eaton's bank was the most profitable in the country at the time, earning 82 cents for every $100 in assets. (An equivalent figure for the Royal Bank, then the second-most efficient financial institution in the country, was 60 cents.) When I asked Eaton how that was possible, he explained that it all came down to speed: multimillion-dollar loans could be granted at favourable terms within twelve hours of application, while the traditional banks took as much as two weeks. At the time, the Alberta bank's assets were growing at an astounding rate of 80 per cent per year.

Speed seemed to be the guiding principle of Eaton's career. Having moved through a succession of West Coast financial institutions at an amazing clip, he helped manoeuvre the granting of the CCB's charter through Parliament in only eight weeks and raised the $22 million cash needed to float the new institution in less than a year. Then, in late 1981, when the National Energy Program and depressed oil prices were forcing most of the companies on the CCB's list of outstanding loans to the wall, Eaton climbed into his Porsche and headed south to California. Instead of condemning his move, the bank's board of directors approved an interest-reduced loan of $1 million to help him settle snugly in Santa Barbara. He pretended to run the bank by long-distance telephone from there, prospering on a chairman's full salary. Most of his energy was redirected to private dealings with his new partner: Leonard Rosenberg, the notorious Ontario-based charlatan whose crumbling trust company empire had been taken over by the Ontario government and who fatally undermined what was left of the CCB's credibility. Their relationship was anything but casual. Rosenberg and his shadowy associates eventually acquired 30 per cent of the bank's shares—three times the legal limit. How any of this was allowed to happen without whistles being blown remained a mystery. On January 25, 1983, the day after Eaton's relationship with Rosenberg was publicly revealed and the ex-patriate chairman was fired from the CCB, Bank of Canada Governor Gerald Bouey inexplicably telephoned *Globe and Mail* reporter Arthur Johnson. In an unprecedented move, he stated for publication that despite the Rosenberg connection, the CCB was at that time "a solvent and profitable bank." That may have been correct technically, but in fact the CCB was on the brink of bankruptcy and nothing would save it. The Big Five bankers pledged $60 million in cash toward the rescue plan, but secretly withdrew their own deposits and credit lines from the wounded institution. The ensuing run on the bank (and later on Calgary's Northland) cost Canadian taxpayers $1.2 billion when the Mulroney government decided to cover all outstanding deposits at both banks.

The faith of most Canadians in the banking system was severely shaken by this and two succeeding blows, this time to the Big Five's credit assessment methods. The first was the decision by Jack Gallagher, the highly influential chairman of Dome Petroleum, to halt interest payments on the $6.5 billion he had managed to borrow from Canadian banks. He had developed Dome into Canada's mightiest energy consortium, entirely with other people's money and without ever paying a cent in dividends or taxes. He marched to his own drum-and-bugle corps, bent on discovering a Saudi-sized reserve of oil among the unforgiving ice floes off Tuktoyaktuk in the Beaufort Sea. He never did find any worthwhile deposits and his enterprise seemed to float mainly on the magnetic attraction of his smile. No ordinary grin, its Cheshire quality moved, if not mountains, then mountains of stock. During a TV interview Gallagher was once asked to confirm the rumours of a significant Dome oil strike. He said nothing but flashed one of his trademark grins. Frantic purchase orders next morning pushed the shares to hysterical new highs, lifting the TSE's energy index by an unprecedented 186 points in a single trading day. My own doubts about Gallagher dated back to an offhand remark he made at the height of his fame when, not knowing how to end our interview politely, I asked him what he planned to do once he had tamed the Beaufort Sea.

"Ah hah..." he confided, with the hooded eyes and stage whisper of a mad scientist, "why, I'm going to irrigate the Sinai desert."

I started inching toward the door, but he wouldn't be stopped: "Much of the sand is really silt, so the eastern third of the peninsula, running from El Arish to Aqaba, could be set aside for nuclear-powered desalinators which could turn the sea water into irrigation systems to transform the desert into a green belt and a new home for the Palestinians." I mumbled, "Great idea, Jack," and skedaddled out of there.

Gallagher never did reclaim the desert, part the Red Sea or find much oil in the Beaufort Sea, but he went on to borrow billions from

Canadian banks to acquire Hudson's Bay Oil & Gas. Dome collapsed under its debt load by 1986, but apart from runs on some Alberta branches of the Commerce and several billion dollars in write-offs, nothing changed. Instead of shaming them into a more conservative diet of loans, the Dome debacle—Canada's North Sea Bubble—served only to whet the bankers' appetites.

CITICORP CHAIRMAN WALTER WRISTON liked to say that "countries don't go bankrupt." He ought to have said, "Countries can't be repossessed. They can, and do, go bankrupt." As one anonymous Third World loans expert quipped, trying to salvage Third World debt was like making love to a gorilla: "You don't stop when you're tired, you stop when *he's* tired." The bankers began to pour gushers of dollars into the Less Developed Countries (LDCs) of Latin America. Many of these deals were clinched by telephone with no investigation on the ground. Even Bob MacIntosh of the Canadian Bankers' Association complained, "If the boards of directors of the banks asked any questions, there is no evidence of it in the numbers." In fact the issue had been raised by at least one director. Gordon Osler, then on the board of the Toronto-Dominion, kept asking bank officials how they could make such huge loans without any agreement on repayment schedules. Told that such schedules didn't exist because the borrowing countries had no idea when they could pay off their debts, Osler became angry. "Their whole attitude was that sovereign countries have never reneged on anything," he later recalled. "I told Dick Thomson at the board's executive committee meetings that the blame is on the bankers. The guy who's borrowing will always take the money. What happened was that the bankers forgot the rules of how to *lend* money. There's no doubt about it."

The six largest Canadian banks had managed to accumulate dubious loans to Latin American countries by 1986 of $27.7 billion (only a tiny percentage of which was secured) and had to build up reserves from other sources to compensate for the losses. At one point the Montreal had a gross LDC exposure of $5.9 billion, a stunning 173 per cent of its common equity base, with its Brazilian loans particularly deep in the Dumpster. The bank's unruffled chairman, Bill Mulholland, boasted it had taken the Montreal 150 years to reach $6 billion in assets, but "now we click that off in less than a year." Only one chairman, Allan Taylor of the Royal, which had been

forced to write off about three-quarters of its disastrous loans to the
LDCs, felt the decency to admit his adventures south of the Rio Grande
had been a mistake. "I have great concern about explaining to my
farmer friends back home in Saskatchewan how in God's name we can
forgive or write down Mexico, yet expect them to pay up or lose their
farms," he said in a 1991 interview. "Is there an inconsistency?
Of course there is. Those loans were a mistake. There will be some
new credit made available to the Third World countries, but we won't
be participating." Taylor also brought in Murray Corlett as vice-
president of credit risk management, to clean up what the newly
appointed officer called the "reckless lending of the 1980s. I would
describe this as a major cultural change. Bankers are traditionally
opportunists. Making them think strategically is a big change."*

BUT ONLY AN ACT OF GOD OR A FORCE OF NATURE could stop the carnival.
Hurricane Reichmann that blew in during the spring of 1992 shattered the bankers' complacency, once and for all.

The Reichmanns accomplished something that had evaded government trust-busters for years: they broke the banking cartel. This
was never a combine in a legal sense, merely the passing on of The
Word—cartel members telling one another whom to help and whom
to avoid. And about the only questions they ever asked of Paul
Reichmann when he demanded more loans was: "Will that be in
Canadian or U.S. dollars?"

"It became an ego thing," explained one senior banker. "You
weren't a big boy if you said 'no' to the Reichmanns. They'd see the
chairman and let out the news that they needed a couple of hundred
million or whatever and didn't want the bank to miss out on this
great opportunity. Not wanting to lose face, the chairman would say,
'Sure, I'll tell my people to fix you up.' The decision was usually
made on the basis of a municipal assessment notice on the building
or project in question, so that when the working bankers got at it, all

---

* There was one small legacy from the LDC caper apart from the lost
  billions. Brazil became a metaphor for risky loans. When nothing but
  generous bank loans could save Ted Rogers's phone company, Unitel,
  in the spring of 1995, a communications consultant named Ian Angus
  came out with the perfect solution: "The banks will have to pretend
  that Unitel is Brazil." They did. At least for a while.

they could do was gloss over the negatives. Of course, when the
Reichmann empire collapsed, it was the same minions who got the
blame, with the chairman accusing them of not having monitored the
situation well enough." That was mainly how the Reichmanns
managed to borrow upwards of $14 billion from ninety-one banks,
without having to show them any balance sheets.

The brothers had arrived from war-ravaged Europe during the
1950s and spent their first twenty years in Canada as modestly successful builders. Then, as if by sleight of hand, they blossomed
overnight into the world's largest developers. Only the occasional
voice was raised against them during their upward climb and it was
almost always raised from the shadows. "They're not really very
different from any other developers," one senior Toronto financier
said of the Orthodox-Jewish Reichmanns. "Just because they wear
beanies, go home at five o'clock on Friday evenings and are always
standing there looking devout doesn't mean that much. In most of
their dealings they tend to be extremely legalistic and not as good as
some of their competitors in observing the spirit of contracts and
agreements. Their behaviour reminds me of a Toronto builder
named Robert McClintock. Bob was a very strong evangelical
Baptist, and that meant he never had any of his subdivisions open on
Sunday. House-buyers would say, 'Well, he must be a very devout
Christian—what a great sacrifice he's making!' They'd be inspect-
ing all the neighbouring subdivisions that had stayed open and had
flags flying and stuff going on, but they'd keep looking over at the
one that was closed. So they would make a point of coming back to
buy a McClintock house on Monday, because they thought he
appeared to be such a good Christian, so honest and straight that he
must be selling better-built houses." The brothers' insistence on
wearing yarmulkes and their strict observance of the Sabbath were
their most widely recognized characteristics; they didn't exploit
their religion, but they certainly took full advantage of their piety.
Paul, the self-acknowledged leader of the clan, had the look of
resigned intensity that characterizes the devout and adhered strictly
to the Orthodox faith. Because Orthodox Jews are not allowed to
operate electrical devices during the Sabbath, the brothers built a
new multi-storey, 7,129-square-foot house in Toronto's Forest Hill
for their mother, Renée, with a lift that ran automatically to each
floor every ten minutes without any buttons being pushed. Only

occasionally did the Reichmanns make a semi-public spectacle of their spending. At a wedding celebration for a niece, each table was bedecked with bouquets of white roses that had been cultivated to come into bloom as the evening progressed.

The brothers—Paul, Albert and Ralph—maintained an air of mystery and intrigue. They employed bodyguards, seldom granted interviews and never answered telephones. (Many messages were taken, only a few calls returned.) They were so discreet that for most of a decade newspapers and magazines had to illustrate stories about them with outdated shots taken twenty years earlier by a *Globe and Mail* photographer. When Albert appeared unexpectedly at the Oakdale Golf and Country Club during a reception for the chief of the Israeli air staff, whose presence had attracted a clutch of press photographers, he spotted the cameramen and patiently hid behind a column for most of two hours. He finally walked out of the room backwards to avoid their lenses.

The brothers belonged to no clubs, would not allow themselves to be listed in *Who's Who* and observed none of the social niceties that fostered business reputations, yet they were widely praised and admired. Paul Reichmann's acceptance by his peers could be dated to November 7, 1985, the day he became a director of the Canadian Imperial Bank of Commerce. Bay Street guru Andy Sarlos called the family "the most honourable people you can do business with. They're creative, yet not impulsive, and can be entrusted with great amounts of money." *Fortune* and other publications listed the Reichmanns near the top of the world's ten richest families—just under the inevitable Arab sheiks and Queen Elizabeth II—reverently noting that they owned no jet aircraft or polo ponies. The magazine was half-wrong about their possessions (the Reichmanns did in fact have a Gulfstream III, later sold to Barrick Gold Corporation) and all wrong about their wealth, estimated by *Fortune* in 1991 at $14.7 billion cash. Their assets at the height of their power were growing at nearly a billion dollars every six months, but the cash was never there.

The Reichmann brothers eventually owned 40 million square feet of prime office space in thirty-five North American cities. Their ambitions had no limits. Paul Reichmann paid $2.8 billion for Chevron Corp.'s 60 per cent stake in Gulf Canada Resources Ltd. in 1985, although he knew nothing about the energy business. He boasted to *Business Week* at the time that the family intended "to be as big in natural resources" as it had become in real estate. By the time the empire attained a daily cash flow of $7 million, the family's borrowing power hovered near $10 billion. It almost doubled after that, a debt which assumed a life and a destiny of its own. The Reichmanns reached that enviable plateau where they enjoyed unlimited and unquestioning access to credit.

The strict cloak of secrecy fostered by the Reichmanns turned out to be not a personal affectation, but their carefully considered operational code. As long as the brothers were able to keep their balance sheets and business methods secret, they could maintain the mystique that they were all-powerful, that their personal fortunes were unlimited and their credit invulnerable. The bankers didn't get a peek at the figures until it was too late. The empire collapsed under its own weight in the 1990s partly because the Reichmanns tried to run it like a mom-and-pop shop with family members making all the decisions. Renée, the Reichmann matriarch, chaired board meetings (which were conducted partly in Hungarian) until her death in 1990. No less a dealaholic than Robert Campeau or Donald Trump, Paul Reichmann subscribed to the same dubious ethics. "What both Trump and Reichmann knew," wrote Peter Foster in one of his well-documented studies of the family, "was that a superhuman image was critical to the banks. Both had set about creating such an image, albeit one was under neon lights and the other set behind a discreet veil. Paul had always produced a dance of the seven veils for the bankers and for the press—a glimpse of asset ankle, a peek at cash-flow calf. But nobody got to see the big picture. To suggest such a thing would have been indecent." Still, the average Canadian, who had to pledge his home and first-born to obtain the chintziest bank loan, was justifiably puzzled why the bankers didn't grow even a tad suspicious, for example, when they agreed to lend the family $105 million as a *third* mortgage on their flagship Toronto building, First Canadian Place. A third mortgage on a house invariably warned of a desperate financial squeeze; office buildings were no different. The banks paid no attention to the warning bells, yet the minute Olympia & York's balance sheets went public it was clear that the empire had no clothes.

Because the brothers were allergic to paying tax, few of their properties were ever cashed out, which meant the brothers had to borrow far beyond their net worth for ready coin. In order to protect their operation, they incorporated a new company for each new building, so that it could be seized by creditors without bringing down the whole empire. The only Canadian bank chairman to balk was Dick Thomson of the Toronto-Dominion, who had the audacity to demand a peek at their financial statements before approving any Reichmann loans. (He did, however, get badly burned on LDCs, Bramalea and the Central Guaranty Trust debacle.) There actually *was* a Reichmann financial statement, kept in a leather-bound loose-leaf file inside Paul's desk; it was rarely shown to outsiders and then only on condition that they take no notes; they were granted only a few minutes to leaf through it. "On a scale of one to ten, I'd say the Reichmanns were an eleven at exploiting the banks by withholding information," a senior former executive of their U.S. operation told New York's *Institutional Investor*. "But then, *nobody asked*." That publication, regarded as the banker's Bible, editorialized: "If over-leveraging of the Reichmann companies was a crime against economic sense, then its lenders stand charged as co-conspirators. For as the Reichmanns became credit junkies, the banks became their eager suppliers, in effect, never checking their references."

The Reichmann companies had reported a stunning operating loss of more than $2 billion by 1992 and according to one insider estimate the family suffered a loss of as much as $15 billion in assets during their meltdown. The enduring self-delusion of the Reichmanns was demonstrated most forcibly by the family's feeble attempts to save its empire. They believed they were so essential to the Canadian economy that the Ottawa and Ontario governments would rush in with financial guarantees. They also managed to con-vince themselves that the bankers, who had filled every one of their past requests with blank cheques, would continue their generous treatment and demand only token guarantees in return. In its original restructuring plan, O&Y offered no meaningful equity to the bankers. At a jammed meeting of the representatives of ninety-one banks in a ballroom of Toronto's Sheraton Centre, a big fuss was made about showing them the family books for the first time. Most of the balance sheets provided turned out to be eighteen months old, con-taining 1990 figures. The world had changed so much during the interval that, for example, the annual cash flow from the Reichmanns' prestigious Exchange Tower (which houses the Toronto Stock Exchange) had been cut in half. With at least $400 million in debt attached to it, the building could no longer carry itself and the creditors moved in. Paul Reichmann seemed to have forgotten the basic real-estate investment rule to borrow long-term funds for long-term assets and short-term funds for quick turn-arounds. Because he believed interest rates would keep falling, he had pegged most of his loans on short-term notes against buildings that he had no intention of selling. That worked fine in a rising market, but by the early 1990s each time he bought more short-term paper, the value of his buildings dropped and the cost of money increased, triggering the spiral that brought him down.

Canada's banks were forced to write off most of their Reichmann loans. The Royal experienced a 90 per cent drop in profit; loan loss provisions for all the banks had to be doubled to $6 billion and their return on equity was cut in half; troubled investors sold off $3.3 billion worth of their bank stocks. All but two chairmen expressed at least faint regret at what had happened. The exceptions were André Bédard, chairman of the *Banque Nationale*, who admitted he'd been extravagant to approve a $500 million loan to the Reichmanns (especially after the disastrous credits he had granted to Robert Campeau and Unicorp) but that his batting average was "still better than most baseball players." (His metaphor failed to strike the desired reassuring note, since any bank that batted a respectable .300 would not survive for long.) The strangest reaction of all came from Donald Fullerton, then chairman of the Commerce. It had been the Reichmanns' lead bank, handling most of their Canadian credit for the previous three decades. Instead of being angry with Paul Reichmann for taking advantage of his long connection with the bank where he was also a director by hanging it with $860 million in questionable loans, Fullerton acted as chief apologist. "The governance procedures were in place," he fulminated. "We got caught at the outer edge of our control limit but not beyond it." Whatever that meant, the Commerce's profit dropped from $811 million to a measly $12 million in 1992.

The Reichmann empire did have solid assets and might have survived had not Paul Reichmann drained its lifeblood with his $3 billion Canary Wharf development in London. It turned into a bottomless money pit. Paul Reichmann believed against all odds that he could could make Canary Wharf sing and turn it into the financial centre of the New Europe. I visited the Reichmanns' agglomeration of luxury skyscrapers, a long seven kilometres from London's financial district, in the spring of 1992. Presumably no one manning the lifeboats at the foundering Reichmann empire had the time to cancel the luxury launch used to woo Canary tenants, because their private vessel still ran from Charing Cross on the Thames. Without asking permission, but posing as a would-be tenant, I boarded the VIP vessel. It was equipped with soft blue sofas and turbo-charged engines that allowed it to cruise at twenty-five knots. We swept through historic London—past Royal Festival Hall, under Waterloo Bridge, past St. Paul's Cathedral, under London Bridge and along HMS *Belfast*, the last of the Royal Navy's cruisers permanently moored on the river. Then the shore view began to deteriorate, with moss-covered piers, derelict barges and rotten pilings that supported long-abandoned docks most London tourists rarely see. Suddenly rising out of the river's mist was Canary Wharf. The day I arrived there was only one crane at work and a lonely gardener was planting purple pansies. The size of the project was breathtaking, especially since it sat in such splendid isolation. It was like running into the Taj Mahal on Baffin Island.

The Reichmanns' master plan had called for construction of an eventual 14 million square feet of office and retail space, with one million square feet being completed annually for the balance of the decade. Only 4.5 million square feet had been finished and less than 60 per cent of it was rented, with fewer than half the tenants having actually moved in. A fifty-five storey marble-clad tower dominated the site, but it was the Reichmanns' extravagant spending that struck the visitor. Everything was brass, stainless steel, oak or mahogany—if it wasn't marble. "Mr. Reichmann ordered marble from thirty different countries, each a pattern and texture designed to suit the appropriate location," a rental guide explained, as I pretended to nod appreciatively. The granite used on the floors of one building had to be "torched by hand" because it proved too slippery in wet weather. The flow of the fountain in the main square was governed by wind sensors to reduce its arc in high winds, so that bystanders wouldn't get splashed. Four fifty-year-old English oak trees had been transplanted to provide summer shade and the Crimean linden trees that lined Canary's entrance had been cultivated in a German nursery for thirty-five years, their roots trimmed bi-annually so they could be transplanted to a premium site like this one. In one still-vacant structure, an eight-storey, plant-filled atrium of about 60,000 square feet provided those with inside offices a more pleasant view.

The mind could absorb only so many details of the builders' Xanadu vision, but it became painfully evident that this was less a development than a monument. No wonder the Reichmanns had to slap mortgages on their profitable North American buildings to finance this palace. Not only did they erect the world's most luxurious office towers on a spit of land far removed from the city's financial core and previously occupied by stray dogs and rats, but to lure tenants they had been forced to buy out their previous buildings and leases. Canary's overhead was running at $45 million a month by the beginning of 1992 and that included no provision for further capital expense. The brothers owned as much empty office space in the financial heart of London as they were trying to rent at Canary Wharf. Conrad Black, for one, sold the buildings where his *Daily Telegraph* was printed to the Reichmanns for $80 million before agreeing to move his corporate headquarters into Canary Tower. (By the time I arrived ten months later, the *Telegraph* property was worth only $8 million.) The City's real-estate market was in a state of collapse, with 33 million square feet of office space remaining vacant. The only practical mass transportation to the Canary Wharf site required extension of the Jubilee underground line sixteen kilometres to Greenwich from its terminus at Charing Cross, which would have cost $3.5 billion. The swampy backwater where the Reichmanns had chosen to build their monument wasn't called the "Isle of Dogs" for nothing. "Paul defied the rules of location," contended Eddie Cogan, the Toronto real-estate entrepreneur. "When you think you're bigger than location, that's when your downfall starts. What Reichmann was a genius at wasn't real estate, it was conning the banks."

Instead of becoming the corporate headquarters of the new European Community,* Canary Wharf turned out to be a concrete-

---

* In yet another case of life imitating art, the entire scheme was remarkably similar to one developed for precisely the same reason by a gangland boss in the 1980 U.K. film, *The Long Good Friday*. In the film, directed by John Mackenzie and starring Bob Hoskins as the gangster and Helen Mirren as his ice-cool wife, Hoskins enlists the help of the New York Mafia to raise the necessary funds for his proposed docklands development. Apparently, writer Barrie Keefe could not conceive of legitimate institutions, like Canadian banks, taking such a risk.

and-marble mausoleum to Paul Reichmann, the man who didn't know enough to tie one end of the bungee cord to his ankle.

NOBODY CRIED FOR THE REICHMANNS, who later attempted to buy Canary back from the banks, with the help of an Arab prince. But in the decade's race to beat the odds against the banking roulette, even nice guys finished last. The best example of a kinder, gentler failure was Reuben Cohen, the reclusive Moncton, New Brunswick, lawyer who quietly built up the country's fourth-largest trust company and almost destroyed the country's financial system when it crashed.

His personal financial debacle (and that of his lifetime business partner, Leonard Ellen, a Montreal lumber dealer) was unusual for its speed and size, even at a time when many of the country's commercial titans hovered near or in bankruptcy. Cohen and Ellen had spun their Halifax-based Central Trust Co. into what was supposed to become the country's largest non-banking financial conglomerate. They almost succeeded. The seventy-year-old Maritimer was worth $200 million by August of 1991 and, if he had accepted any of the many bids for Central Trust's assets then on the table, he would still be rich. Instead, he and his partner believed in their dream so devoutly that they kept buying shares in their faltering company. When the cash ran out, Cohen signed $23 million in personal bank guarantees to add more stock. A measure of how unrealistic Cohen's expectations had grown was the speech he gave to his company's annual meeting on May 26, 1990, just months before Central began to unravel. "I hope that I may be around to address this annual meeting four years hence," he told dubious shareholders, "and I throw out to management the challenge of assets by then of $75 *billion*, and more importantly, profits of not less than $200 million."

But there was no way to keep the dream alive. Even as an insolvent hulk, Central Guaranty still ranked as the country's fourth-largest trust company with 155 branches and $19 billion in assets. "If Central Guaranty had failed," wrote Heather Whyte in the *Financial Post*, "it would have been the largest financial disaster in Canadian history, undermining the value of the Canadian dollar and playing havoc with the economy's already-fragile credit rating." The Canadian Deposit Insurance Corporation set up a $4.3 billion guarantee, its largest ever, to finance Central's takeover by the Toronto-

Dominion Bank. When the TD's chairman, Dick Thomson, closed the deal, Central's stock rallied a notch to 35 cents. The same shares had been quoted at $9.25 a year before and in the interval they had sunk as low as 19 cents. The slide reflected Central's bleeding balance sheets and the fact that many of the group's performing assets had to be spun off to keep the core company out of receivership. Central Capital Corp. (the main holding company, controlled 69 per cent by Cohen and Ellen) emerged from 1991 with a stunning $1.56 billion loss on revenues of $33.6 million and a debt load that reached nearly $2 billion.

Reuben Cohen deserved better. He suffered the same fate as most of the high-flyers of the 1980s, but he wasn't one of them. A kind, shy, generous philanthropist and art connoisseur, he was prudent in his tastes and lifestyle. A gentle slump of a man, with that special quality of taking people at face value that distinguishes Maritimers from their more cynical Upper Canada cousins, Cohen gave up his fortune but never lost his integrity or modesty. "I'm a very dull fellow," he once told me. "I don't ride horses and I don't have antique cars—though the car I do drive is fifteen years old and may soon be classified as one—and the only thing exciting about me was my wife. I'm awfully drab."* After graduating in 1944 from Dalhousie Law School in Halifax, Cohen opened a Moncton legal practice and eventually went into the mortgage business, acquiring Central Trust, which was then a small local firm. Along with Ellen, he merged Central with two Halifax-based firms and the combination prospered, becoming the region's most profitable trust company. But Cohen and, to a lesser extent, Ellen, wanted to be part of the national financial scene—and that involved breaking into Toronto. Their initial attempt took place in 1975, when they purchased a 25 per cent interest in Crown Trust, then the "house" trust company of Bud McDougald, Conrad Black's predecessor as chairman of Argus Corp. Cohen was led to believe that he could buy Crown and became so enamoured of McDougald that his wife pre-

---

* He did have a devoted relationship with his wife, the former Louise Glustein. When she was afflicted with cancer he spent most of her last three years visiting her daily in hospital, holding her hand and stroking her brow from dawn to sunset, too physically and emotionally spent to think about his faltering business affairs.

sented the Argus chairman with his hand-carved portrait etched in enamelled copper on an invented *Maclean's* cover. But McDougald reneged on the deal and Black ended up owning Crown instead. When Black was ready to sell the trust company a year later Cohen bid again, but found himself outmanoeuvred by Winnipeg's Izzy Asper. (The Central partners finally acquired the picked-over bones of Crown from a bankrupt Leonard Rosenberg in 1983.)

Cohen hired Peter Cole, a former Canadian Imperial Bank of Commerce vice-president, in 1986 and told him to expand Central into one of Canada's major financial institutions. Cole fulfilled his mandate with a vengeance. Between the fall of 1986 and the spring of 1989, he negotiated thirty-two acquisitions of major financial firms. The bill for this buying frenzy came to about $2.4 billion, only a fraction ($586 million) of which was paid for in cash. By the end of a growth cycle unmatched in Canadian corporate history, the Central group had gained control of assets worth close to $19 billion and had become the country's ninth-largest financial institution. Cohen's dream had been realized—but at the price of a huge and unmanageable debt. The acquisitive binge had moved so fast Central board members complained that, instead of being given detailed briefings on most acquisitions, they had to read about them in the newspapers.

Cohen finally fired Cole in August, 1990, because the sensible CEO insisted on paying down debt by spinning off some non-core assets, such as a minority interest in Inter-City Gas. Cole also wanted to sell off the whole conglomerate at a considerable profit to Montreal's Bell Canada Enterprises, Inc., then shopping for precisely such a mammoth acquisition. Montreal Trust (a BCE subsidiary) was poised three times to buy Central at ever-decreasing premiums, but Cohen and Ellen backed off. Their dream had become more precious than their credit. At the time, Central's stock was being quoted at $18.75 a share; the two partners could have cleaned up. Instead, as the real-estate market began to disintegrate, many of the loans turned sour and the Central group crumbled. By the spring of 1991, there was little remaining value in the Cohen-Ellen investment. The only way to avoid bankruptcy was to sell off Central's salvageable pieces at sacrifice prices. The Toronto-Dominion takeover of Reuben Cohen's corporate assets—then still worth $9 billion—was the largest single financial transaction in

Canadian history, boosting the bank's asset base by 12 per cent and its mortgage portfolio by one-third.

At the end of his spectacular run, still a proud but a broken man, Reuben Cohen retired to his modest New Brunswick bungalow on Moncton's nondescript Hillcrest Drive, baffled how he had fallen so far so fast and why so many people he trusted had let him down. It was a sad and brutal end to a magnificent dream.

THE CONTRACT BETWEEN CANADIANS and their insurance companies prior to 1994 was that, even if life on Earth remained unpredictable, its three certainties were death, taxes and insurance payouts. Once they died, their surviving spouses, kids, relatives or favourite charities would be taken care of by their policies. That faith was terminally shattered with the bankruptcy of Confederation Life, once the country's fifth-largest insurer, whose roots stretched back to 1871. It turned out to be the largest insurance company failure in North American history. To run a company with a stellar reputation and assets of $20 billion into the ground could not have been easy— even for the crew of misguided incompetents who ran Confederation Life under CEO Patrick Burns.

A self-described "heavy drinker" with a W.C. Fields nose, Burns found his way around Ottawa's restrictive insurance firm regulations by establishing Confederation Trust. The subsidiary operated in a looser regulatory environment, pumping up the company's portfolio with commercial real-estate investments in Ontario cities. When these values melted like Häagen-Dazs in the sun, the company went bust. That was a common enough occurrence in the 1990s; what made Confederation Life different was that it had taken horrendously risky gambles with policyholders' premiums, which it did not legally own and from which it was legally obliged to pay out death and other benefits. That was unforgivable in any business; in a mutually owned life insurance company, it was virtually criminal. That no one was held accountable for the irresponsible and devastating decisions of its executives and directors added potent fodder to the anti-business mood of a growing number of Canadians. Some of Confederation Life's 230,000 policyholders were forced to take heavy losses on the funds they had invested for their retirements, their children's educations and all the other worthwhile reasons Confederation Life's sales agents had given them to buy the policies in the first place.* Paul Cantor, the ex-Commerce executive who was appointed president in October of 1993, got there far too late to salvage the situation. His best efforts were frustrated by Great-West Life's prolonged hesitation about whether it should be a white knight and rescue Confed, or wait and become a vulture. It chose the latter.

More to the point of revolutionary discontent was the highly questionable role played by Confederation Life's board of directors at the time its outrageous real-estate acquisitions were being made. Adam Zimmerman, who joined the board after most of the harm had been done, publicly complained that "the company's control and reporting systems were inadequate to the task" and that the directors "didn't know what was happening and didn't understand, if they knew it." That seemed unlikely at best. In 1989, when most of the questionable investments were being made, Confed's board included some of the shrewdest and most respectable of the Canadian Establishment's luminaries, whose reputations seemed hardly worth endangering by negligence in one of their most important board appointments. They included former Confed chairman Jack Rhind (known for being the only corporate chairman, apart from the mutual-fund guru, Fred Soyka, who rode his bicycle to work); former University of Toronto president Claude Bissell; Mitel Corp. turnaround artist Anthony Griffiths; Toronto great-causes icon George Mara; Montreal corporate legal genius André Monast and some guy called Conrad Black. The responsibility of these and the other directors extended far beyond the duty of most board members. Theirs was an exacting task because Confederation Life was a mutual, not a stock, company. That meant it was literally owned by its policyholders, whose surrogates and protectors were

---

* Until Confederation Life's downfall, there had been only two relatively small life insurance failures: Montreal's Cooperants Mutual Life Insurance Society (with a resultant loss of $180 million) and Calgary's Sovereign Life ($75 million), both in 1992. Alan Graham, the reclusive British investor who ran Sovereign, had first come to Canada as an imported goalie for a Calgary soccer team and ran his company's public relations department with one simple rule: any staff member who allowed the Graham name to appear in print was automatically fired. Graham's favourite charity was helping to preserve a local ceremonial cavalry troop.

supposed to be the directors. Until resurrected by the Confed incident, the time seemed long past when corporate directors could remain imbued with what a British judge had once characterized as "lovable dimness."

The dimness endured. The board had sanctioned Confederation's entry into real-estate deals, many of which bordered on foolishness—to the point where Confederation Trust became known as "a lender of last resort." It was the place where desperate borrowers who had been turned down by careful credit officers elsewhere went for mercy-money. By 1992, two-thirds of the company's assets had been invested in risky real estate. Confed had also become a major player in financial derivatives, the riskiest of investment vehicles that would be used in 1995 by Nick Leeson to bankrupt Barings Bank. Investing policyholders' premiums in the unpredictable swings of foreign currencies, interest rates, commodity prices and market indexes was the equivalent of getting Daffy Duck high on laughing gas to guard Granny's savings.

After a leading American mutual fund (Piper Jaffrey) lost $950 million on derivatives, North Dakota Senator Byron Dorgan compared derivatives to nitroglycerine and introduced legislation in the U.S. Congress to ban their use. Despite these risks, a desperate Confed moved massively into derivatives in 1991 through a subsidiary called Confederation Treasury Services Ltd. A year later, just as the company's financial situation was reaching its point of no return, an astounding $10.3 billion had been entered on its books as "*notional* principal amounts of outstanding contracts," which was the only way the value of derivatives could be measured. By the end of the following year, Confed's investment in derivatives had doubled, reaching an eye-popping $20.4 billion, including $4.3 billion in currency swaps, $9.2 billion in interest rates futures and $5.1 billion in foreign-exchange contracts—the riskiest derivative category. None of these transactions had any intrinsic worth and all were subject to random valuation—Confed might as well have invested in ostrich-egg futures, Dutch tulip bulbs or the South Sea bubble. It might have been tempting for Confederation Life directors to deny any knowledge of these deals, but the amounts were so huge that such a defence is not credible. In fact, Chairman Burns was not only fully aware of these Monte Carlo–style investments, but he actively defended them despite at least one warning from a senior insider. When Frank di Paolo, of Confederation Life's large U.S. operation, visited the Toronto headquarters in November of 1991, it was not a routine courtesy call. A distinguished insurance executive who had spent thirty-five years with Confed, di Paolo rose to be the American subsidiary's chief actuary and then its vice-president of finance. He had been invited to head office to celebrate his retirement. At a corporate dinner, he found himself seated next to the chairman. He took the chance to warn him against the proposed entry into derivatives. "I told him that this business could be very risky, because even though it might—theoretically—be possible for the company to hedge its risk, in a practical sense it could not be done," he later recalled. "I also mentioned that the new Canadian Insurance Companies Act, about to be enacted, did not permit life insurance companies to assume risks other than those 'related to the happening of an event or a contingency dependent upon human life.' Burns replied that no decision had yet been reached, but if the company did go into derivatives it would be through a subsidiary." Di Paolo was shocked that Ottawa's financial regulators did nothing to cool down the directors' gambling instincts until it was too late. "It doesn't take the intellect of a Nathan Rothschild," he concluded after Confed's bankruptcy, "to figure out that if you pay the highest interest rate, you can attract enough deposits and see the trust company's assets grow geometrically. Of course, all that money had to be invested quickly. Hence the shift to derivatives, and to becoming a lender of last resort, modes which inexorably led Confederation Trust—and later Confederation Life—to ruin."

There was a postscript to the Confederation Life affair. Its directors had typically not allocated any funds to pay out the earned benefits of its retired employees. Jack Rhind and Patrick Burns deserved no prize for knowing how to run an insurance company, but they surely earned a special citation for brashness. In early 1995, they demanded a special hearing where they seriously requested the court-appointed liquidator pay them overdue bonuses of more than $1 million. Now, that's chutzpah.

CONFEDERATION LIFE'S FATE was entirely typical of the times. The uncontrolled greed of the 1980s and early 1990s, which eventually brought down most of its practitioners—Cohen, Campeau,

Reichmann and many others—fed the Revolution. It would never have materialized if the banks had not financed corporate treasuries way beyond their ability to repay. The banks, just like the insurance companies that played loose with their depositors' money, were responsible not only for the damage to confidence in their own institutions, but for the withdrawal of confidence in the free-enterprise system as a whole.

Canada's bankers really had been the people's fiscal father-confessors; there was something reassuring about their very presence. Every small town or railway whistle-stop with a bank branch felt it had a future. Then, like the other touchtones that failed during the decade covered by this book, the bankers forgot about the people they had been set up to serve and became instead demi-gods, serving their distorted ambitions and their star customers. Christopher Fildes, writing in the London *Spectator*, neatly summed up what had happened. "It is worrying in more ways than one," he wrote, "to hear international bankers proclaim, as they do, that they sleep like babies. 'Yes,' a City magnate is heard to say, 'these days I sleep exactly like a baby. Every two hours I wake up screaming.'"

III THE POLITICAL REVOLUTION

NINE

THE BLOW-DRIED REVOLUTIONARY

The Mulroney Factor

*"Democracy is the process by which people choose
the man who'll get the blame."*
BERTRAND RUSSELL

I

THERE'S A WONDERFUL STORY about Louis Armstrong who was always being bothered by curious fans asking him to define jazz. "Now tell us, Satchmo," they would ask, "what's jazz all about?" Armstrong would flash his pearly-whites, shrug and matter-of-factly reply: "We play life."

The great trumpeter meant that life—with its unpredictable experiences, its sins committed and omitted, its ruminations, feelings and epiphanies, its span between what you did and what you *wanted* to do—is what dictates the cadence and limits of musical improvisation, which is the essence of jazz.

Some politicians are like that—skilled improvisers who can carry a tune—and none more so than Brian Mulroney. What little ideological content there was to the nine years he spent exercising power flowed directly from the more than a quarter-century he spent trying to grab it. Neither rebel nor reactionary, he probably came as close as anyone to personifying his party's self-negating label: Progressive Conservative. Swinging like a skilled acrobat between the compassionate left and the callous right, between following his reason or listening to his heart, Mulroney opted for a hard-rock allegiance to his gut. "He made decisions with his tummy—it had to *feel* right," confirmed Stanley Hartt, his Montreal friend and legal colleague, who became the prime minister's chief of staff. "When someone would tell him, 'Brian, here's what you should do,' he trusted only the source, not the sounds, those people who sought only to be his friend."

Mulroney's operational code was simple: to advance his personal cause as forcefully as possible; to exercise power at the summit of Canadian politics as long and as effectively as he could. Ideas had nothing to do with it. As he himself confessed during a 1992 year-end interview with the CBC's Peter Mansbridge: "I am not ideologically opposed to anything unless it doesn't work." His use of the double negative may have been unintended, but his self-assessment merely confirmed the even more succinct verdict of Charles McMillan, his chief policy adviser, who told me during a mid-afternoon break in the fall of 1984: "Brian? He's about as ideological as that coffee pot."

Mulroney's were the politics of utility, which covered the barren lands between pragmatism and opportunity. There were certain basic beliefs on which he would not compromise: his opposition to capital punishment, his passionate commitment to having Quebec sign the Canadian constitution, his obsession with improving Canada-U.S. relations, his determined opposition to South Africa's apartheid policy, his support of Israel, his push for regional equalization, his push to further the cause of women in political life and his dedication to the principles of free enterprise. But most of the time, his mind was an open city, unfettered by cant or dogma, committed to political functionalism instead of any grand vision for the country at large.

There was an apparent contradiction at work in the man. His free trade and constitutional initiatives represented nothing less than revolutionary departures from the status quo and a rewriting of the social contract between Canadians and their government. His sponsorship of these risky measures was filled with grievous political risks. Neither policy represented a decision based on conviction. Free trade and the decentralization of Confederation not only failed to qualify as deeply held beliefs, but Mulroney had, before their implementation, taken exactly opposite points of view. Fifteen months before instructing his office to lay the groundwork for pre-liminary free trade negotiations with the United States, Mulroney had told a constituency meeting in Thunder Bay, Ontario: "Free trade with the Americans? There's a real beaut for you. There's a real honey. It's like sleeping with an elephant. It's terrific until the ele-phant twitches, and if the elephant rolls over, you're a dead man." Similarly, he had repeatedly attacked Joe Clark's "community of communities" approach to federalism, which was exactly what Meech Lake and Charlottetown were all about. In his 1983 leader-ship platform he had declared that "no one can make a separate deal with Quebec," yet both accords called for that province alone to be recognized as a distinct society.* "It is against Brian Mulroney's principles to have principles," concluded Robert Chodos, editor of *Compass* magazine.

Pierre Elliott Trudeau once silenced a brave woman, both attrac-tive and young—normally an invitation for him to hold forth at great length—who was trying to plumb the former prime minister's opinion of his successor. Trudeau summed up Mulroney with the curt shot: "Ahh, he's all tactics." That was not true. But it carried a grain of truth. Having spent nearly two decades of political appren-ticeship as a *Bleu* in *Rouge* Quebec (only the imperfectly drafted game laws prevented there being a bounty on him), Mulroney learned that strategy was a survival skill much more essential than articulating any ideology, let alone trying to develop one.

Politicians mated to a point of view or, God forbid, a long-term policy, lost the freedom to move with the turn of events. That there were still a dozen guys around the table willing to throw themselves into the infested moats surrounding the impregnable fortress of Quebec's Liberal machine was far more important than any ideas they might have—unless their brainstorm had to do with fund-raising. In those hothouse days (when being a Tory in Quebec

---

* Under pressure from the media in the 1983 leadership campaign to explain where he stood on the issue of federal-provincial relations, Mulroney grabbed a QuebecAir barf bag while on a flight from Quebec City to Mont-Joli, Quebec, and wrote on the back of it the nine points that summed up his constitutional policy. It was later properly framed and placed in the living room of Peter Ohrt, one of his advisers at the time.

ranked alongside collecting butterflies with an invisible net or believing that Robert Stanfield could fly), policy formation was a luxury. That Mulroney came to office after a long stretch of such internal political exile explained why he was so much better at gaining power than he was at exercising it.

I once asked Alberta Premier Ralph Klein—the Grandma Moses of Canadian politics, in the sense that one is never sure whether the wisdom that spills from his mouth is intentional—what kind of a Conservative he thought Mulroney to be. "I never knew him as a Conservative," Klein replied, without cracking a smile. "I only knew him as Brian." As prime minister of Canada, Mulroney often quoted the admonition of Paris politician Pierre Mendès-France: "To govern is to choose." But what he chose as his most urgent priority (the negotiation of a free trade pact with the United States) went directly against Tory tradition. Its last great proponents had been the nation's most successful Liberals: Sir Wilfrid Laurier and, to a lesser degree, Mackenzie King.

Once safely ensconced in office, Mulroney acted as though the country would be best served if he became the Great Accommodator among political interest groups, heading them off with promises and occasionally with action. This notion—that the sum of all the pleadings by vested interests somehow amounted to an over-arching *national* interest—was dubious at best. It provided neither a common cause nor a shared vision to guide Canadians through a period of revolutionary social change and prompted them to set off in unpredictable and explosive directions.

The direction he chose was a matter of serious concern. By being unable or unwilling to develop a clear vision of the country beyond a more competitive bottom line, Mulroney involuntarily became an agent of the Canadian Revolution described in these pages. He gave Canadians few reasons to participate in public life as a way to advance the national cause. His loyalty to his friends, meanwhile, was an admirable personal trait but a disastrous political one, since it left the impression that those who were active participants in his government were advancing their own agendas and not the national interest. Feeling thus rebuffed, most Canadians retreated into their own worlds, coming up for air only long enough to mobilize themselves in a determined effort to defeat Mulroney, his party and his soul-exempt politics.

What Mulroney failed to achieve as a leader was best described by Adolf Berle, the American lawyer-philosopher, who once noted that effective democratic government must flow from the over-arching values held dear by its leaders. "Only when a political system has decided what is good and what is beautiful," Berle wrote, "can it take the intermediate steps and set the priorities for reaching its goals." No such sequence of priorities existed under Brian Mulroney. Canadians have always had difficulty mobilizing them-selves to deal with crises threatening their country's continued existence because they thought of themselves as a marginal people with few core values of their own. Mulroney did very little to alter that equation. It wasn't so much that his actions were revolutionary, but that they existed outside the context of readily identifiable values, that motivated the nation against him. He was determined to be an interventionist prime minister like no other. But since Cana-dians could not see where he was going they were reluctant to follow him. The Canadian Revolution existed in opposition to the Mulroney Revolution; it was not so much a reaction against his agenda as against his leadership.

STILL, MULRONEY DID HAVE A DEFINITE CAST OF MIND that gave birth to his particular brand of politics. Its governing precepts were there to be winnowed from the torrents of his rhetoric and from the life he had led as Canadian Conservatism's loneliest long-distance runner.

Because of his push-button smile and ham-actor voice, because he had moved so purposefully from being an electrician's son in Baie Comeau to becoming a golden-spurred member of the Montreal business community, his style was inevitably mistaken for substance—or was it the other way around? At any rate, above those Gucci loafers and beneath that ambassadorial coiffure there lurked the small-town boy who had grown up without money or privilege and, in the process, had developed an inferiority complex as wide as the St. Lawrence. His burning desire to put as many miles between himself and his past—both figuratively and literally—was a mistake, because it was only when he abandoned his roots that he got into serious trouble. Brian's youth in Baie Comeau had been dominated by his father's need to hold down two jobs in order to make ends meet. Providing the bare necessities was a real concern and the double shifts represented a genuine sacrifice; it engendered in Mulroney an early respect for loyalty. The two people on earth that he worshipped most were his father, Ben, and his wife, Mila, whose devotion was unquestioned. Of even greater influence on the young Mulroney was the fact that he belonged to a double minority—among the French Catholics he was an English minority and among the English he was an Irish-Catholic minority—and was thus regarded as an outsider by nearly everyone. "What you gotta know about Brian," his best friend Sam Wakim told Richard Gwyn of *The Toronto Star* on election night in 1984, "is that he's spent most of his life shovelling snow." As a two-line character sketch, Gwyn wrote (being careful to confirm that Wakim had indeed said "snow"), this was dead-on. "He's an outsider," Gwyn concluded, "that is, the first prime minister we've had . . . who has never been part of the national governing system, and who, indeed, has spent most of his life fighting it . . . Everyone from a place like Baie Comeau is an outsider when they strike out for the big cities. So are all electricians' sons. So, perhaps deepest in the gut, are most Irish-Canadians."

Growing up in Baie Comeau was the pre-eminent formative influence on Mulroney's life and thought. This was not—as most of his biographers, detractors and hagiographers have maintained—because he sang the occasional song for Colonel Robert McCormick, the proprietor of the *Chicago Tribune,* who visited his town once a year. The image of an eight-year-old Brian Mulroney standing on the piano at the *Manoir* guest-house, singing "Dearie" for the Colonel and pocketing a fifty-dollar bill for his performance (which went straight into his mother's grocery account) was irresistible. That innocent vignette was routinely offered as proof that Little Brian would inevitably grow up into Big Brian who would, half a century later, give Canada away to the Americans. This was sheer bunk. The significance of these musical interludes was not the young boy's fawning performance (every kid enjoys the approbation of adults) but the Colonel's patronizing presence. McCormick owned Baie Comeau, it was his creation and everyone in it owed their living to his whims and fancies. What Mulroney learned, growing up in a company town, was that deference to higher authority might pay dividends—but that *possessing* authority was far better than having to cater to it. The lesson that was imprinted on him early was one that he would, inevitably, come to imprint upon the nation, until its citizens had learned it well and adopted it as their personal creed: deference might be good, but being deferred to was even better.

Before he was ten years old, Mulroney knew that his future lay elsewhere. His call to arms during his rural tour in the 1984 campaign, that Canada was a land of "small towns and big dreams," applied to no one more directly than to himself. It gave resonance to his own life, as it would in a country and decade where so many had left small towns to pursue their dreams. Hard as it was later to recall or even to acknowledge, Brian Mulroney was in 1984 the most popular Canadian prime minister ever elected to office. His rags-to-riches story, his humble roots and his Armani suits, his exquisite tailor-made shirts and his picture-perfect wife, dovetailed precisely with the restless, upwardly mobile, acquisitive mood of the decade. These manifestations of self were not then seen as an impediment, but as an embodiment of aspirations which were, by their very nature, both personal and national.

Baie Comeau at the time Mulroney simmered up in it was a puppy bush settlement far out on the North Shore of the St. Lawrence, offering no beauty and little comfort. Its main cultural facility was the community hockey rink; pollution from the stacks of the Colonel's Quebec North Shore paper-mill had defoliated just about every tree in town. There were only two seasons—winter and August. The little community's plain, hard-working people went to the Taverne aux Amis to have a drink to remember the good old days, then had a few more to forget them. The Mulroney house on Champlain Avenue was cosy and filled with a loving atmosphere, but the town itself was a prison—if you had big dreams. The Mulroneys managed only one holiday each year, a 260-mile trip to Quebec City in the family's 1938 Pontiac. "We would leave at four in the morning—my parents, the six children, the dog, fourteen sandwiches and a six-pack," Brian enjoyed recalling, "to begin a mad race over unpaved roads to catch the ferry at Bersimis, followed by a heroic gallop to catch the ferry at Baie Ste. Catherine—the children crying, the dog barking, my father grinding his teeth and my mother in the back seat saying the beads for the third time." Young Brian left town at age fourteen, first to attend St. Thomas High School in Chatham, New Brunswick, and two years later to enrol in St. Francis Xavier University at Antigonish, Nova Scotia.

There he came under the influence of the co-operative teachings of Father Moses Coady, who implanted the notion in his students that an active social conscience was life's highest goal. Mulroney could recite from memory one of Coady's lectures about St. Francis Xavier's ideal graduates that began: "We want them to look into the sun and the depths of the sea. We want them to explore the hearts of flowers and of fellow men. We want them to be eager to discover and develop their capacities for creation..."

It was stirring, poetic stuff, but the story of how Mulroney became a Tory had more to do with his chances for personal advancement, which were more promising with the Conservatives than within the moribund campus Liberal Party. "The Grits were no fun, they took themselves too seriously," was his ready explanation, but in fact the Tories offered him the chance to run for office and win. Remarkably, Mulroney contested no elections, not even internal party posts (apart from student politics at St. Francis Xavier) until his 1976 run for leadership of the federal Conservative party. He was determined not to have a single defeat noted on his *curriculum vitae*.* The highlight of his time at university was the thirty-six-hour train trip to Ottawa as a delegate to the 1956 Conservative convention which picked John Diefenbaker as its leader and appointed Mulroney as vice-chairman of its youth wing. At about this time Mulroney applied for a Rhodes scholarship and the Nova Scotia selection committee invited the candidates to a formal luncheon, presumably to test their social graces. "I was married and living in Halifax," recalled Patrick MacAdam, his friend from St. Francis Xavier who had graduated two years before, "when Brian called looking for a bed for the night. He was having his Rhodes interview the next day and wanted me to show him which

---

* Less well known is the fact that in most campus elections Mulroney won for his party, he had to face not only the campus Liberals and the CCF, but a splinter movement known as The Order of Obese Occidentals, led by a chunky Richard Cashin, who later became a Liberal MP, Newfoundland union leader and sustaining spirit in the fight to preserve the vanishing fisheries. Cashin, then a close pal of Mulroney's, also caught Mulroney's first love on the rebound. Cashin wooed Rosann Earl after she had left Mulroney heartbroken. The two were married and later divorced.

knife, fork and spoon to use. I had been a ragged-assed kid from Cape Breton Island but had joined the Reserve Officers' Training Corps while at university, and having had to attend a lot of mess dinners, knew about cutlery. So I showed him how to use it and he went off to his selection board." He used the right fork but didn't get the scholarship.

At Laval, which he attended after failing out of Dalhousie Law School, Mulroney came truly into his own. He became leader of the bright coterie of bilingual students who had been drawn to Quebec City, home of Jean Lesage's Quiet Revolution then going on in the province. In its rejection of the established social order of things and its sweeping political consequences, the Quiet Revolution was the most pronounced shift in society to presage the Canadian Revolution of 1985–1995—and it was no coincidence that Mulroney formed his political sensibilities in the one and became the central figure in the other. With a few exceptions, his drinking buddies would later take up senior appointments within Mulroney's government. The political convictions and practices nurtured during this period would be the hallmarks of his time in power.

Mulroney spent a pivotal summer during his Laval days working in Ottawa for Alvin Hamilton, the Tory government's imaginative minister of agriculture* and his brilliant executive assistant, Roy Faibish; he was also a key organizer of the historic First Congress on Canadian Affairs. Both of these experiences widened his horizons, but most of the time he lived in a quiet boarding-house on Rue St. Louis, chasing after nurses and drinking at the Aux Délices tavern. He spent many an afternoon with his political idol and mentor, Daniel Johnson, the father of a later Quebec Liberal premier of the same name, who had taken over Maurice Duplessis's Union Nationale party. During the early 1960s when "Danny Boy," as

---

* Mulroney was no less imaginative than his boss and his enterprise made him single-handedly responsible for the introduction of the prized Charolais cattle breed to the Prairies. The French government at the time refused to share its cattle with Canada, but Mulroney took advantage of the fact that some of the animals were in quarantine on the French island of Saint-Pierre en route to the U.S.; under instructions from Hamilton, he covertly smuggled vials of the bull semen into Canada.

Johnson was then known, was leader of the opposition, he and a reverent Mulroney spent much time together sipping brew and talking politics at La Place de la Fontaine, the ground-level bar at the Château Frontenac. The mentor-apprentice relationship soon blossomed into a genuine friendship which they both enjoyed.

I used to fly into Quebec City two or three times a year in those days to interview Jean Lesage, René Lévesque, Eric Kierans and some of the other cabinet ministers in charge of the Quiet Revolution. I would always try to join Johnson for a drink. Unfailingly courteous, poking fun at me for taking *la grande politique* of the reigning Liberals so seriously, Johnson would expound his own political philosophy, or rather lack of one. I recall him saying one evening after a round of Kir, when I had asked him to define his ideology: "You know, in politics it's very dangerous to have a philosophy. In a democracy you should have politicians who settle the problems that exist, not who set out to prove philosophical ideals." That didn't stop him from having some very definite ideas on Quebec's future within Canada. Johnson was not a separatist, but no other Quebec politician of his time so clearly enunciated the notion of Canada as the home of two distinct societies. "Where the French Canadian nation finds its freedom, there too will be its homeland," he wrote in his aptly titled book, *Égalité ou Indépendance*. He saw Quebec as a culture unto itself that could only survive if it seized control of its economic and social institutions. "Too many people," he told me, "treat the B.N.A. Act like a sacred cow, even though it's been violated many times in closed committee sessions and in hotel rooms during the informal discussions that followed. So why not get rid of it and draft a sixth constitution?" (The other five being those of 1763, 1774, 1791, 1840 and 1867.)

Looking back on those conversations, what strikes me is how much Johnson must have influenced Mulroney. No matter what the weather or circumstance, Johnson always looked impeccable, with not a hair out of place, perfectly ironed pants and shirts so fresh they looked as if they had, minutes before, emerged from the cleaners. During our chatter, Johnson confided that the secret of maintaining effective leadership of a political party was to concentrate on keeping the caucus happy. While Lesage and his circle were spinning grandiose dreams in Quebec City, he was spending three afternoons a week driving about the constituencies in his tugboat-sized Cadillac, clearing the necessary channels for the flood of local patronage that would follow his victory at the polls. In 1966, Johnson astonished everyone but himself by beating Jean Lesage's proud Liberals. He won by applying the vestige of the Duplessis-style politics that had ruled the province for a quarter-century: vote my way and you'll sail over pavement—vote against me and you'll choke on gravel. Johnson believed that the essence of politics was power, not its legal niceties; he felt it was important for political leaders to create a distance around themselves that only the exercise of power can provide. He worshipped all things American, including the presidential system, and had he outlived his first mandate he would no doubt have instilled more U.S. content into his government.

In retrospect, it was obvious that Mulroney had learned the arts of leadership at Johnson's knee (he even briefly worked with the Union Nationale party, although he had previously reviled it as corrupt in campus speeches). Just about everything he did after his sojourn in Quebec City had Johnson's brand on it, from the thrice-daily shirt changes, his emphasis on the value of a contented caucus and the use of a big, black American limousine as a symbol of his authority, right through to his fight to preserve Quebec's distinct-society status and his admiration of the Americans. It was during those one-to-one sessions that Mulroney also became attached to the strategy that became a hair-trigger of the Canadian Revolution: his attempt to convince Canadians outside Quebec to placate that province by accepting a mild form of inequality for themselves and granting it special privileges under a new constitution.

He received his law degree and joined the prestigious Montreal legal firm of Ogilvy, Cope, Porteous, Hansard, Marler, Montgomery & Renault, where he specialized in labour law. With that move, Mulroney had embarked on his time in political purgatory. For half a century, it had meant nothing to be a Conservative in Quebec. The last provincial Conservative administration had lost power in 1897. Local Tories were haunted by their inability to overcome the French-Canadian hostility toward the party since 1885, when Sir John A. Macdonald's Tory cabinet had refused to intercede in the hanging of Louis Riel. As Canada's founding father so unforgettably put it at the time: "He shall hang though every dog in Quebec bark in his favour." J.S. Roy, one of the few Tories from Quebec who managed to get himself elected, complained about his sad lot in the Commons on November 4, 1941: "Any French-Canadian MP of this House who has mixed with the Conservative Party must realize that he is not part of their political family. He is at best a tolerated stranger..."

The only flicker of light in this gloomy tunnel was John Diefenbaker's dramatic 1958 sweep of the country, when fifty Conservative MPs from Quebec were elected. Forty-two of them were French-speaking, which was the same number of seats the Liberals had won in the entire country. It was a stunning upset, since the previous year the Tories had returned only eight (mainly English-speaking) members from Quebec. But their conversion was more apparent than real. The instant Conservatives had been elected thanks to the manipulations of the province's political machine, manoeuvred by Duplessis, who had been anxious to promote his staunchly anti-Liberal stand on "provincial rights." The Conservative MPs elected in Quebec were, to put it kindly, a mixed lot. One of them was on the run from a threatened retribution by a rival gang of Montreal ward-heelers and spent his entire time in Parliament with a revolver concealed in a shoulder holster. He was constantly accompanied by a bodyguard and drove around Ottawa in a bullet-proof limousine. Another, just as he was about to be named as Diefenbaker's chief Quebec lieutenant, was eliminated from the race when he went on a drinking spree that reached its climax when he relieved himself into a potted plant at Montreal's Dorval Airport.* Diefenbaker quickly dissipated his valuable beachhead in French Canada; in the 1963 election his Quebec contingent was reduced to eight seats. Whether it was the result of his ineffective Cabinet from Quebec, which ranged from gentle nonentities like Raymond O'Hurley to noisy ones like Pierre Sévigny, or believing that he could satisfy Quebec's aspirations by issuing bilingual cheques to the federal civil service, remains unclear. (The number of Conservatives elected in Quebec remained at less than four until

---

* This might have been forgiven but for two unfortunate circumstances: he insisted on pulling his pants down instead of merely unzipping them, and he was accompanied at the time by the editor and a photographer of one of Quebec's largest dailies.

1984, when it jumped to fifty-eight.) His youth notwithstanding, Mulroney had been advising Diefenbaker on how to handle the Quebec portfolio. His counsel was shrewd, but seldom followed. After much effort he did persuade the Tory leader to visit Quebec City one Friday evening in 1960 to dine with some of the province's leading opinion-makers. The PM insisted that his office cater the glittering affair at the Château Frontenac, which was made more than a little tense when Diefenbaker's staff ordered a round of steaks for every guest at a time when the practice of eating meat on Fridays was forbidden to members of the Roman Catholic Church.

Mulroney served loyally in the political trenches of Quebec conservatism, displaying the terrier determination for making and keeping friends which would eventually help him take over the party. During the long march toward the victory of 1984, which was Mulroney's finest hour, there emerged a band of brothers (and the occasional honorary sister). They became his personal brigade: Jean Bazin, Michel Cogger, Paul Creaghan, Fred and Gerry Doucet, Bert Lavoie, Patrick MacAdam, Cam McArthur, Michael Meighen, Lowell Murray, Bernard Roy, Jean Sirois, Sam Wakim and Peter White, later joined by David Angus, Arthur Campeau, Guy Charbonneau, Jonathan Dietcher, Janis Johnson, Pierrette Lucas, Frank Moores, Roger Nantel, Rodrigue Pageau and Ginette Pilotte. Precisely how each of them fitted into the push to make their man prime minister—and how each was later amply rewarded—was less important than what held them together. They were a talented crew, bound to one another less by any creed than by their loyalty, inside jokes, jibes at those pretentious pols who held real power (known among them, sarcastically, as "Great Canadians,") and, often as not, by the black cross on the gold finger ring which marked them as alumni of St. Francis Xavier. These loyalists from Mulroney's university days alternated between acting like Green Berets on a search-and-destroy mission and the gossipy knitting circle at the foot of the French Revolution guillotines. They were adept at the crisis management of the political wars that raged around them during their lengthy wait and became superb at putting out the many fires that might have charred Mulroney's eventual candidacy. In retrospect, it was clear that they were a triumphant and fascinating example of the ultimate Canadian heresy: street-smart realists who went into politics for fun and profit.

This was very different from the *weltschmerz* groupies bent on saving the country despite itself, who had assumed the burden of governing Canada in its recent past. These do-gooders believed that in order to conduct the affairs of state one first had to suffer the essential apprenticeship of colonial servitude at either Oxford or Harvard, preferably both. In contrast, the Mulroney brigade knew that there was a lot more clout in a Rimouski beer parlour than the Oxford Union.* The self-selected mandarins who ran Pearson's and Trudeau's Ottawa behaved as though they were operating a miniature Bloomsbury-on-the-Rideau. Aspiring to be intellectuals and Renaissance men, they achieved nothing so well as being dilettantes who couldn't calculate the taxi fare from Mirabel, yet went to bed reciting John Maynard Keynes's General Theory. If you were to ask the Mulroney gang about the General Theory, they'd probably look puzzled, then cite their leader's most seminal thought: "You dance with the one what brung ya."

The Mulroney brigade's organizational command post was the Maritime Bar of the Ritz-Carlton Hotel in Montreal. Its location was less a convenience than a statement that they had arrived. Originally financed in 1912 by a group of Montreal's richest families, who felt they deserved a Grand Hotel of their own, the hostelry quickly became the favoured roost for the city's élite. They lunched in the Oak Room, held debutante parties in the Grand Ballroom, took tea in the Palm Court, dined in the Oval Room and had after-work cocktails in the basement Maritime Bar. Whenever there was rough weather at home, the aggrieved party would move into one of the hotel's luxury suites to drown his or her sorrows in magnums of Grande Fine Champagne de Napoleon 1880, accompanying the salt of their tears with dabs of caviar Astrakhan.†

---

* The only Rhodes Scholar within the Mulroney circle was the Montreal counsel, Yves Fortier, but he was a Liberal and more a personal friend of than a member of his working entourage.

† Some of Montreal's idle rich spent much of their lives at the Ritz; the outstanding example being Elwood Hosmer whose father, Charles, had founded Canadian Pacific Telegraph. During the 1920s Hosmer was driven daily to the hotel, where he would spend the day drinking gin and smoking Corona cigars. Seated in one of the lobby lounge chairs—and often answering nature's calls in the pot of a nearby palm

The Mulroney people met at the Ritz (and occasionally at the Mount Royal Club across the street) to plot a strategy for the federal Conservative Party within the province, dealing in various levels of sincerity with Robert Stanfield, Joe Clark, Claude Wagner, Marcel Faribault and the several nobodies who followed Johnson as leader of the Union Nationale. Despite brave attempts to wrap their Anglo-Saxon tongues around French irregular verbs, neither Stanfield nor Clark had much luck attracting masses of converts. With the election of Pierre Trudeau, Quebec became a more impregnable Liberal fortress than it had been under Sir Wilfrid Laurier or Louis St. Laurent.

Mulroney's most traumatic reality check during this period was the time he spent in the mid-1970s as a Quebec royal commissioner. Along with Judge Robert Cliche, a thoughtful professor-politician and former Liberal lawyer who had become leader of Quebec's New Democratic Party and Guy Chevrette, a farmer's son from Joliette who later became a PQ cabinet minister, the trio was charged with cleaning up the rot in the province's construction industry. The testimony of 279 witnesses revealed the corruption and violence caused by the clash of unbridled unionism and capitalism. People had been stabbed, literally, in the back and one union official had driven his bulldozer into a Hydro Quebec generator, causing damage worth $32 million. The commission's 132 recommendations brought peace to the Quebec construction scene. Its hearings had given Mulroney his first public exposure and had taught him many valuable lessons. There was no better training to become leader of the Progressive Conservative Party of Canada than to be a student of the mayhem that ruled Quebec's construc-

tree—he would eventually pass out, the accumulated droppings and drippings of his day's sojourn around him, his face half-covered by the funny papers that were his favourite reading. Porters would carry him outside where his chauffeur, who had been waiting all day for this moment, would tuck him into the back seat of his limousine for the two-block ride home. This routine was seriously disrupted only once. In 1927, Elwood suddenly decided he had been wasting his life and that the only way to redeem himself was to fly the Atlantic. The attempt ended when his aircraft, *Flying Whale*, crashed shortly after takeoff in the Azores. He and three companions spent three hours drifting in the ocean until they were picked up the liner *Minnewaska*. Elwood promptly returned to his more stable lounge chair at the Ritz.

tion industry. No true-blue Tory at the time recognized any statute of limitations in the internal feuds that gave the party its main *raison d'être*. These vendettas didn't fade like sorrow or fizzle like anger, they just kept on multiplying and spreading poison throughout the entire organization. It was no wonder that compared with the Liberal record of five party leaders between 1887 and 1984, the Tories had gone through fifteen chieftains, and kept themselves out of power most of the century.*

In 1976, Mulroney jumped the gun on his ambitions and ran for the Tory leadership to replace Robert Stanfield. John Diefenbaker, by then his sworn enemy, spoke out against his inexperience; Claude Wagner bribed most of the Quebec delegates, but Mulroney still came in third; the convention picked Joe Clark as the man who had the least number of enemies in the arena. "Bones" was not pleased, especially by charges he had spent so much money on his campaign that it looked as if he were trying to buy the leadership. "That's bullshit," he told *Atlantic Insight* magazine. "I had a pretty sexy, razzmatazz campaign. What the hell's wrong with that? So it didn't fly with some of the delegates. I wasn't a member of the caucus. I didn't have any pros working for me. So what the hell, we made mistakes... Now they all sit around saying, 'He did this wrong, he did that wrong.' Well, I must have done something right. Christ, I came in third and it took the biggest gang-bang in history to stop me."

Shortly after his defeat, Mulroney was formally offered the job of running the Iron Ore Company, the Canadian subsidiary of Hanna Mining of Cleveland, Ohio. Burdened by a $400-million debt, IOC suffered from dismal labour relations with fifty-nine work stoppages in the previous decade, had halted dividend payments and was facing an increasingly competitive market from foreign sources for

---

* Political writer Norman Snider compared the PC Party to "a certain kind of WASP family, where the daughter is going crazy upstairs, alone in her bedroom, the son is getting ready to elope with the Jamaican maid, Mother is drowning her sorrows in gin, but not a word about any of these things is mentioned at the dinner table, and the front porch stays calm. One day Father takes a shotgun to them all, and the neighbours say, 'They were such a quiet, private family.'"

its easily replaceable product. Mulroney was in his element. Unlike previous IOC executives recruited mainly from Ottawa's ivy mandarinate, he had just spent most of a decade as a labour lawyer, negotiating creatively with some of the province's toughest unions. He found himself in tune with the IOC's 7,500 employees who laboured at Sept-Îles and Schefferville and threatened to fire anybody "who thinks I'm impressed by them booting the union around or being rude or kicking people in the ass." Within fourteen months of taking over he had the company operating smoothly in the black. Profits tripled between 1977 and 1981; after he turned the company around, he doubled the pensions being paid to widows of employees. Mulroney himself was well rewarded for his work, with a generous six-figure salary and financing for a twelve-room mansion on Belvedere Road, in the heart of Montreal's ritzy Westmount area. "Where you living now, Brian?" asked Robert Lewis of *Maclean's* when they encountered one another at a Montreal social occasion. "You know the mountain?" Mulroney shot back. "Right at the top! Right at the fucking top!" Another privilege he enjoyed was free use of the IOC corporate jet. Brian Peckford, then premier of Newfoundland, recalled one wild weekend when he met Mulroney in Labrador City at Friday noon. They climbed aboard the IOC jet, spent Friday evening watching the Russia-Canada hockey game at the Montreal Forum; flew to Cleveland on Saturday, where they caught an afternoon baseball game; journeyed on to New York on Sunday morning in time to attend an NFL football game; then flew back to Montreal for the Canada Cup final at the Forum.

He spent many spare hours undermining Joe Clark's wobbly leadership in private, while supporting the Man from High River in public. But that wasn't the main thrust of his activities. Reporters who telephoned the Iron Ore Company's Montreal head office, kitty-corner from the Ritz-Carlton, made light of the fact that it was such an obvious branch-plant operation with only nine full-time employees (including clerks and stenographers) listed on its payroll. They missed the point. What Mulroney achieved during his half-dozen years at IOC was to secure his pride of place in both the Canadian and American business Establishments. By 1982, Iron Ore was spinning off more than $300 million a year into the bulging coffers of its U.S. head office and IOC shareholders collected more dividends under his management than during the previous twenty years. As word of his personal charm and professional accomplishments spread, he began to be invited to join corporate boards. By the fall of 1982 he was a director of ten major companies, including Conrad Black's Standard Broadcasting; the giant supermarket chain, Provigo Inc.; United Provinces Insurance; the Canadian Imperial Bank of Commerce and, predictably, the Ritz-Carlton Hotel Company of Montreal. These were useful instruments to broaden his contacts but none more so than the Commerce, which allowed him a seat at the very marrow of the Establishment's decision-making process.

Equally important were the contacts he made across the border. IOC's parent company had been founded by Marcus Alonzo Hanna at the turn of the century. No ordinary industrialist, Hanna had established Cleveland's Republican electoral machine and for a time ran the city and most of the state of Ohio. One of his best friends and associates had been John D. Rockefeller, the prototypical American billionaire. The Hanna family formed marital and business alliances with other wealthy clans that lasted for generations. Meeting with Hanna's partners and directors brought Mulroney in direct touch with the paladins of American business. As well as the current crop of Hannas and Humphreys, who held control of the company, there was Peter Grace of the New York mercantile family with 1981 revenues of $6.5 billion;* Stephen Bechtel, Jr., head of the San Francisco–based master builders with annual revenues of $12 billion;† Nathan Williams Pearson, who ran the Mellon fortune out of Pittsburgh; Charles Ames, head of the Acme-Cleveland Corporation and William Boeschenstein, chairman of Owens-Corning Fiberglas. They took to the charming young Canadian-Irishman as if he were the son they never had (an impression Mulroney did nothing to dispel), leaving him in the enviable position of having one of the highest-quality business networks on the continent.

---

* For reasons best known to himself, Peter Grace attended most board meetings packing a revolver in a shoulder holster that would swing out whenever he was making a vigorous point. (Mulroney never adopted that affectation, but some of his press secretaries came close.)

† Bechtel's only Canadian director was none other than John Turner, the once and past prime minister.

The Iron Ore Company experience confirmed Mulroney as a politician with a business view of the world. This was a highly significant shift in his career. He came to political office not with the mental bent of a lawyer, but as a successful capitalist, with the economic and social perceptions that entailed. (It was no surprise that he immediately returned to the corporate boardrooms instead of law when he retired from politics in 1993.) No better apprenticeship as an agent of the Canadian Revolution could be imagined than running the Canadian branch plant of a giant American multinational. The experience had muffled Mulroney's humanitarian instincts and diluted his attachment to the sensibilities of his Baie Comeau boyhood. Those distant days became a kind of decorative mantra, called up whenever his social conscience or Canadian credentials were questioned. But his heart belonged to the Ritz. "There are no fancy-pants heroes any more with elegant theories and magic wands," he contended at the time, "just overworked and harassed businessmen, labour leaders and ordinary Canadians who get their hands dirty every day dealing with the pedestrian problems of providing jobs, meeting payrolls and producing products— only to come home at night to learn on TV that some brave new social artist has invented another government plan that will add to costs, increase paperwork and lessen competitiveness." He became vehemently opposed to what he called "the Swedenizing of Canada" and seemed permanently transformed in his political outlook. The Boyo from Baie Comeau had become *le Grand Fromage* on a Ritz.

WHEN HE FIRST ARRIVED IN FEDERAL POLITICS, the pundits fell over themselves trying to credit some recognizable ideology to this upstart who thought he could skip all the intermediary steps and go straight from corporate president to prime minister, without having to run for public office in the interval. None of their efforts to identify his philosophy meant very much, because Mulroney believed that each of Canada's mainstream political parties, his own included, existed not as an apparatus for implementing coherent sets of ideas but as an instrument for the accommodation of personal, regional and national aspirations. Politics was a matter of finding a place for everyone on the picnic blanket.

In the spring of 1983, when he won the Conservative party leadership on a steamy fourth ballot, Mulroney was the lucky recipient of two unbeatable advantages. He was neither Pierre Trudeau—who had by then amply exhausted his welcome with the Canadian electorate—nor was he Joe Clark, whose credentials as a footnote to the party's history had by then been firmly established in the minds of Conservative delegates.

Clark and Mulroney had been linked in the party's mind as alternate leaders for the 1980s, but Mulroney never subscribed to that heresy for one minute. He could hardly bring himself to comment on being counted in the same political category with Clark, yet his rival's record and policy initiatives heavily influenced his own. Mulroney's negative feelings about Clark were based on a deep personal disdain for the man and contempt for the sorry record of Joe Who's brief tumble at the prime ministership. When Clark astounded himself and the universe by defeating the still-charismatic Pierre Trudeau in the spring of 1979, he seemed so stunned by what he had done that he all but threw away his mandate nine months later, as if it were an unwanted child. As he tried, with various degrees of desperation, to preserve his hold on the party, the Clark paradox came into play. Outwardly Joe was incapable of being insulted. One of the many jokes going around party circles at the time claimed that a fan had presented him with a pair of cufflinks.

"So, what happened?" the straight man would ask.

"Damned if he didn't go right out and have his wrists pierced!" came the snickering reply.

But as the stories grew more bitter, Clark emerged from his closet as a paranoid. No imagined slight was small enough to claim his forgiveness—or more important, the forgiveness of his wife, Maureen the bloody McTeer, whose record as the least pleasant and most self-destructive presence ever to occupy 24 Sussex Drive will stand unchallenged through eternity. The daughter of a former Ontario Highways Department employee, she studied to be a lawyer and became a political hanger-on. She was engaged eventually to Tory activist Hugh Segal, but after he lost two bids to be elected MPP for Ottawa Centre, she dumped him. Ever true to her sense of occasion and public show of unswerving support, she gave Segal back his ring on election night with the comment, within hearing of Segal's campaign workers, that she wasn't "about to marry a loser."

She did anyway. McTeer made Clark so nervous that at a

campaign planning committee just before the 1979 election, chaired
by Lowell Murray, it was decided as a matter of policy that
she would have her own tour and itinerary. On the days of her
husband's critical TV debates, she was totally banned from his presence. On Joe's prime ministerial junket to Africa, while he was
signing a protocol in Zambia near Victoria Falls, his pen ran dry.
He took a second one out of his breast pocket and was about to
continue his signature, when McTeer chirped up loud enough for
everyone to hear: "You idiot, that pen has red ink." She bad-
mouthed the Mulroneys, not within the privacy of her home, but in
every Ottawa hair salon and coffee klatsch she visited, thus adding
immeasurably to her husband's burdens by undermining the
working peace respected by both Clark and Mulroney. Her verbal
tiffs with the Mulroneys grew so bitter that when the prime minister's family and retainers were watching the 1988 election results on
television in Baie Comeau, the loudest cheer spontaneously
exploded, not when the CBC's Peter Mansbridge announced the
second Tory majority, but when Maureen McTeer, running as a
Progressive Conservative in the Ottawa Valley riding of Carleton-
Gloucester, conceded defeat.

Clark tried to get by with a set of predictable mannerisms. On
public occasions, he would stick out his chin to make himself look
strong, while lowering his voice an octave to make himself sound
sincere. (No imaginable tactic could have given Brian Mulroney,
who enjoyed natural advantages in both categories, a greater edge.)
But the deadliest aspect of Clark's presentation of himself was that,
when asked a question, he would pause to consider it the way a child
will hesitate before speaking, to test possible answers against
limited knowledge before blurting out the truth. Bad strategy. For
one thing, his words came out raw and awkward, as if they had been
formed by a cookie-cutter. Honest they may have been, but his
pronouncements fit somewhere between post-modern banality and
premature senility. Canadian Conservatives, then and now, preferred
fantasy over reality. They demanded leaders more in tune with
the mindless haze of *The Sound of Music* than the grunge rock
of governing.

There was another factor at work. Mulroney, who had interpreted
his defeat for the PC leadership in 1976 as a blow not only to his
ambitions but to his manhood, had gone through his private night of

the soul—drinking, womanizing and being much harder on himself than any of his enemies ever would be. But he had emerged from that humiliating time as a more mature and grounded individual. Clark had yet to learn from his apprenticeship in purgatory, to undergo the personal soul-searching that would crystallize his character. Still, underneath all that awkwardness Clark was a tough cookie, a charter member of the Chinese water-torture brand of politics, exhausting his opponents by wearing down public support for their positions. He would never set the world on fire (except by accident), but he had a brave spirit, sported a turtle-shell psyche and he never gave up.

When the Tories met in Ottawa during the spring of 1983 to choose a new leader, Clark's glory days appeared to be behind, and as it later turned out, ahead of him. Even his campaign team's remarkable organizational skills couldn't deliver the convention. Its voting arithmetic demanded that the only sure way to defeat Mulroney would have been for Clark and John Crosbie to support each other. But the unilingual Newfie, who privately considered Clark a "platitudinous klutz," could not bring himself to restore the former prime minister to office, while Joe's battered but unbowed pride prevented him from contemplating any move to elevate his rival.

The only other serious contender in the running was Michael Wilson, whose doleful candidacy had about it the brooding diffidence of a man waiting for something that had already happened. His campaign literature documented the false bravado that would become his political hallmark. It featured a photograph of "Our Mike," racket at the ready, with a caption trumpeting: "Wilson is an accomplished athlete and one of the few on Parliament Hill who beats Finance Minister Marc Lalonde at squash." That got the yuppie Rosedale vote sewn up, right there. All through Wilson's leaden leadership speech, the delegates assumed their sermon-enduring position, their mood altering between mild boredom and anxious despair. Wilson came in a poor fourth on the first ballot and walked over to support Mulroney. Or at least tried to: Wilson actually sauntered right past Mulroney's benches and was halfway to the Crosbie section when he noticed his gaffe and retraced his steps. Over at the Clark camp, an astounding 99.5 per cent of his first-ballot strength survived into the second round and his delegate support actually *increased* in the fourth ballot by 234 votes. But it wasn't enough.

Mulroney had the advantages of organizing skill, dedicated operatives spread around the country and a brand of political blarney that proved far more acceptable than the pedestrian mumbling of Joe Clark. Frank Moores, the former Newfoundland premier who took a poll of 1976 delegates, had discovered that Red Tories or Pink Tories did not take to Mulroney. That survey, plus Mulroney's business experience, shifted his position decidedly away from the more liberal side of the spectrum. His positions were not so much flexible as negotiable. He made peace with himself by explaining that he was "a caring, compassionate Conservative on social issues and a fiscal Conservative on money issues." On the fourth and final 1983 ballot, three-quarters of the party's right-wingers cast their ballots for him. The Progressive Conservative Party was his to command at last.

II

THE 1984 ELECTION THAT FOLLOWED turned out to be partly a love-in for Mulroney and partly a posthumous hate-in for the departed Pierre Trudeau. For almost sixteen punishing years, the Liberal philosopher-king had reminded Canadians how ungrateful they were for not appreciating his magical presence. When Mulroney's North Shore *habitant* face hove into view as an alternative it was welcomed like the coming of the green buds at the end of winter. Although most thoughtful voters recognized him as an amiable lightweight, something more fundamental happened during the election that only became clear to me when I attended an early-evening rally at a Calgary shopping centre. It started to rain. Even though he was getting soaked, Mulroney came out bareheaded and began dispensing campaign clichés like after-dinner mints. The audience not only lapped up the performance but umbrellas were collapsed as voters, presumably wanting to be blessed by the same raindrops—or at least not wanting to stay dry while he was getting wet—opted to join their candidate's dampened state. Unlike the remote and sepulchral Trudeau, Mulroney made political currency out of being one of the people; from the homespun values of respect for hard work, thrift and enterprise learned on an electrician's knee, to his dogged climb up the corporate ladder. He was careful to restrain his nostrums, however, before he had climbed beyond sight of the ordinary Canadian. Although he never emphasized rubbing shoulders with U.S. billionaires in quite the same way he recalled rubbing shoulders with the working men of Baie Comeau, neither did he apologize for his achievement. If he was a little slick and a little glib, it was forgiven in the climate of the 1980s. Unlike Trudeau, he had not been born to a Fine Old Family of privilege and did not disdain the wealth he enjoyed. Neither, of course, did he accept the *noblesse oblige* it entailed. If Mulroney represented the bottom-line revolutionary value of every one for themselves, then it was a value shared by that overwhelming majority of Canadians who pushed him through the doors of 24 Sussex Drive.

On election day, he won 211 of the Commons' 282 seats, earning a majority of the ballots in every province, a feat unrivalled in Canadian electoral history. It had been a magnificent sweep, inflicting on the Liberals their greatest-ever defeat. As Mulroney was driven to Government House to be sworn in as Canada's eighteenth prime minister, he took delight in the knowledge that no Liberal held power above the municipal level *anywhere in the country*. The proud new Tory prime minister was determined to prove to himself and his followers that this was not, as the philosopher-scientist Havelock Ellis once complained about a British election, "merely the exchange of one nuisance for another."

It appeared that Mulroney knew best how to touch that microchip in Canadians' souls which silently pleaded that no matter how serious their problems might be, they were not going to let their country go. Liberal leader John Turner's many equivocations during the campaign, including his ambivalence on the Manitoba language question, were no match for Mulroney's shillelagh Canadianism. Few noticed that massive as the Tory vote had been, it was based on extremely vulnerable foundations. The bulk of the Mulroney support had come from Liberals temporarily disillusioned with Trudeau's record and John Turner's shoddy performance. Their continued allegiance was entirely dependent on how favourably they would perceive Mulroney to govern.

Mulroney owed his political existence to being in opposition to Trudeau; his anti-Trudeau policies having defined his bases of

support in both the West and Quebec. But they defined it for altogether different and conflicting reasons. Though his background as
conciliator had allowed him to cobble an alliance of sorts between
the two regions, based on his ability to exploit their shared antipathy
to Trudeau, he offered little by way of vision or value which would
allow them to overcome their antipathy toward one another. This
"hollow man" syndrome was the fatal flaw of the Grand Mulroney
Coalition, based as it was on anti-Trudeau sentiment. An existence
only in opposition to something turns to vapour when that something disappears. Mulroney clung instead to a simpler notion: that
despite their nationalistic impulses, Quebeckers were looking for a
reason to stay in Canada—if they could do so with language rights
intact and recognition of their distinctiveness. And so, instead of
perpetuating Trudeau's toughness toward Quebec, he became the
great conciliator. Mulroney's tough speech on behalf of Manitoba
language rights the previous spring had been designed to curry
favour in Quebec and it had taken extraordinary courage in a party
that still reflected the glow of unreconstructed rednecks. He had also
won support in Quebec for choosing to run in Manicouagan, a
French-speaking constituency that had voted Conservative only
once in the previous fifty years. At the same time, he promised to
wipe out the dreaded National Energy Program and the Foreign
Investment Review Agency, which were hated in the West. It was a
form of levered trading and issue-bundling that had served him well
in labour negotiations and Mulroney saw every reason to apply it
to government.

Mulroney reckoned that the only way to run the country was to
form regional coalitions. That notion dated back to Sir John A.'s
"Grand Alliance of English and French, East and West." Sir Wilfrid
Laurier had realigned Canadian politics, with the Quebec axis
joined to progressive Ontario. Mackenzie King had revived the
West-Quebec partnership and Mulroney hoped to do the same.
Although he had said in 1983, while attacking Joe Clark's mild
flirtations with the Quebec nationalists, that "you don't get to
be leader of the Progressive Conservative Party of Canada by
playing footsie with the Parti Québécois," Mulroney proceeded to
do just that. He believed that the only way to negotiate an alliance
with the province's nationalists was to tame their more radical
impulses through a new-style, decentralized federalism. He

recruited several PQ organizers and such ultra-nationalist candidates as Marcel Masse (who, after a career in the federal cabinet defending Quebec interests through the insistence that Canadian Forces use Quebec maple syrup on their pancakes, would later head one of the independence commissions for Quebec Premier Jacques Parizeau), Suzanne Duplessis and the two Bouchards, Benoît and Lucien. He named former Pequiste ministers and the widow of René Lévesque to Ottawa patronage positions. The payoff for the nationalists was the statement for the Tory leader inspired by his then-close friend Lucien Bouchard, which became part of the speech Mulroney delivered on August 6, 1984, in Sept-Îles, referring to the fact that Quebec had been left out of the 1981 constitutional deal. He pledged that his government would broker a constitutional deal that would allow Quebec's National Assembly to "give its consent to the new Canadian Constitution with honour and enthusiasm."

Mulroney's support for Quebec nationalism provided one of the catalysts for Canada's Revolution. Even before he took office, Mulroney had talked himself into a trap. The Quebeckers who followed his colours went into federal politics to fight for greater Quebec autonomy and try as he might, Mulroney could never satisfy them. At the same time, every gesture toward Quebec worked against his western supporters, who were convinced he was promising Quebec too much. They did not share his enthusiasm for the art of the deal; neither did they understand why the elimination of one wrong (such as the National Energy Program) should require the imposition of another (such as special privilege for Quebec). Mulroney's great miscalculation was his belief that his personal charm and bargaining skills could overcome the tensions this created. By definition they could not, because these tensions ran directly against the grain of the very coalition he was trying to muster. Although this would ultimately lead to the personally and nationally disastrous Meech Lake and Charlottetown accords, the irony is that it was all so unnecessary. Mulroney didn't need to promise anything to the Quebec nationalists at the time. René Lévesque was at the point of abandoning separatism and the nationalists had nowhere else to go, as they were the sworn enemies of the party of Trudeau, and the New Democratic Party had no base in the province. He could have won most of Quebec by appealing directly to francophone Liberals, most of whom were disillusioned with the federal party and who saw Mulroney as one of their own.*

NONE OF THIS WAS APPARENT to Mulroney at the time; none of it was apparent to anyone around him. The only thing that mattered to Mulroney and the party he led was that the coalition seemed to be working, at least for a while. Nothing about his astounding sweep of 1984 pleased Mulroney more—and, as it later turned out, nothing would cause him more grief—than his unprecedented victory in Quebec. He won fifty-eight of the province's seventy-five seats and a greater share of the vote (50.3 per cent) than in True-Blue Ontario (47.4 per cent). The vaunted Liberal electoral organization in Quebec disintegrated in the face of the Conservative leader's inspired onslaught. This was an extraordinary development. In the previous election, the Liberals had swept the province, reducing the Tories to 12.6 per cent of the popular vote and one seat, the lowest margin since 1945, when the party received only 9.8 per cent of the ballot and no seats. Without Trudeau to rally them, the Liberal troops just weren't there in 1984. In contemptuous asides, Mulroney dismissed his Quebec-based Liberal opponents led by John Turner as "Chef Boy-Ar-Dee and his seventy-five noodles." Victory was for him the vindication of all those years spent plotting and hoping. Here was the breakthrough that Mulroney and most pundits believed would allow the Tories to replace the Liberals as Canada's "Natural Governing Party." No longer, he hoped, would Jack Pickersgill, the penguin-shaped guru of modern Canadian Liberalism, be able to dismiss Tory governments as being "like the mumps—something you have to endure once in your lifetime, but when it's over you don't ever want it again."

Louis Riel had received a decent burial at last.

---

* Bernard Roy, Mulroney's chief organizer in Quebec, secretly met every week in the run-up to the election with Pierre Bibeau, Robert Bourassa's campaign director; Bourassa himself ordered his troops to support Mulroney in his North Shore riding.

ONCE IN POWER, MULRONEY DISCOVERED that Canada wasn't the family of benign relatives he wanted it to be. The country instead revealed itself as a loose federation of hard-bitten regions. The newly elected prime minister's triumphant sweep resulted in less a wave of fresh energy and thought than a jetsam of new MPs washed up on Ottawa's shores with no clear destination and unsure how to get there. With most of his agenda, as Richard Gwyn put it, "written in invisible ink," Mulroney won power but he did not gain a mandate. In fact Mulroney did have a platform, and a good one, put together by senior policy advisers Charles McMillan and Jon Johnson. He even occasionally mentioned some of its policies. But nobody paid any attention. It was his cry, "Jobs! Jobs! Jobs!" that struck the responsive chord. "You're going to see tens upon tens of thousands of new jobs being created, just as quickly as a new government can be sworn in," Mulroney bellowed across the hustings. With 2.5 million unemployed Canadians looking for full-time work, nothing else mattered.

As he had done before and would do many times again, Mulroney damaged his reputation by having to retreat from his own hyperbole. By promising so much he was forced to trade between manoeuvrability and credibility—a deadly political option. In making that rash jobs promise, Mulroney had over-estimated the enlightenment of his friends in the private sector, believing they would respond to his call for a national crusade to modernize the Canadian economy and renew their entrepreneurial spirit. He bought his own rhetoric and believed that the Liberals had been deliberately destroying the economy by lowering the number of available jobs. Worse, he subscribed to all those super-cilious Chamber of Commerce valedictorians, Business Council on National Issues acolytes and Mount Royal Club habitués who had told him how the floodgates of capital investment would open once the voters had dumped Pierre Trudeau. He had done everything they asked—changed the investment climate, moved fiscal conser-vatives into power, declared Canada open for business—but nothing much happened.

The sour mood took a while to crystallize. Immediately after the election Canadians felt good about themselves and their country. Most citizens were pleased with their lot and their post-Trudeau prospects. Not just the mood but the very rhythm of Canadian politics seemed to change. The feeling of renewal and satisfaction at having finally kissed off sixteen years of Trudeau arrogance were comparable to the initial euphoria of Charles II's Restoration. Seldom, if ever, before had the nation's vested interests been so unanimous in their political preference. Ottawa's political newcomers were buoyed by their belief that much in government might be difficult but nothing was impossible. Ottawa journalist Roy MacGregor (later one of Mulroney's severest critics) reported that the nation's capital was beguiled by the new leader's style. "Like Ronald and Nancy Reagan, Brian and Mila Mulroney appear to radiate such middle-class sentiments as family, church, neighbourliness and earned success. Broad smiles, laughing eyes, crinkling nose and soothing voice may not have much to do with policy. But in terms of pure image there may be enough charm in the Mulroney family to buffer the deficit indefinitely." Gerald Caplan, a former secretary of the New Democratic Party and subsequently one of Mulroney's enemies, was filled with admiration for the new PM's political skills. "The man," he declared, "is a wonder." It was not only Mulroney who was guilty of hyperbole in the post-election euphoria.

Mulroney had demonstrated that there was nothing "natural" about Liberal hegemony and that the Conservatives could form a national government just as well as the Liberals. But few Tories, least of all their leader, had thought through the second part of that equation: govern, yes, but with what priorities? The air was filled with the scrip of political slogans, but the currency of political ideas remained remarkably devalued. One reason for this surprising lack of dynamism was the tension between the politicians and the senior civil service. Most bureaucrats had not been entirely happy with Trudeau and his people, but the two groups understood each other and found self-interest in supporting their mutual endeavours. The Tories remained outsiders. The bureaucracy was not committed to Mulroney, but neither was the new government captured by its senior mandarins in the way both Diefenbaker's and Clark's had been. The onus shifted to the prime minister. The bureaucrats, the good ones, waited for their marching orders and hoped the freshly minted PM would declare where he intended to lead

the country.* Instead, his office kept such a tight grip on the government's agenda that even many of the new cabinet ministers and their
staff felt they were little more than glorified messengers.

"One of the really, really striking things about the Mulroney years
was what happened to the public service," maintained Michael
Pitfield, who had been clerk of the Privy Council under Pierre
Trudeau. "We had built up a mythology based on the example of
Norman Robertson and Bob Bryce, a sense of high mission and a
belief in certain values, so that when a minister wanted to do this or
that, there was a process of trying to gauge whether that was within
the rules of the game. Sometimes, the prime minister himself
couldn't get things done the way he wanted, appointing a friend as
an ambassador, for example. But in the world of fear that came in
with Brian Mulroney, even the most senior public servants were
constantly being told: 'If you're not prepared to do it, I've got half a
dozen people who would like to have your job and we can put them
in there tomorrow morning.' All of a sudden people would do things
as ordered and there was no rudder. The rules that had been built up,
the checks and balances, went out the window."

Canadians had respected Pierre Trudeau for his decisiveness, but
in the tentative Ottawa climate he inherited, Mulroney started
slowly, then wound down. Allan Gregg, his pollster, had advised
him that Canadians wanted above all else an end to the bickering,
finger-pointing and federal-provincial shoot-outs that had marked
the Trudeau period. National reconciliation became the govern-

---

* A good example of how directionless Ottawa felt occurred in the
Department of Finance, which ought to have been at the forefront of
change. Mickey Cohen, its deputy minister, had been asked by
then–prime minister John Turner in 1984 to draw up an economic
agenda. The department did, working most of the summer to produce
a weighty, multi-volume document. The Liberal leader was defeated
before it could be presented to him. The new finance minister, Michael
Wilson, ordered an economic agenda of his own. When the brain trust
at Finance read Mulroney's campaign speeches, they decided that
little had changed from his predecessor. Having no orders to the contrary, they slapped a new title and cover on their previous study, *A New
Direction for Canada: An Agenda for Economic Renewal*, and presented it to Wilson. It became the finance minister's cornerstone of
Conservatives' economic policy.

ment's religion, Mulroney its high priest. His operating principle followed the axiom of medical pioneer Dr. Thomas C. Cullen who, when asked by one of his patients what he planned to do in a forthcoming operation, replied: "As little as possible—and as much as necessary." That turned out to be lethal advice, because it got translated into a lack of decisive action. The government lost its momentum; the people, who had been demanding change, saw only delay. Departmental initiatives were shunted off to commissions and study groups. The imaginative economic policies suggested by advisers McMillan and Johnson were shelved. "If there is anything lacking around here," complained Don Mazankowski, the most capable of Mulroney's ministers, "it's innovation."

The public grew restive because of unfulfilled expectation and the only explanation offered by the media were the personal flaws of Mulroney himself. The rebellious mood accelerated as the government began to suffer from bloopers major and minor. Mulroney had told a Hamilton radio interviewer, Tom Cherrington, that (unlike Trudeau) he would not charge the state with the costs of a nanny. The name of Elizabeth MacDonald subsequently appeared on the payroll of 24 Sussex Drive. Into the breach stepped Fred Doucet, the senior adviser to the prime minister, to explain with a straight face that MacDonald was not a nanny, she was an employee who "interfaced with the children on a habitual basis." At the same time, Transport Minister Don Mazankowski was fantasizing in public about "bringing romance back to train travel." Weeks later Finance Minister Michael Wilson tabled the first of VIA Rail's eviscerating cuts. In succession like a speeded-up Keystone Kops two-reeler, seven cabinet ministers were fired (or resigned minutes before they were told to leave) for stupidity, conflict of interest, dishonesty or all three.* The way these crises were handled was reminiscent of former Israeli Foreign Minister Abba Eban's jibe that, "for a government to repeat its mistakes is permissible—but not mandatory."

---

* They included Defence Minister Bob Coates, Fisheries Minister John Fraser, Minister of State for Transportation Suzanne Blais-Grenier, Industry Minister Sinclair Stevens, Minister of State for Transportation André Bisonnette, Public Works Minister Roch LaSalle and Supply and Services Minister Michel Côté.

Tom Kierans, head of the C.D. Howe Institute and one of the few thoughtful iconoclasts within Canada's business community, offered this explanation: "Mulroney's background left him totally unsuited to deal with the country's problems; especially from Ottawa, which is like passing into a spaceship, it has so little to do with how Canadian society actually works. You can't go from the corporate boardroom to the prime ministership and know what the hell you're doing. Mulroney may have been qualified to negotiate free trade, but he had no more idea how to reform social policy than how to fly to the moon. He sat there, isolated in this crazy vacuum called Ottawa, listening to all the special-interest groups as if they represented the country, or any part of it. He got out of touch. The country was changing—race, creed, colour, male-female—and most of the people he talked to were totally irrelevant. He didn't have any touch-stones. I mourned his lack of political sensibility."

Within eighteen months of coming to office with the largest mandate ever, the Tories were trailing badly in the public opinion polls. "Just a year after their victory," wrote Robert Fulford, the editor of *Saturday Night*, "the Tories were in disarray. They had become a kind of national joke, somehow transformed from tri- umphant conquerors into rather pitiful incompetents. Their actual mistakes were not in themselves calamitous. What mattered more was the atmosphere in which the Tories, and particularly the prime minister, dealt with these issues. They hesitated, they fudged, they issued contradictory statements, then contradicted themselves again. By their incompetence they managed to turn each issue into a ques- tion of integrity. It quickly became obvious that the government had no reservoir of goodwill on which to draw."

So many things went wrong so quickly for Mulroney that it brought to mind the curse of Sir Robert Borden, whose embattled administration suffered similar travails, climaxing in 1916 when the Parliament buildings burned down. "What else?" Borden demanded, as he watched the flames consume his office. "What else can happen to this goddamned government?"*

---

* Joe Clark wrote at length to Brian Mulroney in 1985, warning him about some of the trends that threatened to overwhelm the Tory administration and how they might be reversed. For a text of the Clark letter, see Appendix 2 (Sincerely, Joe).

MULRONEY'S TRADE, TAX AND CONSTITUTIONAL policies represented fundamental changes in the way the country had operated for the previous 120 years. Introducing shifts of that magnitude without the necessary massaging of public opinion left most Canadians puzzled, angry and ultimately, rebellious. Mulroney had pledged to encourage national reconciliation, economic renewal, social justice and constructive internationalism. He did all four, but his agenda was soon overtaken by events and instead of calibrated steps along a legislative ladder, his government lurched from crisis to crisis to crisis.

One of Mulroney's political liabilities was his tendency to take personal control of his ministers' many pratfalls. At flash points in past administrations, prime ministers such as King, St. Laurent, Diefenbaker, Pearson and Trudeau would cut away from their politically bleeding colleagues, demand their resignations and then carry on, as if they had never even known their names. Mulroney too often backed his offending ministers beyond reasonable doubt as to their competence or honesty and as a result, he became a national lightning rod. His time in office turned out to be a long siege marked by few calm interludes.

A conservative by temperament and inclination, Mulroney might have been expected to hunker down and do as little as possible. Instead, he behaved like an obsessive beekeeper, walking around the buzzing apiary of Canada punching holes into every hive he could find. More often than not, he was stung by the bees he had set loose. Mulroney turned out to be the most radical of Canadian prime ministers—in the precise meaning of that word, as one who "goes to the root of things and advocates fundamental changes." Mulroney was condemned for being a political opportunist, and he was—yet he spent much time and energy championing causes that carried no political benefits, only electoral costs.

Mulroney had long been preoccupied with making Canada's economy more competitive. He subscribed to the dictum attributed to Abraham Lincoln: "You cannot help the wage-earner by pulling down the wage-payer, or help the poor by destroying the rich." The problem was that such ideas ran against the reality of Canada's economy in the early 1990s, which was in the harshest recession since the 1930s. Nothing else mattered but creating new jobs, but as French President François Mitterrand had earlier pointed out, "Employment no longer responds to governments—and I mean governments in the plural." Mulroney promised too much, which placed him in the impossible position of trying to please an electorate with federal fiscal resources that had become not just modest, but extinct.

It became more apparent the longer he stayed in office that his style was out of step with the times. As a labour lawyer, he had concluded dozens of negotiations by gathering the contending parties in a locked room to bash a few heads together and cut a deal. Everyone then walked out arm in arm, the dispute settled, the factory gates reopened. But countries aren't factories and the body politic is a fragile creature. His style of bargaining required lightning adjustments which threatened people's sense of security. His lawyer's habit of treating each case *ad hoc* meant his government's various policy initiatives seldom reinforced each other. For example, it was perfectly valid to argue that deficit reduction created jobs and that the billions poured into Hibernia created jobs, and Mulroney supported both—even though they contradicted one another.

Canadians grew suspicious of the way Mulroney exercised power as they lived through a series of national debates which were mainly negotiated behind closed doors. That mood was encouraged by his threats—such as that September, 1992, day in Sherbrooke, Quebec, when he tore up a sheet of paper representing the Charlottetown Accord and shouted: "If we vote 'No,' we rip up these historic gains!" His boasting didn't help, either, such as his declaration that he was solely responsible for Canada's first-place ranking in a United Nations quality-of-life survey ("Canada is number one. Not number fourteen or forty-one. Number one! Not bad for a guy from Baie Comeau!") At the same time he crowed about how affluent he had made the country, he came to personify the malignant recession that blighted the land in the early 1990s, a trend made worse by the public's perception of his and Mila's luxurious personal spending.* As the cumulative effect of these suspicions grew, almost nothing Mulroney did found favour with the voters. His administration's

---

* Despite accusations that the Progressive Conservative Party paid for his furniture, Mulroney personally spent $211,796.68 for most of the interior decorating and furnishing at 24 Sussex Drive, as documented by the exchange of letters reproduced in Appendix 3 (Paying His Way).

pratfalls brought to mind the refrain of blues singer Albert King: "If it weren't for bad luck, baby, I'd have no luck at all."

DESPITE THIS SOUR MOOD, IT WAS one of Mulroney's greatest achievements that during the nine years his MPs shared the toboggan slide of his popularity ratings, there was never a caucus revolt.* He achieved this rare harmony by spending an extraordinary amount of time and energy wooing his own troops. When he and Mila finished a gruelling tour of eastern Quebec in the summer of 1992, they learned of the death of Mona Darling, the wife of the oldest member of the Conservative caucus, Stan Darling. The Mulroneys flew by government jet to the northern Ontario town of Burks Falls and arrived, un-announced, during the funeral service. Mulroney was fond of Darling, but he was also aware of the message his surprise attendance would send to Tory backbenchers: "If Brian will take that much trouble to salute old Stan, he'd do it for me." And he did. Nearly every backbencher had his own story to tell. The late Bob Wenman, MP for Fraser Valley West, had been in Brandon, Manitoba, on a private visit in 1991, for example, when his father called to tell him that his mother had died suddenly; within the hour, while the senior Wenman was still on the line notifying other family members, Mulroney was on the phone to Brandon expressing his sympathy.

Mulroney retained the loyalty of his troops, in the face of enemy fire by the opposition and the press, with a lot more than phone calls. Next to his family, Mulroney had no higher priority than his caucus. The PM could get tough, such as the time he insisted that the caucus sanction the rights of homosexuals to serve in the armed forces. "All right," he told them, "statistics tell us that 10 per cent of the population is homosexual, and since we in the Conservative Party are representative of the population, there are at least twenty gays in this room. Am I wrong? Is there a flaw in my logic? Are you ready to deprive these people of their rights?" His bravura performances at the Wednesday caucus meetings were rated for their rhetorical "blarney

---

* Prior to the Bloc Québécois defections late in his term, there was only one resignation—backbencher Patrick Nowlan—and two expulsions—David Kilgour and Alex Kindy. The two Alberta Tory MPs had refused to support the GST.

index" by some of its pranksters, who held up score cards like figure-
skating judges, yet his consultations with caucus were genuine and
policies were often changed on the spot; the connection with his parliamentary group had a healthy two-way flow to it. He asked each MP
to write him an annual letter, outlining any complaints or recommendations. He read each missive and dictated personal replies; he also
invited caucus members for breakfasts at 24 Sussex Drive and tended
to their welfare as though they were extended family. "You can only
weather the violent attacks to which I was subjected if your caucus
tells you none of it is true," he once explained. "If *you* have to tell *them*
it's not true, you're in trouble. Under the British parliamentary system, it doesn't matter what the press gallery thinks of you, or even
what the country thinks of you, so long as your caucus continues to
support you. Then you have time to regroup. What happened to Joe
Clark at the Winnipeg review in 1983 had nothing to do with the party;
he resigned because he understood that his caucus wouldn't follow
him. They saw him every Wednesday, and figured he wasn't a leader."

While the caucus support strengthened Mulroney's hand inter-
nally, it left him overly protected from what was happening in the
real world beyond Ottawa's ramparts. By capturing the hearts and
minds of his followers, he allowed little room for them to convey to
him the mounting anger sweeping the land. Few whispers of
Revolution were heard in Mulroney's corridors of power.

Mulroney was further protected from voters by his personal staff,
which at one point swelled to more than 200. They often acted as if
their main responsibility was to keep him away from ordinary
people with genuine problems. Even his forays into the hinterland,
designed to establish contact between the governor and the governed, were scripted so tightly that Mulroney resembled a pontiff
being shunted around in his hermetically sealed Popemobile. Events
were scheduled in such trivial detail that a simple elevator ride
required a manifest, vetted and in triplicate. A day's timetable could
run to sixty pages, which made for orderly prime ministerial proces-
sions but left hardly a minute for spontaneous mingling.*

---

* For three typical itineraries, see Appendix 4 (The Presidential PMO).
  Mulroney's presidential style was partly because he appeared to be governing alone. A 1992 Gallup Poll showed 34 per cent of Canadians
  couldn't name a single Mulroney cabinet minister.

Nothing was left to chance. His advance team was told he would never wear a hat of any kind, that he did not want to be touched, hugged or kissed in public and that he never, ever jumped on trampolines or caught footballs. He was to appear perfect, not a hair out of place, shirts freshly starched, pants pleated sharply enough to cut Wonderbread. When Mulroney hosted a nationally televised economic conference in Ottawa in 1985, Mila called his office to tell them there was an air vent over his head. "It's blowing his hair all over the place," she complained. "Turn it off!" One aide was bold enough to tell her: "Look, it's not that terrible for people to see his hair out of place. He's human. He's not made of plastic—his hair flutters in the wind." Not that wind; the vent was shut. Dress codes even applied to country retreats with Cabinet. There he would dress down for television, becoming aggressively informal by donning a sweater. Unfortunately, the sweaters he chose (or had Mila choose for him) looked straight off the rack from the Via Condotti in Rome.

Mulroney did not want to appear too human in public, especially on formal occasions, in case it weakened his authority. Faced with the routine chore of laying a wreath on a cenotaph, for instance, he would rehearse every vowel and consonant of his body language— when to turn left, whose hand to shake, how vigorously to shake it. He told himself this was necessary to maintain the dignity of his office and to avoid offending anyone's sense of history or protocol. That may have been his motive, but he succeeded in making himself look as though he were encased in concrete.

His immaculate conception of politics sprang from those long sessions with Daniel Johnson of Quebec's Union Nationale, who had taught him that political leaders reassure their subjects by not appearing in the least vulnerable. There was nothing much wrong with this heroic notion in its time, except that by the 1990s it had become dated. It was a Mulroney paradox that his *rigor mortis* poses for the public were so patently phoney, while in private he was warm and amusing, especially when he trotted out his self-deprecating wit. "I try to avoid popularity like the plague," he loved to tell friends in his second term, "and I've been reasonably successful at it." Joking about his patronage, he would say: "We practise neither nepotism nor extravagance at 24 Sussex. It's true, we did put in a dumbwaiter, but it was the least we could do for Uncle Larry." At the 1987 parliamentary press gallery dinner, just after reports of his Gucci shoes had been published, he began by apologizing he was late. "We had a family crisis," he explained. "Nicholas was lost for three hours in my shoe closet. The kid obviously doesn't have much sophistication. We found him in the Wallabee section . . . When I heard about *The Globe* article on my loafers, I didn't pay much attention. I thought it was just another negative story about my staff."

He invited a few friends to his country residence at Harrington Lake every New Year's Eve, always including Governor-General Ramon Hnatyshyn and his wife, Gerda. At the 1991 party, when Mulroney was down to 12 per cent on the public approval meter, Hnatyshyn tried to console him with a story. "When I was energy minister in the Clark government in 1979," he recalled, "I was working eighteen hours a day. I got a call from Saskatoon to come home right away, because my dog—my old, faithful retainer of eleven years—had just died. When I got home, the kids wanted $285 in cash to provide perpetual care for the dog in a nearby animal cemetery. I agreed, but a few weeks later the local CBC station exposed the fact that the cemetery was all a scam.

"To prove their point, the camera zoomed in on the headstone of my dog, which read: 'Tippy *Hynythishin*.' Having misspelled my name, they as well had provided no care, perpetual or otherwise. My whole political life flashed before me. Who was going to vote for a boob who had parted with $285 like a village idiot? Well, I received a hundred letters of support commending me for being an animal lover. I even got an offer of an honorary life membership in the Saskatoon Kennel Club."

At this point in his story, Hnatyshyn turned to the prime minister and said: "Brian, you're only 12 per cent in the polls. I can arrange to have your dog killed."

Mulroney looked hard at his black poodle and in feigned sympathy, told his favourite pooch: "That's it, Clover. I love you, but you're a goner."

IT WAS A RARE MOMENT of fun. Mulroney's tenure was characterized by few high points and many troughs—none lower than his feelings about the loss of the Meech Lake Accord. Few entries in his private journal were more emotional than the one for January 13, 1991, when he first expressed his anguish at having lost the Meech Lake Accord six months earlier.

"Last night I told Mila of an enormous sadness in my heart that I have carried since Wells's decision to sabotage Meech Lake," he wrote. "It is like a dark cloud that smothers the joy one would normally associate with the privilege of being Prime Minister of such a great country.

"For thirty years, I have felt that the successful resolution of the question, 'What does Quebec want?' would solidify the federation once and for all. The danger with 1981–1982 was that, unlike 1867, Quebec was no longer a willing partner in the agreement on Confederation. Indeed, by proceeding without Quebec, Trudeau gave rise to a new argument that Quebec could perhaps one day make, that since they never signed the 1982 convention they were neither morally nor legally bound by it. Accordingly, they would claim, 'We are not in violation of national or international law if we secede, because we never formally accepted the Constitution in the first place.' Such an argument by Quebec in regard to the B.N.A. Act would have been nulled back then. Twice, in 1987 and then again in 1990, we achieved unanimity, although the 1990 document was qualified by Newfoundland and Manitoba.

"Meech was not perfect and it no doubt would have given rise to some controversy in the future. But by signing Meech, Bourassa truly became a Canadian and would have been forced by circumstances to defend his signature—hence Canada—against the onslaught of the anti-federalists. His enthusiasm for fence-sitting would have been dramatically lessened, because by signing the document he took himself off the fence forever. History would have viewed him as a Canadian nation-builder. Wells destroyed the Bourassa position and the Bourassa legacy as a Canadian nation-builder. Wells may well have forced Bourassa into a process where the nation that emerges is not Canada, but two Canadas, both diminished and forever banal, as living proof of the failure of honourable compromise.

"When reason is replaced by ideology, the essential dynamic of a federation as a living, changing political entity has been fundamentally stunted. The greatest irony of Canadian history may turn out to be the one underlined by Jack Pickersgill privately. Namely, 'Pick' says it was a Québécois, Louis St. Laurent, who engineered the compromises that in 1949 enabled Newfoundland to enter Confederation. It was a Newfoundlander, Clyde Wells, who repudiated the compromises in 1990 which encouraged Quebec to leave

Confederation. All of this does not lessen my own personal sense of grief for Canada. The experience, since June, has been like a death in the family and I have not been able to shake fully the feeling of loss. To have come so close twice and to have it snatched away so needlessly, to satisfy the vanity and arrogance of a few who have themselves failed to bring unity when they were in office, is like a throbbing pain that refuses to go away..."

One person who wasn't the least surprised by Clyde Wells's reversal was Mila Mulroney. She had kept her eyes on the Newfoundland premier during the signing ceremony for the Meech Lake Accord and, on the drive home to Sussex Drive, she told her husband: "He's going to betray you and betray the country. There's something in his eyes that I don't like, that doesn't ring true." She was Mulroney's sanctuary during the toils and troubles of the Canadian Revolution, intuitively comprehending the rebellious mood sweeping the land much better than he could. Thirteen years his junior, but politically mature beyond her years—and in most ways, wise beyond her station—she was his *de facto* chief adviser and character reader. Brian Mulroney was a loner who couldn't stand being alone, and the only person he trusted with his secrets was his wife. With her outgoing manner, crinkling nose and expensive outfits, she played the role of Canada's glamorous First Lady to the presidential prime minister, but she could also be tough. She set boundaries on Mulroney's restless ambitions, rhetorical excesses and diverse impulses, because she alone could contradict him without bruising his ego. She was also very funny.*

Mulroney was persistently criticized for wanting to be loved instead of respected. This was a basic misunderstanding of the political process; sometimes, making the right enemies is essential and making—or rewarding—the wrong friends can be deadly.† The

---

* For the text of Mila Mulroney's speech to a Tory insiders' gathering at the Tulip Valley Motel in Wakefield, Quebec, just prior to her husband's resignation, see Appendix 5 (Gentlemen, That Reminds Me).

† When Voltaire was on his deathbed, an attending priest asked whether he was ready to renounce the Devil. The great sage looked surprised, then shook his head. "This," he whispered, "is no time to make new enemies."

gridlock of distrust that enveloped him grew out of his own insecurity. Despite his quick wit, sartorial elegance and compulsion for civility, he never managed to communicate warmth except to those genuinely close to him. Mulroney remained a politician in search of his own approval. It took him several weeks, for example, to fully realize that he had actually won the 1984 election and was the prime minister of Canada. He recalled responding to a letter from Fidel Castro congratulating him on his election sweep a month earlier: "I remember very clearly thinking, 'I must be prime minister,' because I was signing a letter to Castro and it dawned on me that this was not something I did every day." Perhaps it was such ambivalent feelings that drove him so often to edit his memory and rearrange the past.

MOST OF THE PUBLIC'S PERCEPTIONS of Mulroney were filtered through the Canadian media, whose suspicions of his character were matched only by his suspicions of their motives. Smelling the scent of blood on unkept promises, sensing their prey approach the trap built upon their own exaggerated praise when he was first elected, parliamentary press gallery reporters began to lie in wait for Mulroney. Most reporters just plain didn't like him—he didn't share their cosy paradigms; he had not come up through the appropriate apprenticeship. Almost to its last member, the press gallery shared the sensibilities and prejudices of Trudeau's Ottawa; while its members claimed to agree with the public's disdain for the Liberal regime, it had in fact become their familiar home. It was the land beyond Ottawa, which was strange and alien to them, that had given them Mulroney. Unlike Trudeau, whom the media claimed (rightly) to have created, Mulroney had won the election all by himself. He was an interloper who owed the press nothing, which doubled their fury. Furthermore, Trudeau had always, much as he was the creation of the press, affected a disdain for it. Trudeau was not one of them; he sprang from a different culture and class which allowed him to exploit the distance of power between himself and his critics. Mulroney lacked such distance. He stressed his common roots, not his corporate connections. He read his reviews and remarked upon them—angrily and publicly— which showed the press his soft underbelly. He claimed to be just like them, which allowed the press to treat him as shabbily as they habitually treated one another.

This confrontation contributed significantly to the government's inability to communicate its intentions—vague as they were—so that gradually, no matter what Mulroney said or did, his message was filtered through the personal animus of the media. Within months of his taking office, the press would pay far more attention to the size of his clothes closet than the size of the national debt. That set the stage for one essential precondition of a revolutionary climate, which is the demonization of authority.

It was a decade when perception took precedence over reality and the messengers became the message. The media's operational code switched from access to aggression, from objectivity to objecting. Instead of interpreting personalities and events, journalists became players in Canadian politics. The trend originated with Bob Woodward and Carl Bernstein, the two *Washington Post* reporters who uncovered the Watergate scandal that deposed Richard Nixon. The problem was that instead of being another Woodward or Bernstein, who brought their quarry to ground with enormous amounts of research, most journalists succeeded only in aspiring to be Robert Redford and Dustin Hoffman, who portrayed them in the glamourized Hollywood film version. The line between news and entertainment grew increasingly fuzzy. So-called "investigative reporting," with a few exceptions, meant imposing a predetermined narrative to a story, with a villain being unmasked whether the evidence warranted one or not. No one, for example, seemed to sense any contradiction in attacking Mulroney for cravenly seeking popularity at a time when all the evidence showed he was pursuing the least popular agenda since Genghis Khan. "I'm not sure that Mulroney got a fair shake from the media," said former CBC national news reporter Christopher Walmsley. "In the 1980s, Ottawa was invaded by scores of young, new reporters eager to make their reputations. Few had a decent, fundamental grounding in political science, economics or history. This basic lack of education showed, and still does. There were many, myself included, who wandered around Parliament reporting on subjects we really didn't understand. It wasn't fair. It wasn't very good journalism, and I left because it was like that."

Mulroney certainly displayed little neutrality on the subject. "Anybody who goes to the Montreal *Gazette* library [for example] and pushes a button to call up what they've written about me in the past ten years will not find one favourable adjective," he complained. "I bet even Hitler had someone write a favourable adjective about him in a decade—maybe he said hello to somebody one day, and it was recorded. What happened was a conspiracy of weakness, a collapse of professional ethics in the Ottawa journalistic fraternity where anyone who wanted to say a single favourable thing about me was knee-capped by the knee-cappers, so it became fashionable to be on the other side." Apart from his press clippings, Mulroney's evidence was an unpublished survey by Peter Snow, a professor at the University of Western Ontario Graduate School of Journalism that showed 53 per cent of 118 national journalists surveyed thought of themselves as being close to the NDP and Liberals, while only 11 per cent identified with the Tories.

But the problem was much more complicated than that. For one thing, the affiliation of press gallery members did not, according to the polls, vary widely from the sentiments of the Canadian public at large. After the first few run-ins, Mulroney rarely made himself available to the press. He didn't hold a single news conference in Ottawa between January 18, 1987, and March 20, 1989, a record equalled only by one other head of government, President Ramiz Alia of Albania. "Many reporters tended to regard anything Mulroney said or did with a mixture of suspicion and cynicism—he rarely received the benefit of the doubt," wrote Allan Levine, the Winnipeg academic, in *Scrum Wars: The Prime Ministers and the Media*.

Fed up with what he considered to be a raw deal, Mulroney periodically announced to his inner circle that he was finished with the media and henceforth would never again look at a newspaper or watch the television news. His resolve occasionally lasted a whole day, but never into the late evening. Unknown to all but Mila, he went to sleep on a special, speaker-equipped pillow that allowed him to listen to the short-wave radio news long into the night. "It's a little flat plastic thing which tucks under, so the whole pillow talks to you," Mila explained. "I rued the day he got it, but I had to eat my words because once or twice that stupid little radio saved the day. We were at the Commonwealth Conference in Kuala Lumpur when Brian happened to tune into a BBC press conference that Margaret Thatcher was giving, in which she retracted her support of the sanctions against South Africa she had previously supported in Brian's presence, which helped him deal with the issue the next day."

Mulroney was not just an avid media consumer, he was, as Robert Sheppard wrote in *The Globe and Mail*, "a news junkie. He snorted stories and commentary as if it were the kind of stuff that gets seized at the border."* He hated journalists, but never stopped trying to influence or anticipate them. It was an inside joke among his advisers that if they wanted to change his mind on an issue, they would hint that Craig Oliver had been overheard discussing it with Mike Duffy and the pair thought the government ought to reconsider its policy—in the direction the adviser wanted.

Among Mulroney's least favourite journalists was Don McGillivray, a columnist for Southam News. There was a subtext involved that the prime minister knew nothing about. When Mulroney would wax eloquent about the francophone contribution to Canada, he would sometimes invoke another great Tory, the Hon. Pierre Sévigny, who had "left his leg for his country on the shores of Normandy during the Second World War." Sévigny's leg was actually in McGillivray's living room. After the war, Sévigny used an artificial limb which eventually wore out and had to be replaced. The McGillivrays lived down the street and his daughter found it in the garbage. She dragged the artificial limb home because it looked interesting. McGillivray used it to stoke his living-room fireplace. He never interrupted the PM's colourful anecdote, but to the rhetorical question, "What would I say to Pierre Sévigny, who left his leg in France?", McGillivray was often tempted to reply: "Tell him it's in my living room and it makes a good fireplace poker." Among Mulroney's severest critics was Allan Fotheringham, the *Maclean's* columnist, who had once been a close friend and had given Mila a croquet set for her birthday. "Sometimes," she later confessed, "I feel like giving the goddamn croquet set right back to him..."

---

* His interest in the media was truly obsessive. I remember being told a story by a man called Hyslop who had interviewed him on a local television station, deep in Hammond Organ country around Chatham, Ontario. Hyslop happened to mention to the prime minister that his sons were learning French and that one of them was the camera operator. When he returned to speak to the Chatham Rotary Club a year later, Mulroney was interviewed by someone else, though the same camera operator was on the set. As Mulroney left, he walked by the camera stand, and said: "So, how's my French connection in Chatham?" The operator was left gasping in disbelief.

Mulroney's most infamous quote was his explanation to Jeffrey Simpson, Graham Fraser and Susan Delacourt of *The Globe and Mail* how he had planned the timing of Meech Lake to give it the best chance of approval. "It's like an election campaign; you count backwards," he recalled. "I said, 'That's the day we're going to roll the dice.'" Ironically, Mulroney had telephoned William Thorsell, the newspaper's editor-in-chief, offering to be interviewed because he felt that the press had not given him enough credit for hammering out the Meech agreement. "The interview was amiable, and from our perspective, deliberately so," Simpson recalled. "We knew that with Trudeau, for example, it was often best to be aggressive, since that might elicit the most information. With Mulroney, it was obvious that he loved to talk about himself and his triumphs. Since he had just recorded one, or so he thought, and had phoned Thorsell to brag about it and relive it, we deliberately decided to offer him soft questions so that he would be relaxed, self-congratulatory, and revelatory—which of course he was. The rest, as they say, is history."

Television provided the dominant image of Mulroney. He came to office just as TV was becoming the media of instant record, with CNN and CBC Newsworld keeping the country on constant alert. Every Canadian living room became a whispering gallery, with political events flashed from coast to coast as they happened—well, not quite as they happened, since each tightly edited item was squished between the reporter's commentary. Public information was so condensed that there was no shade of subtlety or nuance, with news bites reduced from an average of one minute in the early 1970s to twenty seconds by the 1990s. At the same time, there was something unnerving about Mulroney whenever he appeared on television. The camera's glass eye made him act like a small-town boy awed by having become prime minister. His eyes darted like minnows from one lens to the next, his mouth forming a tight loop that betrayed the fact he was running scared.*

---

* Worried about his television image, Mulroney invited well-known New York speech consultant Dorothy Sarnoff for a secret taping session at Harrington Lake in the summer of 1986. Her verdict, announced to Mulroney's communications director Bruce Philips: "This guy is probably the greatest communicator in the world of politics today, better than Reagan or Thatcher, and he can do it in two languages."

Television is always a witness for the prosecution. It is an X-ray of character, reflecting the grave and complex quality of inner disposition. To survive its exposure requires a rock-solid sense of oneself, which was never Mulroney's long suit. Television is a hot medium that works best for those who speak in cool, passionless tones; it is not the ideal arena for a fiery orator like Mulroney.

"THERE WAS A DISTASTE in the gallery for ostentation, extravagance and especially gross patronage," wrote *Sun* newspaper columnist Douglas Fisher, one of the most thoughtful Ottawa journalists. "Even on his first run at the Tory top, Mulroney had been wildly extravagant. In power, he engrained his profligate image." Nothing damaged Mulroney more deeply than the patronage he dispensed to his friends and supporters. Late in 1984, some of his closest buddies—Patrick MacAdam, Guy Charbonneau, Sam Wakim, Michel Cogger and a few others—were having dinner in the Senate Speaker's Gallery, where the wood panelling is carved with Latin inscriptions. Late in the evening they were speculating what the words meant, when they were brought up short by Wakim, who announced: "I don't know about you guys, but I was never that good in Latin. The way I see it, this stuff on the walls means: *Thank God for patronage!*"

Within the first year of taking office, Mulroney had made more than 1,000 political appointments.* There was nothing haphazard about the process. Yukon, for example, had eight one-hundredths of Canada's population and received eight one-hundredths of the job hand-outs. The first three directors Mulroney named to the board of Canadian National were a black man from Toronto, a Ukrainian farmer from Draper, Alberta, and a francophone woman from northern Ontario. No one's nose was too dirty for the trough. Few MPs gave Mulroney more trouble than Winnipeg's Dan McKenzie, who was unalterably opposed to bilingualism and had, in fact, been fired by the PM as a parliamentary secretary. But when McKenzie retired before the 1988 election, he agreed to take on the onerous responsibility of becoming a one-man task force to report on the prospects of economic association between Canada and the

---

* For a breakdown, see Appendix 6 (You Had An Option).

Caribbean islands of Turks and Caicos, advertised in tourist brochures as "The Islands of Perpetual June."

What made Mulroney's patronage orgies worse than those of his Liberal predecessors was the fact that he had come to power promising fundamental reforms. "They have dishonoured the system," he said of the Grits, "and it shall never happen again with a Conservative government." Even as he was attacking John Turner for rubber-stamping Trudeau's final paroxysm of patronage, Mulroney's own patronage machine—skippered by his deputy leader, Erik Nielsen—was already operational. A full two months before that memorable televised election debate, Nielsen was recruiting provincial advisory committees to suggest the names of eligible Tory patronage appointees and had already planned for the dismissal of eleven serving federal deputy ministers and six senior diplomats. Seven weeks later—and still twelve days *before* the televised debate—Nielsen sent out letters urging the provincial committees to round up patronage candidates.* Although he portrayed himself in his autobiography, *The House Is Not a Home*, as the slayer of "patronage, political favouritism and influence-peddling, wherever I found them," Nielsen not only greased the process, he didn't do that badly by it himself. He asked Mulroney to appoint him chairman of the National Transportation Agency, a seven-year appointment that carried a salary of $143,000 (later raised to $155,000) plus $44,000 in fringe benefits; on top of a special retirement package and his $40,000 parliamentary pension. Refusing to work out of the agency's offices in Hull, Quebec, Nielsen rented a luxurious suite in downtown Ottawa, for $333,490 a year—at government expense.

Mulroney made many good appointments, but they were outweighed by the sheer volume of his bad ones. Denyse Patry, his former secretary from the Iron Ore Company of Canada, for example, was appointed to the board of the Canada Council although her only administrative experience was founding the Baie Comeau chapter of Weight Watchers. When a Tory municipal politician named Gayle Christie was named to the board of Air Canada, she confessed to a reporter that her only relevant experience was being *able to drive a*

---

* For Nielsen's secret memo suggesting future patronage slots and how the system would work under the Tory government, see Appendix 7 (Sincerely, Erik).

car. The strangest attempt at Tory patronage took place on June 25, 1984, just after the Liberals had chosen John Turner as their leader and Jean Chrétien seemed to be facing an uncertain future. Fred Doucet, who was then Mulroney's chief of staff, recorded his thoughts that day: "Just came back from Stornaway, where I suggested to Brian that possibly he would like to check with Jean Chrétien since our news is that Jean is having a tough time settling for the terms that Turner is offering him. My suggestion is based on the fact that there's nothing to lose. We call Jean and suggest to him that he would be well looked after later, in terms of an appointment. If Chrétien stays with the Liberals and accepts Turner's offer, there would still be some gains in that Chrétien would see a measure of kindness extended his way in these, his tough times—and this would help us either way. We don't think he will accept any of the offers [but] we think there are some points to be made by chatting with him and we're going to do that tonight...[Mulroney] has now spoken with Jean Chrétien and confirms our suspicions that indeed, he is not very happy, he's a pretty disgruntled man, but however bad that might be, he still remains a Liberal . . . We still think that there was something positive in chatting with him."

Those Mulroney supporters that didn't share directly in his wealth of patronage shared the wealth available to Ottawa lobbyists. Operating below the radar range of public opinion, they minted fortunes from the sale of access to the PM and his ministers. Harry Near, once an aide to Pat Carney, made so much money lobbying that he built himself a pretentious mansion in Rockcliffe Park, the ritzy Ottawa suburb. His mansion-warming, attended by most of Cabinet, produced one of the great quotes of the Mulroney era. Harvie Andre, who as minister of corporate and consumer affairs was one of the lobbyists' chief targets, stepped into the marbled foyer of Near's Alcazar and mused aloud: "I've never understood why it's so much more profitable to *know* Harvie Andre than to *be* Harvie Andre." Among the most successful lobbyists was Gerald Doucet (Fred's brother), who started out with Frank Moores's Government Consultants International, but sold his one-third share to Pierre Bourque for $1.2 million in 1989.*

---

* For a sampling of Doucet's fawning correspondence with Brian Mulroney, see Appendix 8 (Thou Swell).

CANADIANS HAD EXPECTED BRIAN MULRONEY to be their king, father, confessor, sugar daddy, favourite uncle. They expected it because he had promised all that, and more. As with the initial flush of any romance, there was a willing disregard for obvious truth. Mulroney was none of those things: he was an ambitious power-seeker with a flawed understanding of the country; he was a masterful deal-maker who had cobbled together an unworkable coalition based on an impossible premise; he was a well-intentioned road-paver, a charmer, a high-stakes player who rolled the dice and lost.

He projected onto the country the same divided loyalties that warred in his own psyche, attempting to marry the nationalism of Quebec with the regionalism of the West. It was a hybrid mating that could bear no fruit. It led directly to the rise of the Bloc Québécois in the East and the Reform party in the West. It was the inescapable result of his own history and experience, but the Mulroney option was a Revolutionary mixture that eventually blew his party—and the delicate Canadian political balance—asunder.

Canada, with its regional and linguistic tensions, was always a powder keg; Mulroney was the lighted match.

TEN

JOHN TURNER

The Iceberg of the Revolution

He was defeated by one man alone, himself.

SOME POLITICIANS, LIKE BRIAN MULRONEY, Preston Manning and Ralph Klein, were agents of the Canadian Revolution who propelled it along or who surfed it to power; others, like Joe Clark, Bill Vander Zalm and Audrey McLaughlin were its victims destined to have the Revolution roll over them. And then there was John Napier "Chick" Turner, whose life and motto for the decade might well have been taken from the historical spoof, *Start the Revolution Without Me.*

Turner was the prime minister-in-waiting on Bay Street for eight frustrating years and the real McCoy for only seventy-nine days; a 37:1 ratio of hope over experience. This about matched his role in the Revolution, which was that of an indispensable bit-player, like the iceberg in a *Titanic* movie. His significance was limited to being there through most of 1980s, providing a daily *tableau* of political ineptitude and personal *angst*. Had he managed to mobilize himself, the Liberals would have become a welcome haven for voters disillusioned with Mulroney's stewardship. As things turned out, Turner—engraved on the public mind as a has-been before he ever-was—proved to be one of the Revolution's more significant

265

failures. Like the iceberg that remains eight-tenths under water, Turner seldom showed a fraction of his talent. The brief moments of inspiration he displayed were more than offset by the vast energies he dissipated, squandered and submerged.

Canadians have few expectations from their governments (if they're good, things get worse a little more slowly), but there's an unwritten understanding that the prime minister should be able to cross the street unaided and head for the right desk before settling in for a day's work. Turner never quite qualified.

He had the best damn credentials in the business, but found it difficult to connect his self-image with his real self. He talked fast and loose, like some McLuhanesque disk jockey, but underneath that flash and footwork he was never comfortable with the niceties of the political craft. When he dragged his party down to an historical low of forty seats in 1984, for example, it was Mulroney and not Turner who wrote sympathetic notes to many defeated Liberal candidates. At any public gathering Turner behaved as if he were attending a defensive-driving course, peeking over the shoulder of the person he was talking to and visibly pondering whether to charge off into a faster conversation lane. His aggressively hunched shoulders and the restless darting of his cobra's head all promised action, yet he was about as spontaneous as a cathedral Mass. His trademark gaze—Caribbean-blue eyes issuing the feral command, "Love me, goddamn it"—quickly lost its currency on his journey from political exile to political exile.

This jumpiness in his own skin was a metaphor for his political instincts. Turner always seemed out of sync with the events and moods swirling around him. He had considerable difficulty deciding when to switch from being an agitator to being a statesman and while he could occasionally master either incarnation, poor timing made him a disaster at both. Ironically, if he had got it right and become an active agent of change, he could have led the Revolution or stopped it in its tracks. As it was, he spent most of his time like a shortwave radio, tuning in and out to some distant, wavering frequency. At a Commons reception, parliamentary reporter Michael Vaughan extended an invitation for Turner to appear on CBC Radio's showcase political program, "The House." The Liberal leader looked around to see who else was at the party, distractedly murmuring, "Yeah, yeah, the house, the house..."

Finally, his wife, Geills, nudged him: "John, THE HOUSE, THE HOUSE."

He seemed to lock on to her frequency for a moment, then told Vaughan: "Oh, yeah, sure, we'll have to have you over to the house sometime, Mike..."

His slips of the tongue were legendary. While campaigning in Guelph during the 1984 federal election, he said, "I've been talking to doors and they tell me..." ["I've been knocking on doors and people tell me..."] Though basically good-natured, he could also be surprisingly insensitive. When the Victoria writer Bruce Hutchison was mortally ill, he was visited by columnist Allan Fotheringham, who quickly realized his old friend was dying. When he got back to Toronto, Fotheringham telephoned Turner (who was also a pal of Hutchison's) and advised him to visit Bruce as soon as possible. Turner straightaway picked up the phone. "Bruce!" he bellowed. "Allan tells me you're dying. Want to come and see you." Hutchison, who was failing rapidly, gathered up his considerable dignity and replied: "Fotheringham isn't going to tell me when to die. *I* will decide that."

Turner's problem was that life had come too easy. Most Canadian politicians must work hard to earn the intellectual, professional and regional credentials to claim the prime ministership—credentials that were simply handed to Turner. His rugged good looks, his élitist upbringing and diverse geographical background, his high-octane education (Oxford, Sorbonne), his remarkable exploits (Olympic runner, favourite dancing partner of Princess Margaret) and his career achievements (minister of finance and minister of justice) were precisely the ingredients for a leader expected to grasp the torch from Pierre Trudeau. When he resigned from the Trudeau cabinet in 1975 and moved to Bay Street, the shift was accepted merely as a private-sector sabbatical from his upward political spiral.

Like Charles de Gaulle, who decamped for three years to Colombey-les-Deux-Églises before being called back to command a troubled republic, Turner retired to Toronto and its fabled restaurant, Winston's, where he was found at Table 23 nearly every lunch hour. There he was surrounded by business leaders fed up with Pierre Trudeau's "socialist" shenanigans and *Louis Quatorze* style of government, who saw Turner as their best bet for a resurgence of their own influence. Turner seemed to them the ideal leader: experienced in parliament, sympathetic to big business, bound to few ideas of his own (always dangerous), bilingual, tough, smart and, above all, what they called "a True Liberal." And so those captains of commerce at Winston's, men with not quite enough chin and too much cuff, persuaded Turner that the country would be his to command.

THE JOHN TURNER WHO ASSUMED CONTROL of the Liberal Party in 1984 turned out to be very different from the Kennedy clone who had wowed them in Parliament a decade before. Those many Winston's lunches had failed to feed his grasp of contemporary realities. Turner returned to the political wars like a jazz musician who hadn't played his instrument for most of a decade and had lost his spark of excitement, spontaneity of impulse, empathy and rapport with audiences. Apart from his erratic style, Turner had abandoned the party's traditional recipe for power. He casually jettisoned the formula that had kept the Liberals in power for most of the century, a loose sort of "sedate populism" which had allowed the Grits to strike a marketable balance between élitism and egalitarianism. Instead, Turner was too cosy with the cuff-linked crowd at Winston's so that what remained of his popular instincts had been dulled and outdated. From the start of his leadership in 1984, the Liberals split into warring factions that agreed on nothing except that he should be replaced. Some of Turner's more enlightened advisers, like Senator Keith Davey, John Payne and Ray Heard, tried to get him to act moderately. Instead, Turner compensated with an alternative agenda of his own. His attacks on Canada's business Establishment during the great 1988 free trade debates cost him the corporate support he had so long cultivated and shifted his party to the left of the NDP, where it wallowed like a wounded dinosaur. It was a lurch in the proper direction, given the times, but Turner never moved beyond that single issue to consolidate his hold on the revolutionary impulses sweeping the nation. Perhaps he had lost the ability to improvise; for the most part he gave the impression that he didn't care—or cared too much.

Turner responded to events like one of those frigid creatures locked inside a glass souvenir paperweight. The perpetual snowflakes swirled about him, but the little man gazing through his protective shell was unaware that the seasons beyond it had

changed. No wonder they called him "the ice man." During the leadership convention to replace Pierre Trudeau, which he won in a
walk, Turner betrayed his ignorance of Canada's new reality by
complaining to a friendly journalist: "The boys tell me the mood of
the House is pretty sour. When I was there, we were all friends. We'd
play poker together." At Vancouver's Bayshore Inn on election night
in 1984, he spotted a Liberal functionary who had been his fraternity
brother at the University of British Columbia. Turner went over and
hugged him. "Hey, remember the songs we used to sing?" he
enthused, then broke into a chorus of "Oh What a Time We Had with
Minnie the Mermaid." He insisted on referring to his personal
retinue as "guys," though half of them were women. At a garden
party held at Stornaway in 1986 for the Ottawa press corps, he
looked down at the red pumps worn by television personality
Pamela Wallin and quipped: "Well, Pammie, bet those shoes have
been under a lot of beds in their day." * His locker-room expletives,
his 1950s lingo, his unfashionably cut suits, foot-long cigars and
habit of patting women party officials on the bum, reduced him to
being a leader who, in Jeffrey Simpson's phrase, "promises us all a
better yesterday."

Like its leader, the Liberal Party had been flying on automatic for
a quarter-century, its policy matrix having been set at the Kingston
Policy Conference in 1960. But Turner made little effort to revive
policy discussions and became pathologically indecisive, usually
making the wrong decision and making it too late. On the seminal
issues, his every policy twitch seemed to be based on the last piece
of advice he heard; the trick was to be the last "guy" in. On the day
before he was due to be interviewed on his constitutional position by

---

* Two years later, when Wallin was host of the CTV program, "Question
  Period," she invited Turner on as a guest and thirty seconds before they
  went live told him she was going to ask some tough questions. Giving
  substance to one of Ottawa's more prevalent rumours, she asked him,
  with a look of feigned innocence: "There have been suggestions, I
  guess, is the best way to put it, in the town of Ottawa, and this is a very
  small world in a little fish bowl, that you have, or potentially have a
  drinking problem..." Turner's mumbled denial ("Yeah, I like a good
  party and I've enjoyed myself over the years, but I have never allowed
  any pleasure or distraction to interfere with doing the job...") did little to
  disarm the rumours.

Claude Ryan, then editor of *Le Devoir* (the equivalent of reciting the catechism before the Pope), Turner was asked by his assistant, Stewart Langford, to define his position. "Look, Langford," he replied, "you know all about that stuff. What is it?" His kinetic energy charged most of his pronouncements with more voltage than they deserved, yet few of his statements reflected the man's sophistication or even his education. When René Lévesque died, an aide phoned him at home asking for a reaction, which had been requested by *La Presse* in Montreal. "He was a goddamn separatist, why do we have to say anything?" was the leader's inspiring response. "Just write something, I don't care what you say." A few days later Turner attended the former Quebec premier's funeral and, on the way back to Ottawa, complained to the aide: "You know, that Trudeau really is an asshole. He dominated the funeral, even though I was there and so were Bourassa and Mulroney. What the hell is going on?"

Turner made his biggest gaffes early in his leadership by agreeing to make nineteen high-level patronage appointments on behalf of the departing Pierre Trudeau. At the same time, he lamely dismissed French-language rights in Manitoba as "a provincial initiative with provincial solutions." And he called the 1984 election much too soon. Instead of taking advantage of the summer visits from the Queen and the Pope, occasions that would have allowed the nation to see him at his gracious best, Turner flew to London, asked Elizabeth II to postpone her trip and, despite strong advice to the contrary by most of his inner retinue, called an election. It was a grievous error. Canadians had not taken the measure of his new administration; only 40 of the 282 riding associations had Liberal candidates in place (the Tories had completed 240 nominations and the NDP, 115); the party's national director, Gordon Ashworth, had been fired but not replaced, and the election apparatus came under the control of Bill Lee, a lobbyist and former air force group captain who had never run a national election or even a single riding campaign. The new Liberal leader was so anxious to cut ties with his predecessor that only one of Trudeau's advisers (Tom Axworthy) was retained. Carefully crafted transition books were ignored and no peace treaties with the Jean Chrétien camp were attempted. Turner trimmed the Trudeau cabinet from thirty-seven members to twenty-nine, but then reappointed twenty-four ministers to the same portfolios. He thus could present himself as neither an agent of change nor a guardian of continuity.

Turner insisted, as part of his anti-Trudeau stance, on discarding pollster Martin Goldfarb of Toronto and recruiting his own, Angus Reid of Winnipeg. Goldfarb, who at that point had two Liberal functionaries, Tom Axworthy and Michael Kirby, on his payroll, went ahead anyway and drafted a weighty, "for the leader's eyes only" document, for which he charged the party an unauthorized $225,000.* At one point he attacked Lee for hiring Angus Reid, "that two-bit westerner," and begged Lee to rescind Reid's contract, since so many of Goldfarb's American clients had been sold on his services by being told that he advised Canadian prime ministers. The quality of Goldfarb's counsel could be judged as outside this planet by one telling bit of advice in his strategy paper. "Mrs. Turner can do a great deal to soften Turner's image," he seriously suggested, "and make him appear more like an ordinary, everyday person." While Goldfarb's memo contained more of such reassuring pap, Reid had correctly read the country as being angry with the Liberals and about to endow Brian Mulroney's Tories with a decisive majority. "I find it hard to believe that we could slip any further," Reid wrote Turner in a secret memorandum on August 6, 1984, "but in light of the significant cloud of doubt that presently surrounds this campaign, I fear that we are in danger of losing all credibility." Eventually Lee was fired and Keith Davey was brought in to take his place. Davey had earned his title, "The Rainmaker," during two decades of masterminding half a dozen victorious Pearson and Trudeau campaigns. When he was appointed to salvage the remnants of the Turner campaign, he received a telex from Doug Richardson, the Liberal candidate in Saskatoon-East: "There's been a terrible drought out here all summer. But it rained the day you were appointed." Announcement of the Davey move was handled in typical Turner fashion. He was electioneering aboard a B.C. ferry at the time, safely insulated from the press in the pilot-house, pretending to steer the ship. When reporters heard about the Davey appointment, they wanted the leader's comments. He wouldn't climb down to face them, so the media refused to board the campaign buses, and a simple situation deteriorated into a headline-grabbing confrontation. Davey did

---

* Goldfarb was incredibly generous with himself. In 1994, for example, the company he controlled paid him a salary of $1.2 million—$20,120 more than Conrad Black earned that year.

manage to stabilize the campaign and restore morale among campaign workers. That didn't win the election, but it probably saved the Liberal Party from oblivion. He also persuaded Trudeau to speak out on behalf of Turner—once. The Montreal meeting, hardly a triumph of the democratic process, was aptly described by *Globe and Mail* columnist Jeffrey Simpson: "Requested in panic, given with reluctance, crafted in indifference, the speech was a loon's cry before the terrible storm."

During the 1984 campaign, Turner and Mulroney quickly learned to expect the worst of one another and they were seldom disappointed. Turner's Waterloo—and the turning point in the 1984 election—was the televised English-language debate that allowed the Tory leader to cut his opponent off at the hip. Mulroney's admonition, "You had an option, sir," is entered in the lexicon of Canada's defining political moments. Less well-remembered is the fact that the Liberal leader brought the attack on himself. The debate had been droning on for more than an hour, clearly headed for a draw, when Turner—recently savaged in public and private for making the outrageous Trudeau patronage appointments—launched a pre-emptive strike against Mulroney. Referring to the inappropriate jokes Mulroney had made about appointing Tories to the public trough, Turner began an unrehearsed ploy. "We have this patronage issue," he said. "Mr. Mulroney has told his party that every job would be made available to every living, breathing Conservative."

"I beg your pardon, sir," Mulroney interrupted, hardly believing his luck.

"I would say, Mr. Mulroney," Turner went on, unaware he was about to throw away his political life-jacket, "that on the basis of what you've talked about—getting your nose in the public trough—that you wouldn't offer Canadians any newness in the style of government."

Mulroney bore in with the magnanimous air of a hippo hunter who finds a petrified bunny in his sights. "Mr. Turner, the only person who has ever appointed around here, for the last twenty-odd years, has been your party, and 99 per cent of them have been Liberals... The least you should do is apologize for those horrible appointments. You, sir, owe the Canadian people a profound apology for having indulged in that kind of practice with those kinds of appointments."

"I told you and told the Canadian people," Turner replied, releasing the last buckle on his flotation device, "that I had no option."

"You had an option, sir. You could have said, 'I'm not going to do it. This is wrong for Canada and I'm not going to ask Canadians to pay the price.' You had an option, sir, to say no, and you chose to say yes, to the old attitudes and the old stories of the Liberal party..."

"I had no option..." Turner muttered, to himself as much as to the television cameras, the blood running through his shoes. The 1984 election was over. The Liberals dropped a hundred seats; the Tories won the largest plurality in the country's history. In two and one-half months, Turner had at least temporarily destroyed the most powerful political machine this side of pre-thaw Albania.

WITH THE LIBERALS AT A LOW EBB, the moment had come to set the party on a new path. Had Turner restored Canadian Liberalism during the next four years to its roots as the party that protected the poor and underprivileged, reflected middle-class aspirations, fulfilled ethnic expectations and initiated fresh political ideas, he could have aborted the Canadian Revolution in its gestation and become a national hero. Instead, by trying to turn the Liberals into an ultra-nationalist movement that would have made Mel Hurtig nervous, he became, at least politically, a bum.

To add to his troubles, Turner suffered from the worst staff since Benito Mussolini's tank corps, which was sabotaged by squadron commanders so jealous they ended up firing live shells at one another. Turner's senior aides entered into Byzantine conspiracies against real and imagined foes in the caucus, the party and members of their own revolving ranks. Turner unwittingly encouraged this paranoia with a casual management style based on unspecified lines of command. He would often assign two advisers to the same task without telling either one they had a clone. An iron curtain was drawn around his office by two senior aides, nicknamed the "Thug and the Jug": the misguided principal secretary Peter Connolly (Thug) and his immature deputy, Doug Kirkpatrick (Jug). The main culprit was Connolly, whose advice usually did more harm than good and made unnecessary enemies for the leader.

Because he alienated the party's traditional financial supporters, Turner's office was so broke that trusting staffers often had to take rainchecks in lieu of wages and placed travel for political assignments on their personal credit cards. "A siege mentality prevailed in Turner's office," recalled Ray Heard, the former managing editor of *The Montreal Star* and head of Global News, who did a twenty-month stint as Turner's director of communications. Heard, who had worked on Fleet Street, compared Turner to Sir Anthony Eden, so meticulously groomed for a British prime ministership that proved beyond his capability. "Both laboured in the shadow of greater men and each ruled for only a few months. They shared good looks, and there was a lot in common in their family backgrounds and psychological make-ups. It must have been very damaging to their self-esteem to see themselves—and be seen by the public—as always 'the next-best men.'"

Turner's wife, Geills, was a talented and intelligent woman (who was, incidentally, a crack photographer), but she ranked hot on the heels of Maureen the McTeer in any contest for Political Wife from Hell. During one election campaign, she decided that she would fly back to Toronto from Vancouver, where she had tired of watching her husband kiss babies and pat bums. She was comfortably ensconced in the first row, window seat, of Air Canada's first class, her accustomed due (as her husband was prime minister, she is entitled to fly first class on Air Canada free for the rest of her life) when a woman carrying a crying child was seated next to her. "There's no damn way I'm going to fly across the country with a mewling brat beside me," she proclaimed, loud enough for even steerage to overhear. There were no alternate seats and the captain, called in to negotiate, finally lost his patience. "I'm not going to take this flight if this woman is here," he declared to the applauding passengers. Geills finally disembarked and headed directly for the Air Canada counter, where she staged such a screaming match that a Turner aide was despatched to the airport with instructions to do something, "or we'll lose the mothers' vote."

As it unilaterally jettisoned such hallowed dogmas of Canadian Liberalism as its historical affinity for lower tariffs, Turner's crusade against free trade in the 1988 election made for great television, but it never evolved into a sustainable campaign. Turner sounded unconvincing as he machine-gunned his way through the midnight jottings of some overworked speech writer. His Tarzan declamations on free trade ("Me tear up treaty!") were hardly credible, since he had always supported greater American investment in Canada and compared to the black plague such nationalist measures as the Foreign Investment Review Agency and the National Energy Program. It was suggested that he fought against the Mulroney initiative mainly because Lloyd Axworthy, Sheila Copps, Herb Gray and few other Liberal progressives had reluctantly supported Turner on Meech Lake in exchange for his opposition to free trade. Sympathetic advisers had wanted Turner to deliver a nightly emotional tirade on the evils of free trade while wearing a body mike and pacing in front of a giant Canadian flag, in imitation of U.S. General George Patton hectoring his troops. It was a small mercy, in that unmerciful campaign, that they were overruled.

Turner's battle against free trade enraged his former pals on Bay Street. Alf Powis, then CEO of the mining and forestry giant Noranda Inc. and a friend of Turner's, declared the Liberal leader was "dead wrong" and that, even though he was a card-carrying Liberal, it would be "a national tragedy" if the Canadian people rejected the free trade agreement. That was mild compared to other reactions. "No one anticipated that Turner would turn into such a mad dog— it's one thing to want to be elected, but to screw your country in order to win, that's just disgusting," declared Jack Fraser, head of Federal Industries Ltd. in Winnipeg, who was also vice-president of the continentalist Business Council on National Issues. As usual, Conrad Black insisted on having the last word: "Not since Maurice Duplessis embarrassed the Liberals and amused himself by accusing his opponents of importing 'Communist eggs' from Poland, has a leader of a major Canadian party inflicted upon his electorate such an avalanche of sulphurous falsehoods and banalities." The critics notwithstanding, Turner became comfortable with his new-found nationalism and played well in the election's televised debates, decisively outclassing Brian Mulroney who found himself defending the status quo. "Turner achieved a grace when he talked about the country, its history, and its geographical challenge," wrote Graham Fraser, in his history of the campaign. "It was a speech that rang true to the patrician nature of the man, his love of canoeing, his awkward, old-fashioned qualities that sometimes made him seem hopelessly out of date." On election day, November 21, 1988, Turner was beaten for the second and final time, though his nationalist appeal did manage to double his party's Commons seats from forty to eighty-two.

Because of the hiring climate he created for himself during that campaign, when it was hard to tell whether he was fighting the Conservatives or the business community, Turner couldn't find a decent job once he decided to leave politics in the spring of 1990. Betrayed by one of their own, Bay Street slammed its door in his face. The sole exception was Ontario Premier David Peterson, who retained his friendship and made sure that he was seen sitting beside Turner at the 1990 Liberal leadership convention in Calgary.

During his tortured half-decade as leader, Turner's tragedy was embarrassingly personal. He was defeated by one man alone, himself. With the only party that could offer the country an alternate government in the hands of a confused and confusing politician, whose main accomplishment was his knack for making the worst out of each bad situation, John Turner became the Canadian Revolution's most effective recruiting sergeant.

ELEVEN

PHANTOM OF THE CANADIAN OPERA

Trudeau's Revenge

*"To be a revolutionary is first of all to make sure of
permanence and of good reception.
After which intellectual masturbation is permitted."*
GRAFFITI, SORBONNE, MAY 1968

H E MAGICKED US. Like the lead player in *The Phantom of the
Opera*, Pierre Elliott Trudeau seemed elusive and unfath-
omable, yet master of the music of the night. He remained that
paradox, an egotist with ideals, who revealed his fellow players
to themselves. Masked and huddled in his cloak, he mysteriously
controlled the melodrama of Canadian politics, threatening anyone
who stood in his way until he was brought to heel by age, circumstance and the exhaustion of his doctrines. But he lingered in the
wings long enough to confound his successor with his booby-trapped
legacy, and his ghostly, chain-rattling appearances provided the
spawning grounds for Revolution.

Even if he were no longer running the country, Trudeau could still
sway its perceptions. It was less his cause than his passionate conviction that attracted followers in an age that had come to despise
opportunism and suspect pragmatism. This exquisitely stubborn
man never yielded, age having permanently set his face into the
carved alabaster mask of some distant Crusader. He went on performing the task he had always done, which Norman Mailer once
described in another context as "the indispensable psychic act of a

leader, who takes national anxieties so long buried and releases them to the surface, where they belong."

Whenever the constitution he had breech-birthed into existence was threatened by change or reform, as it was during the Meech Lake and Charlottetown accord debates, he took on the guerrilla tactic of husbanding his resources for a single, dramatic strike, the elements of noise and surprise making up for his non-existent constituency. Trudeau had gone underground for three years after leaving power, never saying a public word. When he emerged, rhetorical guns blazing, he vigorously undermined the political support for Mulroney's constitutional crusades. A member of the French-Canadian Establishment by birth, upbringing and bank account, Trudeau paradoxically became the embodiment of populist defiance.

That incarnation took form most forcefully on October 1, 1992, when the former prime minister spoke passionately for fifty minutes to a gathering of cronies about the perfidies of the Charlottetown Accord. The venue he chose was La Maison du Egg Roll, in Montreal's working-class St. Henri district. A Chinese joint that offered all-you-can-eat buffets for $6.95, it was the perfect setting for a grass-roots rejection of the constitution. The stage had been deliberately chosen to emphasize his message that those not specifically mentioned in the accord would, as he put it, be relegated to the "bottom of the heap—the little, obscure people without rank, like many of us." His interventions prompted nearly half of undecided Canadians to weigh against the deal.* He was not at all bothered by the fact that his criticism was unacceptable to most Quebeckers. As with his implementation of the War Measures Act a generation earlier, his intervention would heighten Quebec nationalist sentiment, but in his lexicon of values that was worth no more than a shrug. John Ciaccia, a Quebec cabinet minister, accused him of "fanning the flames of bigotry," while Jean Paré, editor of the fortnightly *L'Actualité*, wrote, "his attacks might move a few in Quebec who are nostalgic about the past. It is a concentrate of thirty years of

---

* The article Trudeau wrote in *Maclean's* attacking the Charlottetown Accord increased the magazine's newsstand sales fivefold and pushed the value of the Canadian dollar down by more than 1 cent on the world's currency exchanges.

his worst calumnies dribbling with contempt for an insecure society that could never quench his thirst for power. Outside Quebec, Trudeau finds himself in the company, amongst others, of marginals and extremists to whom he gives not leadership, but a justification for their prejudices."

In a television age when most celebrities felt lucky to last more than a season, Pierre Trudeau's hold on the Canadian imagination was only magnified by his absence from power. Long past his prime and with no task left undone except to defend the history he had made, he cast himself in the role of the country's beleaguered conscience. He was listened to partly because his beguiling appearance as the Phantom of the Canadian Opera was so convincing, partly because he was willing to rattle Brian Mulroney's chains, but mostly because he played to the prejudices of English Canada. He brought out the worst in English-speaking Canadians, exposing their anti-French and anti-Catholic biases and regional jealousies. His tactics would never have succeeded if Canadians had not been primed for revolt, lacking only a credible authenticator of trends already in motion. Outside Quebec, Trudeau was hailed for putting down Quebeckers and their nationalist aspirations; inside Quebec, he was reviled for being, as columnist Lise Bisonnette put it, "unreal, pathetic, a sore loser—one is nevertheless moved by this powerful man's raging and sad look at his vanishing dreams."

The Trudeau constitution, the one he wanted to leave untouched, had provided the Canadian Revolution with its Magna Carta. The Charter of Rights and Freedoms, passed into law in 1982, prompted the country's citizens to contemplate their past dues, re-examine their current entitlements and set out their future aspirations. The Queen herself had guaranteed the people freedom of conscience and religion; freedom of association and assembly; and freedom of thought and expression, including freedom of the press. To progressives, the Charter represented the greatest possible advance in the protection of civil liberties; to traditionalists, it was a backward step that signified the further Americanization of Canada in allowing the judiciary undue influence over Parliament. Whatever the verdict, the formula for Revolution had been set. The Charter was above all a contract between individual citizens and the state. This had an unintended revolutionary effect: with the Charter, the circle of tolerated governance had grown smaller until it incorporated each individual as a sovereign entity. Every citizen now constituted a nation of one.

This sense of personal autonomy was magnified by the citizens' ability to challenge governments under the Charter, which exponentially increased the influence of interest groups. They were in fighting trim by the beginning of the Mulroney years, endowed with the authority (and federal grants) to confront the political system. They did this through broad, nation-wide organizations formed to trumpet their own, narrowly focused policy options. Almost overnight, the parliamentary politics of brokerage that had made Canada governable was replaced by often conflicting, extra-parliamentary agendas set by its noisiest petitioners. "Pluralism has run wild," warned John Meisel, the Queen's University political scientist. "We have become so blinded by the notion that there is no national interest, only special interests, that we are incapable of pursuing policies designed to be of general benefit to the whole community." Politicians had to relearn their craft. The party system seemed marginalized, as priorities had to pass muster not only with cabinet and caucus, but with the anticipated lobbies of the interest groups, whether of the right or the left. The most powerful of these pleaders were the Business Council on National Issues, which believed its briefs ought to be Cabinet directives, and the National Action Committee on the Status of Women, which believed it *was* the government. Neither group was as inclusive as it maintained. The powerful BCNI became so identified with major corporate powers that small and regional businesses formed their own competing pressure groups. Under the militant and persuasive leadership of Judy Rebick and Sunera Thobani, the NAC grew increasingly distant from the concerns of mainstream, middle-class women. When General Motors of Canada appointed Maureen Kempson Darkes as the first woman president of its Canadian subsidiary, NAC spokeswoman Maureen Layland responded with less than sisterly solidarity. "She's white, isn't she?" sniffed Ms. Layland. "Skin colour brings privileges. The appointment will make no difference to women of colour, immigrant women, women with disabilities, aboriginal women, or single female parents." That chilly comment brought Margaret Wente, editor of *The Globe and Mail Report on Business* magazine, to respond: "Gender feminists and socialists, who sadly, are the only feminists we hear from these days, believe that [in order] to be virtuous, a woman should have as many minority attributes as possible. If white and privileged, she must apologize that her experience of the world is cruelly limited by her background. Virtue also requires a certain set of narrowly-prescribed beliefs and behaviours, beginning with the belief that the market system is evil, individual achievement suspect, and big businesses are instruments of human oppression."

Trudeau's Charter spawned a citizenry that wanted the *process* of consultation, but the *results* of leadership. That impossible expectation of government contributed much to Brian Mulroney's unpopularity and to Trudeau's ability to influence events from beyond the political grave. His resurrection was not limited to his constitutional crusades. At various points during the Mulroney years, Trudeau exercised *de facto* control of the government's priorities. Nearly every move that Mulroney made while in office was governed not by his own budgets, but by Trudeau's fiscal legacy. During his sixteen years in power, Trudeau turned the nearly balanced books he had inherited into a $38.5 billion deficit and increased the national debt by 1,200 per cent, from $17 billion to more than $200 billion. By the time Mulroney took over, less than 15 per cent of the annual budget was made up of discretionary spending, so that he was robbed of any manoeuvring room to pay for the many promises he had made.

Trudeau consulted almost daily with his former deputy prime minister, Senator Allan MacEachen, who regularly brought parliamentary business to a halt by rallying the seventy-three senators appointed by Trudeau to vote against the government. The Red Chamber was Trudeau's government-in-exile, where such Liberal warlocks as Jack Austin, Keith Davey, Jerahmiel Grafstein, Michael Kirby, Leo Kolber, Colin Kenny, Joyce Fairbairn and Royce Frith obstructed pivotal Tory legislation including free trade, the Goods and Services Tax and the drug patent bill. The Trudeau-appointed constitutional whiz, Senator Eugene Forsey, explained the unelected body was justified in thwarting the will of the electorate if it did so in the national interest, adding somewhat mysteriously: "It's because I'm a John A. Macdonald Conservative that I sit in the Senate as a Pierre Trudeau Liberal."

IT WAS TRUDEAU'S FAILURE TO INCLUDE his birth province in his constitutional delusions that baited the trap for Mulroney's later bid to enter the history books as the prime minister who had brought Quebec into modern federalism.* An enduring mystery of the Meech Lake debacle was why Mulroney would willingly stake his career on a legal accord that voters didn't understand or especially want in the first place.

Mulroney got so bound up in the process partly because of his conviction that such an accord would vanquish thoughts of separatism once and for all. But apart from that simplistic notion, the main reason was best articulated by the PM at a private breakfast with Bob and Elizabeth Dole at 24 Sussex Drive in the early winter of 1989. Dole was then senior senator from Kansas and the Senate minority leader (he would later become a Republican presidential candidate); his wife had served as secretary of transportation in the Reagan administration and as secretary of labour in the Bush Cabinet. On a semi-official visit, they had asked the prime minister to explain what Meech Lake was about. As he later recounted, he answered: "Forget Canada. Let's assume that the United States decided to have a new constitution in 1982 and all the states met with the federal administration for an extended period of time. Finally, they did come up with a new document. But it was not endorsed by New York, California and Texas. That's approximately the equivalent of Quebec's population *vis-à-vis* this country.

"It gets better," Mulroney continued. "In those negotiations, the governors of the fifty states wound up with the power to override every provision of the U.S. Bill of Rights and all decisions of the U.S. Supreme Court." Elizabeth Dole, a one-time candidate for the U.S. Supreme Court, couldn't hold herself back.

"Are you telling me," Mulroney quoted her as saying, "that the governor of Mississippi would have been given the right to overrule Supreme Court decisions on issues of civil rights?"

"That's exactly what I'm telling you," Mulroney shot back.

"Who did this?" she demanded.

"Guess who?" was the triumphant reply. "Pierre Trudeau, the same fellow who today is demanding perfection in the Meech Lake Accord!"

---

* At the same time, Trudeau indirectly controlled what was happening inside the Liberal party. He undermined John Turner's leadership, especially after the Bay Street lawyer jumped aboard the Meech Lake submarine; when Jean Chrétien first took over the party, he admitted to checking his speeches with Trudeau before delivering them.

That little history lesson left out the fact that the accord quickly became less of a constitutional deal than a symbol of all that had gone wrong with the country's politics. It was easy enough to blame Brian Mulroney, who started the Meech Lake process, or Clyde Wells, who ended it. But the real culprit was Pierre Trudeau, for having made it necessary. Trudeau had originally used language rights as the instrument to open up the country to Quebec. He hammered through the Official Languages Act, which permitted Quebeckers to speak French with federal officials wherever they lived, and appointed franco-phones to major economic portfolios, proving conclusively that in office they were no worse than their anglophone counterparts. His crackdown on the FLQ had fanned the fires of Quebec nationalism and triggered René Lévesque's 1976 victory over Robert Bourassa's Liberals. In the Quebec referendum that followed, the separatists were beaten on Trudeau's pledge of "renewed federalism." Two years later, he patriated the British North America Act from London without Quebec's participation or consent. That move also cast in concrete the rigid amending process, requiring provincial unanimity within three years, that ultimately helped kill the Meech Lake agreement.

Probably Trudeau's most harmful legacy was entrenchment of the "notwithstanding" clause, which allowed dissenting premiers to override the Charter of Rights. It was invoked by Bourassa to implement the 1988 language bill prohibiting outdoor signs other than in French, in defiance of the Charter's guaranteed freedom of expression.* Trudeau later publicly admitted that the Charter was "fundamentally flawed because of the override clause."

Trudeau's conviction that individual rights always had to be protected from the tyranny of the majority clashed head-on with the inclusion of collective rights, as proposed by the Mulroney government's reforms, which would have entrenched the distinctiveness of Quebec and the First Nations. That approach subtracted nothing from individual rights, and the distinct society clause in the federal proposals explicitly took into account Quebec's anglophone minority. But Trudeau couldn't bear having his sacred document touched.

---

* The extent of Brian Mulroney's opposition to the Quebec legislation became the subject of an intense correspondence he had with Conrad Black. Their private letters are reproduced in Appendix 9 (Sincerely, Brian).

CANADIANS HAD ALWAYS BEEN OF TWO MINDS about Pierre Trudeau. They admired themselves for having had the nerve to elect, on four occasions, such a fabulous smartass; but they also hated themselves for having been seduced by a supremely detached Jesuit who acted as if his grandeur grew in direct proportion to his aloofness. Compassion cast little light on his interior landscape. As powerful as Trudeau's discourse proved to be (someone described his style of government as "despotism tempered by epigram"), his words were less compelling than his body language, which at times could be deafening. He was the dancing man, sliding down banisters, dodging (or slugging) picketers, pirouetting behind the Queen's back. He was Billy the Kid, pole-vaulting onto platforms or standing his ground, thumbs hooked in belt loops.

Despite his penchant for making outrageous statements and dressing in what then passed for outlandish political costumes—leather coats, desert boots, loose-flowing capes and thonged sandals—Trudeau appeared a lot more daring than he really was. Unable to classify him as a man of the left or right, most Canadians were satisfied to think of him as a voice of the hidden potential within themselves. When he finally decided to quit as prime minister in February of 1984, the jubilation about his going was mixed with a feeling best described in an essay on the demise of a rival by the Parisian critic, Jean de la Bruyère. "It is a great loss," he wrote to a friend. "He was a good man and deserved a longer life. He was talented, reliable, resolute and courageous, faithful and generous. Provided, of course, that he is really dead."

Although he was judged—at least in retrospect—as having been some sort of political wizard, Trudeau was able to squeeze out only a two-seat margin running against the comatose Robert Stanfield in 1972 and seven years later, he was defeated by Joe Clark. Although they didn't run against one another, Trudeau was never able to come anywhere near Brian Mulroney's appeal on the hustings. In the 1984 campaign, which was Mulroney's best outing, he won fifty-seven more seats than the Liberal leader ever won in his best campaign; in Mulroney's worst showing (1988), he still got fifteen more seats than Trudeau at the height of Trudeaumania (1968). Based on that record, which is the ultimate bottom line for politicians, Mulroney could never comprehend why Trudeau was regarded with such awe while he was dismissed with so much contempt. During Trudeau's sixteen years in power, twenty-one ministers resigned, compared to thirteen from the Mulroney cabinet in nine years; there wasn't much to choose between them on patronage either, especially in their last month in office when each appointed hundreds of hard-core partisans to government jobs.*

It was difficult to compare their spending habits, because yet again Trudeau had set things up to absolve himself and condemn his successor. Trudeau timed implementation of the Access to Information Act, which allowed journalists to examine politicians' expense accounts, to take effect just as he was leaving office. Mulroney and his ministers were its first potential victims, while Trudeau remained exempt from scrutiny. Particularly galling to Mulroney were the public opinion polls from 1988 onwards that showed Trudeau consistently running ahead of him in popularity 55 per cent to 14 per cent in April of 1991, for example), even though Trudeau was by then into his seventies and seldom budged from his art-nouveau mansion on Montreal's Pine Avenue. Mulroney comforted himself with sarcasm. "I suppose if you're Pierre Trudeau," he said, "it must be kind of difficult to get up in the morning and look in the mirror and know you've seen perfection for the last time all day." But Mila was more direct. "I want to know," she once told me, "why people keep saying Trudeau is such a great intellect. Because he quotes Nietzsche? I could train Nicolas to quote Nietzsche if I wanted to. This does not make someone brilliant. The two keys that can unlock any door are intelligence and good judgement. Trudeau had no judgement. In sixteen years he took a strong country and damaged it. Also, I don't understand how this short, little ugly pock-marked man became a sex symbol. And here's Brian, with his wonderful deep voice, those beautiful blue eyes, his generous nature and wonderful sense of humour..."

---

* Trudeau made these appointments in such haste that nineteen of the most senior postings had to be promulgated by John Turner, his successor; Yvon Pinard was made a Federal Court judge so hastily there wasn't even time for the usual consultation with the Canadian Bar Association and warhorse Bryce Mackasey was named Canadian ambassador to Portugal before Lisbon could officially whinny its objections.

TO MULRONEY IT SEEMED THAT his predecessor had not so much elevated the office of prime minister as crippled anyone bold enough to
occupy it after him. To Trudeau, battling the constitutional accords
was only half the fun. He continued to influence social policy as
well, possibly on the grounds that phantoms have to keep busy, or
they vanish. At a private Ottawa dinner party on April 6, 1988, held
to mark the twentieth anniversary of his assumption of power, the
former prime minister laid out a political agenda for the 1990s. "For
too long," he proclaimed, "we have experimented with the dark side
of excellence. For too long this country has suffered from politics
that stresses economic efficiency instead of social fairness—and it's
in that direction our party must make its next policy thrust."

The notion of social fairness as a political issue had been lost
during John Turner's stewardship of the party and was not revived
under Jean Chrétien. "When we talk about the dark side of excellence," explained Senator Jack Austin, the intellectual godfather of
the idea, "our concern is with the loss of tolerance, the absence of
compassion and the downgrading of fairness, as expressed in this
neo-conservative age. There has been a hard edge in Brian
Mulroney's pursuit of national competitiveness and a subsequent
dilution of optimism among Canadians. In contrast, Liberal policy
for forty years was based on the politics of optimism through the
emphasis on equality of opportunity." Austin, who had once been
Trudeau's principal secretary and later became his minister of state
for social development, expanded the notion. "The Tory approach,"
he claimed, "depended on benefits trickling down from a process
that inevitably strengthened the already strong. Instead, governments must return to the animating idea of fairness. A country is not
a business and a government should stand for much more than economic efficiency."

Trudeau was criticized for being a man of the past, but in response
to such accusations he would shrug and say, "I suppose Pythagoras
was yesterday's man also, but two and two still equals four." He
was impartial, criticizing Jean Chrétien ("he knew his limitations")
with the same throwaway arrogance he applied to Joe Clark
("headwaiter of the provinces") or Brian Mulroney ("a sniveller, a
constitutional pyromaniac").

Whatever his faults, Trudeau understood the cold grammar of
power and refused to succumb—or even recognize—the existence

of the momentary pushes and pulls of a country in turmoil. Like the Phantom, he staked out his ground and dominated the stage. His Charter permanently transformed the relationship of Canadians to their governments; his reckless budgets left the country in such dire debt that only a wave of political reactionaries, the style of leaders he hated most, could clean it up. His pivotal contribution to the defeat of the Meech Lake and Charlottetown accords was a flash of triumph, but could in retrospect turn out to be a national tragedy. It seemed either result would be fine with him. "I'm quite prepared to die politically, when the people think I should," he ruminated on one occasion we had together. "Politicians should be like Trappists, who go around in monasteries and the only words they can say to each other are: 'Brother, we must die one day.' I think this is true of politicians. The world is so full of a number of things, I'm sure we could all be as happy as kings."

The last time I saw him was at a Montreal reception in the spring of 1995 and I recalled, twenty-seven years earlier, standing beside a Liberal matron at another reception in Ottawa's Château Laurier. Just before Trudeau came through the door, she stiffened and turned to her many-chinned husband with the whisper: "What if I faint when he comes in?" The husband cut her in two with a look of complete disdain, his eyes rolling heavenward, searching for relief. But when Trudeau finally loped past and happened to shake the man's hand, he hugged his wife and started quietly to cry.

Looking at Trudeau a generation later, the only connection to his charismatic past was the gorgeous young woman draped over his arm. He seemed less feisty and more introverted, a philosopher-king without a kingdom. As in the third act of *The Phantom of the Opera*, when the protagonist is brought to ground and his magical powers depart him, Lucky Pierre was gradually abandoned by most of his groupies and disciples. He had not changed, but the country had.

Then I remembered my theory about Pierre Trudeau being the character in an opera and realized that the fat lady hadn't sung yet. I turned to tell him. But he was gone. Once a phantom, always a phantom.

TWELVE

END OF ENTITLEMENT

Goodbye, Charlie Brown

*"His response to Judy Rebick was to evacuate a
perfectly good supper."*
BARBARA AMIEL ON HER HUSBAND, CONRAD BLACK

To BE A NEWFIE IS TO BE A SURVIVOR. Newfoundlanders are a great people because they have a way of surviving without ever becoming victims. There is about them an exhilarating, nose-thumbing air of tempting the fates that ceaselessly try to bring them down. Their great spirit, fed by muscular Darwinian impulses, has allowed them to claim with brassy validity that they are a race apart. But in the decade between 1985 and 1995, there was a real possibility they would become an endangered species.

The human tragedy that played itself out on the Rock in the first half of the 1990s threatened not only the livelihood of the jobless fisheries workers and their families, but promised to decimate a unique way of living. To fish, as anyone who does it even as an afternoon's sport will know, is a serious business that gets in the blood; doubly so if your earnings depend on it. Richard Cashin, who headed the Atlantic Fisheries Task Force that issued an eloquent report to the Mulroney government in 1993, put it best when he wrote: "The sea is to those who fish what the land is to those who farm. The relationship of the harvester to the elements—the sea or the land—is more than economic, it is organic. It is how one gains a sense of place, of belonging and of accomplishment."

A people's culture depends for its sustenance on perpetuating the way of life that gave it birth. With the Rock's ground fisheries not just dormant, but extinct for the foreseeable future, the loss of work was not the equivalent of a mere factory closing in Ontario or a sawmill going bankrupt in British Columbia. Most of Newfoundland's outports depended entirely on the fishery, so the collapse of the resource meant the ruin of communities—not just the death of dreams, but the end of yearning.

To suggest that Newfoundland's tragedy was a microcosm of what was occurring across the country, or what might someday happen in the rest of Canada, was a gross exaggeration. But in one way at least there was a significant connection. Despite some initial transition payments from Ottawa and the declining benefits of unemployment insurance, Newfoundlanders realized that nothing would save their situation except their own efforts. That meant establishing local micro-industries: an Arctic char hatchery at Daniel's Harbour; an eiderdown business at Main Brook; a silviculture installation at Gander Bay; a fish silage plant at Leading Tickles; a massive compost heap at Lockston; a conversion of the old CN line that ran across the island into a tourist hiking trail.

Not one of these ventures reversed the downward spiral of the local economy, but their mere existence signalled a clear lesson to the rest of the country. The age of entitlement had come to an end; it was time to dig in and look after your own.

In a country that had amply earned its label as a "nanny" society, few trends could be more revolutionary than this. Canadians had grown up in the comforting belief that nothing which could be imagined was impossible, that life from generation to generation would become ever more bountiful, that governments would magically provide the fiscal infrastructure for such a Disneyland world. The expectation was based on the concept of universal access to government largesse, the snoozy notion that anyone who was born or became a Canadian automatically inherited the manna of heaven. By inference, those who dared question such blessings, by advocating that "special" rather than "universal" benefits be conferred, were accused of having horns on their heads and dismissed as reactionaries.

The idea that governments would take care of every need of its citizens became the unsigned social contract Canadians took for granted. Each of the national political parties approached this obligation with only marginal variations. Historically, the Tories had tended to be the most restrained in their approach, pledging that they would do everything for voters from birth to death. The more activist Liberals extended that pledge to keep everyone out of harm's way from womb to tomb. The New Democrats didn't believe in such artificial limits; their pledge "comfort zone" stretched from erection to resurrection.

The elusive definition of Canadian identity came simply to mean universal social programs. A pamphlet published in 1991 by Ontario's Ministry of Intergovernmental Affairs synthesized the essence of Canadian citizenship: "A national system of health care, an array of income support programs, free public and secondary education, and affordable post-secondary education are claims that all Canadians make on their governments. Taken together, these programs represent and symbolize Canadians' sense of themselves as members of a community where solidarity and mutual responsibility are fundamental social norms."

The Canadian Revolution was a response to diminishing expectations in a country that had thrived on raising them. Canadians' slow-burn realization, that their entitlements were running out and would never be honoured again, became a root cause of the decade's revolutionary impulses. Infinite demands on governments at all levels had collided with overdrawn fiscal resources. No matter how worthy the cause or the recipient, Canadians were thrown back on their own devices, and it was hell. The notion of fending for themselves without the security of government support represented a basic shift in the Canadian character. It was an attitudinal Revolution of no mean proportions.

The easy money which Ottawa and the provinces distributed had actually run out two decades earlier, though no one had paid any attention. Ever anxious to rent voters by buying their ballots, Pierre Trudeau, Brian Mulroney and nearly every provincial premier had poured out a Niagara Falls of largesse, having mortgaged the farm in the process. Canada had for years been selling off national assets to maintain a style of living for its citizens that they could no longer afford. Viewing the country's overdrawn accounts, the Wall Street gnomes who determine international credit ratings stood ready to bestow on Canada the dubious Third World status of a Zaïre with polar bears.

According to the Canadian Council on Social Development, the country by 1990 was spending $121 billion for social programs by all levels of government. At a time when rising debt loads were even larger than this staggering amount, this level of spending was clearly unsustainable in the long run; what was worse, it was costing an inordinate amount to move income between classes. Then, suddenly in the spring of 1995, the country woke up: a pending receivership, like a hanging, had wonderfully concentrated even the pickled minds of politicians. Governments prepared to abandon the entitlements which had nurtured and protected their citizens. The sorry state of the country's finances was documented most dramatically by the Vancouver Board of Trade's $35,000 Debt Clock, organized by Darcy Rezac in 1990, recording for all to see the increase—second by second—in the country's mortgage. (In mid-1995, it was rising at $1,400 per second.)

The idea that the state owed its citizens a living had a hard time dying. As the political scientist Alexander Brady once observed: "The role of the state in the economic life of Canada is really the *modern history* of Canada itself." The hoary cliché about there being no free lunch, trumpeted righteously by conservatives ever since the country first took on the responsibility for social welfare back in the mid-1920s, sadly turned out to be true. Any nation like Canada that had consumed more than it had earned would have to pay back its debts by earning more than it consumed.

The disillusionment with Brian Mulroney's government was largely propelled by the public realization that, despite his grandiloquent promises, the state could no longer deliver the goods. The money just wasn't there and his pledge that social spending was "a sacred trust," however well-meant, had therefore been hollow. Voters became disillusioned with the system because they realized that no future politician could ever deliver the goods again. It was one of those awful, stark epiphanies that touch a population once in a generation or so. Santa Claus was dead; looking after yourself was the only way to go.

But the retreat from entitlements was not easy for governments to make. The national news agenda was captured by public interest groups trotting into camera range shuffles of starving street kids, flotillas of dispossessed fishers and parades of gay and lesbian activists—all, rightly, lamenting their loss of entitlements. It was always easier to depict the effect of lost welfare than the reason it was needed in the first place.

No one suffered more grievously from having to watch these flickering television images than the media mogul Conrad Black. "It would be hard to avoid the conclusion," he wrote, "that we are a society composed entirely of battered wives, molested children, humiliated ethnic groups, exploited workers and other groups despised for their sexual preferences or cultural attributes, all festering in a spoiling environment. In Canada, government-designated victims outnumber the entire population because of the possibility of accumulating conditions of victimization, like food stamps." If only that kind of rhetorical flourish, for which Black was justifiably famous on both sides of the known universe, had been the end of his rant. It was not to be. Barbara Amiel, his columnist-wife, was fortunate enough to witness the denouement of her husband's agony. Writing in *Maclean's* on March 6, 1995, she reported: "About a month ago, I was watching television one night when I came upon a group of talking heads including the feminist Judy Rebick. Rebick was talking about the terrible plight of the dispossessed in Canada, specifically women, single mothers, minority persons and other ill-treated groups in our land. I let out whoops of laughter. The only ill-treated groups in Canada I can see these days are hard-working Canadians of every socio-economic class who fork over a lot of their money to the government so it can subsidize Rebick's various causes.

"'Please,' said my husband, Conrad Black, who was recuperating from the 'flu. 'Please change the channel or I'll be ill.' I thought he was joking, so I carried on watching. Finally, someone asked another guest on the program how Canadians were going to take care of those people who couldn't make it in Canadian society. The answer given was that all Canadians who worked and looked after themselves in this unfair land of ours ought to be responsible for one person who didn't. I was in stitches of laughter. This, I thought, was why going to Bedlam was considered entertainment in earlier centuries. Then, I heard a groan. 'Oh, no,' said my husband, 'that's what Canada has come to. At birth, each Canadian will decide whether to

be a member of the productive or nonproductive classes.' He went to
the bathroom...[When] I noticed my husband was still absent, I
went into the bathroom and found him lying on the floor looking
green. He has a strong sense of Canadian patriotism and seeing the
decline of rationality in Canada's political debate is a deeply
unhappy experience for him. His response to Judy Rebick was to
evacuate a perfectly good dinner."

Some *tableaux* require colourful commentary to amplify their
message; others, such as the image of Black on the white marble
floor, are best departed in silence.

CONRAD BLACK'S VANTAGE POINT may have been unique, but his views
were shared by others. "English Canada has become a crèche, a permanent daycare," thundered Scott Symons, the expatriate Toronto
novelist. "Everybody wants to be looked after. Everybody wants
their little bottle of milk. Everybody wants their nipple. How utterly
inconceivable! This is a disaster that will not be repaired in one or
two years. It will take a generation to climb out of the hole we have
dug for ourselves." Such rush to judgement may have sounded hysterical, but it was undeniable that once the attainment of social
objectives becomes divorced from national savings or increased
productivity, the entitlement culture breaks down. By the end of the
decade, entitlement to public-sector largesse had become more of a
privilege than a right. The reversal of what Canadians expected from
governments came into focus most clearly with Jean Chrétien's
approach to the social policy system the Liberals had been most
instrumental in creating. The Paul Martin budget of 1995 shifted the
definition of the state from social protector to social regulator,
claimed McGill political scientist Antonia Maioni. She told a
Queens University symposium in the fall of 1994: "It replaces the
notion of universality with the notion of means test. It shifts the
concept of Canadian society from collective to individual responsibility. We are heading toward a social safety net that puts more
emphasis on economics and less on social well-being and the question that needs to be answered is, how much of a mythology or ideological shift are Canadians prepared to accept?"

To appreciate the revolutionary nature of that shift in mythologies
requires some history. The Canadian welfare state had been inaugurated in 1927 with the introduction of old age pensions, payable (at

one dollar a day) to those citizens over seventy years of age who qualified by a means test. It was a time when the poor depended less on government assistance than the patronizing charity of the rich, there being a widespread belief that poor people were indolent, alcoholic or suffering from some fatal character flaw and deserved to be isolated in obscure dwellings at the edge of towns designated for "the wayward and the helpless." Although the 1933 Regina Manifesto of the Co-operative Commonwealth Federation had called for universal entitlement under socialism, the government-sanctioned notion of universality dated back to a seldom-remembered political crisis that took place in Ottawa during the early years of the Second World War. In 1941, the Liberal government of the day had passed a primitive Unemployment Insurance Act and established a Committee on Post-War Reconstruction, whose research adviser, Leonard Marsh, had studied at the London School of Economics under Sir William Beveridge, the author of several controversial British reports that recommended universal welfare measures. Back home, Marsh advocated "a charter for social security for the whole of Canada," the foundation of a welfare state. Nothing much happened to these suggestions until a Gallup poll showed the Socialists overtaking the Grits. In the provincial election of August 1943, they had come within four seats of taking power in Ontario and in 1944 did elect a government in Saskatchewan.

By the autumn of 1944, Mackenzie King, the Liberal prime minister who was a grand master at squatting on both sides of every political fence, had come to fear that massive postwar unemployment would drive Canadian voters into the embrace of the CCF. In order to co-opt "the approaching socialist hordes," he diverted the Liberal party's traditional managerial priorities to helping "the common man," as ordinary Canadians were then called. Advised by Marsh and others, Minister of Reconstruction C.D. Howe proposed that government provide a basic social welfare net and maintain "a high level of employment," urging adoption of "a total security program designed for the modern industrial state." It was all part of the revolutionary doctrine, pioneered by the British economic guru John Maynard Keynes, that governments could stimulate the economy during times of recession through loose monetary policy and public works spending. Approved by Cabinet, the C.D. Howe proposals were published as the "White Paper on Employment and Income" on April 12, 1945. They enshrined the idea that Canadian governments should be the prime factor in the creation and disposition of wealth.* Before Ottawa passed the Family Allowance Act, which in 1945 established the first baby bonuses, the federal health and welfare budget amounted to only 2 per cent of national revenues. The architect of Canada's expanded social net was Paul Martin, the late father of the Chrétien government's finance minister, who had been a delegate to the League of Nations in Geneva in 1938. A gutsy reformer and consummate politician, "Oom-pah," as he was known, spent forty years gliding around Ottawa, his right arm constantly at the ready to pump an out-stretched hand or pat a back. His advocacy of universality carried the day. Paul Martin's influence on postwar fiscal thinking is hard to overestimate: he served in the cabinets of four Liberal prime ministers and ran unsuccessfully three times for his party's leadership. It was entirely appropriate that when he died in September 1992, it took four bishops and a dozen priests to officiate at his funeral service—and that his casket was borne by a troop of seventy-five red-caped Knights of Columbus. It was less the burial of a man than of a generation.

Martin's personal influence and the philosophy of the White Paper dominated the thinking of Canadian administrations in the postwar years. George Hees, who was a leading member of the 1957–1963 Diefenbaker Cabinet, recalled that no one even thought of questioning costs when Cabinet was approving yet one more welfare measure. "It was never a problem," he remembered. "There was money coming out of our ears. Diefenbaker, like every other leader at the time, thought you could spend your way into power, and since national income was more than doubling every decade, nobody cared how much new programs added to expenditures. The money would always be there."

The problem most industrialized governments encountered when following Keynes's advice was that, while his theories called for stimulative intervention in lean years, it also called on governments to tighten the money supply and reduce their spending when times

---

* News of this pivotal policy declaration was almost totally ignored by the Canadian press, because the report was published on the same day U.S. wartime president Franklin Roosevelt died—and got all the coverage.

were good. This proved impossible in the competition for electoral power and race for Cold War supremacy. Successive Liberal and Tory federal governments expanded the notion that massive intervention in the economy was part of their mandate, which proved to be the ideal medicine for purging capitalism of its defects without tempting the voters to sample socialism.

Universality, the glorious notion that everyone was entitled to every program offered, was a very Canadian and wonderfully egalitarian idea, even if it was being constantly abused. Revenue Canada figures for a typical year in the 1980s showed that 500 Canadians earning more than $1 million each were collecting an annual $2.1 million in pensions, while another 250 with a combined gross income of $438 million claimed child-care tax breaks designed for people on low incomes. While social policy reformers on the right tended to point the finger at welfare abusers from the poorer classes, it was also the entitled rich who were draining the system of its funds. Montreal millionaire Peter Curry, for example, had married his son's youthful baby-sitter and had children by her. He boasted that he was collecting the baby bonus and old age pension at the same time and that he needed neither.

Despite its abusers, universality was part of the benign and compassionate Canada that existed for most of four decades following the Second World War. It seemed perfectly natural to help out the economically underprivileged; universality removed the stigma from receiving benefits and it seemed only fair for the richer provinces to pay sacrificial endowments (called equalization payments) to poorer regions for the sake of the national interest. This political orthodoxy left unquestioned the fact that Canadians had to pay a premium (through tariffs, subventions and subsidies of all kinds) for retaining their independence from the United States. "Like all liberal ideas, the Canadian experiment made heavy demands on selfish nature," wrote Michael Ignatieff, the brilliant Canadian-born commentator, writing in the London *Observer*. "A small élite of federal civil servants and politicians made Confederation work by acting as if the whole country was as virtuous as they. Yet the costs of virtue were high and could be borne only so long as the long summer of the postwar boom continued. By the early 1970s, liberal politics was coming apart everywhere in the face of hard times. The neo-conservative revolution that brought Margaret Thatcher to power encouraged taxpayers everywhere to believe that all public expenditure was a net reduction of their private welfare."

The music stopped with the Mulroney years—though it really should have been turned off by Pierre Trudeau. Between 1980 and 1984, the Trudeau government's annual deficits climbed from $12 billion to $36 billion, even though exactly what Canadians got for all that money remained a mystery. Trudeau's guiding principle of social welfare seemed to be his offhand smirk: "What's so great about work?" It was the legacy of debt, more than any other factor, that crippled Mulroney's time in office. It forced him to sponsor such lethally unpopular measures as the GST, derail the country's railway system, slash unemployment insurance benefits, abandon the promised daycare program and so on. Mulroney never had the luxury of launching the kind of social initiatives that earn political points and produce electoral rewards. Caught in the cusp of the Canadian Revolution, he was dealing with a public that still thought its support was auctionable. Ottawa's largest single expenditure during his tenure was the more than $40 billion paid annually as interest on the national debt.

Pressed by his opponents on the issue of Canada's universal welfare programs, Mulroney unequivocally declared during the 1984 election that they were "a sacred trust, not to be tampered with." Scarcely three months later, asked whether these programs were exempt from the fiscal review he had just announced, his finance minister vehemently protested: "No. That's why everything's on the table. The bullet has to be bitten." Shortly afterwards, Mulroney admitted that while medicare remained sacrosanct, all other measures would be reviewed. "Are we making proper use of taxpayers' money," he rhetorically demanded at a press conference, "by giving a bank president who makes $500,000 a year the baby bonus?"* Universality was in the process of being replaced by a safety net, designed to catch those who stumbled through the cracks of self-sufficiency. The issue came to a head in the new government's first budget, tabled on May 23, 1985. The document's governing dilemma was that less than 15 per cent of federal expenditures could be classified as discretionary; everything else

---

* This was not a very apt metaphor. No Canadian bank president was young enough to have children who qualified for the bonus, and none earned as little as $500,000 a year.

was already spent on debt interest, transfer grants to provinces or direct social payments to individual Canadians. In order to begin whittling down the deficit, the decision was made to attack indexation, the practice of automatically boosting social payments with cost-of-living increases, which had been the accepted norm since the mid-1970s. Implementation of de-indexing family allowances and old age pensions would have saved the federal treasury $6 billion over six years, if the cost of living rose by more than 3 per cent a year. The bureaucrats at Finance recommended offsetting the impact on the elderly poor through doubling their added cost-of-living increment in the Guaranteed Income Supplement.

That helpful notion was rejected and the Mulroney government went ahead with its de-indexing scheme, while at the same time reducing corporate taxes and, in effect, doing away with capital gains taxes by introducing a $500,000 lifetime exemption. The budget broadcast the unmistakable message that the Tories would kick old age pensioners on fixed incomes in the groin, while allowing millionaires to claim tax-free exemptions for the money made by their money. The audacious measures caused a storm of fury across the land. It was the opening salvo in a revolution that would eventually relegate the Conservative Party to the scrap heap of history. The perception that Ottawa had turned against the old and the needy crumpled the Mulroney government's popularity in one of the steepest ratings declines ever to hit a Canadian political party. The Canadian Council on Social Development estimated that de-indexing would relegate 250,000 more Canadians to existence below the poverty line. Pensioners' groups launched letter-writing campaigns and marched on Parliament Hill, while Bernard Richard, the head of the New Brunswick Senior Citizens' Federation, spoke for his generation when he declared that the budget "stinks and sucks." The Commons turned into a daily inquisition for the government benches as opposition MPs condemned the budget. Surprisingly, the outcry was echoed (in more moderate language but carrying the same message) by the very business groups that had urged Mulroney to reduce the deficit. The Business Council on National Issues, the Canadian Chamber of Commerce and the Canadian Organization of Small Business, fiscal archangels all, attacked the government's conservative agenda while primly disassociating themselves from the very policy they had so strenuously advocated. That was the final insult, as far as Mulroney was concerned, but for two weeks neither he nor Wilson backed down from their budget.

The budget was supposed to demonstrate not only that the Tories were fiscally responsible, but that Brian Mulroney was decisive. He had departed caucus early on June 19 for lunch at 24 Sussex Drive when a few seniors who had gathered around the main entrance spotted Mulroney leaving the building. They swarmed over to where he was standing. After a few minutes of friendly chit-chat, the prime minister found himself looking down at a spunky Ottawa sixty-three-year-old named Solange Denis. "You lied to us!" she shouted. "You made us vote for you, then Goodbye, Charlie Brown. If you do anything to the pensions you won't get back in three years..." Not realizing this was the defining moment of his administration, Mulroney mumbled a lame: "I'm listening to you, madam..."

Denis, who was fighting for her husband's $277 monthly pension, would not be denied. As every television-news footage editor and headline writer in the country took up her cause, the brief exchange gained iconic proportions. The camera angle had made Solange Denis appear even smaller than her actual height of five feet, four inches, yet she humbled the political giant who recently had earned the largest majority of any elected leader. To make it worse, when Mulroney got home that day he found his gloomy-faced boys lined up at the door waiting to ask their father if he was really going to take the money away from the old woman they had seen on television. It was too much. Eight days later the government caved in, restoring fully indexed pensions, nicking instead the businessmen whose organizations had proven so disloyal. The incident had made it clear that the "sacred trust" Mulroney had pledged to uphold was there for the breaking; meanwhile, Michael Wilson's credibility had turned into a mirage. The government's honeymoon had been terminated. More to the point, Canadians realized how vulnerable this apparently all-powerful Tory government really was: to launch a revolution against them seemed as difficult as seizing a telephone booth.

AFTER THAT EARLY REVERSAL, THE MULRONEY government did not follow the examples of either the Reagan or Thatcher administrations and disassemble the social welfare system. While baby bonus payments were terminated in 1989, they were replaced by a relatively generous program of child tax benefits for the poor. Though it was attacked as such, this move didn't really signal the end of universality since a refundable child tax credit program had first been introduced by the Trudeau government back in 1979. Under Mulroney, clawing social benefits back from higher-income earners enforced a kind of equality; the tax system was the dominant instrument of social policy. The problem was that routine adjustments became major incidents because of Mulroney's unyielding addiction to hyperbole. Only four months before the 1989 budget, he told a group of Prince Edward Island seniors that as long as he was prime minister, "social benefits, particularly benefits for the elderly, will be improved, not diminished." A few days later he confessed to a Quebec City press conference he would never sign an accord that would have the effect of threatening his mother's pension. Fifteen weeks later he did just that. The 1989 budget's clawback provisions cut in half old age pensions for anyone earning over certain minimums.

The least efficient of the social programs was unemployment insurance. It often seemed as if the whole country ran on pogey; actually only one-third of Canadian families collected UI payments. When Frank McKenna became premier of New Brunswick in 1987, he discovered that his province had 128 fish plants, each geared to the number of work weeks its employees needed to qualify for UI. Municipal employees in Quebec were enrolled in the same club, which meant that by investing $4.2 million in salaries, the provincial government could create an $8 million UI obligation for the feds. In the village of Newport on the Gaspé Peninsula, only 200 of 2,148 inhabitants worked in winter, while everyone else collected UI and went snowmobiling. McGill University economist William Watson cited the case of Larry Duchesne, a Prince Edward Island politician who took summer furloughs from his job as provincial leader of the NDP so he could qualify for UI and save his party $4,000. This was enough to keep it operating in the black.

And so it went. Owen Lippert, who wrote a report on UI abuses, compared the ethics involved to the statistical finding that factories covered by fire insurance had more frequent fires. This was not because fires were carelessly set, but because less was spent on fire safety equipment. Similarly, the presence of a UI safety net (or "hammock," as Conrad Black preferred to call it) allowed people to invest less in education, training and job-hunting. The Tories promised twice to reform the UI system and were given the ideas to do it, but backed away each time. It was too hot a political potato.

IT WASN'T UNTIL PAUL MARTIN tabled his second budget in 1995 that the situation began to change. Before the Liberal finance minister's father died in 1992, he had told his son at one of their final family gatherings, "I was the father of Canada's social revolution; you will create the country's economic revolution." That was what the son set out to achieve. The half-dozen finance ministers who served in the Trudeau and Mulroney cabinets had based their budgets on hope rather than reality and limited themselves to marginal reductions of obvious extravagances. They never dared make the kind of deep cuts that would force Canadians to downscale their expectations. Martin broke that psychological barrier, partly because he had no choice: the international money traders were in ambush, waiting to turn Canadian dollars into pesos. More significantly, he had wanted for some time to detonate a cultural turnabout. "Central governments such as Canada's," he told me during a 1992 interview, "have become too small to deal with the big, global issues, yet they remain too large and distant to deal with problems of local concern. So the challenge is to redefine the role of the central government as an institution that can do a limited number of things well, instead of continuing to pretend it can do everything for everybody." That turned out to be the budget's guiding philosophy. The document began to thaw public policy from its twenty-year deep freeze. Martin was convinced that most of the country's fiscal troubles dated back to the OPEC crisis of 1973, when Pierre Trudeau had tried to isolate Canada by claiming it could withdraw into itself and operate on oil prices lower than the rest of the world's. "From then on," Martin maintained, "we stopped evolving. When Mulroney took over, he had a tremendous mandate at just the right time, but didn't understand what he was supposed to do with it. By the time he did understand, during his second term, he had lost four crucial years and it was too late. You can't thrust change onto a country without leading the cultural shift that would make it acceptable."

It was that cultural shift which allowed Martin to float a budget past Canadians that made Mulroney's "Charlie Brown" budget seem like a gift from Santa Claus. The Mulroney years had served to heighten Canadians' anxieties about rising deficits while convincing them that governments were the worst possible agents of their reduction. Canadians finally were willing to accept the fact that universality was dead. Martin realized he had to present nothing less in his budget than the blueprint for a social and cultural revolution that would drastically alter the way Canadians viewed government. Among the first of the senior Ottawa bureaucrats to comprehend that fundamental shift was Tony Manera, the CBC president who immediately resigned in protest. "This will change the definition of public broadcasting in Canada," he warned, stunned by the $360-million cut the Mother Corp. was being asked to absorb over the following three years, especially since the Liberals had promised this would never happen. Apart from his courage in standing up for his principles—which Patrick Watson, supposedly the embodiment of broadcasting integrity, never exhibited during his three years as CBC's chairman—Manera realized the CBC would soon exist only in a brutally different and much-reduced fashion. That he seemed shocked by this development was understandable, but radical change in value systems is exactly what revolutions are about; Manera was not just flogging a dead horse but a buried one.

No provincial premier attacked the Martin budget more harshly than Ontario's Bob Rae, who was understandably upset about the disproportionately high transfer payment cuts from Ottawa. It was Rae, more than any other politician, who placed the document in its proper perspective when he declared that it "literally ends the Canada that we've known."

An Angus Reid poll for Southam News showed most Canadians believed Martin's $6 billion budget cuts didn't go far enough. Although the toughest budget in living memory, an astounding 69 per cent of Canadians thought it was "on the right track."* Popular

---

* One reason it was "on the right track" was that the Liberals had done what they always did best: stolen their ideas from any competing party that had achieved some resonance with the voters. During the King, St. Laurent, Pearson and Trudeau eras, that meant appropriating the platforms initially of the CCF and later of the NDP. In 1995, the Grits borrowed their ideas from Reform and just like the old days, carried Reform supporters to their banner along with their rented ideology. The Reid poll showed that 73 per cent of Reform party members approved the Liberal approach—even though their leader, Preston Manning, had the week before presented an alternate budget of his own.

support of the Martin initiatives represented an extraordinary condemnation of Michael Wilson who, during almost a decade as finance minister, had never once tried seriously to tackle the deficit. Paul Martin took a very different tack. "People who think governments today can give up because there's an election coming," he said, "simply don't understand the overwhelming degree of national will by Canadians from coast to coast to clean up the balance sheet and make this country sound and to not pass on to the next generation the terrible legacy that we have inherited and created." Once convinced that cost-cutting at the federal level was the way to go, most Canadians wanted to proceed as fast as possible. Four in ten respondents surveyed by Reid thought that Ottawa was reducing the deficit too slowly, while a surprising 83 per cent believed there would be a lot more cuts in the future. "Paul Martin effectively sounded the death knell of the traditional liberalism that Canadians have experienced for most of the post-Second World War era," accurately concluded David Bercuson, the University of Calgary historian.

In a way, the Canadian Revolution had come full circle. Creation of the social safety net had been a radical act at the time of its inauguration in the mid-1940s, just as its demise became a revolutionary process in the mid-1990s. In both cases the federal budgets merely reflected a deep shift in attitudes toward the role of government. The C.D. Howe initiatives were as much a result of cultural deference as the Martin budget was the result of cultural defiance. During the intervening half-century, Canada had turned into a different place, and Canadians had become very different people. Maude Barlow, the combative head of the nationalist Council of Canadians, got it right when she concluded after a post-budget tour of Canada: "The federal and provincial people all use the same term for what's really happening. They talk about 're-inventing government.' Their real message to Canadians is: 'You're on your own, Bud.'"

IV FLASHPOINTS

THIRTEEN

REBELLION: WEST

Riders of the Purple Bile

*"A revolutionary should neither look nor act like one
to get ahead in Canada."*
PRESTON MANNING

T HE DWELLERS OF CANADA'S PLAINS, foothills and western shore
had sat there every damn night for the whole decade, impatiently surfing the channels. Their nervous systems had been strained
beyond endurance as they watched the familiar procession of newsmakers and commentators: prime ministers who promised the moon,
academics who promised wisdom, furtive politicians who promised
the truth, economists with Coke-bottle glasses who promised the
apocalypse. There were the pundits who smiled smugly over place
names like Medicine Hat or Moose Jaw; CBC anchor-persons who
looked like stewards on British Airways night flights; profound
editorialists from Quebec who knew everything except how to smile.
These annoying creatures hogged the television screen to debate
one interminable topic: what Quebec wanted in order to stay in
Confederation, or what it didn't want so that it could leave.

This exercise in futility was more revolting than revolutionary, but
every once in a while (especially in rural Saskatchewan) a frustrated
farmer would lose control and blast his television set with a shotgun,
letting go with both barrels just to be sure. It particularly itched the
trigger-fingers when the constitutional wonks got that "Bingo!" look

in their eyes and explained exactly why Quebec was a "distinct society"—fighting words to Westerners, who felt so markedly distinct
themselves that they should each belong to an individual nation-state
of their own. Unlike Hans Johst, Hitler's censor of plays, who claimed
to reach for his revolver upon hearing the word "culture," these
confounded Westerners reached for their twelve-gauge upon hearing
the word "distinct." It got so bad that George Richardson, the
merchant prince from Winnipeg, maintained the easiest way to spot
genuine Westerners was by deafness in their right ear.

The sentiment these anonymous marksmen represented was not
"anti-Quebec," as Montreal and Quebec City columnists were so
quick to aver. Anti-Quebec was the talk in Legion halls and at meetings of Western separatist splinter groups, after the press went home.
Except for noxious pockets of anti-French and anti-Catholic prejudice, which certainly did exist, most of the anti-Quebec feeling was
based less on religion or language than on the Westerners' stubborn
conviction that all provinces and all citizens should be equal. It
didn't matter how often well-meaning politicians explained that
endowing Quebec with official "distinct society" status merely recognized existing differences and did not bestow any implied superiority. The sharpshooters were expressing their sense of outrage, not
so much at Quebec, but at the longstanding refusal of anyone in
authority to listen to their equally legitimate beefs and lamentations.

Many Westerners were happy to dip their kids in French immer-
sion and were intrigued by living in a bilingual country, but they also
wanted an equal say in how Canada should operate. Statistically, this
request did not seem out of place. The four western provinces had a
million more residents than Quebec and their gross domestic
product was 20 per cent greater. But Quebec's dominance reflected
more than mathematics. Ever since the founding of Confederation,
Quebeckers had demonstrated an uncanny ability to play the politics
of self-interest, voting as a bloc and controlling the federal administrations that became dependent on their ballots.

The Canadian Revolution started slowly in the West, like the
meeting and marrying of many drops of rain sliding along a wire to
form one steady trickle. By the mid-1980s, the West's various grievances—some historic, some petty, but most deeply felt and well-jus-
tified—had turned that trickle into a stream and the stream into a
river, fed by a ferocious craving to be heard.

FRONTIERS ARE PLACES TO ESCAPE TO. Their emptiness creates a state of mind where one seeks to be lost and rediscovered. Living on the frontier—which in central Canadian terms, means anywhere west of Mississauga—signifies existence on the edge of undiscovered potential, in oneself as much as one's environment. That sense of possibility endowed most Westerners, whether generations old or newly arrived, with heady feelings of new energy that turned them into dreamers. When those dreams collided with the stereotypes held dear by the nation's power arbiters of the Toronto-Ottawa-Montreal axis, revolutionary thoughts began to stir. Ignorant of the lively culture that had developed in the land of the setting sun, Canadian centralists still regarded their country as an Atlantic nation whose western backyard was endowed with not much more than wheat, oil and scenery; a land that stretched through monotonous flats to the mountains and some distant other shore. (They similarly saw Japan as a country to the east of Europe, instead of to the west of Canada.) Never in a thousand years would they realize that the West was every bit as developed and cosmopolitan as Ontario or Quebec.

The West's revolutionary mood evolved not because of such ignorance (most Westerners took it for granted) but because their discontents multiplied without ever being debated, much less resolved. Isolated from the national (which is to say, Toronto) media, Western advocates were ignored except for the occasional caricatures similar to those accorded witch-doctors in Africa. The central Canadian élite could never accept the notion that Westerners were anything more than bubbas in the boondocks, whose lives were consumed in envy of the lucky few plugged into Action Central in Toronto, Ottawa and Montreal. Most Westerners did not want to weaken the centre or gain official recognition of their distinctiveness. What they did want with increasing ferocity was control over *their own destiny*, which they felt had been abandoned by a country that had mobilized its best and brightest to satisfy the demands of Quebec, without ever realizing that another large chunk of geography had aspirations that were just as urgent and just as valid.

Westerners had no familiar framework to understand the inexorable impulse of French Canadians toward self-determination, so they interpreted each of Quebec's gains as the hot breath of rejection. They reacted accordingly. This was particularly true of Premier Robert Bourassa's notorious Bill 178, which outlawed the use of

English on outdoor signs. The bill was introduced after an earlier law, which outlawed the commercial display of English both inside and outside, was struck down as a violation of human rights. Quebec simply opted out of the Charter, justifying its insistence on the "collective right" to protect its own language. This was interpreted in the West as an attack on the individual rights of English-speakers. Official bilingualism had always required the generosity of the West and, for the most part, it had got it. West of Ontario, the population who spoke French as a mother tongue was a tiny fraction of the population; many more times that number learned French as a second language. The enactment of Bill 178 was a signal to Westerners that their attempts at accommodation were futile; their sense of fair play had been violated and the social contract with Quebec was torn beyond repair. For some, particularly those who advocated a reactionary brand of Western chauvinism, it was a signal that the West should itself separate from Confederation. "There's a revolution going on," editorialized Ted Byfield, publisher of *Alberta Report*. "Western Canada more than ever intends to assert itself. If Quebec starts acting seriously about getting out, there's going to be people in the West asking the same question."

THE ROOTS OF WESTERN ALIENATION stretched back to when the territories originally joined Confederation. British Columbia, as an established colony, entered on its own terms, demanding construction of the CPR to seal the bargain. The great Canadian plains had no such leverage. Eventually divided into three provinces, the land was acquired directly from the Hudson's Bay Company, which sold territory lands to Canada in 1870 for $1.46 million in cash, a grant of 45,000 acres around its 120 outposts and another land grant of 7 million fertile acres in the West. "We have quietly and almost without observation, annexed all the country between here and the Rocky Mountains," Sir John A. Macdonald boasted to a colleague. It was true. Neither the HBC factors nor any of the settlers then occupying the territory were consulted, or even officially notified, of the buy-out. The land was held "for the purposes of the Dominion," which meant that Canada retained ownership of all natural resources. This included the land, most of which was given away by Ottawa either to the HBC, to railway builders as construction subsidies (including the 1.3 million acres of Saskatchewan which were granted to railroad promoters who didn't build a mile of track) or to settlers. By 1930, when natural resources were handed over to the three provinces, they found themselves with minority ownership of their own surveyed territory. (Alberta held title to 18.1 per cent of its land; Manitoba, 12.8 per cent and Saskatchewan, 4.6 per cent.) This act of land piracy by the federal government was the Prairie equivalent of Quebec's Conquest, with a similar sense of historic grievance. "Western alienation anchors in this tap root," explained Ralph Hedlin, the Calgary writer and economist. "Western Canadians were taught right from the beginning that they were helpless to resist when their interests were in conflict with 'the purposes of the Dominion.' They found confirmation in struggles related to rail rates, the grain acts, transportation, tariffs. The National Energy Program of 1980 replicated, in oil resources, the plundering of the land resource, confirming the power and the greed of the central government that imposed it."

The plains were populated mostly by immigrants from Europe who, once settled, provided a rich market for central Canadian goods. This pattern of colonial development was cast into law by the protective tariffs of Macdonald's National Policy. Until the late 1950s considerable investment was made in the Prairies and British Columbia, although the decision-making, the venture capital and the profits tended to come from, and return to, the U.S. and Central Canada: the development of Alberta's oil gushers and natural gas fields, sparked by the 1947 Imperial strike at Leduc; the delineation of Saskatchewan's valuable uranium and potash deposits; the carving out of Alcan's $1 billion aluminum empire at Kitimat, B.C.; the construction of the pivotal Trans-Canada Pipeline; the emergence of forestry mills and metal smelters in northern and coastal British Columbia. But after the 1950s, most investment dollars shifted to Ontario, where the nation's industrial future was being forged, and to Quebec, where the struggle for national unity was starting to be fought. The West went into an economic slump. Wheat sales, which in postwar Canada had accounted for one-tenth of the country's gross domestic product and a third of its exports, came to make up only 1 per cent of the GDP and less than 4 per cent of overseas sales. The oil patch in Alberta and the mining and forest industries of British Columbia flared for a while, then went into remission. As its economy declined by virtue of political and economic considerations beyond its control, the West began to feel a deepening sense of isolation from the national decision-making process. This grew particularly bitter after the 1963 defeat of John Diefenbaker and his Prairie pro-consul, Alvin Hamilton. For one brief shining hour, while the man from Prince Albert had ruled, the West's concerns had been moved to the top of the national agenda. But Lester Pearson reversed that. He never championed the Western cause and the Liberals won only six of the 192 Prairie seats they contested in the four general elections fought under his leadership.

For a while it looked as if that estrangement would end when Pierre Trudeau became Liberal leader. The three Prairie provinces had given him eleven seats in his first election, creating a new national majority. (At the time, Liberals also had fifty-seven MLAs in four provincial legislatures.) But it quickly became clear that the West had misread Trudeau. Because of his emphasis on the "One Canada" theme, many Westerners thought he intended to get tough on Quebec. Instead, Trudeau was tough on the *provincial* Quebec government, but conciliatory to Quebec in *federal* politics to the point where Westerners felt he was intent on turning Ottawa into a French-speaking technocracy. Trudeau tended to govern as though the country were divided into Upper Canada (Ontario), which he ruled; Lower Canada (Quebec), to which he catered; and Outer Canada (all the rest), which he ignored.* Westerners still flash with anger when they recall the havoc spread by the Trudeau government's National Energy Program, which obliged Albertans to sell their crude at half the world price in order to subsidize Ontario's manufacturing sector, a step that cost the province revenues of $4.6

---

* At one of his early cabinet meetings, Trudeau was being briefed about how restless French-speaking citizens in Manitoba had become and how this could turn into a political threat to him. "Surely," he retorted, "there must be somebody out there we can hang." At Calgary's Petroleum Club in those days they were cracking up over a story that had James Coutts, the prime minister's major-domo, deciding whether to run in Alberta as a Trudeau Liberal. He flew to Calgary, dressed up in an appropriate Western outfit so that he wouldn't be recognized and went to the toughest bar in town. There he yelled out, "Trudeau is a horse's ass!" A cowboy sitting nearby immediately punched him in the face, sending the delicate Coutts reeling across the room. As soon as he recovered, Coutts shook his head in disbelief and muttered: "I didn't realize this was Trudeau country!" "It's not," the cowboy replied. "This is horse country."

billion a year. Visiting the oil patch in those days was like walking into a laundromat at midnight and being confronted by one of those functioning crazies who corner people with their real and imagined woes. Alberta Premier Peter Lougheed appeared on national television and threatened to cut oil shipments flowing east through a series of embargoes (60,000 barrels per day every six months) until the NEP was lifted. Trudeau's Prairie support had evaporated by the mid-1980s, while several separatist parties sprang into existence. From their apogee of twenty-seven western seats in Trudeau's first election, the Liberals had fallen to two seats by the time of his last.

In contrast to Trudeau, Brian Mulroney cared deeply about maintaining the Western leg of his ruling coalition. On election night, 1984, when the Tories had swept every seat in Alberta and won thirty-seven of the fifty-six seats in the three other Western provinces, Harvie Andre, elected in Calgary Centre, boldly declared: "We have reconstructed the old Mackenzie King coalition of Quebec and the West. We will not easily give up or squander either side of that combination." Good as the future minister's word, Mulroney promptly signed a Western Accord which eliminated the reviled National Energy Program. He scrapped the punitive and unprecedented federal taxes on provincial oil and gas, moved the National Energy Board to Calgary, established a Western Diversification Office with headquarters in Edmonton and a budget of $1.2 billion, signed a Western Procurement Initiative that significantly boosted government purchases in the region, reduced freight rates and deregulated the transportation industry, did his damnedest to sell more wheat (without ever asking why he should) and appointed a quarter of his senior cabinet ministers from the West. On a trip to Winnipeg in the summer of 1985, Mulroney unilaterally declared the official end of Western disaffection: "You've got one-third of the Cabinet and half the seats on the Priorities and Planning Committee. You're at the decision-making centre of Ottawa. Western alienation is dead."

Hardly. Mulroney spent an inordinate amount of time and energy jetting from Red Deer to Prince George to Comox to Saskatoon and back again, but he never got the message. Western Canadians did not want the prime minister to arrive in their home towns to repeat the compulsory salutation about how glad he was to be "*out here* in (fill in the blank)," as if he had been disconnected from his Ottawa life-support system and couldn't wait to be beamed back to Mission Control at 24 Sussex Drive. While more federal dollars and greater cabinet representation were welcome, that wasn't the answer either. Provided with an impressive phalanx of first-line cabinet ministers: Don Mazankowski, Joe Clark, Jake Epp, Pat Carney, Harvie Andre, Ray Hnatyshyn, Charles Mayer and Bill McKnight, most Western commentators wrote them off as having been put in place primarily to sell federal positions in the West, instead of acting as defenders of Western causes at the centre. At the same time, Ottawa poured a gusher of subsidies into Western agriculture. Some categories, like assistance to grains and oil seeds, were up six and one-half times over the previous government's payouts. Still, by the fall of 1990 Prairie farmers were going bust while harvesting the second-largest crop in history. It was not an issue that grabbed much time on the television news, yet throughout most of the decade, Canadian agriculture was in a crisis yet nobody, including the men and women who worked the earth, had the faintest notion how to solve it. During the first six of the Mulroney years, special government aid to Western farmers totalled more than $17 billion. According to the Paris-based Organization for Economic Co-operation and Development, which produced statistics on its members' activities, each job in agriculture cost Canada $100,000 in subsidies, which was five times higher than in the United States or the European Community. Canada's 105,000 grain farmers were the country's most expensive citizens; Canadian agriculture received more subsidies than all other industries combined. In 1989, for example, farmers pocketed $3.3 billion from the federal government (while all industrial programs amounted to $2.7 billion) and received another $2 billion from provincial treasuries. These amounts were staggering, yet most farmers resented being beholden to governments for such generosity. They were all too aware that they were victims of an international system based on only the vaguest connection with the laws of supply and demand.

The real quandary of Canadian agriculture was not the size of the subsidy, but that subsidies were not resolving the problem. In Saskatchewan, the Christian Farm Crisis Committee estimated that one-sixth of the province's 60,000 farmers lived on the edge of bankruptcy, their land and equipment liable to seizure by banks and other financial institutions. About 4,000 grain farmers were being forced off the land every year. More cash wasn't the answer, but with each season the agricultural protest movement grew more desperate. "We can't quite decide whether we want to punish our farmers for being involved in such a volatile business, or support them because the international situation isn't their fault," complained Professor I.C. Stabler, head of the agricultural economics department at the University of Saskatchewan. "We've subsidized them, but we've done it begrudgingly on a year-to-year basis and after the fact—so that farmers who plant in one season haven't the faintest notion what they're going to receive for their crops, while their counterparts in North Dakota know a year ahead. Everyone recognizes that we've created a problem of overproduction and that it would be in everybody's best interest to solve it. But there's no popular support for doing anything quick or drastic."

Subsidizing agriculture wasn't the only Mulroney policy that backfired. The inefficient shipyard of Marine Industries Ltd. in Sorel, Quebec, received a $263 million federal bail-out when it couldn't complete its contract to build three naval frigates, yet the feds reneged on their promise to spend $317 million at the Versatile shipyard in Vancouver to construct the Polar Eight icebreaker for the defence of Canada's sovereignty. At the same time, Ottawa contributed $558 million to build a wildly uneconomical heavy-oil upgrader in Lloydminster which, after suffering heavy losses, was abandoned by Ottawa six years later. Part of the problem was Mulroney himself. He had done all that was humanly (and fiscally) possible to make the West love him, but his failure had more to do with his inability to connect with the Prairie ethic. "I just don't have a lot of respect for Mulroney," declared John Masters, founding partner of Canadian Hunter, one of Calgary's most successful resource companies, "and I suspect that something like that is acting on the Alberta people. He certainly has come through with pretty nearly all the things we could reasonably expect in the way of assistance and support from Ottawa. I just don't like the way he's run the rest of his business. He could do anything for me and I'd still say, 'Mulroney, you're a wimp. You did that just to buy me.' I don't detect any ring of sincerity or strength of purpose in the guy." An even more direct critique came from Gurston Dacks, a political science professor at the University of Alberta in Edmonton, who accused the prime minister of being too self-satisfied: "He expects a choir of angels to break out singing whenever he speaks. That's contrary to the Western style, which expects people to be more self-effacing."

By the late 1980s the citizens of Canada's plains found themselves caught up in such a series of contradictions that a revolution seemed the only way out. Westerners' faith in individualism translated itself into faith in free enterprise and the invisible hand of the market. Yet, caught in a web of international subsidy wars, the farmers of no other North American region became more dependent on government hand-outs. The West also found itself caught in the revolutionary re-orientation of Canada. Explored and developed on an east-west axis, Mulroney's free trade initiative had turned the country ninety degrees so that the flow of just about everything began to run in a north-south direction. For central Canada this resulted in scores of manufacturing plants moving south of the border; for the West it resulted in the re-examination of the very roots of their Canadianism. British Columbians began to feel more affinity with the Pacific North-West, which formed a casually defined enclave called Cascadia. On most days, British Columbians felt closer ties to the dragon-nations of the Pacific Rim than they did to Ontario. As Allan Blakeney, a former Saskatchewan premier, put it, "Separatism is something people here feel rather than think about. But there's no doubt that most Westerners are concerned that the essential bargain of Confederation has not been kept by Ottawa."

ANY CENTRAL CANADIAN UNDERSTANDING OF THE WEST necessarily starts with the explanation that no such region exists. It was barely possible to encompass the three Prairie provinces into a term such as "the plains," but it was silly to include British Columbia in such a grouping. British Columbia was better understood as an appendage of the country, rather than as an integral part of it. The province operated strictly according to its own rules, which were made up as it went along—or as the Pacific folk preferred to put it—as their world unfolded.

There never was much evidence in the province of the down-home neighbourliness of the Maritimes, of the righteous self-obsession of Quebec, of the arrogant superiority of Ontario, of the Hallmark optimism of Manitoba or of the rugged Howdy Doodyism of Alberta. British Columbia was where it rained most of the time and residents were uncertain whether it was God trying to wash the province clean of its sins, or to sweep it out to sea. It was not a very Canadian place. People played as hard as they worked and there was little evidence of the Protestant ethic that made this country what it used to be. British Columbians were lacking in modesty and in the deference to authority that had characterized Canadians everywhere else. The province's most successful citizens were proud of their accomplishments and instead of trying to hide them, flaunted their wealth, their buffed biceps and their mates.

The province was different because everything was so polarized, with little sense of Canadian moderation or compromise. That trait was best illustrated by B.C.'s provincial governments, which alternated more sharply from far left to distant right than any other administration in the country. Even religious observances were subject to the provincial bent for acrimony. When the government installed a prayer room in the provincial legislature, it was immediately taken over by a coven of local witches, a Satanist and a couple of garden-variety Victoria pagans.

Few British Columbians know much about their own history, yet there exists a strand of shared thought and experience which reached back to their economic beginnings and helped to explain the province's divisive nature. It started in the bunkhouses of the early fur traders, railway builders, miners and loggers. They were mostly independent-minded labourers, from the idled factories of northern England and the shipyards of Scotland, who worked long hours in life-threatening jobs. Powerless and frustrated, they dreamed of creating a new, more equitable, social order. On the other side were the bosses, rugged free-booters who owned their mining and logging concessions and were determined to squeeze every ounce of muscle from their underpaid workforce. They resisted unions as long as possible and yielded not an inch in the battle for greater profits. Contributing to the problem was B.C.'s choppy terrain which allowed only a tiny agriculture sector, thus forfeiting the solid and ameliorating influence that farming usually brings to politics. "People who come from the land can exercise a significantly stabilizing force," maintained Peter Pearse, a professor of forestry at the University of British Columbia, "but all we had was free-wheeling entrepreneurs and the aggressive drifters who came here to work for them. The heritage of all that friction is that our right-wing parties are more reactionary than anywhere else and our left-wing parties are more socialist—and there is nothing in between." The historical struggle between labour and bosses provided prime breeding ground for a revolutionary attitude that would start in the West and work its way eastward through the course of the decade.

There was no better example of this Great Divide than the government of William Vander Zalm, who served as the B.C.'s premier from September of 1986 to April of 1991. A self-proclaimed loose cannon who recognized no boundary between church and state (on such issues as abortion, for example), he stretched credibility to its breaking point. After a dozen resignations shook his cabinet, Vander Zalm's followers were winnowed down to marginal misfits and rednecks from bumper-sticker country.*

My favourite encounter with the British Columbia premier took place in the summer of 1987, when the Commonwealth Conference was being held in Vancouver. Nathan Nemetz, then the province's chief justice, hosted a formal dinner party for Lee Kuan Yew, most senior of the attending prime ministers, who had ruled Singapore with an iron fist since 1959. Much of the Vancouver Establishment was on the guest list and Bill Vander Zalm had been asked to propose a toast to the distinguished visitor. Despite his Great White Hunter good looks his face somehow lacked definition, as if it were painted on a balloon; his eyes were as unfocused as billiard balls. Most remarkable was his body language: the flashing semaphore of his piranha-perfect teeth, the enigmatic duck of his head and his arms parked akimbo. They signalled a man who would not accept any assessment of himself except his own. Just before we were ushered in, the premier sidled up to me and whispered, as if to confirm a rumour he had once heard: "This Singapore—is it in the Commonwealth?" I allowed that it was. He rewarded me for this delicious secret with a dazzling flash of molars, then took his place

---

* Out of this turmoil came the momentum to establish a free-enterprise alternative to Mike Harcourt's New Democratic Party, then in Opposition. Called the Pacific Party, it was co-founded by Ed Odishaw, a leading Tory lawyer and his wife, Theresa; Gowan Guest, a former principal secretary to John Diefenbaker; and Jim McLean, a one-time regional director of the Social Credit party. The Pacific Party (PP), inevitably labelled "the Pee-Pees" by the media, was making some headway and decided to create a youth wing. When a certain irresponsible journalist labelled that offspring "the Wee-Wees," the party slid into oblivion.

at the table and delivered a depressingly spirited toast to the Far East dictator, with whom he got on exceedingly well.

During his five years in office, Vander Zalm demonstrated the attention span of a squirrel, enunciating policies at the drop of a microphone with little benefit of forethought. This political surf-boarding was best caught by former premier Dave Barrett, who described Vander Zalm's operational code as: "Ready! Fire! Aim!" Throughout Vander Zalm's stewardship, the province's button manufacturers were kept busy with such entries as: "Gay Florists Against Vander Zalm," while T-shirt merchants flogged a design that showed a smiling, hairy monster rising from a swamp with the caption: "It came from Holland!" The premier appeared unruffled by all this and continued to flog his gardening video, host his Sunday radio phone-in show, hawk authentic copies of his wife's headbands at his Fantasy Gardens gift shops and lecture the few survivors in the echo chamber of his Cabinet.

Vander Zalm's downfall was the direct result of the conflict-of-interest scandal surrounding the sale of his private theme park. Only the editorial cartoonists grieved his downfall, but his reign was not without significance. The Canadian Revolution may have been a new phenomenon in the rest of the country; in B.C. it had already become a way of life. As the Revolution took hold elsewhere, more and more Canadians began to behave like British Columbians, who had long since abandoned faith in government and transferred that trust to themselves or their chosen special-interest groups. The Left and Labour continued to hold sway because they amounted to little more than pressure groups. Talk-radio hosts such as Rafe Mair had more credibility in the province than elected leaders, perhaps because Vander Zalm had blurred the distinction between entertainment and public policy. In any event, British Columbians regarded government as something to protest, to cajole or to ridicule, but seldom something to command their respect.

WHAT VANDER ZALM DID FOR THE West Coast, the CF-18 did for the Prairies. Winnipeg was the Vienna of Canada, a city which had lost its empire. Its appeal was best described by local architect Charles Brook, who said: "It's a great place to live, but I wouldn't want to visit." Once the lively and prosperous centre of Canada's grain trade and the gateway to the West, Winnipeg had been bypassed: first, by construction of the Panama Canal, which robbed it of much transcontinental rail traffic, and later, by the federal government decisions to move many of its agencies to other cities, including relocation to Montreal of the Air Canada repair shops and the VIA Rail maintenance yards. The decline was supposed to be reversed in June of 1986, when Bristol Aerospace of Winnipeg emerged as pre-ferred bidder on the $2-billion maintenance contract for the Canadian Armed Force's jet fighter-bomber, the CF-18. There had been much delay and controversy over the contract, but a team of seventy-five independent experts had found that the Bristol proposal was technically superior and $65 million cheaper than the rival bid by Canadair Ltd. of Montreal. The Mulroney government had recently sold Canadair, then a Crown corporation, to Bombardier for a fraction of its real value. (The purchase price for the debt-free company was $120 million, which Bombardier could have recouped through sale of the land alone that accompanied title to the firm's impressive design patents and manufacturing facilities.) As rumours began circulating in Ottawa that Bristol might not get the contract, Patrick MacAdam, in charge of the PMO's caucus liaison office, sent Brian Mulroney a memorandum warning there would be "a helluva fire-storm" if the contract went to Montreal. On Halloween morning, Treasury Board President Robert de Cotret confirmed the rumours. (The announcement had been delayed in order to allow Grant Devine, the Tory leader in Saskatchewan, a clear run in the provin-cial election on October 20.)

Suddenly, the CF-18 contract was no longer about maintaining jet aircraft; it was a slap in the face to Western Canada. The plains exploded. The alienation aroused by a clearly political decision to favour Montreal over a superior bid from Winnipeg undermined the Tory government's carefully nurtured policies of reconciliation. Frank Lawson, owner of Mother Tucker's Electronics in Winnipeg and a former president of the Manitoba Young Conservatives, erected a sign in front of his store that accurately summed up the sentiment: "MULRONEY, TAKE YOUR POLITICS, TAKE YOUR CONTRACT, TAKE YOUR B.S. & SHOVE IT!" Manitoba New Democrat Premier Howard Pawley vigorously protested the deci-sion and threatened not to co-operate in any constitutional talks, although next year he did sign the Meech Lake Accord. David Elton of the Canada West Foundation compared the Quebec favouritism of the CF-18 deal to the National Energy Program, since "in both cases a national party made the hard decision on the basis that, to any government, central Canadian seats are life-and-death, while Western Canadian seats are a luxury."

The sense of anger and betrayal that grew out of the CF-18 decision was made worse by the fact that the West no longer had a partisan apparatus through which it could funnel its frustrations. Such Prairie protest movements as the federal wing of Social Credit, the Progressive Party and the United Farmers of Alberta and Manitoba had either vanished or, like the NDP, been co-opted by labour unions and Eastern intellectuals. The choice of Quebec for the jet fighter maintenance program, against the advice of Mulroney's own experts and at considerable extra cost, convinced Westerners that his goodwill was worthless. Out of that discontent emerged Preston Manning's Reform party, which held its founding convention in 1987. Within a few years of its founding, this vintage expression of Canadian populism swept the government of the day right out of Western Canada. It was the first time in history that an aircraft had spawned a political party.

THE WAY TO SPOT A POPULIST movement is by the empty Kentucky Fried Chicken buckets used as collection plates at the end of each rally. Western populists were people who took seriously the messages in greeting cards. They were generally against big government, gays of any gender and abortions of any description; opposed to anything in print except dollar bills; they hated vegetarians, cappuccino drinkers, environmental wackos, femi-Nazis and gun control advocates, who had all blended in their imagination into a turbanned Mountie ordering a *café au lait* in French at the Legion hall.* Non-believers were dismissed as élitists, a category that included anybody with more than two independently programmed brain cells to rub together or the capacity to consider more than one point of view. But there was a streak of decency to be found in Reformers

---

* The most explicit explanation of the Reform party's stand on abortion came from Edmonton North MP Ron Mix, who told a party forum that "a woman should pay the price for an unplanned pregnancy. When the woman lays with the man, she has made her choice. Sexual intercourse isn't all fun and games." Neither, by the sound of it, is the Reform party.

also, of belief in the Christian faith and the importance of earning your own way, the shared legacy of life on the homestead. "Populist parties are like oil wells, tapping reserves of pent-up energy," noted Sydney Sharpe and Don Braid in their book about Reform, *Storming Babylon*. "Every generation or so they release the anger of Canadians in a geyser of frustration directed mainly at the country's political and economic élites, the people who claim to know best. Populism is always angry, often negative, and never friendly to the status quo."

The growth of Reform may have been sparked by the CF-18, but it had been a cause looking for a movement years before it became a party. Preston Manning had long pounded the pavements and highways of Alberta, gaining support for his vision of a reformed Canada where the regions would hold as much clout in Ottawa as the central provinces. He rejected separatist talk as irresponsible and sought to play off the positive energy of Western sentiment, as demonstrated by his original party motto, "The West wants IN" (a phrase coined by Ralph Hedlin in an *Alberta Report* column). But this historical sense of grievance was freshened by the daily CF-18 headlines to give his party momentum. Pollster Angus Reid recalled driving along Vancouver's Marine Drive when he spotted a Reform rally. "You could see the anger in the faces of these staunch Reformers and the commitment they had to this new cause of really being mad as hell and standing up and telling people. It's the emotion of Reform that's the most extraordinary element in this whole story."

Even if he looked like a fugitive from the third trombone chair in Lawrence Welk's band, Preston Manning was perfectly cast as Reform's founding leader. He was not a great orator nor an impressive stage presence, but he had that Bible-thumper's perfect cadence that made God seem to bear witness to his message. In the party's early days he reached all the way back to Louis Riel, whose firebrand tradition he hoped to emulate. "Louis got hanged in the end," he'd say, as if he were taking the audience into his confidence. "But we don't talk a lot about that. It doesn't help membership sales at the end of our meetings." His confidants cursed the fact that Manning wrote his own speeches, because that took him away from the essential business of organization and policy planning. But Presto! knew exactly what he was doing. His test of successful populism was that people would recognize in him a man free to speak his mind and his conscience. Any hesitation between thought and word would signal to his audiences that some ghost writer or pollster might have been involved in the process, which would never do. "We believe in the common sense of the common people," was his guiding principle.

The Reform message spanned the Prairies and scaled the Rockies, eroding the once-impregnable Tory bastions in Alberta and the B.C. interior. Manning's absence of charisma prompted competing politicians to dismiss him as a temporary and overblown phenomenon. They forgot that the Reform leader had to do little else except be there, providing Western voters with a voice of their own. As *The Globe and Mail*'s Miro Cernetig wryly commented, after observing the passions at one large Reform rally: "Any politician who can turn lack of charisma into his biggest asset is no amateur."

The son of Ernest Manning (who had parlayed his religious beliefs into twenty-five uninterrupted years as Alberta's premier), Preston was an active member of the evangelical Alliance Church of Canada, which forbade homosexual practices, placed women subservient to men and only married mates who had entered into a personal relationship with Jesus Christ. It has also been said, in jest, that its adherents would not make love while standing in case the Lord thought they were dancing. Manning claimed to have kept his religious beliefs apart from his politics, but the Holy Spirit was his boon companion. Everything he stood for was rooted in his evangelical beliefs, even if his sense of brotherly love did not prevent him from using blood-thirsty political imagery. "We like to think of Western Tory MPs as a herd of buffalo, lumbering along, and ourselves as a small but growing pack of wolves," he once explained to a party gathering. "We can't take the herd in a head-on situation— we'd be trampled—but should one of them grow old, or lame, or infirm, then we'll pick them off." Manning did not go as far as his father, who once claimed, "Giving to the individual societal benefits such as free medicare breeds idleness, causing breakdown in the relationship with God." But he came close. He wanted to eviscerate medicare (by introducing a two-tier system), welfare, non-white immigration, multiculturalism, women's lobbies and bilingualism. Reform membership grew most animated in opposition to the three "Gs": gays, gun control and government spending. While their platform was not against equal opportunities, Reformers were staunchly opposed to any state guarantees of equal results. Manning's disciples claimed that he was simply championing populism over élitism. Whatever, Manning's ideology faithfully reflected that of his followers. "The typical Reformer," charged Michael Peers, the head of Canada's Anglican Church, "only trusts people who, 'Look like me, think like me, talk like me, and preferably come from within three miles of where I come from.'"

Manning was well aware that he was leading a revolution, but he knew enough to tie it in with his geographical whereabouts. "A revolutionary should neither look nor act like one to get ahead in Canada," he confided to an adviser. To Westerners who had lost confidence not only in politicians but in representative democracy itself, he offered an alternative: the replacement of parliamentary *representation* with parliamentary *delegation*. This meant elected MPs would act solely as their constituencies' surrogates, reflecting the electorate's views rather than those of the party or even their own personal conscience. "We're reverting to a more active notion of citizenship than the purely electoral and representational theories encompass," Ralph Hedlin wrote in his privately circulated Calgary newsletter. "The Reform party has seized on the idea of delegated representation because it has a strong resonance in Western Canada. The co-operative movement provided a training ground for direct democracy and planted the will to define, determine and direct our own destiny. Ingrained in this determination was an anti-state bias and a commitment to decentralized decision-making and local control. In the Reform version of democracy, the people, not Parliament, are supreme." This was a praiseworthy but not entirely practical suggestion. At the same time, Westerners became convinced that what they needed was a Senate that followed the advice of Alberta farmer Bert Brown, who had ploughed the letters "E-E-E" into his fields outside the Calgary airport—referring to the Reformer's ideal Senate with an Equal number of senators from each province who were Elected to be an Effective counterweight to the Ontario and Quebec-dominated Commons.

On national unity, the central issue of the decade, Manning insisted that Quebec should make up its own mind about remaining in Canada on terms no different from any other provinces, or leave. That insistence on provincial equality undermined the two-nations theory that had characterized negotiations with Quebec for a generation. It wasn't gentlemanly, in fact it was downright unfriendly, but it accurately reflected Western Canada's tough attitude. "Either all Canadians, including the people of Quebec, make a clear commitment to Canada as one nation; or Quebec and the rest of Canada should explore a better, but more separate, relationship between the two," Manning insisted.

The night before Ontario went to the polls in the fall of 1990, Conrad Black hosted a private dinner for Manning with four dozen of Canada's wealthiest at the Toronto Club. Manning's forty-minute speech made a profound impression and Black's Vancouver-based CEO, David Radler, became one of Reform's most successful fundraisers. "We in Toronto and Ottawa have too often paid the price in the past of ignoring centrifugal* political movements," Black told me afterwards. "I thought it was time for us to see that Manning isn't some lunatic from the nether regions and for him to see that we're not a bunch of plutocrats with horns and cloven feet. He is also the only politician in the country who makes an intelligent case for redesigning Canada's structure and wants Quebec to join us, but makes the sensible point that if the province won't play, there is life for Canada after Quebec."

Encouraged by such attention, Manning began to think he might be able to copy the achievement of his idol, Abraham Lincoln, whose Republicans replaced one of the old-line parties. That meant going national. At a convention held in Saskatoon during the spring of 1991, the party dropped its successful slogan, "The West Wants IN," and decided to run candidates everywhere. It was a brave option, but it severed Manning from his power base. "He received more national attention than ever before, a lot of it on television, and it hurt him," wrote Kenneth Whyte, editor of *Saturday Night*. "Millions saw him at his non-telegenic worst, blinking and squawking through thirty-second spots." Proclaiming his sincerity by favouring the kind of blue Fortrel shirts that politicians stopped wearing for televised appearances at least two generations ago,

---

* He meant *centripetal*. A centrifugal force drives from the centre or axis in an outward direction, whereas a centripetal force drives from the outside toward the centre. In Manning's view federalism was a centrifugal force which required the centripetal counter-force of Reform to bring it into balance.

Manning persevered and in the 1993 federal election came in third behind the Liberals and Bloc Québécois, with 19 per cent of the vote and fifty-two seats.

This was a remarkable achievement for a regional party on its first electoral run. (Reform fielded a candidate in the Alberta by-election that resulted in Deborah Grey becoming the party's first MP, while the late Reformer Stan Waters became the first, and likely the last, elected senator. But the party had not seriously run in federal elections prior to 1993.) Almost as soon as his troops walked into the green-carpeted Commons, however, their impact began to fade. They reversed the Trudeau aphorism that MPs become "nobodies" the moment they walk fifty paces *off* Parliament Hill; Reform MPs were the toast of their local Rotary clubs but became toast of a different kind the moment they stepped *onto* the parliamentary precinct. Polls revealed that instead of being a triumphant expression of Western populism, Reformers had become the "Why Not?" Party. Pollster Allan Gregg said: "When I polled people and asked, 'Would you support the Reform party?' they would say, 'Sure, I'd think about it.' So I would ask, 'Why?' And the response would inevitably be, 'Why not?' The passion had evaporated."

The real barrier to Reform's long-term success was its inability to embrace a plausible role for itself within a political system divorced from its populist roots. Jean Chrétien's Liberals stole most of Reform's thunder by adopting many of its cost-cutting measures, while Manning's own reputation suffered when it was revealed, contrary to his claims to personal frugality, that the party had paid for his clothes and taken care of other expenses without an accounting. Disillusioned disciples publicly complained about his autocratic control of the party apparatus and his inability to impose personal discipline. "Reform is in a bruised and delicate state," wrote Ottawa columnist Anthony Wilson-Smith. "Leader Preston Manning—the rock upon which Reform was built —spends his time drag-racing on the information highway, careening from electronic town-hall meetings to announcements of 1-900- telephone numbers with barely a pit stop to check his voice mail."

Then a rival populist came riding out of the West to challenge Manning on his home turf. Ralph Klein, the homespun premier of Alberta, was a Canadian politician like no other. Fully bilingual (English and bar-room), he paid no attention to party labels but nearly everything that Manning had talked about, Klein was able to *do*. "I look at politics only one way and that's through people," he told me in 1995. "Administering a province is totally separate from politics. My style is to run the government the same way I run my house. My wife, Colleen, and I are very frugal. We live in a three-bedroom, 1,200 square-foot bungalow in Calgary's Lakeview district, which is a normal kind of working-class neighbourhood, and have a small condo in Edmonton, not in a luxury building. We've always operated on the premise that we pay our bills. I'm obsessive about our family's credit rating. It's sacred; it's our good name." That kind of animating philosophy may not earn a place on any political science curriculum, but it was Prairie populism on the hoof. When Klein was first elected premier in 1989 (he had previously been a teacher, a television reporter and three-time Calgary mayor) it had been rumoured that he'd purchased a $500,000 home, spent another $1 million renovating it and then bought a $400,000 penthouse in Edmonton. "None of it was true, of course," Colleen Klein emphatically pointed out. "That's the old school of politics when people expected leaders to have such things."

His approach to *Kleinpolitik* was to wander into the beer parlour at Calgary's St. Louis Hotel and plumb people's thoughts. "It smells of deep-fried chicken, chips and cigarette smoke but you find everybody there," he explained. "Union leaders, the odd judge, Hutterites, cops, Croations and Serbs, even a lawyer or two. I feel at home there. But I also feel comfortable at the Petroleum Club." * Klein reinvented Alberta society, turning his province into a laboratory of balanced book-keeping. Every public sector expenditure was cut to the bone, right down to removing 40,000 of the 100,000 bulbs that lit up the legislature buildings at Christmas. Alberta wasn't the only province to balance its budget, but it was the only one that did it without raising taxes, which Klein considered to be "the easy, cowardly, brainless way out." He eliminated politicians' pensions, reduced public service salaries and drastically cut their numbers, launched a determined effort to allow the option of privatized

---

* During the 1992 Alberta Tory leadership campaign, Rick Orman, a former provincial energy minister running against Klein, was asked how he thought the province might best balance its budget. "That's easy," Orman shot back. "Ralph just has to return his empties."

medicare and eliminated the province's $3.4 billion deficit. He did away with many school districts and hospital boards, slashed grants to higher education and dissolved any government service not justified as essential. Despite the fact that some of Alberta's poorest citizens suffered in the process, Klein never stopped insisting that those who truly needed help were getting it. He was not against welfare, he claimed, he was against welfare as a way of life. He believed that everyone "should benefit from the work experience" and was happy to spend provincial funds on education and job retraining. "But if they're able to work and tell us that they'd rather not, that welfare is their God-given right," he warned, "then I'm sorry, they're out of here." (Often literally, as welfare recipients were handed a bus ticket to British Columbia.) When I challenged him to deny that his actions eroded the concept of universality, he told me without the hint of a smile: "We have good highways," he maintained, "so there *is* universality in some things. People expect to have good roads, right? Some things are fundamental to the taxpayer." Subject closed.

Klein sounded serene and confident by the mid-1990s, as he harvested an unprecedented (73 per cent) approval rating from Albertans. He felt no need to pepper his discourse with the annoying edge of impatient righteousness exhibited by Preston Manning and the Reformers. In his heart, he knew he was right. Whatever the final verdict on his stewardship, Ralph Klein had hitched his wagon to the Canadian Revolution. Klein had at his core no philosophy deeper than the simple expedient of giving the voters what they wanted, which at that red-hot moment meant government paying its own way. In allowing Albertans to launch their own revolt, instead of trying to ignite one at the centre, Klein rescued innumerable television sets from death by buckshot. The riders of the purple bile could now return to their preferred way of dealing with the federal government, which was to ignore it in hopes it would go away. As Bob Edwards, the witty editor of the *Calgary Eye Opener*, had written in 1908: "Without the periodic scandals at Ottawa, lots of decent people in the West would never hear of the place."

FOURTEEN

REBELLION: EAST

The Bouchard Sanction

"This is what separated us from you: we made demands.
You were satisfied to serve the power of your nation and we
dreamed of giving ours her truth."
ALBERT CAMUS, LETTER TO A GERMAN FRIEND

I

WHEN I FIRST ARRIVED IN CANADA from wartime Europe in 1940, we were only allowed into the country by promising to buy a farm from the CPR. We did that and for five years my parents worked fifteen acres of irrigated loam near Freeman, Ontario, from sun-up to sunset. I attended school at the time, but often accompanied my father on his 4:00 a.m. expeditions to sell our vegetables at the Hamilton farmers' market. Exiled Jews from a Nazi-occupied Czechoslovakia, we lived immersed—or more accurately, drowned—in a WASP-dominated world. Toronto was bicultural then: British and Irish; except for the bankers, who were Scottish.

I never subscribed to the benevolent notion of the country as a "cultural mosaic" which was supposed to differentiate Canada from the American "melting pot." The nation's ethnic structure had been set in place during the first decade of this century, when a million immigrants chose the western plains to make their last, best stand. It had been a perfect arrangement: the WASPs got in on the kill of the construction and manufacturing booms, while we "bohunks" (all of us tended to be grouped as "D.P.'s" or "Uke-aranians") had

patronizingly been allowed to maintain our way of life—just so long
as we ploughed the soil, did the most menial jobs and restricted
public displays of our culture to folk dancing on Dominion Days.
This point of view was most brutally articulated as recently as 1978
by Bryce Mackasey, a former Trudeau cabinet minister. During an
election speech defending the country's immigration policy, he
asked: "Where would we be without the Italians, the Czechoslovaks,
the Portuguese, the Greeks and Lebanese? Who would do the dirty
work, dig the subways, mine the mines and sweep the floors . . . ?"

Where indeed, since sheer numbers had muted such prejudice. No
ethnic or linguistic flavour dominated the Canadian crock-pot.
Every six years or so during the past two decades, nearly a million
immigrants from Asia, Africa and other non-white countries had
arrived on Canada's shores. The WASP and francophone bloodlines,
kin and traditions had been overwhelmed by waves of newcomers of
every class and stock, dreaming big dreams about new lives in wide-
open spaces. Canada's founding societies remained in charge—as
evidenced by the all-white, mostly male leadership of politics and
business—but they were no longer in ascendancy. A new and radically different country was being born.

Perhaps the most profound Revolution of all was the wane of the
WASPs. The White Anglo-Saxon Protestants who once ruled every
aspect of Canadian life had been, in certain metropolitan districts
and economic sectors, reduced to a visible minority; roast beef had
become an ethnic dish. Canada had turned into a multinational (or
post-national) country, not in the abstract of government edicts or
sociological hocus-pocus, but in the visible facts plain to anyone
walking the streets of Montreal, Toronto or Vancouver.

The politically correct notion of Canada as the home of two
nations had outlived reality. Only die-hard constitutional reformers
still maintained that one society (Quebec) was distinct while the
others, by default, were indistinct and somehow interchangeable. To
people outside Quebec, this "two nations" model had always been a
sociological theory which meant not very much; to Quebeckers, it
meant everything. To have their own language and culture officially
recognized meant the difference between being a proud nation or
just another marginal tribe with cultural curiosities. "Quebec sovereignty is not about resentment against English Canada," Lucien
Bouchard, its most articulate proponent, kept insisting. "It's about

two nations which need to go their own way politically to give them-
selves the kind of society they both need and deserve."

It had been a wonderful dream, this Canada with two founding
nations calmly coexisting as they evolved toward the twenty-first
century. But by the mid-1990s, Canada had almost as many cultures
as postal codes and nothing added up to peace in our time. "Nobody
can dwell any longer inside a zoological garden in which you preserve yourself as a species unaffected by changes in ecology,"
declared Dr. Vivian Rakoff, chairman of the University of Toronto's
department of psychiatry. "The world's ecology is changing drastically. Like it or not, we're all blood brothers now."*

Equality of treatment, which became the axis of the Canadian
Revolution, was plainly incompatible with any form of officially
sanctioned privilege based on language, ethnicity or length of
tenure. The time had come to acknowledge that liberalism and trib-
alism were terminally incompatible. "For the tidal wave of new
immigrants," wrote Michael Ignatieff, "Canada is more a land for
the realization of private dreams than for maintaining the old
compact between founding races. No common identity was provided for the millions of new Canadian immigrants other than a
weak vision of mutual multicultural indifference."

The collapse of the two-nation theory outside Quebec moved
debate on Canada's future to new ground. Deprived of its founding
myth, Canada by the mid-1990s had become a land with a common
past but no common history.

---

* There was a strange codicil to all this. In their 1991 meeting at Whistler,
B.C., the provincial premiers unanimously voted to accept the concept
of self-government for Canada's First Nations. That was a daring initiative because no one—Indian leaders included —knew exactly what that
meant. In contrast, Quebec Premier Robert Bourassa had been denied
any form of special status for Quebec. Yet at Confederation, Quebec had
been granted distinctly different rights in at least three sections of the
British North America Act, including language and the use of civil law.
"The distinct society we're asking for," Bourassa would explain with
impatient zeal, "is not a society of privileged citizens. It is a society with
a different culture, a society with a different legal system, a society with
specific institutions." But the same premiers who had readily given precisely that kind of distinct status to the natives withheld it from Quebec.

That troublesome new factor, which understandably triggered a revolutionary mode on both sides of the issue, was at the heart of the 1995 Quebec referendum: if Canada had abandoned its historical *raison d'être* as one country, should it become two? This was much more than a partisan struggle or ideological contest; this was a fight to the finish for Canada's future.

The mood of English Canada had turned hard and uncompromising, reminiscent of the old Chicago blues refrain, "I told you I love you—now get out!" There had been too many false alarms. Confederation was supposed to have caved in when René Lévesque was elected in 1976 and again when he called the referendum four years later; the sun was never supposed to rise again once the Meech Lake Accord had failed; hell was going to freeze over when Canadians voted to reject the Charlottetown Accord two years after that.

EVER SINCE THE QUIET REVOLUTION of the 1960s, Quebec and the rest of Canada had been dealing with one another in a series of confrontations seeking, but never finding, the ultimate compromise between French dreams and English impatience. Federal politicians sacrificed their larynxes, careers and budgets trying to find an answer to the eternal puzzle: what does Quebec *want*?* More of everything and less of nothing was the simple answer; a more useful question would have been: what does Quebec want *to be*?

Quebec's case was put forth by Robert Bourassa, who represented his seven million citizens with maximum clout and minimum risk for most of the decade. Being neither convinced as a federalist nor convincing as a separatist, he was distrusted by both sides—the ideal Canadian political posture. He would usually come down on the side of Canada, but he also understood that Quebec could achieve the most through the theatre of the absurd. He was uninterested in rekindling the glory snuffed out on the Plains of Abraham; his were the politics of the bottom line and the computer spreadsheet. His "profitable"

---

* For one thing, Quebec's nationalists wanted to legitimize their own version of Canadian history. The Bloc Québécois tabled a bill in the Commons in 1994 calling for annulment of the guilty verdict against Louis Riel 109 years earlier. "Riel was hanged because he was francophone and came to the defence of a distinct society," claimed Bloc MP Suzanne Tremblay, inventing some instant history of her own.

approach viewed federalism as a chance to push his province into an equal technological partnership with the rest of Canada. Bourassa would meanwhile unequivocally declare that Quebec must be a nation without becoming a state—whatever that meant.

He was precisely the type of enlightened conciliator that Alexis de Tocqueville had in mind when he wrote that "it behooves moderate men to ensure the success of a moderate republic." Despite his raging pragmatism—or perhaps because of it—Bourassa viewed the political process as a voyage of infinite and unexpected contingencies. It was entirely fitting that Brian Mulroney and he should leave the scene within months of each other. One of the stranger partnerships in Canadian political history, they were good friends and staunch allies. At about the same time the Baie Comeau lawyer was defeated by Joe Clark for the Tory leadership in 1976, Bourassa was bounced out of office by a triumphant René Lévesque. The two men faced down their personal humiliations over long lunches at the Mount Royal Club and formed a bond that was never broken.

The basic assumption in the endless negotiations with Robert Bourassa held that no matter how Quebec and the rest of the country settled things, French and English Canadians could find a way to muddle through. Quebec nationalists remained as bound to their creed as their forebears had once been to Rome, but inflammatory rhetoric aside, Quebec's position could be reduced to the conviction that only political independence (or the next thing to it) could guarantee the long-term survival of Quebec's language and distinctive way of life.

The problem was how to create two "nations" and still have one country. The solution inevitably reduced itself to a formula resembling the famous quip of Montreal comic Yvon Deschamps: "We want an independent Quebec within a strong and united Canada." *The Globe and Mail*'s Andrew Coyne noted a similar phenomenon: "If the famously canny voters in Quebec persist in the delusion that they can be both independent and part of Canada, it is because for thirty years they have been told precisely that, not only by their own leaders but by political élites in the rest of Canada. Lucien Bouchard's bizarre proposal for political and economic union to follow secession is only the last in the series."

Although they professed purity of thought and action, Quebec's nationalists believed in at least six degrees of separation: indepen-

dence, sovereignty, autonomy, special status, separation and sovereignty-association. Separatist Pierre Drouilly, a University of
Montreal sociologist, speculated that the real problem with the
sovereignty option was that it always required a "Yes" vote. Since
Quebeckers had an unbroken record dating back to 1942 of voting
"No" in provincial and national referenda, he predicted certain
victory if the referendum question were reworked to read: "Don't
you disagree with the idea that Quebec shouldn't be a non-sovereign
state?" Or more simply: "Do you agree that Quebec shouldn't
become a sovereign country?"

According to the polls, the independence option most acceptable
to Quebeckers was sovereignty-association. It was also the least
practical. Its most telling critique came from the late constitutional
gadfly Senator Eugene Forsey, who dismissed the idea as "a horse
that won't start, let alone run; you can no more negotiate sovereignty-association than you can negotiate sour sugar, dry water,
boiling ice or stationary motion." Forsey was right. Even in a
country that officially described itself at birth as a "self-governing
colony," sovereignty-association was an unworkable oxymoron. As
former Ontario Premier Bob Rae never got tired of pointing out:
"We already have a political union with Quebec. It's called Canada."
These were solid, rational arguments; but nobody promised the
rational would necessarily carry the day. "Quebec has no opinions,
only emotions," as Sir Wilfrid Laurier had noted.

The supreme irony of the Quebec independence movement was
that its leaders intended to finance the breakup of Canada with
Canadian dollars. Even if English Canadians were mutton-headed
enough to extend their currency to the newly created republic, it was
simply unworkable for two sovereign states to share their money.
Several countries (mainly Panama and Liberia) used the American
dollar as official tender, but their balance-of-payments positions
were so dismal that no functioning monetary union actually existed.
Similarly, the nine former French colonies that combined their monetary destinies by forming the West African Monetary Union had to
impose severe foreign-exchange controls to prevent capital flights.
The world's only functioning monetary union was the partnership
between Belgium and Luxembourg, but the population of the tiny
principality was only 4 per cent that of Belgium's and it regularly
ran budget surpluses. The great experiment in forging a monetary

union had, of course, been the attempt to negotiate use of a common currency within the European Community. Paradoxically, those negotiations forced participating countries to face an even higher degree of political integration.

According to Jacques Parizeau's propaganda, the transition to Quebec independence would be so smooth hardly anyone would notice. The only real change, one assumed, would be in his own status. Instead of being the lowly premier of an important province, he would become the exalted president of a marginal republic, able to arrive at the United Nations with the *fleur-de-lys* proudly fluttering from the fender of his limousine and to bore the Assembly with one of his avuncular lectures blown through his moustache. Parizeau would at last be officially installed in his Quebec City presidential palace, instead of merely living in a donated house with pretensions of becoming one.

MOST REVOLUTIONS ARE DEDICATED to the destruction of the upper classes who control the means of production. Quebec's Quiet Revolution, started under Jean Lesage in 1960 and still simmering thirty-five years later, had precisely the opposite effect in mind. The idea was for the province to create its own élites to grab control of its major institutions, so that Quebeckers would seize command of their economy and culture. Few Canadians outside Quebec realized how fundamental a change that required. For more than a century the resident cardinals, cocooned in the splendid isolation of their celestial palace at the foot of Dominion Square, had decreed that material matters be left to the English. This created an impenetrable Anglo network that operated out of Montreal's Mount Royal Club, aided by the more mundane power-wielders at the Mount Stephen and St. James's clubs.* It was during the Quiet Revolution that a genuine middle class began to emerge, consisting of an adventurous few who branched out of the traditional career paths of priest, lawyer or doctor. For a time, the Anglo institutions paid no attention. Of Canada's Big Five banks, for example, only one—the Montreal—had a French-Canadian executive of vice-presidential

---

* The St. James's was said to have two classes of members: those who wished they belonged to the Mount Royal and those who were glad they didn't belong to the Mount Stephen.

rank or higher. (He was a talented, bilingual M.Comm. graduate with the wonderfully appropriate name of Pierre MacDonald.) Lesage's Quiet Revolution, carried on by every Quebec premier that followed, was specifically aimed at creating an indigenous managerial class, its policies aptly summed up in the slogan, *Maître chez nous*. The new Quebec business tycoons, mostly trained at Montreal's *l'École des Hautes Études Commerciales*, were the natural successors of the notaries and bishops. Within one generation, corporate CEOs had become Quebec's role models and a new and vibrant bourgeoisie had taken over. This was dramatically documented in the spring of 1995, when the authoritative business magazine *Affaires Plus* published its annual list of the fifty most powerful Quebeckers. All but four of those named belonged to well-established Quebec families; of those who didn't, two were Jewish. WASP influence had not just waned, it had vanished. Ironically, it was the U.S.-Canada Free Trade Agreement that set some leaders of French Canada's business community on a course of championing Quebec's independence. The CEOs, traditionally federalist, realized that they no longer had to depend on English Canada for markets or technology. The FTA had eliminated once and for all their feeling of operating under some form of Toronto-based trusteeship.

Such circumstances, including the fact that the prime minister had come from Quebec for all but twelve of the previous forty-seven years, made it difficult for the separatists to maintain the myth that Quebeckers were somehow subjugated by *les maudits anglais*. That didn't stop them, of course. Just before the 1994 provincial election, Parti Québécois Vice-President Bernard Landry told the Parisian magazine *L'Express* that Quebec "is the western world's last colonized nation." He added, presumably with a straight face, that "its population has endured a cataclysm comparable to the Chernobyl nuclear catastrophe." (A slight overreaction to the impending loss of the Nordiques, *n'est-ce pas,* Bernard?)

MY COMPANION WAS ONE OF those wonderful Montrealers of a certain age, connected with the political élites in Ottawa and Quebec City and trusted by both; partly because they shared his passion for minor French cheeses but mostly because he had been a useful interlocutor between the two cities and two cultures. In many ways he was the last of his kind. Independently wealthy, he had spent most of his life in public service, just as second sons of Anglican vicars in nineteenth-century England once joined the army—both as a duty and as an interesting way to spend one's life. Unlike most Canadian politicians and bureaucrats, he retained a firm notion what his country was and ought to be; he wanted to help create a very different Canada, but a Canada all the same.

We had not seen each other for a couple of years and were sitting at the bar of the Atlantic Pavilion on Sherbrooke Street, trading apprehensions about Canada's future. He said something after our third cup of coffee that I could hardly credit having heard. "The thoughtful Quebec nationalists," he had remarked, with the casualness of a weather forecast, "not only take separation for granted but they have a kind of lingering regard for English Canada, because they know they weren't treated all that badly. They're saying now that the English shouldn't be absorbed piecemeal into the United States through the gravitational economic pull that will strengthen dramatically once Quebec leaves. They believe we should start the process of a calculated liquidation of English Canada by negotiating sovereignty-association with the U.S. at the same time Ottawa is signing a similar treaty with Quebec. That way we'll preserve some clout, instead of ending up as nine states represented by 18 out of 118 senators in the U.S. Senate."

I would have dismissed that chin-dropping comment—made in 1990—as both silly and wildly premature from any other source. From my friend, who had waged many political battles to keep the nation together, it seemed a warning worth heeding—especially considering it had been given before the defeat of the Meech Lake and Charlottetown accords and well before the elections of the Bloc Québécois to Opposition status in Ottawa and the Parti Québécois to majority government in Quebec City.

The warning was certainly supported by the evolution of Jacques Parizeau from an avuncular professor to a die-hard revolutionary. The first time I met Parizeau was in the 1960s, when he was a member of Premier Jean Lesage's entourage. As I walked into his office, he was doubled over at his desk in a fit of belly-pumping laughter over the premier's pretensions. Parizeau explained that Lesage had just ordered him to write a speech for a rally that night at Levis, across the river from Quebec City, "specifically designed to impress Harold Wilson." (Wilson was then prime minister of the United Kingdom and Lesage required British parliamentary approval to abolish the Quebec legislature's upper chamber.) Parizeau rightly considered the mission absurd. He was an intellectual's intellectual, throwing off such barbs as, "I was aware of the quarrel between Reynaud's mistress and Daladier's mistress in France and its influence on French national defence, before knowing who the prime minister of Canada was." But even then, even before his famous 1969 train journey to Banff when he became a separatist, he had a bias against the English. It probably dated back to his early twenties, when he crossed Canada with a friend. They were chatting in a Winnipeg bar when somebody yelled at them to "Speak white!" He broke his right hand in the ensuing fist-fight and its little finger still juts out at an awkward angle.

In the interval, Parizeau had become more confident, more powerful, more articulate and much more cynical. His idea of great government seemed to extend no further than exacting revenge for the British conquest of Quebec in 1759. He had become such a true believer in separatism that he gave the impression of not caring a whit how it was achieved or what Quebeckers might suffer in the process. His jaded approach was captured in his remark to the *Los Angeles Times*: "Get me a half-dozen Ontarians who put their feet on the Quebec flag and I've got it." His cynicism was best exemplified during an off-the-record briefing of foreign diplomats when he compared Quebec citizens following their approval of his referendum question to lobsters trapped in a pot.

In 1995 he supported the same platform of sovereignty-association which had caused him to resign from the Lévesque government in 1984; that spoke volumes. As Norman Webster, the wise Montreal *Gazette* and *Le Devoir* columnist, noted: "Jacques Parizeau isn't trying to fool all of the people all of the time, just fifty-one per cent of them . . . once."

DESPITE THE AMPUTATION of a leg, Lucien Bouchard dominated the strategy of separatism and propelled its progress. A master of desensitizing Canadians to the possibility of Quebec independence, he became the dark angel of Canadian politics. A complex, paradoxical figure, his loyalties were as changeable as the hues of a pigeon's pout. He had been a loyal Liberal, influential enough to be named vice-chairman of the party's Quebec political commission by Pierre Trudeau in 1968; he then switched to being a loyal follower of the Parti Québécois from

1973 to 1984, but changed allegiances again and became a loyal Canadian when offered a plum ambassadorship; he later also became a loyal Conservative, occupying the senior positions of secretary of state (which meant, ironically, that he presided over the 1988 Canada Day celebrations), environment minister and political minister for Quebec. He abruptly abandoned the Tories at the most crucial juncture of their mandate in 1990 to become the loyal leader of his own separatist party. Bouchard regarded political parties as vehicles to be used and discarded at will. He was not for sale; but his loyalty could always be rented if the price were high enough. Asked by a reporter from *Le Journal de Montréal* about Parizeau, his closest political ally in 1995, Bouchard answered: "I have great admiration and affection for him—to the extent that one can have affection for others in politics." It was a revealing reply, hinting at a bedrock belief that people in politics merely used one another and that no real friendships or loyalties were possible.

His bond with Mulroney ought to have been an exception. The two men had been friends since law school at Laval, where they were self-described soul mates. They complemented one another: Mulroney, the man of action; Bouchard, the man of thought. Their lives had become intertwined at every turn. In 1974, Mulroney had Bouchard appointed chief counsel to the Cliche Commission looking into violence on the Quebec labour scene. A decade later, the freshly coined prime minister of Canada appointed his pal to Canada's most glamorous overseas posting, ambassador to France. When asked how the French would respond to such an inexperienced diplomat, Mulroney replied: "When they're talking to Lucien Bouchard, they're talking to Brian Mulroney."* At the gala dinner in Quebec City during

---

* Bouchard's four years as Canadian ambassador to France were notable for three reasons: he successfully mounted the 1985 and 1987 summits of *la francophonie*; the embassy's expenditures under his stewardship shot up 71 per cent; and while representing Canada he abandoned his wife, Jocelyn, to conduct a flaming affair with CBC French-language TV star Denise Bombardier, who left her husband and young child behind in Montreal to live with him in an apartment off Embassy Row. His greatest protocol *faux pas* was to propose a toast at the first gathering of the embassy's two hundred employees: "To Quebec-France relations!" Quickly correcting himself, he switched his salute: "To Canada-France relations!"

the 1985 Shamrock Summit, Mulroney had proudly introduced
Bouchard to U.S. President Ronald Reagan as "the most eloquent
French Canadian I know." When Bouchard married Audrey, his second wife, in 1989, Mulroney hosted the reception; when Bouchard's
son, Alexandre, was born, his first call was to his friend Brian.*

For Mulroney, the split with Bouchard during the last days of the
Meech Lake negotiations was particularly painful, because it violated his motto for life and politics: "You dance with the one what
brung ya." Nothing hurt him more during the nine years he spent in
office. Mulroney knew that politics and gratitude were strangers, but
believed that friendship was not negotiable. The split between the
two men ran so deep that Mulroney instructed Mila that, should
Bouchard show up at his funeral, she must stop the service until he
left the church.

LUCIEN BOUCHARD'S POLITICAL quest seemed limited to Quebec's aspirations, but he was much more complicated than that. For one thing,
he sought legitimacy from the very country he was in the process of
attempting to dismantle. Any political movement such as his Bloc
Québécois, which championed no greater cause than destruction of
the system that gave it birth, was bound to have trouble in the legitimacy department. But the withholding of political legitimacy was
an alien concept to Bouchard, who could not understand the criticism. "The Bloc Québécois has been on the federal scene for more
than three years, but until recently we were ranked alongside the
bizarre and outer fringes," he complained during the Chrétien
government's first throne speech debate.

"He was a man of multiple personalities and each had its own
agenda, often contradicting the others," recalled Arthur Campeau,
who was his international environment adviser. "I would start a

---

* Brian Mulroney didn't flinch in his loyalty to Bouchard, but Mila had
her suspicions: "When he left Jocelyn and married Audrey, Brian had a
little reception for the family at 24 Sussex, but I chose not to be there. I
just had other things to do. I didn't like the way it had been handled.
After the split, Audrey would go to my hairdresser and it was funny how
we kept being scheduled at the same times. Once she came into the
room where I was having my hair done, with tears in her eyes, and told
me: 'I'm really sorry about what happened.' I said, 'Look, Audrey, I
have no problem with you and I wish you and the baby all the best, but
as far as I'm concerned, Lucien does not exist.'"

meeting with one Bouchard and end it with another. He was given to shifting from one frame of mind to another without even realizing that he had, reinventing history as he went along. While environment minister in times of fiscal restraint, he never bothered justifying his expenditures because his friend Brian would make sure he had his way. He had many mood swings, when his cool logic frequently overwhelmed his emotions. This enabled him to convince himself of the Big Lie: he was totally convinced, for example, that he never betrayed Mulroney, but that it was the other way round."

Bouchard depended on Mulroney to get himself elected the first time, but campaigned brilliantly and successfully in 1992 to defeat the Charlottetown Accord, in 1993 to elect fifty-four members of his Bloc Québécois and in 1994 to help push the Parizeau government into power. He saw an independent Quebec as a practical option, not as some kind of miraculous solution or nostalgic dream. "We are seeking sovereignty," he told the first annual convention of the BQ in Montreal on April 7, 1995, "because it is absolutely essential, like the ripening of a fruit, like reaching adulthood, like the opening of a river into the ocean. *It is necessary, because we are a people.*"

Former Ontario Premier David Peterson had been attacked for comparing Bouchard to Hitler, but a transcript of his actual remarks showed him to have been much less vitriolic and much closer to the truth: "If we want to build a whole political structure on resentment, Bouchard's building of his campaign on the basis of Quebec's humiliation has another parallel. I mean that of Hitler, who built the whole Nazi movement on resentment of the humiliation of Germany after the First World War."

THE DEFINITIVE SUMMARY FROM INSIDE the Mulroney circle of the Bouchard defection in the spring of 1990 was the biting comment of Stanley Hartt, then the PM's chief of staff. "Lucien turned himself into a human car bomb, designed to go off at a time and place when it would do the most damage," Hartt told me. "He acted when he did because he saw, for the first time, that there was a way for the Meech provisions to work and thus disarm Quebec separatism. The tactic of not coming to see his friend to talk things over was deliberate. He saw a chance to make himself both a hero and a martyr at the same time and a chance of eventually catapulting himself into being Parizeau's successor. That's what he did. I don't know anybody else like that. And I'm glad."

II

BECAUSE LUCIEN BOUCHARD'S DEFECTION raised suspicions that he had betrayed his oath as a minister of the Crown in helping Quebec separatists to destabilize the government of Canada, most of the people around him kept notes, journals and diaries of their involvement in the unfolding events. From those documents and personal interviews, I have attempted to reconstruct the essential elements of Bouchard's dramatic defection.

In the spring of 1988, Jean Charest invited Bouchard to a private dinner at his home in Hull to meet the younger francophone ministers: Pierre Blais, Pierre Cadieux and Bernard Valcourt. They jointly told the Canadian ambassador to France that the prime minister needed a Quebec lieutenant to entrust with the affairs of the Quebec caucus and that he was the caucus choice. Bouchard resigned his post at the end of March and returned to Canada to be sworn in as secretary of state and appointed to the important Priorities and Planning Committee of Cabinet. "Quebec must be a distinct entity in the federation," he told the media. Interviewed by William Johnson for the television program, "Sur la Colline," Bouchard announced he would run for the Tories in the June 20th by-election in Lac St.-Jean. In his Montreal Gazette *column the next day, Johnson reported: "Asked about his past as a Pequiste, as someone who gave speeches for sovereignty-association during the 1980 Quebec referendum campaign, he said he no longer believes that Quebec will ever be independent and that he is working sincerely within the framework of the Canadian federation."*

Despite endorsements from Premier Bourassa and Corinne Côté-Lévesque (René Lévesque's widow), the by-election went badly because Bouchard concentrated on constitutional, instead of local, issues. His chief of staff, Luc Lavoie, and the party's Quebec director, Pierre-Claude Nolin, were sent in to help. Although he seldom campaigned in by-elections, Brian Mulroney made an exception and also spent three full days in the riding, spread over two visits, once accompanied by his daughter, Caroline, and the other time by Mila. He campaigned hard for his friend, promising $50 million for a new road to James Bay and a $120-million development fund for the region. "I need Lucien in Ottawa—send him to me!" he implored. Bouchard won the riding with a 6,200-vote margin and, six months later, was promoted to the prestigious Environment portfolio. Then the defection began:

Ottawa–Toronto
February 14, 1990:
Paul Terrien, a PMO speech writer, informs Stanley Hartt, the PM's chief of staff, of his discomfort with the "Quebec nationalist" tone of the speech Bouchard is planning to give to the Empire Club in Toronto. Hartt instructs Terrien to persuade Bouchard to deliver a speech that is more federalist in perspective. But Bouchard agrees only to shorten his text, refusing to modify its tone. He informs Terrien that he is a Quebecker before he is a federal minister and that his stay in Ottawa is coming to an end. Terrien warns Bouchard that the speech might embarrass the government, to which Bouchard replies: "In any event, Paul, you know that my objective is to go into Quebec politics." While discussing his Empire Club speech, Bouchard tells L. Ian MacDonald, the Mulroney biographer and chief PMO speech writer: "I think Brian is screwed with the Meech Lake Accord; it's not going to go through."

Ottawa
February 23:
Mulroney shuffles his Cabinet and Bouchard picks up the added responsibility of political minister for Quebec.

Gatineau, Quebec
March 13:
"The meeting of the Quebec Caucus at Meech Lake was a long one with several interventions, some of them very emotional, on the issue of what we would and would not do if Meech was not ratified," Jean Charest notes in his journal. "At the end of the meeting, Bouchard, as the Quebec lieutenant, rose to sum up. He made a short but precise speech to emphasize the need for the Quebec Caucus to offer its full support to the PM's initiatives to save the accord. He emphasizes that the Caucus should support all efforts to implement the accord until June 23, 1990 and if not approved, the Caucus could then weigh its options."

Fredericton, New Brunswick
March 21:
Premier Frank McKenna introduces his companion resolution to the Meech Lake Accord in the New Brunswick legislature.

Ottawa–Vancouver
March 22:
In a national television address, Brian Mulroney explains his proposal for a Commons special committee on the New Brunswick
Companion Accord. Bouchard is in Vancouver, attending the
"Globe 90" environmental products conference. He is upset by
the McKenna proposals, particularly its "promotion of linguistic
duality" clause. (The clause would make the federal government
responsible for the maintenance of both languages in all regions,
including the protection of the English language in Quebec.)
Bouchard is distraught and phones his mother. "That's it, Lucien,"
she tells him. "It's time for you to come home now." The next day,
Deputy Prime Minister Don Mazankowski announces the government's intention to strike a parliamentary committee to study
McKenna's proposals.

Ottawa
March 25:
During a dinner at the residence of Camille Guilbault, deputy chief
of staff of the PMO, the guests (Consumer and Corporate Affairs
Minister Pierre Blais and his wife, Chantal; Lucien and Audrey
Bouchard, Jean Charest and his wife, Michèle Dion) are discussing
the prospects for Meech when Bouchard leaves the living room to
take a call from Mulroney. Upon his return, he says they discussed
how to give the McKenna resolution some running room and agreed
that Jean Charest would make the ideal chairman for the parliamentary committee studying the issue. Charest is confused, not
knowing what to make of the offer, but Bouchard insists, reiterating
that he will give "Jean" his full support. Charest finally agrees to
accept the position.

Camille Gilbault later tells Lucien she is worried by Benoît
Bouchard's doubts over Meech. Bouchard replies: "Camille, you're
not worrying about the right Bouchard. You should worry more
about me!" She confides to a colleague that Lucien has lately been
acting very "volatile and feverish," alternating between "positive
and very negative moods" and that at one Quebec ministers' breakfast meeting he had openly expressed his hostility toward Michael
Wilson, accusing him of "controlling everything, not listening to
anybody and manipulating the prime minister."

Montreal
April 5:
Renegade MP François Gérin, who has been threatening to leave the
Conservative Party, tells *La Presse*: "The Quebec electorate is ripe
for a separatist vote at the federal level. We will have to consider
sending to Ottawa MPs who will work exclusively toward defending
Quebec's interests."

St. John's, Newfoundland
April 6:
Clyde Wells revokes the Meech Lake Accord in the legislature,
prompting Bouchard to respond: "One can imagine a situation
where English Canada would have to choose between Quebec and
Newfoundland."

Ottawa
April 27:
Jean Charest and Lucien Bouchard meet following Question Period
and Charest tells him he thinks he will recommend changes to the
unanimity requirement on Senate reform. Charest tells Bouchard
that his committee will probably not recommend adoption of a
clause for the promotion of linguistic duality. (The final report,
however, makes precisely that recommendation.)

Ottawa
May 4:
Charest's committee hearings begin with his announcement that he
already has a draft report, but will discuss it with representatives of
the three parties before distributing it to the full committee. A copy
of the plan is given by Charest's brother, Robert, to Bouchard and
Patricia Dumas, his chief of staff.

Mont-Tremblant, Quebec
May 5:
At a Conservative caucus meeting, Mulroney discusses with
Bouchard any possible defections among Tory backbenchers and
reviews progress of the special committee. That morning, *Le Devoir*
publishes a story quoting Bernard Landry, vice-president of the Parti
Québécois, saying that between twenty and twenty-five Tory MPs are

ready to bolt the party. Bouchard assures Mulroney that it's all nonsense and that he knows nothing about it, repeating his comments—
at Mulroney's request—in front of Tory Caucus Chairman Harvie
Andre. At the end of the meeting, Camille Guilbault tells Jean
Charest: "Lucien is behaving like a yo-yo—he is constantly changing his mind."

Mont-Tremblant, Quebec
May 7:
Jean Charest meets with Bouchard to discuss the draft of his report.
Bouchard expresses satisfaction with the plan and agrees with the
strategy designed to bring Manitoba and Newfoundland on side.
Significantly, he expresses no concern with inclusion of the clause
on the promotion of linguistic duality.

Mont-Tremblant–Montreal
May 8:
Bouchard takes part in the regular breakfast meeting of Quebec ministers and gives a favourable review of Charest's draft report. He
does not attend a subsequent meeting of the full Quebec caucus and
something mysterious seems to happen at this point. When Pierre
Blais talks to him privately shortly after the ministers' meeting, he
finds Bouchard's opinion of Charest has suddenly been reversed.
"He was anxious to leave and was very concerned about the contents
of Jean Charest's report," Blais notes in his diary. "He shrugged off
my suggestion to phone or meet with Jean."

That evening is the last time Mulroney and Bouchard meet as
friends. They attend a dinner at the Ritz-Carlton for the fifteenth
anniversary of the Cliche Commission. Mulroney gives his faithful
lieutenant a lift back to Ottawa on the government's Challenger jet.
They spend most of the evening together, but Bouchard never
mentions having any doubts about the Meech process or his ability
to stay on as minister.

Ottawa
May 9:
Marcel Danis, the Mulroney government's sports minister, makes a
startling discovery. He is advised of meetings between Parti
Québécois Vice-President Bernard Landry, Jacques Bouchard (a

political aide to Lucien, but no relation) and the separatist Tory MP François Gérin. The objective of these meetings, he is told, was the formation of a "Bloc Québécois" in Ottawa with the help of the Parti Québécois. Invited to the meetings were PQ organizers and Tory MPs deemed to be "nationalists," like Louis Plamondon and Nic Leblanc. Danis is also invited, but declines to attend. Danis later meets Lucien Bouchard in the Commons lobby and tells him it is unacceptable for one of his aides to attend secret conferences with Landry. Bouchard replies that he was aware of the meetings but didn't take them very seriously. While visiting St. Paul de Varennes school in his riding a few days later, Danis meets Bernard Landry, who asks him to be a Parti Québécois candidate in the upcoming provincial election. When Danis declines the invitation, Landry offers to make him a Quebec ambassador. Danis, who subsequently becomes federal minister of labour, informs Mulroney's people of the encounter only after Bouchard's subsequent defection. When asked why he didn't sound the alarm earlier, he replies: "Look, I was there as a junior minister from Quebec, dealing with the leader of the Quebec caucus. It's widely known that the PM helped him all through his life, made him ambassador, cabinet minister, Quebec leader, gave the reception for his wedding and was supposed to be his best friend. Christ, I couldn't pick up the telephone to tell him what I'd heard. He would have thought I was crazy. I thought, 'I've got to give Lucien the benefit of the doubt.' "

Jacques Parizeau attempts to destabilize the federal government by personally telephoning Quebec backbenchers to persuade them to defect and form their own party. Mulroney and his people believe the main reason for this activity was to hinder ratification of the Meech Lake Accord, because once passed it would have remedied Quebec's absence from the 1982 constitutional agreement and undermined much of the separatist's *raison d'être*.

Ottawa
May 10:
As Canada's minister of the environment, Lucien Bouchard prepares to attend the Bergen Conference in Norway where fifty countries will be asked to set goals to reduce carbon dioxide emissions, the leading cause of global warming. Canada's delegation includes former PQ Premier Pierre-Marc Johnson and Arthur Campeau, a

former Montreal law partner of Mulroney who was appointed by him to be special adviser on international affairs to the environment ministry. Before he leaves Ottawa, Bouchard has a long meeting with Clerk of the Privy Council Paul Tellier.

Tellier's account of the visit differs substantially from the version that Bouchard later describes in his autobiography. "During our conversation," Tellier observes, "Mr. Bouchard expressed his preoccupations about the linguistic aspect of the constitutional question and regretted that, as minister of the environment, he had to be away at a time critical in the evolution of the constitutional issue."

Prior to his departure for Europe that evening, Bouchard meets with Bernard Roy, Mulroney's close adviser, at the Château Mirabel. "During our dinner, we spoke of various subjects, including the constitutional issue," Roy recalls. "According to Lucien, the prime minister was particularly skilful in this kind of discussion and he still thought it possible that there would be a favourable denouement to the impasse. He expressed his reservation about the federal government's obligation to promote linguistic duality in Canada and therefore in Quebec. To him, if such an obligation was the price that Quebec would have to pay to obtain the accord's acceptance by all the provinces, this price would be too high. He would fight to stop the federal government from forcing Quebec's hand."

London–Bergen
May 11:
Bouchard flies to Heathrow, where he is met by his executive assistant, Martin Green. During the evening, Bouchard appears preoccupied about Tellier and tells Green that the prime minister places too much faith in his clerk of the Privy Council. Bouchard seems worried about the upcoming meeting of the PQ executive in Alma to celebrate the tenth anniversary of the 1980 referendum. He plans to send a telegram to the assembly and repeatedly asks Green what he should say in his message. Green tries to discourage him, insisting that a simple word of welcome would be enough. Bouchard then flies to Norway in the late afternoon, where he immediately teams up with Pierre-Marc Johnson. The former Parti Québécois premier is concerned by Bouchard's increasingly erratic behaviour. In conversations with third parties, Johnson is later heard to make such comments as: "Lucien arrived at Bergen like a mad dog" and "Minister

Bouchard's behaviour is suicidal—the Scandinavians, the Germans, the British and the Americans are all against the position he has directed Campeau to take." (At the conference, Bouchard wants Canada to adopt the extreme position of completely eliminating carbon dioxide emissions before the year 2000.)

Bergen
May 14:
Bouchard begins the day by telling his staff to hold all calls from Ottawa. His executive assistant, Martin Green, accompanies Bouchard on a six-hour walk around the city. Bouchard tells him his life story and presents his theory that Quebec and Canada cannot co-exist. He claims Parizeau is not a real Quebecker and reminisces about René Lévesque. He tells Green he must send that telegram to Alma. Later in the day, Bouchard's deputy minister, Len Good, and Arthur Campeau brief Bouchard, but the minister is not receptive to anything Campeau has to say. Bouchard later tells Green: "I know why Arthur's here. He's not here to work for me, he's here for the prime minister, to watch me." In a long conversation with Green later that evening, Bouchard reveals that René Lévesque had told him, "One day you will be one of those who will replace me." Green observes that Bouchard appears to believe this off-hand remark has the power of prophecy.

Johnson and Bouchard dine privately. Johnson asks him whether he feels it's really appropriate for a federal minister to send a telegram of support on the tenth anniversary of the Quebec referendum. Bouchard replies that the meeting was being held in his riding and that he had been urged to write the wire by Marc-André Bédard, a former justice minister in the PQ government of René Lévesque. Johnson then tells Bouchard that he should emphasize René Lévesque's role, in order to provoke Jacques Parizeau. Johnson initially believes that Bouchard's emotional state caused him to act without regard for the telegram's consequences, but later concludes that his actions were not innocent but intended to make a big splash.

Ottawa–Paris
May 15:
The Charest committee approves its draft report. Charest unsuccessfully attempts to contact Bouchard, who is holding himself

incommunicado. Although the Bergen conference is not finished, Bouchard leaves abruptly and flies to the French capital, where he meets his wife, Audrey, and his son, Alexandre. Canadian Embassy official Marc Lortie meets the minister on his arrival and Bouchard stays at Lortie's apartment on rue Saint-Dominique. He categorically refuses to take calls from Ottawa, including an urgent message from his own chief of staff, Patricia Dumas.

Ottawa–Paris
May 16:
Camille Guilbault is the only one who manages to reach Bouchard in Paris. He tells her that he feels "tired and disconnected." She tells him she has sent the Charest report by courier and asks him to get back to her if he has any problems with it. She speaks a second time with Bouchard that evening. He confirms having received the document but says he is too tired to read it. It is their last conversation.

Ottawa–Paris
May 17:
Martin Green arrives at diplomat Lortie's residence to find Bouchard in an enraged state. Bouchard says he has read the Charest report and feels betrayed. He says he had assurances there would be no compromises regarding Meech. Bouchard tells Green: "Meech is dead, it's over!" Many calls, including those from Charest and Benoît Bouchard, go unanswered. The committee report is tabled in the Commons; Tory MP François Gérin resigns from caucus in protest and announces he will sit as an independent.

Paris
May 18:
Green returns to Lortie's apartment in the morning to find Bouchard and his press secretary, Micheline Fortin, working on the draft telegram to Alma. Bouchard seems depressed and exhausted. Green and Fortin leave the apartment for lunch. At the restaurant, Green discovers that she has a draft of the telegram and asks her to show it to him. As she hands it over, she mentions that Bouchard specifically ordered her not to show it to him. After reading it, Green declares: "This is a letter of resignation—if Lucien sends this, he'll have no choice but to resign." Green has Fortin call Bouchard to express his

concern. Bouchard sends a message back: "Tell Martin: thank you, I understand." Green takes the next plane back to Canada in disgust and frustration. "I loved the guy," he says of Bouchard. "He really betrayed me. I have nothing but disdain for him now."

Fortin sends the Alma telegram via the Canadian embassy. It contains Bouchard's explosive words: "René Lévesque's memory will unite us all this weekend. He was the one who led the Québécois to realize they had the inalienable right to decide their own destiny."

Ottawa–Paris
May 19:
Clerk of the Privy Council Paul Tellier finally reaches Bouchard, who is interrupted while having a shower. Tellier asks Bouchard to withdraw the telegram, which has been reproduced on the front page of every Quebec newspaper. Wrapped in a bath towel and dripping over Lortie's kitchen floor, Bouchard shouts: "I don't give a damn about the telegram! The Charest report, that's the problem. You knew I couldn't accept these changes. Wait until Monday, things will be happening!" At no time does Bouchard attempt to phone his friend Brian Mulroney to discuss his dilemma.

Paris–Montreal
May 20:
Bouchard and his party fly back to Canada. Just before take-off, Camille Guilbault reaches Micheline Fortin and asks why the PMO was not informed of the telegram. "If I had told you," replies Fortin, "you would have ordered me not to send it." Aboard the plane Bouchard meets the Trudeau-era finance minister, Marc Lalonde, and Martial Asselin, a Conservative senator, who both applaud the Charest report much to Bouchard's discomfort. When Bouchard arrives at Mirabel, he speaks to no one—including his chief of staff, Dumas—and heads for Ottawa.

Ottawa
May 21:
A PMO strategy meeting to deal with the Bouchard sanction is held in Room 218 of the Langevin Block. Present are PMO functionaries Bernard Roy, Stanley Hartt, Marcel Côté, Tom Trbovich and Norman Spector, plus Senator Lowell Murray and Luc Lavoie, a

former chief of staff to Bouchard who left that position to work for Mulroney. Lavoie describes a long meeting he had with Bouchard the previous night, in which Bouchard announced his intention to resign because of the controversy surrounding the telegram. Bouchard said he was insulted when it was suggested that he apologize to the prime minister.

Bouchard meanwhile meets with Tellier, who tries to persuade him not to resign because of the great harm it would do to the government and his friend Brian Mulroney. Bouchard remains adamant, but agrees to talk with Bernard Roy—who, along with Mulroney, had been his chum at Laval. Roy writes in his journal shortly after that historic and final meeting:

"I endeavoured to convince Bouchard that only the government's political opponents would benefit from his resignation, making the chances of ratifying the agreement even more remote. He should therefore postpone his decision until after June 23rd. [The deadline for ratification of the accord.] I pointed to the fact that his sworn enemy, Jacques Parizeau, had already exploited the sending of the telegram for partisan reasons, commenting on the contents of the message on television with an ironic tone that was not necessarily flattering for Bouchard. Bouchard did not budge, in spite of my efforts to bring him to show a minimum of loyalty to the prime minister. I reminded him of everything that he had done for him: his appointment to the Cliche Commission, as ambassador to Paris. Nothing worked. According to him, he had sacrificed much, personally and professionally, when he responded to the prime minister's call to enter politics. On balance, he did not feel he had any debt to the prime minister. He stressed that he had paid a heavy price after having entered politics. He told me of having been ostracized by his family and friends and of having been criticized in the English media, which always brought up his separatist past.

"During our discussion, he was very aggressive towards the Charest report and criticized the government for having been weak and letting itself be manipulated by Chrétien. When I told him that he himself had urged Charest to become chairman of the committee and that Charest had repeatedly tried to reach him when he was in Bergen to discuss the contents of the report before its publication, Bouchard said he never received any message from Charest, except in Paris after the report had been published. He said he had been tricked by the report, which contained many unacceptable recommendations imposed by Chrétien as a condition for the support of the Liberals. He told me he had thought about his decision to resign and that his decision could not be changed. He stressed the fact that his gesture was purely a personal one and that he had no intention of trying to convince other Conservative members to follow him.

"When I suggested that he should at least have the courtesy of seeing the prime minister before making his resignation public, he answered that he hoped he would not have to, so he could avoid a painful confrontation that would unavoidably result from his refusal to reconsider his decision."

Bouchard returns to his office and Roy informs Tellier of his unsuccessful conversation. The two men drive to 24 Sussex Drive to brief the prime minister. Roy tells Mulroney that the reasons invoked by Bouchard to justify his resignation were not convincing and seemed more like an excuse to quit. His impression is that the decision had been taken a long time before and that Bouchard had deliberately chosen this moment to act, using the Charest report as an excuse.

Minister of Consumer Affairs Pierre Blais calls on his friend Bouchard later in the day. "It was a holiday [Victoria Day] but there seemed to be feverish activity," his diary notes. "Three employees working on a document on two computers. Lucien seemed empty, exhausted, tormented. Upon seeing me, a bit taken aback, his first words were 'I'm resigning—come in!' He informed me that he had spent some time with Roy, but had finally decided to tender his resignation. I tried for an hour and a half to dissuade him, using every argument possible without success. Lucien told me that the Charest report was a delusion, that it had been concocted following negotiations between Jean Chrétien and Stanley Hartt, and that he was sure Quebec was getting 'screwed.' I begged him to wait until after June 24th and told him he had no right to do this to his friend. As a last resort, I asked him to remain in caucus so as not to destabilize the government; since Gérin resigned the preceding Friday, some other MPs could follow him and this would prejudice the government. At 7:30 p.m. Lucien was called to 24 Sussex. As a lawyer, I had the feeling of having missed the appeal of a lifetime . . ."

The final meeting between Bouchard and Mulroney is curiously lacking in drama. For one thing, apart from his worries that the

Meech Lake Accord seems to be unravelling, Mulroney is facing a horrendous personal problem. Dimitrije Pivnicki, Mila's seventy-year-old father, is critically ill with a massive brain tumour. Mila has moved into a Montreal hotel to be near him and the family agrees to let Mulroney decide whether surgery should be risked (doctors give Pivnicki a 15 per cent chance of survival). The PM is constantly visiting the hospital and worried about the family crisis during the final days of Meech. On the day Bouchard decides to resign, Mulroney has given the go-ahead for what turns out to be a successful operation. He is awaiting the results when his one-time soul mate walks into his study to end their thirty-year friendship. They conceal their overwhelming emotions and deal with each other as the strangers they have become. "As you have already conveyed to Paul and Bernard that you have no intention of modifying what is profoundly unacceptable conduct for a federal minister, I have no choice whatsoever but to demand your resignation immediately, which I am now doing," Mulroney pronounces, in the dry tones of a judge delivering his verdict. "You are no longer a member of my government. There will be the appropriate exchange of correspondence. I have no idea why you did this; one day we will know." The Bouchard defection, he later tells a friend, was like being shot in the back of the head.

The prime minister then walks his former comrade to the door and whispers a goodbye. Then he has a final word: "You may want to reconsider resigning immediately from the caucus, which you may not want to do because there are so many Quebeckers involved. You've encouraged the whole caucus to stay and fight for Meech and here you are quitting for no apparent reason that I can see. You are now walking out and you may want to spend time in the caucus trying to sort this out with them."

Pierre Blais returns to Bouchard's office that night to warn him that he's making a serious mistake; that he's leaving the ship at the most inopportune moment and that if he truly held the success of Meech to heart, resigning was the last he should do. "I left Lucien in the wee hours of the morning, overcome by a great sadness," he notes in his journal. "In spite of his expressed desire to remain 'good friends,' something snapped and will remain so for a long time."

Ottawa
May 22:
Luc Lavoie arrives at Bouchard's office at 8:00 a.m. to find that his
lengthy resignation letter—which has just been made public—has
long before been translated into English, a job that must have taken
days. "I then understood the extent to which I had been personally
duped and betrayed," he tells a friend. "I felt sick because of what he
had done and I said to Lucien, 'Politics clearly is not made for tender
hearts.'"

Bouchard assembles his parliamentary staff at 9:30 a.m. and tells
them he is resigning. He gets on the phone in an attempt to persuade
other Quebec Tories to follow him into a new party. A few do, but
most of the Mulroney caucus remains loyal.

Ottawa
June 9:
The Meech Lake Accord is approved by the premiers without a word
or comma being changed, just as Mulroney vowed that it would be.
Phoned by reporters, Bouchard has no comment.

Winnipeg–St. John's
June 23:
The Meech Lake Accord, after being talked out in Manitoba and not
taken to a vote in Newfoundland, legally dies at midnight.

Ottawa: Postscript
Some time later:
The Vancouver Sun's parliamentary writer, Peter O'Neil, asks the
departed minister whether he feels like a traitor to his country.
"Traitor?" Lucien Bouchard rears back in surprise. "Traitor? Traitor
to what? My country is Quebec."

FIFTEEN

REBELLION: RED

The First Nations Triumphant

"They're waiting for us to go away."
ANTHROPOLOGIST SOL TAX

INDIANS HAVE ALWAYS BEEN the ghosts of Canadian history. The original First Nations were not conquered in battle like the American Sioux nor, with the exception of Newfoundland's Beothuks, were they hunted for sport to extinction like the Tasmanians. Still, their lives and spirits were torn apart by the arrival of the Europeans. They became the Palestinians of the New World, displaced within their own homeland, forced to live in enclaves under the rule of an intrusive majority of "newcomers." The various First Nations made much history but wrote down little, depending upon their hallowed oral tradition to sustain collective memories and myths. Early European historians treated them as an amorphous, out-of-focus backdrop, not far removed from local vegetable and animal life, and deserving of a similar fate. Their aspiration to decide their own destinies became a rubric kept deliberately out of their reach. Most non-native Canadians treated Indians* as

---

* I hesitate to use the term "Indian," because of the negative connotations of the Indian Act, Indian Agents, Cowboys and Indians, etc. But I go along with native author-journalists Brian Maracle and Dan Smith, who

quaint barbarians, their delight in native culture limited to watching them perform a token rain dance at the Calgary Stampede or puff a pretend peace pipe at a county fair.

All of that changed during the decade covered by this book. No group gained more benefit from, or participated more fully in, the Canadian Revolution than the First Nations. Fuelled by white guilt that stressed the plight of discontented minorities, the Indian cause suddenly became fashionable. Given an expanded base of public support and blessed by a new brand of native leaders who rejected the Uncle Tonto approach of their predecessors, the First Nations came close to setting—or *up*setting—the national agenda.

Bertrand Russell, the eminent British philosopher and mathematician, once defined power as "the production of intended effects." He meant that many people in society have influence, but they do not exercise power unless they can actually change the course of events. Leaders of the First Nations took that advice to heart. They ceased acting like the ghosts they had become, and started instead to behave like the warriors they had once been. No outsider could predict if they recognized any limits to their lively sense of reparation. The befuddled politicians who dealt with them knew only one thing, that nothing could stop them.

It may seem a distorted verdict to speak of Indian gains when so many failed to achieve a better life for themselves. The 1995 statistical summary of Canada's aboriginal population went like this: 603,000 Indians belonged to 605 bands living on 2,370 reserves; another 405,000 non-status Indians lived off the reserves; there were some 196,000 Métis (of mixed Indian and white blood) and 52,000 Inuit. At the end of the decade, as at its beginning, living standards on the reserves were dismal, amenities absent, health care intermittent. Kids from reserves had a better chance of going to jail than of

---

have written extensively on the issue. "When my Cree and Mohawk friends stop using the word 'Indian' in their everyday conversation, then I'll stop using it in print," wrote Smith in *The Seventh Fire*. I feel the same way. Rather than imposing a rigorous orthodoxy on the term, I have opted to follow contemporary usage, which includes First Nations, aboriginals and natives when referring to the various indigenous peoples of Canada; with distinctions drawn between the Innu, Métis and Indian populations.

going to high school. According to the Assembly of First Nations, 62 per cent of reserve Indians and 58 per cent of non-reserve Indians were on welfare; family income on reserves was just over half the Canadian average. Native unemployment rates were running between 70 and 90 per cent and the suicide rate of young males was five times the non-native equivalent. Nearly half of reserve homes had no central heating. To be a Canadian Indian was to be dispossessed.

But collectively, the First Nations' accomplishments were daunting. They stopped dead in its tracks the $12.7 billion Great Whale hydro-electric mega-project on their lands in northern Quebec; they organized the putsch that culminated in Elijah Harper's dramatic veto of the Meech Lake Accord in 1990, thus altering the direction of Canadian history;* they became a key element in slowing, or even halting, the forces of Quebec separatism. Premier Jacques Parizeau was mindful of the risks involved when the grand chief of the northern Cree, Matthew Coon Come, repeatedly warned that the Quebec Cree had just as much right as Quebeckers to choose their future and were not inclined to follow the Parti Québécois to oblivion. "Our land is our memory," Coon Come proclaimed, and that was that—particularly since the land he was talking about contained most of the province's electricity source.

At the same time, the First Nations won the right to self-government, which was proposed under the rejected Charlottetown Accord and later granted by the Chrétien administration. Their claims to the land that had once been fully their own and, in many cases, had not been surrendered by treaty, were being heard and were beginning to be honoured. Even if no amount of money or territory could compensate for the way Canada had historically mistreated its aboriginals, they stood to gain billions of dollars and

---

* It will be endlessly debated whether the Meech Lake Accord was killed by Harper, who refused to grant the unanimous consent of the Manitoba legislature which was needed to meet the accord's deadline, or by Newfoundland Premier Clyde Wells, who did not put the issue to a legislative vote. The clear answer was both. The actions of the one permitted the decision of the other; acting in tandem, they deep-sixed the hard-won agreement.

millions of acres. From a political perspective, the negotiations granted the various First Nations *de facto* status as self-governments; a status which was recognized when they signed treaties with the Europeans and which they insisted had never been relinquished. It was testament to how far the Indian cause had moved out of the shadows that these land claims became a dominant Canadian concern in the 1990s. Although they were here first, for more than a century the preoccupations of natives had ranked last on government agendas.

THEN CAME OKA. THE ARMED STAND-OFF at Oka, a place previously known only for its delicious cheese in the round, had as little to do with the ownership of a local golf course (its official *casus belli*) as Elijah Harper's obstruction of the Manitoba legislature had to do with constitutional reform. The issue in both cases was a down payment on more than a century of lapsed dignity and pride.

The Mohawks' resolute stand at Oka in the summer of 1990, the first armed conflict of the Canadian Revolution, was the ultimate expression of the shift from compliance to defiance. Instead of bowing before the onslaught of armed white authority, for seventy-eight days the Warriors stood up to every physical and mental pressure Canada's Second Nation could muster against them. They would not be moved. One combatant—Quebec Sûreté Corporal Marcel Lemay—was killed when he was shot in the torso during a dawn raid on July 11. For eleven weeks, longer than the modern-day stand-off between natives and whites at Wounded Knee, rebellion was the order of the day. As the siege grew longer and tempers grew shorter, the First Nations went on an unprecedented spree of protest across the country. Roadblocks were set up where freeways crossed reservations, railway crossings were blockaded, hydro transmission lines were torn down and Alberta's Peigans even attempted to reroute a river. Persuasive elements within the native community objected to such guerilla tactics, but there was no disagreement about their aim, which was to further the cause of aboriginal self-government.

The deferential Indians of Canada's past had learned how to negotiate at the end of an Uzi. "They demanded what no responsible government could ever concede—that Canadian laws no longer apply to them and that the Mohawks' community be recognized as a separate nation-state," complained Bernard Roy, the former Mulroney *aide-de-camp* who became the chief federal negotiator in the crisis.* Mohawk conditions included the right to enter into free trade arrangements with other countries, exemption from Canadian personal, corporate and sales taxes and the ability to levy tariffs on goods and services passing through their territory.†

The original barricades were erected to block a golf course extension, which had been approved by the town council of Oka, onto a grove of trees known as The Pines. Because it infringed on what the Mohawks claimed as sacred land, the Warriors dug in to validate their position. In a sympathy move, Mohawks from the nearby Kahnawake reserve put up traffic barriers on the Mercier Bridge, a vital commuter link to Montreal. That became a flashpoint as the sacred right to land ran head-on against the sacred right to commute. The fires burned nightly as mobs convened to hurl spit, insults, Molotov cocktails and rocks at natives crossing the bridge. A few Mohawk elders and children were sent to hospital suffering injuries and with no successful end to negotiations in sight and both sides becoming increasingly intense, the situation threatened to escalate. Robert Lavigne, chief of the Quebec Police Force, confessed by mid-August that he was beaten. "We are incapable of maintaining peace and order, and to enforce the law with the resources we have," he told a hurriedly convened news conference. "Quebec is in the midst of the most important crisis in its history." The Canadian armed forces were requested to aid civilian power by the government of

---

* The federal position had been immeasurably weakened by the fact that the Department of Indian Affairs at the time was under the direction of Tom Siddon, a cabinet bumbler best described by Newfoundland Liberal MP George Baker as being "like an ambulance chaser, only in his case the ambulance is always chasing him."

† Since the Mohawk territory was bisected by the Canada-U.S. border and included a small slice of New York State, recognition of their claims might conceivably have prompted the U.S. to send in a peacekeeping force, with Canada contributing three of its junkyard destroyers to patrol the St. Lawrence. That would have had an unintended benefit—after-dinner speakers would have finally been robbed of that nauseating cliché about the world's longest undefended border.

Quebec. Three infantry battalions, with artillery, engineers and signals elements, descended on Oka.*

The incident quickly gained worldwide notoriety. As the international press descended on Oka, the surrounding forests filled with strange moon-men carrying satellite dishes on their backs. In the late twentieth century, this was confirmation that something cosmic was happening. Observers arrived from the Paris-based International Federation of Human Rights, as did U.S. presidential candidate Jesse Jackson and the template-stamped American television anchors, whose teeth, hair and booming voices sanctioned the event as history on the hoof. The Oka stand-off also signalled the coming-of-age of CBC's Newsworld, whose blanket coverage became a factor in the siege itself. "Television transformed a real situation into a surreal scene," wrote *Ottawa Citizen* columnist Roy MacGregor. At the outset of its military operation, National Defence held a tele-vised news conference to explain the nature of their mission, the Mohawk defences and their own (seemingly unstoppable) forces. The threat of the enemy's defences proved to be wildly exaggerated, it was a piece of political theatre which had more effect on the Canadian public than the Mohawk enemy, who watched it live on television with scorn. During the conflict, the Mohawk Warriors monitored the army's movements through television sets propped up on tree trunks; the army watched the Mohawks on television sets in command posts. Oka became a war by scrum. As both soldiers and Warriors seemed as concerned with their television image as with their supposed enemy, the camera saved the day. No combatant was willing to be the first to open fire against the other—not with the chance that Canadians would witness the salvo from their living rooms." This not only had a restraining influence on the authorities and the Warriors, but it also had an energizing effect on those who were watching from home. It was a kind of power—to

---

* Along with two women tourists seeking the Trappist monastery where they make the cheese. Agnes Jones from Oakville, Ontario, and a Hungarian relative were waved through all but the final barrier between the army and Mohawk warriors. The two women spoke nothing but Hungarian to the guards at each checkpoint, until they were finally questioned on precisely what strange Indian dialect they were using—and were turned back, cheese-less.

use Bertrand Russell's definition—which Canadians had never before enjoyed exercising.

The army in the field behaved with exemplary caution. Initially they dismantled the bridge barriers and, in the first week of September when there was evidence of internal dissent between militants and civilians on the reserve, they moved in to restrict the Mohawks' operating perimeter. Eventually squeezed into the reserve's substance abuse treatment centre, thirty of the remaining Warriors, along with a hundred Mohawk women and children (and attending press groupies) were surrounded. The siege was lifted on September 26, but the image lingered: masked and armed Warriors, looking like PLO commandos in the furnace of battle, facing scrubbed soldiers with locked bayonets. Thirty-two Mohawks were convicted for offences committed during the dispute, while another thirty-four were acquitted. No one was specifically charged with the death of Corporal Lemay.

To the frustrated commuters of Montreal, the stand-off was a symbol of lawlessness, anarchy and that Things Had Gone Too Far. But to almost everyone else, the confrontation at Oka was recognized as the agonized cry of a people turned desperate by their inability to gain a meaningful place in the national polity or conscience. The First Nations leaders vowed that unless significant changes were made, such incidents would happen again. At the crucial Charlottetown conferences of 1992, Chief of the Assembly of First Nations Ovide Mercredi threatened to block any deal that failed to recognize aboriginals as a "distinct society," a gambit which forced the premiers to allow his organization observer status at the talks. In the world after Oka, Indian leaders were no longer willing to remain wards of the state and would never again be tagged as soft and deferential.

HAVING WRITTEN A THREE-VOLUME HISTORY of the Hudson's Bay Company, I documented many instances during the three centuries of the Company having taken advantage of Indians. The Bay minted a fortune by trading pots, axes and blankets with the Indians in exchange for furs, a transaction so weighted in the Company's favour that it often returned as much as 50 per cent in annual dividends to its investors. The Company claimed that its presence was a positive influence, since Canadian history provided one of the few instances of the white man's commercial ambitions coming to terms with an indigenous population without much bloodshed. That was true, so far as it went. There were documented instances of Bay traders keeping Indians (and later Inuit) alive during periods of malnutrition and epidemics. But their motive was partly the realization that starving natives wouldn't be out on the trap lines turning a profit for the Company. Although relatively peaceful, a cultural gap pervaded the fur trade. The HBC regarded the animals and the natives alike as mere units of production. To the aboriginals, hunting was a spiritual experience. They saw themselves as part of an interlocked universe in which animals were treated as their relatives. They meditated with sacred "keepers of the game" who told them where to hunt and later sought the animals' permission to kill them. When the Hudson's Bay Co. factors demanded that the Indians slaughter virtually every furry beast in the forest, they destroyed the spiritual balance of Indian life. The worst abuses occurred in the early 1800s when liquor became the currency of the fur trade. The booze itself was a throat-searing mixture of raw, 132-proof gin (two-thirds alcohol by volume), flavoured with a few drops of iodine or a squirt of chewing tobacco to make it look more like rum. The traders diluted this foul mixture with water and Indians tested it by spitting it into a fire. If the flames flared, it was okay; if the fire sputtered out, they demanded a stronger brew.*

The sudden upheaval to Indian life by the fur and whisky trade can never be redeemed, but to dismiss the mistreatment of the natives as ancient history was neither right nor fair. Many contemporary Canadians felt it defied common sense to be made to feel guilty and pay reparations when they had no personal hand in the appropriation of native lands. Such thinking failed to take into account the fact that they still enjoyed the fruits of that act, from the land they occupied to the resources they consumed. It also failed to recognize the fact that Indians traditionally operated on a different calendar, where yesterday's wrongs are only aggravated—not eased—by the passage of time.

For government negotiators, dealing with the Mohawks at Oka — or native insurrections at the many other flashpoints across the

---

* This was the origin of the term "firewater."

country—proved to be a novel experience. Dealing with a people who had nothing left to lose, they found that none of the existing arbitration rules applied. One of the problems in settling land disputes arose from the fact that, with few exceptions, the only documents providing a written history of each land claim were written by European colonizers. It was a great disservice that oral statements by aboriginals were not recorded as evidence, since in many ways their early oral cultures were more highly evolved than those of the invading Europeans. Native bands would stage four-day miracle plays from memory and family heads could recite prayers by the hour without missing a syllable. Even when there was documentation proving that Indians had surrendered territory, some of the treaty provisions their ancestors had signed belonged to the lowbrow burlesque of Mel Brooks's *Blazing Saddles*. One agreement negotiated around 1870 by Manitoba Lieutenant-Governor Sir Adams George Archibald with local Cree and Ojibwa chiefs provided that they and their descendants, in exchange for their territory, would receive a new suit every three years in perpetuity. As late as 1969, Ojibwa Chief David Couchene accepted as his treaty right a blue serge outfit with red stripes down its trouser legs, complete with brass buttons, gold braid and a black bowler hat—all made, incidentally, by the prison tailor shop at Kingston, Ontario.

The Royal Proclamation of 1763 by George III of Britain recognized aboriginal title, directing that lands and resources be acquired from aboriginal peoples only by the Crown and only by treaty. Although this instrument had been binding on the Crown for more than 200 years, it was given a fresh impetus by rulings of the Supreme Court in the mid-1980s which recognized that aboriginal title existed by virtue of their long possession of the land—in other words, whether or not the Europeans recognized their ownership through treaty. This forced the governments to begin a series of land claim negotiations which were overwhelming to contemplate. Georges Erasmus, the former chief of the Assembly of First Nations, flatly declared that ownership of half the country was under dispute, including—if you added up all the existing claims—110 per cent of British Columbia. The Nisga'a band in the west-central part of the province, for example, claimed 2,400 square kilometres of land, timber and fishing rights—plus an extra $4.3 billion in compensation for lost revenues from forestry, mining and tourism in the interval between losing their historical land rights and the reclamation of the same. That claim was exceeded by the Ojibwa in northern Ontario, who demanded $80 billion on similar grounds. By 1995 nearly 1,000 claims were being processed by Ottawa and provincial governments, with the issue promising to become one of the hottest political topics of the late 1990s.

Unresolved land claims held the potential of becoming the fuse for violent protests that would make Oka seem like a model of passive resistance. Oka had lanced the boil of centuries of pent-up anger and resistance, allowing a younger and more militant breed of native leadership to express open defiance against Canada, which they regarded increasingly as an occupying power. No longer were the First Peoples willing to play a cigar-store stereotype. Their shift from deference to defiance was among the most profound of the Canadian Revolution. "The countries you came from, kicked you out—you came here because you couldn't make a living and you had nowhere else to go," Bill Wilson, chairman of the B.C. First Nations Congress, told a non-native audience at a 1990 meeting in Victoria. "And what did we natives do? We welcomed you. Stupid mistake. Really silly mistake. We should have killed you all." With talk like that, the future promised not only more Mohawk Warriors, but the mobilization of such militias as the Rosedale Fusiliers, Westmount Irregulars and Shaughnessy Skirmishers.

NATIVE RAGE WAS UNDERSTANDABLE when set against revelations of what had happened at the government residential schools administered by the churches until the late 1970s. The sexual and physical abuse that took place in the name of the Europeans' God was beyond imagination. Native children forced to attend these institutions were not only deprived of their culture and language, but many were raped, beaten and systematically tortured. During the trial of Arthur Plint, who had been the lay supervisor of the United Church–administered Alberni Indian Residential School in British Columbia for twenty years, it was revealed that he had repeatedly abused children as young as six years old. When he was finally brought to court at the age of seventy-one, he showed no remorse. Sentencing him to eleven years in prison, B.C. Supreme Court Justice Douglas Hogarth labelled the residential system as "nothing more than institutionalized paedophilia." Robert Mason Lee described in his *Globe and*

Mail column what happened in one isolated valley in B.C.'s Cariboo
country: "The Indian Agent and the priest would roll into the village
each autumn to take the children away in cattle trucks. One proud
and defiant woman told me her brother saw the trucks one day and
ran for the hills. He holed up for three days, living on a chocolate bar
and his wits, while they sent the dogs after him. When he was captured and returned to the school he hanged himself. He could not
face the sodomy. He was eleven years old."

Paradoxically, the residential school experience became a source
of Indian pride and strength. The gradual recognition during the
mid-1980s that the schools were responsible for patterns of family
dysfunction in reserve life, from alcoholism to abuse, gave an
opportunity for many bands to organize a response. These ranged
from community-operated treatment centres to legal actions against
the school operators and the governments, providing a focus which
helped many bands regain their self-esteem and forge political
organizations in the process.

OKA TRANSFORMED THIS GROWING SENSE OF PRIDE into one of open hostility. Few native leaders—in particular the younger firebrands—
would recognize Canada as anything but a foreign regime. The
Chrétien government's unilateral 1994 declaration recognizing the
aboriginals' inherent right to self-government attempted to accommodate this sentiment within federalism. At least in theory, aboriginals would be responsible for their own affairs on their own
territory. This recognition—which had formed part of the defeated
Charlottetown Accord—was the essence of the legal reality ever
since Supreme Court rulings a decade earlier, but it was belatedly,
and somewhat dilutedly, given life by Ron Irwin, the most activist
Indian Affairs minister since Chrétien himself held the portfolio in
the 1970s. "It's time to bring dignity, honour, self-reliance, and self-
government to a people that have been held, not necessarily in
bondage, but certainly as supplicants under an Indian Act that is
archaic," Irwin said as he announced the gradual dismantling of
his department.

Dan Goodleaf, a forty-five-year-old Mohawk who was deputy
minister of the federal Department of Indian Affairs at the time,
presided over the dissolution of his department with an energy born
of anger, justifiably roused by some of the bureaucrats' patronizing

ways. "As a Mohawk from Kahnawake, I consider Montreal a
suburb of our reserve," he told me in a 1994 interview. "If I had my
druthers, my department would vanish much faster than the current
timetable, but you don't simply take away without having some
replacement for an essential conduit between government and aboriginal people. Seven years ago, the department had a complement
of 6,000; today I'm down to 3,400 and there will be even more
reductions. As it is, 84 per cent of my budget is managed directly by
First Nations, but that doesn't mean accountability is being lost.
We're not proposing to just hand out five billion dollars without
reporting structures, but it will be the receiving communities that
become responsible for doing the proper accounting." Goodleaf was
understandably sensitive to charges that the aboriginals had no tradition in dealing with either democracy or capitalism. "Hell," he
said, "we Mohawks were part of the Iroquois Confederacy, which
once operated a highly sophisticated system of trading and governance across the continent."

Doing away with the Department of Indian Affairs amounted to
nothing less than a declaration of First Nations independence that
would have vast and continuing repercussions in the country at
large. The institutionalized paternalism of the Indian Act was being
buried at last. "We are now plotting our own destinies, setting our
own agendas," declared Jerome Morin, chief of the Enoch band west
of Edmonton. "We are determined. We know what we want —nation
to nation—a bilateral process with the Canadian government."

That notion of natives as a countervailing force to government got
its fiercest workout in the fight against the $12.7-billion Great
Whale hydro-electric project in northern Quebec. Long the dream of
Quebec Premier Robert Bourassa, who christened it James Bay II,
the mammoth undertaking was supposed to divert five rivers and
flood almost 5,000 square kilometres of Cree and Inuit hunting territory to produce 3,168 megawatts of electricity for export. While in
political exile after losing the 1976 election, Bourassa had written
Power from the North, in which he described in minute detail how
the project would be built and financed, even postulating the
damming of James Bay as a reservoir for freshwater exports to the
United States. As soon as Bourassa returned to power in 1985, he
rushed to Washington and Wall Street, enlisting high-profile U.S.
businessmen and politicians as the scheme's supporters. He told the

Americans, who were then nervous about the safety of their Middle
East petroleum supplies, that James Bay would produce by the
1990s an annual hydro equivalent of 212 million barrels of oil. In
addition, Bourassa promised that Quebec, being a "trustworthy
ally," would "never pull the switch" on any export deal. James Bay
II quickly became Bourassa's political holy grail. "Northern waters
are to Quebec," noted Lysiane Gagnon, the columnist for Montreal's
La Presse, "what oil is to Alberta: an invaluable natural resource, a
precious source of energy, a tremendous economic asset. This is why
the development of the province's water resources has always been
Mr. Bourassa's main project—the only one, actually, that he holds
with real conviction." For the 17,500 Cree and Inuit who inhabited
the lonely shores of Hudson Bay and James Bay, the fight against the
project was not some form of ideological challenge to the authority
of Quebec; it was, plain and simple, the defence of a way of life. The
Quebec City negotiators never seemed to realize that life was not a
commodity to be bargained away. Their offers were the equivalent
of the citizens of Quebec being told by a group of outsiders that they
would be financially compensated for the forced removal of the
benefits of living in Quebec, including their food, their churches,
their culture halls and their sports arenas. "It's a matter of the Cree
trying to preserve a way of life that depends on what the territory
provides," insisted Robbie Dick, chief of the Cree band at Great
Whale. "The premier seems to have suggested that it doesn't matter
if you kill a thousand people—here are seven million people who
need this [electrical power]. Is he God?"

New York State, James Bay II's most important customer, was
unhappy because it needed the electricity (presumably, to power all
those Canadian factories moving into its northern precincts after the
free trade agreement), but Cree lobbying was so effective that the
state had to find alternate sources. Cree leaders became the darlings
of Manhattan's activist scene. "So effective has been the environmental lobby of the Cree," reported the authoritative Ottawa-based
newsletter *Environmental Dimensions*, "that Bourassa's cherished
Great Whale project has as much hope of financing—yet alone
construction—as George Custer had at Little Bighorn." What
helped trigger the death of Great Whale was not only the New York
State turnaround, but the Mulroney government's decision to autho-
rize a two-year environmental impact study by a trio of Quebec

academics. Given the fact that the chosen commissioners were a philosopher (Paul Lacoste), a specialist on the effects of heavy metals on aquatic life (Claude Delisle) and an oceanographer (Grant Ingram), the outcome of their deliberations was so predictable that they never actually filed a report.

Another element in this explosive mix was the aboriginal claim to northern Quebec territories, including the site of the Great Whale project, in the event of Quebec separation. "What a lot of stuff," ridiculed Jacques Parizeau, adding: "They're going to walk off with the dams under their arms! Pretty soon we'll read in one-inch headlines, 'Sovereignty makes you bald.'"* In the winter of 1994, Parizeau officially killed the Great Whale project, hoping as a result to win the loyalty of Matthew Coon Come, who had become his most ardent and most articulate opponent. The ploy only made the Cree more determined than ever to buck the separatist dreams of the Parizeau crowd. "There will be no annexation of ourselves or our territory to an independent Quebec without our consent," Coon Come declared. "We Crees do not think of borders as sacred. We are part of the land. There is no other place in the world where everything, every hill, every stream, every fork in the river is named in Cree. *Eenou Astchee* [the Cree homeland] is the centre of Cree civilization, and it is inconceivable that we would cease to care for it."

On a militant note no Canadian Indian would have dared use in public before the advent of the Canadian Revolution, Kahnawake Councillor Billie Two-Rivers told a 1994 conference in Montreal, pointing at a group of Quebec separatists in the audience: "They have no land to separate with, it's that simple. I mean, how much land did they bring? They brought a bit of dirt behind their ears and around their necks and between their toes. So maybe they can separate only with that."

Within the space of a decade, Canada's First Peoples had moved from the shadowed margins of society to its boiling centre and had come to constitute the most aggressive and active critics of the power class. Governments were forced to respond to Indian demands for territory and self-determination, while attempting to cope with the rise of a new separatist force in the country which was,

---

* So does federalism. I know these things.

unlike Quebec, thinly scattered across the land. The Marxist writer Antonio Gramsci described a force like the Indians as the most difficult for a state to pacify. A dispersed minority engaged in political activity has two advantages, he wrote in his *Prison Notebooks*: "It has the capacity to destroy the war potential of the dominant nation from within and it compels the dominant military force to thin out and disperse itself over a large territory, thus nullifying a great part of its war potential." Suddenly the words of University of Chicago anthropologist Sol Tax seemed not so ridiculous. Tax, who spent much of his life with North American Indians, once sat on a knoll overlooking an Indian village and jotted down in his journal a seminal realization: "They're waiting for us to go away."

SIXTEEN

ELECTION 1993

Epitaph for the Two-Party State

> *"It doesn't matter who gets elected.*
> *We still end up with a government."*
> ANONYMOUS

M OST OF CANADA'S POLITICIANS WERE SO BEREFT of moral authority by the spring of 1993 that, even when they admitted they'd lied, nobody believed them. With Brian Mulroney deep into the fifth year of his second mandate and the Liberals, led by Jean Chrétien, yet to face the people, there was a smell of election in the air. But the prevailing mood was best expressed by the anonymous observer who grumped, "It doesn't matter who gets elected. We still end up with a government." Voters narrowed their choice according to the least negative alternatives, as in: who's worst, who's second-worst, who's left? The burden rested on the party leaders to recapture the interest and allegiance of those who would cast ballots. This could no longer be accomplished by the traditional gambit of windy rhetoric, "sincere" calls for "renewal" or whatever else came up on the campaigner's poll-driven cue cards.

The 1993 election was significant in the calendar of the Canadian Revolution as a moment of closure and catharsis. It marked the end of Canada's tradition of brokerage politics and it buried, at least for the time being, the two-party system that had been the norm since 1867. At the same time, it provided a catharsis in the way it punished

the Revolution's unindicted conspirators. Two powerful new movements, Reform in the West and the Bloc in the East, soaked up
regional anger and altered the calculus of Canadian politics. The
Progressive Conservatives suffered the worst defeat of any ruling
national party in the country's history. The New Democrats vanished
from contention, as did Mel Hurtig's stillborn National Party. Jean
Chrétien's Liberals earned a majority, but would have to reverse
their ideology to hang on to it.

The day after he announced his resignation in February of 1993,
Brian Mulroney found himself on the CNN network with one of those
Ted Turner droids with a low hairline, deep voice and nothing much
in between. "Rumours have reached us," intoned the interviewer,
"that when you retire, you've been offered a job doing American
Express commercials on TV. How do you react to that?" Without
missing a beat, Mulroney held up his right hand as if grasping a
credit card, looked straight into the camera and advised, "Don't
leave home without it." His ability to turn a slight into a joke was
typical of his good humour upon leaving office. Though the date of
his leave-taking had been postponed four times, he believed that his
plan to hand over the leadership at a convention on the weekend of
June 11 gave his party the best chance of renewing its mandate.

Mulroney's decision to leave was triggered by his original pledge
to serve only two terms and his inability to raise his personal
approval rating above the mid-teens. He wore his polling results like
a leper's bell. "These days, if you're unpopular it means you've
done the tough things," he told Pamela Wallin on the CBC's 1992
year-end interview. "Beware the popular politician. It means he
hasn't done a single thing except tell you what you want to hear." He
tried to take the poison out of the system with him. It had been
Mulroney's original intention to leave office in mid-1990, following
approval of the Meech Lake Accord. When that didn't happen,
Mulroney sought to become the secretary-general of the United
Nations. Senator Lowell Murray, who had headed the constitutional
negotiating team, warned that Mulroney's departure would be followed by the defection of so many Quebec Tory MPs to the Bloc
Québécois that "the disintegration of the government" would not be
"weeks, but hours away." Then came the Oka crisis, the Gulf War,
the stormy passage of the GST legislation through the Senate, the
beginning of the Recession and the establishment of the Bélanger-

Campeau commission in Quebec, which recommended a referendum on sovereignty. Having survived this succession of crises, Mulroney was determined to retire by the fall of 1992, but his plans were cancelled by the referendum that followed the unexpected agreement on the Charlottetown Accord. The deciding date then proved to be January 28, 1993, when Jean Chrétien delivered the first of two major speeches outlining the Liberal platform in such detail that Mulroney felt it locked him into the leadership for the upcoming election. The Tory strategists' greatest fear had been that their unpopular leader's departure might prompt the Liberal caucus to dump *le petit gars de Shawinigan* and substitute New Brunswick's Frank McKenna. Apart from that strategic consideration, Mulroney quit because he couldn't think of a good reason to stay. "Hell, I can't even generate a good demonstration any more," he told me at the time. "I've spent my energy on some reasonably exciting causes, but I've run out of new ideas. When I first was elected to this job, I was younger than Bill Clinton when he moved into the White House. Then I had all that enthusiasm and generated all that hope, but now the party must be regenerated by a new leader who can win. I'll be fifty-four in March and for thirty-eight of those years the Liberals have been in power, which is not a hell of a great record. The only way you change that is by handing the new leader the keys to the kingdom." Those "keys" included a bulging party war chest ($2.3 million collected in 1992, cash reserves of $7 million and a $10-million line of credit with the Royal Bank), a supposedly well-honed campaign organization and the opportunity for his successor to shine during the Tokyo photo-ops at the Group of Seven summit in July.

But Mulroney didn't help his party's cause when he took twenty aides along on an expensive and largely ceremonial international farewell tour that featured a boar hunt in Russia with Boris Yeltsin. He further diminished his stature at home by a patronage orgy during his last six months in office that included more than five hundred appointments of friends, party faithful, his hairdresser, his hairdresser's wife and his baby-sitter to public-service positions, including fifteen cronies to the Senate.

Unlike most prime ministers who were regarded as statesmen the minute they left office, Mulroney's announced resignation on February 24, 1993, opened a dyke of venom; his name had become an adjective for everything that was wrong with the country. "It's reached the point that people blame him if their cars don't start on winter mornings," commented Lysiane Gagnon in *La Presse*. "No Canadian politician wanted more urgently to bind the people to him," wrote Richard Gwyn in *The Toronto Star*. "By the formal measure of electoral victories, none in modern times fulfilled that purpose more triumphantly than did Mulroney. None, in substance, failed so utterly . . . There never was any bonding because, all along, Canadians have sensed there was no core inside him to which to attach themselves, only the hollowness of the pursuit of power. He got the power. He never got the people." Sheila Copps demonstrated her customary generosity of spirit with her observation that "the only nice thing to say is that he's leaving." The opposite point of view was expressed by the *Financial Post*'s David Frum, who called Mulroney "the most effective PM in modern history" and lamented that "through it all, the man with patience and even humour, bore the most scurrilous, cruel, ignorant and unjust criticism."

The most sentimental of Brian Mulroney's journeys was the trip home to Baie Comeau for the last time as prime minister. "Only if you lived in a place like this fifty years ago," he reflected, "did you know what real isolation means, a real sense of community. The place was frozen-in all winter, no roads, one little airline that no one could afford to take . . . I started here. I'll finish here."

WHEN MULRONEY JOKED about handing his successor "the keys of the kingdom," the recipient he had in mind was a wispy self-confessed wood nymph from British Columbia named Avril Phaedra (Kim) Campbell. Just before he left, Mulroney had named her minister of national defence. As she was even less qualified for the post than its usual hapless occupants, the decision was made presumably so she could use the line, "Don't mess with me; I've got tanks."*

She turned out to be one of those rare politicians cursed with an unerring instinct for her own jugular. She would be prime minister

---

* She made at least one fateful decision as defence minister that would cost her the image of being a fresh thinker. Instead of cancelling the Tories' $5-billion contract for the acquisition of fifty EH-101 helicopters, she only marginally reduced the number to be purchased, and thus lost the votes of both the program's supporters and its opponents.

for only 132 days, yet she occupied some pride of place in the Revolution. Like Aleksandr Kerensky, who temporarily appealed to both moderates and revolutionaries in the Russia of 1917, she was a transitional figure representing change without upheaval. Her failure not only shattered her own party but allowed the darker agents of the Revolution—Lucien Bouchard and Preston Manning—to claim the power that threatened Canada's national integrity.

She was an unlikely agent of destruction. Kim Campbell's conversation oozed from her like overripe Brie; yet, upon first meeting she seemed smart, wonderfully irreverent and above all, different. I tested these traits when we had Sunday brunch at the Crystal Room in Victoria's Empress Hotel. She came into the hall, attended by a headwaiter awkwardly trying to execute something between a bow and a curtsy, all the while walking backwards. The first thing I noticed about the approaching minister of national defence was that she walked toes out, like a platypus. She had a beatific smile and blue eyes that even Michael Wilson would drown in. While we went up to grab a bite at the buffet, I casually tested her sense of irreverence. "So," I asked, as she was bending over the cracked crab, "where were you conceived?"

"On top of a timber lookout near Port Alberni," she shot back, as she piled the Dungeness on her plate.

Then a youthful-looking forty-six years of age, Campbell gave the impression of being both gregarious and lonely. (Her favourite greeting card, she told me, carried the message: "You don't seem very grouchy for someone who never has sex.") She was warm and open, until I challenged so much as a sliver of her beliefs or agreed with a single one of her critics. Then she became brittle as flint.

She told me she loved music, that next to politics it was the most essential part of her life. She was a capable cellist, although she didn't take up the instrument until her thirtieth birthday;* she was also the only person I had ever met who could intelligently diagnose Bill Haley and the Comets. ("He was really on the cusp, still heavy

---

* One of her more notable gaffes was the impromptu speech she once gave to a crowd of hungry street people on Vancouver's skid row. "I know that a lot of you have faced disappointment and loss in your lives," she intoned with great empathy. "I have, too. I wanted more than anything to be a concert cellist."

on the saxophone, but the brass were beginning to decline.") The
significance of her musical inclination only hit me later, when I
watched her speaking French to a military delegation in Ottawa and
realized that even though she sounded letter-perfect, she was
reading every word and comma from a prepared text. What was
remarkable about the performance was her mastery of the language's cadences. It was her musical ear as much as her mental
agility that allowed her to grasp other languages so rapidly—and
would later get her into trouble in unrehearsed exchanges with
Quebec journalists.

By the time we were into our second buffet course, Campbell's
mood had softened a bit. She was decidedly coquettish as she confessed, "I've got a strong streak of wood nymph in me, the way I was
raised. There's a kind of mystical quality about the West Coast that
forms everything you do, and I feel that my grandfather's family,
although they were Scots Presbyterians, truly were of this place.
My grandfather was an environmentalist before his time. He was
instrumental in having the fish ladders built on Sproat Lake. He was
a hunter, but my grandmother canned what he shot. He was very much
in tune with the land." She had studied political science at UBC, supported herself during the summers by skinning halibut at a Prince
Rupert packing plant ("I still can't eat it") and worked the mayon-
naise line at Kraft's Vancouver factory. After an unhappy stint as an
obscure member of the Vancouver school board and an even unhap-
pier sojourn as a Social Credit backbench MLA (she ran for the party
leadership but secured only fourteen votes), she switched to federal
politics and won Vancouver Centre in 1988. Her upward political
mobility then became spectacularly swift. She was named minister of
justice and attorney-general of Canada, having spent just sixteen
months at a law firm (including her articling period), a leap that had
taken Pierre Trudeau a full quarter-century to complete. What I recall
most clearly from that interview was that she seemed stumped only
once, when I had asked about her shortcomings. "Well . . ." she began.
"I mean, I'm not always right. I mean . . . let's see, what *are* my shortcomings? Now that will sound really *arrogant*, if I can't think of any.
I know! I don't like using the telephone. Ask my staff, they'll tell you,
'Oh, she doesn't like using the phone.' I guess one of my biggest shortcomings, believe it or not, is that I'm very shy around people. This
may seem strange to you, because I'm sitting here telling you the story

of my life, but I'm playing a role. I have a reason to be here. If this were a blind date, I would be much more shy."

At first nearly the entire Tory party saluted her colours. Until Jean Charest volunteered to make a race of it, no other candidate wanted to risk running against her for the leadership. Campbell, who had joined the Progressive Conservatives only four years earlier, seemed to be a shoo-in to win the party's mid-June leadership convention and become the country's nineteenth prime minister, the first woman to hold the office. Lengthy political apprenticeships don't guarantee political leadership, but it is certainly an advantage for prime ministers to have a feel for the country and party they hope to lead. Campbell had demonstrated neither. She moved to the top of the polls not because of her enduring love of her country, but because of her country's brief crush on her.

The mystery of her rapid ascent was explained by the fact she was the candidate most identified as an agent of change. Her support was based on her combination of gender, age and geography. The idea that a Clinton-generation woman from British Columbia could become the magic bullet for the Tories was as brilliant as the Tory thinking a generation earlier, when a calm, dependable Maritime premier with long governing experience was thought to be the winning combination. The difference was that Robert Stanfield turned out to be by far the more successful politician of the two.

Since these were considerations beyond her control or credit, Campbell was quick to discount tokenism as a factor in her victory. "I would like to think," Campbell said, "that whatever I do, my gender will be part of what goes into my outlook. But nobody should ever say, 'Oh God, we've got to have a woman! Well, there's Kim.' That's what they did in the NDP. That's tokenism. And it's very insulting, a dead-end for any group that wants to be liberated." Her protests to the contrary, Kim Campbell benefitted from the post-Charlottetown consensus that the last thing Canada needed was another guy in a suit. As the most famous photograph of her proved, she was most assuredly not a guy and and she was certainly not in a suit, other than the birthday variety. Such irreverence fit the times. Long before Mulroney resigned, she was interviewed by an earnest CBC type who wanted her to confirm or deny that she planned to run for his job. "Life is unpredictable," Campbell replied. "I might run, or I might take up with a gigolo and move to Brazil."

Topics of substance were barely touched in the Conservative leadership contest, which was entirely about personalities and decided such issues as whether Kim was really cuddlier or whether Charest preferred pancakes to waffles. The Tories had learned nothing from the referendum the previous October. Less than eight months earlier, the country had rejected the established order of things. Canadians were demanding a totally new style of leadership. Campbell kept promising to deliver just that, but the voters eventually saw just another Mulroney in a skirt. At first, Campbell seemed to understand that for anything to change, the Old Boy network that dominated Canadian politics would have to be replaced. Yet, she inexplicably placed herself in its hands. Mulroney-vintage lobbyists and backroom operators like Pat Kinsella, Paul Curley, Pierre-Claude Nolin, Allan Gregg, Norm Atkins, Bill Neville, Jodi White, Nancy Jamieson and John Tory ran her campaign. At one point, twenty-seven members of the Tory caucus were working the phones to steer delegates her way; not a new voice among them.

Her idiosyncrasies were turned against her in a brutish leadership struggle; her enemies painted her as lacking in feminine virtues because she was a childless woman who had been twice divorced—despite a Statistics Canada report which showed that about half of Canadian families were divorced, blended or otherwise Osterized. Campbell had hoped to demonstrate to delegates that if they were serious about winning the next election, the Tories had better join the twentieth century (before it was over) and subscribe to an inclusive human agenda. But what ultimately swayed the party her way was a very different consideration. The Tory brain trust figured that in a choice between a Liberal from Quebec (Jean Chrétien) or a Tory from Quebec (Jean Charest), most Canadians would probably cast their ballots for Chrétien, since the country had just spent a troubled decade under another Tory from Quebec (Mulroney).

The night of the nominating speeches, Campbell supporters were milling about like bulls in the pens at Pamplona. Her people came on strong to the rock rhythms of INXS's "New Sensation," but Campbell's speech was delivered to the stately cadence of Bach's "Te Deum." Throughout her campaign, she had made it clear that she was ready to accept the leadership only if it came on her terms. Above all, she wanted to be free to drop verbal bombs on command. But at some point before the convention she abandoned her resolve.

The only bomb that night was her wooden delivery of a leaden speech. Her traditional appeal for votes quieted any doubts about her willingness to behave like an Old Boy.

Charest, who seemed to be always having a bad-hair day, didn't do much better. He appealed for support on the freshness of his youth—but instead of appearing young, he seemed merely to be untested, which was worse. Too smooth by half, he sounded like the cocktail-bar pianist who substitutes warbling for soul. His campaign had been bound by the high catechisms of Tory orthodoxy: devotion to God, family, country and Quebec's place in Confederation. He looked like a politician and sounded like a politician, which meant that neither he nor any of the other politicians stood a chance against the extraterrestrial appeal of Kim Campbell.

In the summer doldrums that followed, Campbell prepared herself and the country for the fall election. However lofty the illusions or grand intentions that had brought her into office, she soon realized that being prime minister meant she had to be both Mary Poppins (making that nasty fiscal medicine go down) and Mary Magdalene. She turned out to be neither and found nothing more inspiring to talk about than balancing the budget or auditing the cost of the Mulroneys' used furniture—hardly a sense of purpose to set loose Canadians' new-found capacity for self-fulfilment.

ON THE LIBERAL SIDE, Jean Chrétien led a party dubious of its choice. He had assumed the leadership in 1990 mainly because it was his turn; the Liberals had never deviated from alternating English-and French-speaking leaders and John Turner's term had expired. The only high-profile options were Sheila Copps and Paul Martin, disqualified by the accident of their mother tongue. (Martin lived in Montreal but was born in Windsor.) Although Chrétien assured anyone who would listen that he wanted an election "the better the sooner," he was hardly ready to assume the burdens of high office. Chrétien had been around forever, having been first elected to the House of Commons when John Kennedy was still in the White House and Harold Macmillan occupied 10 Downing Street. There had been six more presidents and five more prime ministers since, but familiarity did not necessarily breed consent. True, there was something reassuring about Chrétien's *patois* accent, his avuncular charm and his Jean-Paul Belmondo smile. But that had to be tempered by a reminder of Chrétien's political shortcomings. He rose through the ranks of the Liberal Party by being well-briefed, fast on both feet, aggressive, tart and by hiding behind his peasant mannerisms whenever the going got tough. Tracing his performance in the nine cabinet posts he had occupied, it was clear that most of his policy initiatives consisted of mild groping toward orthodoxy. His record betrayed no evidence of original thought; that was not unusual among Liberal politicians, but his real problem was that he had never been a leader. Being a nice guy wasn't enough.

It was ironic that the Tories were in the political cellar but hardly a murmur was heard against Brian Mulroney among his caucus members; while Liberal MPs and senators, whose party topped the polls, were lukewarm at best about Chrétien. He had been unable to mobilize his troops in any policy direction or even mount a concerted attack against the Tories. The party that Chrétien had inherited from Turner was a dispirited residue from the political wars, innocent of policy, philosophy or any purpose other than survival.

The fabric of Chrétien's politics was like a veil, translucent but not transparent, serving to protect the inner man from exposure to a wider constituency. His convictions seemed negotiable, giving the impression of profound detachment. Chrétien appeared to move through many worlds without fully belonging to any but his own. He regarded the grip of ideology as a dangerous trait in a politician, believing that progress flowed not from commitment to ideas but from the pursuit of alternatives, through adjustable tactics that permitted the gradual reconciliation of differences. "The art of politics is learning to walk with your back to the wall, your elbows high, and a smile on your face," he stated in his ghost-written memoirs, perfectly defining his standard operating procedure. An interesting counterpoint was provided by John Rae, the Power Corp. executive who was Chrétien's 1993 campaign manager. "Jean has always been much more thoughtful than people give him credit for," said Rae. "He looks at things historically, philosophically and practically." Chrétien could be very practical. In the 1968 election, after he gave a speech in a small town in the British Columbia interior, the riding chairman asked him to greet someone who was about to switch to the Liberals. Chrétien told the fellow: "So, I understand you're going to vote Liberal for the first time in your life."

"Yeah," came the reply. "Trudeau will put the damn frogs in their place!"

"A vote's a vote," Chrétien shrugged, and walked away.

His greatest strength was that just about every Liberal in the country owed him something,* but his biggest problem was Quebec. His old-fashioned, pea-soup persona was bad enough; the televised image from the Calgary leadership convention, where Chrétien hugged Clyde Wells for killing the Meech Lake Accord, was the modern equivalent of hugging Macdonald for hanging Louis Riel.

To fashion an election platform, Chrétien called a Liberal policy conference in the autumn of 1991 at Aylmer, Quebec, just across the river from Ottawa. The meeting was based squarely on the 1960 Kingston Conference which had resurrected the Liberal party, also then in opposition under Lester B. Pearson. That conference had been organized by Mitchell Sharp, vice-president of Brazilian Traction, Light and Power Co. Ltd. (today's Brascan) and a former deputy minister of trade and commerce in Ottawa. (Chrétien's mentor since 1966, Sharp also helped organize the Aylmer think-tank.) Kingston not only provided new blood for the party, but also moved its centre of ideological gravity decisively to the left. Tom Kent, former editor of *The Economist* and the *Winnipeg Free Press* and destined to become Pearson's chief policy adviser, set out most

---

* David Anderson, who later became revenue minister in Chrétien's first cabinet, was one such example. "He gave me the Pacific Rim National Park," said Anderson. "When I was a Liberal backbencher and he was the minister responsible for national parks. I asked him to visit the west coast of Vancouver Island and when he did, he brought no boots to walk into the wilderness. He borrowed my mother's, which were a full size too small for him. We arrived at a little dock on Nitinak Lake and there was Charley Edgar carving a dugout canoe. I said to myself, 'God, this has got to be my day. I accidentally bring the Minister of Indian Affairs to the only dock in the world where an Indian is chipping a dugout canoe!' The fog was rolling, the mist was rolling, the rain was rolling, we were sitting around a sputtering little campfire and I thought, 'This is awful, Jean will never believe this should be a park. This is just a grim bit of the west coast.' But he did it and now the Pacific Rim National Park is so popular that in the summer the reservations system has to be closed for hours at a time. I was impressed that he took the trouble to come out and have a look instead of just parroting the decisions of his department."

of the radical ideas that catapulted the Liberals back into office in his paper, *Towards a Philosophy of Social Security*. In contrast, the Aylmer conference rejected the ideas of such pink Liberals as Lloyd Axworthy and opted instead for Roy MacLaren's continentalist, free-market approach. The party's strategists decided to fight the next election on economic grounds, reviving the old slogan: "Tory Times Are Hard Times."*

ELECTIONS ARE A PECULIAR PHENOMENON. They capture the political landscape of a nation at a frozen moment in time. Kim Campbell went into the campaign with the highest approval rating of any Canadian political leader in three decades; just six weeks later she was running a poor fourth and facing defeat in her own riding. She later blamed her dramatic slide on being tarred by Brian Mulroney's legacy, on having recruited the wrong advisers and on being forced to seek votes in a time of fiscal restraint. She failed to acknowledge that her run for office was so clumsy it could have been played by Woody Allen in drag. Her descent was due to her transformation on the campaign trail, where the wood nymph turned into a wooden cigar-store Indian. Her rigid, school-marmish lectures and dehydrated disposition would have got her kicked off a Texas line dance, let alone an election campaign.

The enduring mystery of her fall from grace was why Campbell had allowed it to happen. It was all so unnecessary. For example, her biggest problem had been the absence of positive policies, yet a workable platform was at her disposal. Before he left office, Mulroney had a throne speech written based on position papers from key government departments. The proposed measures were carefully geared to avoid any negative impact on the federal treasury. The centrepiece was a detailed plan to drop most existing social programs and replace them with a guaranteed annual income. Although

---

* The motto dated back to R.B. Bennett, a hard-rock Tory from Calgary, who had been Canada's prime minister for the worst of the Depression years. At one postwar election rally, Liberal leader Louis St. Laurent repeated the slogan, pointing out that conversely, Liberal times were good times. A heckler yelled out: "It's a coincidence!" The prime minister nodded and replied: "Ah yes, my friend, but which coincidence would you rather have?"

she claimed to represent change, when presented with such a positive innovation, Campbell instead set the dominant tone of the campaign on the day she dropped the writ by musing about a jobless economic recovery and holding out no hope of reduced unemployment in the 1990s. On the first day of the actual campaign she reiterated her pessimistic forecast. The next morning she acknowledged that she was planning to cut social programs, but would not provide details and made it appear the whole welfare net was up for grabs. She started to feud with the media corps, withdrew into an uncommunicative cocoon and told one reporter who asked why she wasn't offering Canadians some hope that the reporter needed a hearing aid. Her credibility crumbled. She blathered on endlessly about the deficit being a time bomb she vowed to defuse, but pledged not to increase taxes and refused to specify any social program cuts. What she was telling voters, in effect, was, "Trust me." That was a deadly rejoinder, the one message Canadians in the troubled autumn of 1993 were not prepared to believe from any politician.

She tried to deflect questions about social programs by pointing out that an election campaign was no time "to get involved in very, very serious issues." Then, just to make sure that her extraordinary gaffe would be noticed, she went on to emphasize that elections are "the worst possible time to have that kind of dialogue because it takes longer than forty-seven days to tackle an issue that's that serious." It was an appropriate Freudian slip when she climbed into an aircraft flight simulator in a Montreal factory and said to herself, loud enough to be overheard, "I haven't crashed yet, but I have no idea where I'm going." The actual crash took place in mid-October, when her campaign aired TV ads that made fun of Chrétien's partial paralysis of the face. The commercials had been put together by pollster Allan Gregg and advertising agency executive Tom Scott. Their colossal error in judgement, which only played to public disgust at Tory arrogance, was compounded by a lag in communications. It took exactly nine seconds for members of the British Columbia campaign team to agree unanimously over breakfast that the Chrétien ads were in abysmal taste and had to be yanked, but the message didn't reach Tory headquarters in Ottawa until late that afternoon. The Liberals, in contrast, had a rapid response team headed by Senator (later Governor-General) Roméo LeBlanc and communications whiz Peter Donolo, which monitored the leaders' tours on a minute-by-minute basis. The Chrétien road team had a well-crafted response to the ads before the Conservatives even realized the extent of their blunder.

During a brief stopover at Kelowna, British Columbia, the Tory leader unwittingly made a prescient prediction. "I'm not computer literate," she complained, "and it worries me. I'm working very hard to get re-elected because, frankly, if I get thrown out of office, I'm not sure I can find a job." Delivered in jest, it was the most honest moment of her campaign.

The televised debate brought the leaders together for the first (and last) time of the campaign. Meant to be the election's highlight, it failed to provide a defining moment. Preston Manning spoke almost entirely in slogans, his Howdy Doody chin flapping at the hinge. He was smooth as a seaside boulder (any guy who wears ties as awful as his couldn't be all bad); but his pinched, sophomoric sincerity soon wore thin. Lucien Bouchard, leader of the Bloc Québécois, looked like one of those swarthy opera villains whose stage entry is inevitably heralded by a profondo chorus of low-register trombones. He seemed impatient with the whole process, exasperated by the notion that he, the future president of Quebec, should have to put up with this charade. At one point, he attacked "the imperialistic ambitions of the federalist government." Audrey McLaughlin seemed the most comfortable. Maybe she knew she had nothing to lose; more likely she felt so balanced and collected because alone among the candidates, she spoke out of conscience rather than obligation. She was the only free spirit on stage.

As was her wont (or wonk), Campbell talked far too fast for any human mind to follow. "I have a very clear plan to eliminate the deficit!" she bellowed every few minutes. Visibly peeved that it took all this guff to win an election, she projected the idea that there should be a tenure track for prime ministers and that she should be on it. Even though Allan Gregg had once postulated that the only way for an incumbent to lose a debate was to eat a live rat on stage, Kim managed it without the snack. Jean Chrétien's eyes gave off a distant lunar glow as he tried to concentrate on the questions he was being asked. When in doubt, like an old-time preacher getting into theological difficulties, he looked heavenward and intoned: "It's in the book! It's in the book!" waving his little red pamphlet. (Mao would have been proud.)

ONE OF THE MINOR MYSTERIES of the 1993 election, indeed of the entire decade, was why the New Democrats—who by rights ought to have been in the vanguard of any Revolution—got thrown on the tumbrel. Unlike the Liberals and Conservatives, the NDP (and CCF before it) had traditionally been populist movements whose members and leaders felt they should be loved for the enemies they made. They squandered their political lives demanding open-ended absolution for their utopian dreams of a more equitable Canada. They turned their socialism into a high religion instead of high economics, which made for low politics. But their righteous refusal to dilute their purity of purpose alienated the mildly reform-minded members of the mainline parties who might have otherwise been tempted to join up, leaving their fate in the hands of dyspeptic academics. While Canadian socialism often acted as the conscience of the country, it seemed destined never to govern it.

Ed Broadbent, who led the party from 1975 to 1989, came the closest to reversing this philosophy, claiming that "social democratic politics involves both principles and power; to argue only for principles is narcissistically self-indulgent." But he never won more than the forty-three seats his party gained in 1988. Audrey McLaughlin, who succeeded him, limited herself to what party insiders referred to as "the reject and preserve" agenda—rejecting the corporate ethic while trying to preserve Canada's social net. Best remembered for her lament that "the hardest thing in most Ottawa men's pants is their cellular phone," she worked long hours but pioneered few new policy directions. She set the tone of her stewardship when she confided to an aide that she wouldn't hire anyone who had served on her leadership campaign because "if they worked for me, they can't be very good." In the 1993 campaign NDP support fell from 20 to 7 per cent, with only eight of forty-three incumbents re-elected. By the following spring, NDP support had bottomed out at 4 per cent in the polls. With the Ontario New Democrats routed and the British Columbia New Democrats in deep doodoo-dom, it looked as if Roy Romanow's New Democrats in Saskatchewan would be the party's only surviving flag carrier. This was either despite, or because of, the fact his ideology had as much bite as light beer that's been left out too long in the sun. Canadian socialism had thus returned to its birthplace, although its radicalism was measured in the parts per million when set against the original Regina Manifesto, signed by J.S. Woodsworth in 1933.

ON ELECTION NIGHT, the country's three largest regions voted for self-interest in three different political directions. The decimation of the Progressive Conservatives—from 169 seats to two—temporarily reduced the party to a cult with no power base, no money and no new ideas. Mulroney's coalition of Quebec and the West, which had held during the 1988 free trade election, lay shattered by the subsequent constitutional quarrels. The election wrote an epitaph for Canada's existing two-party state.

The party leaders who most visibly challenged the status quo with their own dark agendas, Preston Manning and Lucien Bouchard, were rewarded with major gains; fifty-four seats and Official Opposition standing for the BQ and fifty-two seats for Reform. They had leapt above marginal status by their contrary role in the Charlottetown referendum. Nothing the Liberal leader said or did during the campaign challenged anything or anybody, but Chrétien left the impression he could deal with the nation's awesome problems—that if he wasn't an agent of change, he might at least be an agent of managed change. Among disillusioned voters, that elicited enough support on election night to grant him 178 seats.

THE BRITISH STATESMAN Benjamin Disraeli once observed that a good politician has to know both himself and his times. That aphorism went a long way toward explaining Jean Chrétien's long-lasting popularity following the 1993 election. Except for killing the EH-101 helicopter deal and the Pearson International Airport expansion, he accomplished virtually nothing during his first twenty months in office. Yet according to the polls, the public approval of his performance ranked the highest ever recorded by a Canadian prime minister, a love-in that extended nearly halfway through his mandate. He knew how to spend power and personified the values Canadians wanted in their leaders: parsimony, humility and above all, the ability to operate government without being constantly in people's faces—the skill to run the country without frightening the horses. "They do nothing but do it with great grace," commented Tony Wilson-Smith in *Maclean's*. "Policies are defined by what is not done, rather than by what is."

Chrétien was all too aware that politics was unpredictable, but he also knew that he could bask in the comfortable pew of having no national rivals. He could thus follow the Napoleonic dictum that no leader should ever interfere with an enemy while he is in the process of destroying himself and used his popularity as a licence to perpetuate the same smug patronage he had so vehemently attacked in Mulroney. He went even further, authorizing expenditures of nearly a quarter-million dollars by the foreign affairs department to lobby the Organization for Economic Co-operation and Development to appoint as its secretary-general Donald Johnston, the president of the Liberal Party and its chief financial officer. He gave his niece a job in the PMO and appointed his nephew Raymond as ambassador to Washington. The son of the governor-general (himself a Liberal Party hack) was put in charge of Maritime patronage. His son-in-law, André Desmarais (married to Chrétien's daughter, France), was awarded a billion-dollar contract to operate a satellite-TV network over the objections of federal regulators. Had Mulroney tried even one of the tricks, there would have been blood on the streets.

In fact, as the Chrétien years progressed it became increasingly difficult to differentiate his government from its predecessor. Apart from Chrétien's unapologetic use of patronage, there were similarities in policy. Chrétien had severely criticized Mulroney for fishing with President George Bush at Kennebunkport, yet he played golf with Bill Clinton in Halifax. While in Opposition, Chrétien had mounted devastating attacks on such Mulroney policies as the GST, free trade, NAFTA, CBC budget cuts and reductions in transfer payments to the provinces, yet once in office he reversed not one of these initiatives. Instead he cut federal welfare and social service payments to 1950s levels and reneged on his election promises to increase immigration, support cultural sovereignty or allow more free votes in the Commons. "As the months go by," wrote Barbara Yaffe in *The Vancouver Sun*, "it becomes ever clearer that Jean Chrétien is an Old Boy, practicing an outmoded style of politics. In many respects he is what we feared—yesterday's man. Ultimately, this will be his downfall."

THE 1993 ELECTION MAY HAVE BEEN THE FINAL ACT of the Revolution. Two new regional parties were formed from the broken shards of the Mulroney coalition. The brokerage role played by the old politics of élite accommodation had been rendered obsolete. There had been little grace in the campaign and an absence of feeling that anything enchanting, or even vaguely desirable, might be happening. Canadians figuratively stormed the walls of Parliament and razed its chambers clean of all but a few traces of the politics they had come to hate. Having lost their touchstones and their faith in the process, voters in Quebec and the West were no longer willing to merely replace one set of discredited politicians with another. Instead, they opted for a revolutionary option: by replacing representation with delegation, sending regional surrogates to Ottawa to fight on behalf of their particular, rather than national, interests. Elsewhere, the voters opted for their least offensive and least activist choice: the languorous Liberals. The composition of Parliament ensured that the Liberals would be goaded into action only in response to the populist pressures of its regional parties. Reform set the agenda on social spending and deficit reduction while the Bloc set the agenda on Quebec; it was left to the Liberals to mediate between existing priorities.

The decade had taught voters to make choices that left open an interplay of possibilities and a window on hope. Their electoral choice reflected this; sadly, their leadership did not. The entire concept of political leadership is meaningless if it amounts to little more than pandering to the latest opinion poll, opposition demand or reactionary impulse, but that was how the Chrétien government managed to stay afloat. Meanwhile, the Revolution continued to be without national leaders who could *feel* what issues mattered to people and direct those feelings into positive action, which is the essence of enlightened politics.

But that wasn't true on the provincial scene. Ralph Klein in Alberta, Mike Harris in Ontario, Gary Filmon in Manitoba, Frank McKenna in New Brunswick, John Savage in Nova Scotia, Gordon Campbell (the premier-in-waiting of British Columbia) and, to a slightly lesser degree, Roy Romanow in Saskatchewan were all following a similiar political agenda. Theirs was the Revolution's fallout of defiance, translated into political action. From their accurate reading of the public mood, the premiers had made the connection between grass-roots populism and the people's anger at free-spending governments. It was an anti-élitist movement, only most of the élites targeted were in the public service.

In such circumstances, the country spawned few heroic politicians. A welcome exception was Brian Tobin, the federal fisheries minister. His stand against the Spanish trawlers overfishing the slimy turbot may not have been that heroic—in the sense that he never left dry land—but his take-no-prisoners attitude personified Canada's new defiant posture. The brief turbot war was one of the rare times Canadians had fired shots in anger on their own behalf. The armed intervention on the heaving North Atlantic was significant because, for once, Canadians felt proud to be cast as aggressors. True, the four bursts of .50-calibre bullets were aimed wide of the bow of the *Estai*. But Canadians didn't customarily use machine guns to impose their will; they never drew lines, even invisible ones on water.

No matter how hard Ottawa pretended the contrary, the Law of the Sea didn't support its actions. The Spanish fleet had been fishing beyond Canada's jurisdiction. But once the diplomatic niceties were exhausted, Canadians proudly stood up for what they felt was right. The strength and dignity exhibited by Brian Tobin, a one-time parliamentary Rat Packer whose previous reputation had been for noise rather than eloquence, helped buoy public acceptance. But it was the national shift from deference to defiance that had sealed the bargain.

It was, however, an isolated example of Canadians being proud of their politicians. If politicians started spending more money on day care than on helicopters, if single moms got the same tax breaks as corporate raiders, if safeguarding the environment became as important as throwing a span of concrete across the Northumberland Strait to turn Prince Edward Island into a destination resort—if a few enlightened measures like that came seeping through the system, then Canadians might start trusting it again. Until then, they were prepared to keep their governments on a short leash and chokechain. The Revolution had only rid Canadians of one set of politics and one set of attitudes toward power. It had not yet replaced them with an enduring alternative. The Chrétien government was about caretaking; for the time being, Canadians looked to places other than government for care-giving. Eliminating the deficit was a necessary part of any future government, but it proved to be more of a bureaucratic necessity than a spiritual destination.

EPILOGUE

Slouching Toward the Millennium

*"If there is one safe generalization in human affairs, it is that
revolutions always destroy themselves. How often have
fanatics proclaimed: 'The Year One!'"*
ESSAYIST WILLIAM RALPH INGE

TEN YEARS AFTER THE JOURNEY that began this book, I was in the
air flying back to Vancouver from Toronto. As the Pearson
International Airport runway lights fell away and we began the
arched passage across the plains to the Pacific and home, it hit me
yet again: this is not a country; this Canada we call home is a continent. How in heaven's name can anyone govern a continent? Or
even pretend to? How can anybody fashion policies that will meet
the divergent imperatives of an unemployed Newfoundland fisher-
man, an upwardly mobile Markham broker, an oil-patch roughneck
and a Vancouver craniosacral therapist? As Samuel Goldwyn used to
say: "In two words: *im-possible*."

Viewed from my 30,000-foot aerial platform all that piss and
vinegar spent bickering over constitutional crumbs seemed about as
relevant to Canadian daily life as the mating habits of Brazilian killer
bees. What mattered was that, unlike most industrialized countries,
the glorious hunk of geography which we claim remained authentic—
and ours. Sure, the idea of drawing our national identity from the land
had become an obsolete concept from the first day we logged on to the
Internet. But the land was still our beginning, the source of our spiri-

tual sustenance, whether we worshipped it from the porch of a toy cottage on a crowded lake, the cockpit of a sailboat or at sunset from a bench in a city park still reverberating with the echo of the children's daytime hooting.

The aircraft was sizzling along at cruising altitude with Toronto far behind us, appropriately faded into an indistinct smudge of flickering shadows. Just before the clouds cut off my view, I could see the tapestry of central Ontario's market-garden farms draped over low ridges, marching toward the horizon where I mentally mapped the rivers that had first brought the voyageurs inland in their quest for adventure and fur. I visualized the back roads that twisted away from the country of the mind into the real Canada—brooding, silent and inaccessible, an empty land filled with wonders.

Below me, one belief system had given way to another. Despite appearances, the country was more than a collection of Potemkin city-states on the tremulous edge of an uncertain millennium. During the previous ten years Canadians had reinvented themselves, from deferential nerds living in a quiescent and faintly colonial society to articulate and astonishingly defiant arbiters of a sophisticated nation-state. The Protestant ethic had become as rare as the Sunday suits and crinoline skirts that had symbolized it. In its place Canadians had substituted an ethic which was more suited to the reality of their lives. People had moved from a preoccupation with values as the source of experience, to experience as the source of values.

Great institutions can only be reformed by stealth or by revolution. Canadians had tried both and it was difficult to judge exactly when, or if, the Revolution had run its course. Canada takes a lot of killing and its historic cycles have a way of coming most sharply into focus at a distance. Canadians feel outrage most acutely when they conceive the gap between possibility and reform.

To authenticate the Revolution's final outcome will take another decade or more. As Mohandas Gandhi wisely observed: "A non-violent revolution is not a program of seizure of power. It is a program of transformation of relationships, ending in a peaceful *transfer* of power."

That had been very much the process of the Canadian Revolution, 1985–1995.

Just about every faith and tradition we had held sacred was in play. The *status quo* had fallen to its demise through the chasm that sepa-

rated illusion from reality. Gone was certainty, the idea of being able
to depend on the past as a guide to the future. Gone also were the
dated notions of deferring to authority and allowing representatives—
even elected ones—to make the significant decisions. Experience had
made it impossible to believe any longer in responsible politicians,
pious priests, sensible Royals, trustworthy lawyers, peace-loving
peacekeepers, reliable bankers, principled businessmen or honest
diplomats. As they sank in the quicksand of 1980s greed, they dragged
down with them much of the corresponding faith in politics, religion,
monarchy, government, business or the law. Like it or not, Canadians
had no choice but to accept the dictum of University of Toronto political economist Abraham Rotstein, who had written that "much will
have to change in Canada, if the country is to stay the same."

The only thing left unchanged by the Revolutionary Decade, it
seemed to me as I flew west, was airline food—an oxymoron if there
ever was one. I was aboard a privatized aircraft bound for a privatized
airport. The gap between business class and steerage had widened, as
had every other social and economic dividing line in the country,
especially the distance between the governors and the governed. The
cities, towns and villages I was passing over had been deconstructed.
The train stations had been mostly closed or turned into museums, the
bank branches were no longer places of fiscal worship, the churches
found their most faithful flock among the hungry who crowded their
basement food banks, the army drill halls were shuttered, the local
MP's office was just another franchise, no more worth visiting than the
Tim Horton doughnut shop next door.

TO DARE AND DARE again is the secret of revolutions, but Canadians had
no tradition of being either daring or revolutionary, so they had impro-
vised. Instead of the endless search for a national identity, they opted
to assert their own identities. Not since frontier days had there been
such a surge of self-reliance, such determination by a people to exercise more control over their lives.

It was a giddy feeling, to be alive in the interval between casting off
obligation and taking on responsibility. Instead of feeling as if they
were carrying the Precambrian Shield on their shoulders, Canadians
took a break from lugging around the cumbersome baggage of their
national virtues and became most untypically Latin, finding strict

morality tedious, tidy living boring, frivolity endearing and passion inviting. Personal identities were up for grabs as people yearned to transcend their birthright. They tended to agree with Woody Allen, who equipped: "I don't want to achieve immortality through my work. I want to achieve it by not dying." In practical terms, this meant having some fun on the way through, cramming into a lifetime as many experiences as one could and letting the after-life take care of itself. "Deference is absolutely at odds with these transformational tendencies slowly establishing themselves in Canada's culture," noted Michael Adams, head of the Environics polling firm. "Suddenly, we can give ourselves to the future by divorcing ourselves from the past—jettisoning the old-fashioned reflexes of deference and blind loyalty."

The problem with Canadians' new-found liberation was that, left untended, it could easily turn into anarchy: collective conscience finds few outlets in the mere defiance of authority. Selfish bedlam was not what most Canadians had in mind. The aspect of deference worth preserving was the civility that usually accompanied it. While they were firmly set against the old style of leadership, Canadians were determined not to abandon the mutual respect that had always separated them from Americans. They longed to recapture the feeling of community that had animated such events as the Grey Cup, the Stanley Cup, Montreal's Expo '67 and Vancouver's Expo '86, which had turned collections of strangers into tribes. The achievement which most lent itself to unity and common purpose during the decade had been the 1992 World Series win by the two dozen Latinos under contract to the Toronto Blue Jays. It was a great victory, but not quite the moral equivalent of building the CPR—though, as Grant McCracken, an ardent Jays fan and cultural anthropologist at the Royal Ontario Museum, pointed out: "If we Canadians can identify with twenty-five ball-players who are not obviously Canadian, then we can identify with anybody—even each other."

WHILE I FEAR FOR OUR common future in a culture of self-interest, I take heart in the conviction that a collective purpose is bound to emerge at some indeterminate point in the future, when more Canadians learn to encompass within their daily striving the quest for a more spiritual outlook. A longing for this was documented in a survey published by

Maclean's on Canada Day in 1995. Allan Gregg, last seen throwing himself under the Kim Campbell campaign bus, was back in business reporting the startling notion that "given a choice, many Canadians appear to place spirituality on a higher level than they do having sex on a regular basis." While I do not personally subscribe to this dictum, two-thirds of Canadians surveyed said the notion of being "a good person and finding spiritual fulfilment was 'more and more on their minds lately.'" It was natural for Canadians to want to tend to their own spirits in the absence of a national soul, I reflected, and perhaps it was about time the values that Canadians really cared about—co-operation, tolerance, genuine gender equality and civility—sprang from the people's hearts, instead of their crumbling institutions.

Jetting over the Rockies, a thrill no matter how frequently that route is flown, I thought how often we fail to appreciate the value of a relationship, an event or an experience—until it's over. The time had come, it seemed to me, to take better care of our patrimony. My mind, as always, floated to my favourite jazz metaphors. I thought the best advice for Canada had been rendered by Eubie Blake, who had played ragtime piano at most of the New Orleans cathouses. When Eubie was celebrating his one hundredth birthday, he told a friend: "You know, if I'd realized I was going to live this long, I'd have taken better care of myself."

Blake died the next day. Still, it seemed like wise counsel. Being a Canadian isn't a nationality, it's a condition. When citizens of Japan or Sweden declare their nationality, it's a self-defining statement. Citizenship in Canada is an act of faith, a promise of potentials that will take generations to realize. Canada was built from the beginning on dreams as well as appetites. Too often—as a nation and as individuals—we have decried what we lack instead of celebrating what we have. Revolution or not, to most of the world's troubled citizens, Canada still appears to be blessed with the mandate of heaven.

ACKNOWLEDGEMENTS

Like all my works, this is a journalist's book. Though it has become a much-maligned profession, I have always believed that journalism is an honourable craft which requires no apologies. As this volume illustrates, I have attempted to imbue the chronicle of how Canada changed between 1985 and 1995 with the bounce and bravado the events themselves deserve.

The case I have tried to make was that during the ten years under review, the country was transformed into a very different kind of community, and Canadians into a very different kind of people. The Canadian Revolution did not cause that change; change caused the Revolution. It had to do with a fundamental shift in the way Canadians viewed their leaders. Values took precedence over issues; strength of character trumped personality.

It was not a tidy process, with many groups and individuals being hurt or displaced and everyone headed off in their own direction. By the end of the decade, very little could be taken on faith, since there was no longer any sustaining reservoir of trust to draw on. That precipitous decline of trust in most of the society's once-sacrosanct touchstones is this book's essential sub-text. "Canadian Revolution" ceased being an oxymoron because, faced with a betrayal of trust on a massive scale, Canadians began fashioning their own belief systems. The resultant shift in social values rejigged the elements of the Canadian character—from Deference to Defiance—thus defining the Revolution and summarizing this book.

IT HAD ORIGINALLY BEEN my intention to write about Brian Mulroney's term as prime minister, though this was not *ever* conceived as being an official or sanctioned biography. While Mulroney was in office, I was granted access to some of his thoughts and papers. But that was a prerequisite, not a hindrance, to writing an objective biography.

I decided to write this book instead of a Mulroney biography because I became convinced it was a much more urgent and interesting endeavour. I also happen to believe that it's far too early to make any definitive judgements about the Mulroney stewardship. At the same time, I heeded Philip Roth's warning that "every biographer has two nightmares—one is that everybody gives out the same story; the other, that everybody gives you a different story." My initial probes made it clear that this would apply to a Mulroney book: Everyone, including its subject, seemed to have a hidden agenda that had little to do with writing an authentic chronicle of the period.

This was a long way from the Mulroney mood on February 15, 1976, when we first discussed the possibility of my doing a book about him, should he become prime minister. "I wouldn't want a puff job," he said at the time. "As a modest student of history, I find myself so god-damned frustrated by asking, 'What was the guy really like? Did he look after his family? Did he swear? Did he get drunk?' The only Canadian prime minister who comes across as a human being is Sir John A. Macdonald and if I were lucky enough to be in that position, I would not object at all to people reading about warts and failings. They're all a part of me."

My, how things change.

ANY LIST OF TRIBUTES to friends and colleagues responsible for the merits of this book must be headed by Robert Mason Lee, who was my editor, wagon-master and morale booster from the first rough drafts to the final galley proofs. He is an extraordinarily sensitive soul with a discerning eye, keen wit and a great ear for cadence. Knowing he will be editing this, I must ration my adjectives, but he was superb in every way, and I am eternally grateful for his care and his caring. This book would not exist without him.

I was inspired, creatively and personally, along the way by Ritva Marjatta Karajaoja, a talented anthropologist from Finland, whose spiritual magic cast its spell. I must also express my deeply felt gratitude to Doug Beardsley, Ray Heard, Lyall Knott, Robert Lewis, Theresa Odishaw, Vladimir Plavsic and Jamie Weinstein—who believed in me.

I wish to thank Irshad Manji, now an author in her own right, who did a dozen of the book's most important interviews and commented valuably on the manuscript. I owe much to many others: Cynthia Good, the publisher of Penguin, whose enthusiasm, compassion and incisive suggestions inspired me at every turn; Michael Levine, who doubles as my lawyer and friend, for thinking up the title; Marina Martin and Steve Sharpe for articulating the theme's initial thrust; Brian Bethune for his genius fact-checking; Mary Adachi, for once again applying her trustworthy exactness and good humour to the book's copy-editing; Ted Rushton of the Gallup (New Mexico) *Independent* whose itinerant wisdom proved immensely valuable; and the following librarians for generously allowing me to intrude on their thoughts and shelves: Basil Guinane, Mary Jane Culbert, George Serhijczuk, and Robin Selz at *Maclean's* as well as Theresa Butcher at the *Financial Post*. Fran McNeely, my executive assistant, deserves a very special tribute for her patience, highly evolved sense of the absurd and hard work. She is a rare and valuable character and I am proud to work with her.

This book owes its existence to many others; only the responsibility for its imperfections is fully my own. (Even these I prefer to blame on my blue iguana.)

THE DECADE OF THIS BOOK was a confusing, stressful time, especially as pre-millennial anxiety set in and most people ceased believing in the politicians and other low-lifes who kept announcing there was a light at the end of the tunnel. As far as most Canadians were concerned the tunnel had been boarded up long ago and if there was any electric flicker, it likely came from some guy as befuddled as everyone else, flashing an S.O.S.

I was that guy in the tunnel, trying to illuminate the path we've taken and even flash ahead a bit to light our uncertain future.

PCN
January 1994–July 1995
Deep Cove and Kitsilano, B.C.

APPENDICES

APPENDIX 1

THE LAST SUPPER

The following is the guest list for the "last dinner" held at Winston's on May 5, 1992 for John Arena. The restaurant had figured prominently as the well-greased hub of the Toronto élite for the preceding three decades; the departure of host and owner, John Arena, marked the passing of the collective influence for these fabled few.

Alexander, Lincoln
Andrews, William
Arena, John
Barbetta, Frank
Barnicke, Joseph
Bigliardi, George
Black, Paul
Bougain, Pierre
Brandt, Andy
Bratty, Rudy
Brown, Arthur
Burns, Latham
Cardy, Gordon
Carter, Emmett
Cogan, Eddie
Coombs, Maurice
Coutts, Jim
Creighton, Bruce
Creighton, Doug
Creighton, Scott
Deacon, Campbell
DePencier, John
Donato, Andy
Donkin, David

Duffy, Graham
Eagles, Stu
Elliott, Fraser
Farrow, Grant
Ferreira, John
Ferroni Carli,
   Enric'Angiolo
Foster, Robert
Fotheringham, Allan
Francis, Robert
Gerhardt, Hans
Godfrey, Paul
Godsoe, Peter
Grubmeyer, Hans
Jackson, Bruce
Jackson, Ernie
Johnston, Don
Knight, Doug
Kosiancic, John
Kraus, Wolfgang
Lovely, Larry
MacLaren, Roy
MacMillan, Tom
Maxwell, John

Maxwell, John (Orso)
Maywood, Charles
McCarthy, Leighton
McCutcheon, Jim
McDermott, John
McGiverin, Don
McKeough, D'Arcy
Metcalf, Fred
Mills, Dennis
Mitchell, Ron
Munro, Raymond
Odette, Ed
O'Conoghue, Paul
O'Hagan, Dick
Powell, John
Pyette, Les
Reid, Tony
Sarlos, Andrew
Schwartz, Gerald
Smart, Allan
Steward, Hartley
Thornhill, Fred
Tighe, Jim
Turner, Rt. Hon. John

APPENDIX 2

SINCERELY, JOE

Once the bitterest of rivals, Joe Clark sought to advise Brian Mulroney early in the Progressive Conservative mandate of trends and issues which would later precipitate a revolt against the government. In this letter, Clark cautioned against the prime minister's excesses, warned of bureaucratic resistance and complained of the internal sniping and gossip flowing from the PMO. Mulroney was to later champion the cause of the African National Congress in his keynote address to the United Nations.

July 2, 1985

The Right Honourable Brian Mulroney, P.C., M.P.,
Prime Minister of Canada
Prime Minister's Office,
Room 309S, House of Commons,
OTTAWA, Ontario
K1A 0A2

PERSONAL AND CONFIDENTIAL

Dear Brian:

Thank you for the invitation to speak frankly about the Government. On balance, I think we have started very well, but we need to plan carefully from now on. I am attaching comments under separate headings, but want to emphasize three observations which I consider most important—they concern the reputation of the Government; the quality of support for your leadership; and the need to control our agenda.

First, we were elected to be both national and new. So far, we have been remarkably successful as a national government but the "patronage" issue has tarnished our "newness"; among other things, it has distracted us from defining ourselves in terms of the real changes we have accomplished—on the deficit, energy, federal-provincial relations. We must consciously develop, and convey, a distinctive "reform" reputation for the government.

Second, you have extraordinary personal support from our Caucus in Québec. They see their future in terms of your success. However, I am troubled by the degree to which the support of others, outside Québec, is of your function as Leader; it is almost impersonal. On reflection, that is not surprising, because most MPs have not been through crisis with you, as a peer. On the Manitoba question, during this Budget, and naturally during the election, you were their Leader more than their colleague. If that Leader-Caucus relation is impersonal, it could break under pressure. There'll be a lot of pressure before 1988, and we have to build in a sense of collegiality.

Finally, we have three major obstacles to controlling the agenda:

(a) our inexperience at setting collective priorities;

(b) the ease with which outside events, including the Opposition, can blow us off-course; and

(c) most importantly the habit of the Public Service running the Government. Changing Deputies won't matter unless we give Ministers the resources and the authority to set policy in fact. I think that requires more exempt staff, and more planning by Ministers; it may also require substantial changes in regulations and legislation governing the Public Service.

I was most impressed by the frankness you inspired at the full Cabinet last week. The following observations are offered in that spirit, and in the context of my belief that the first nine months have been very successful.

More personally let me say how much I admire the sense of optimism and leadership you have brought to the Party and the country. The issues will get tougher during the rest of the mandate, but the real test was to put your personal stamp on the country, and that has been done and well done.

> With best wishes,
> Yours sincerely,
> Joe

(Encl.: Addendum)

ADDENDUM

Protecting Ministers

The Jeffrey Simpson thesis—that Brian Mulroney undercuts his colleagues—could become conventional wisdom. Many people believe that Mike [Wilson] and Jake [Epp] have been seriously diminished by the [old-age pension de-]indexing episode; and the implication is that you did not do enough to support them. I can think of nothing but time to turn that around. In the meantime, you must be extraordinarily careful that nothing you say or do lends credence to that thesis.

Personal Relations

We have dispelled most of the tensions of the 1983 Convention, and I have found members of the PMO, like Bernard Roy, Fred Doucet and Bill Fox to be increasingly helpful in creating a reputation of team work. However, there is too much speculation about the relations between us. That speculation unsettles the Party and hurts the Government and the damage could grow as we face tougher issues. Naturally, I keep my own counsel, but I find it debilitating, in light of my conduct since the Convention, to still be subject to sniping. I enjoy my work as Secretary of State for External Affairs, and appreciate the opportunity you give me to influence the broader direction of the Government. But, if I am to continue, I will need your help in stopping that corrosive speculation.

Trade

I urge you strongly to leave Trade exactly where it is. The Department has made the adjustment, and is beginning to perform well. A major change would disrupt everything again. A minor change would suggest a major one is coming, and re-ignite the speculation which has been so troublesome. Changing Trade again would be seen as being indecisive and incompatible with our desire to enhance trade. In the modern world, we cannot separate politics from economics. The people in External are good, and getting better. Naturally, their performance and their reputation suffer when Ministers of the Government gnaw away at them. . . .

Media Relations

Our media strategy has enjoyed enormous successes. But it has inspired a suspicion in the Gallery that is more dangerous than the adversarial relation Trudeau developed; and it concentrates too narrowly on (a) you; (b) the Ottawa Gallery; and (c) Montreal. You are the Government's leader and best performer, but no one can stand the strain of being the whole show. In the House, you consciously delegate questions. That spirit should be brought to national media strategy, making deliberate use of the particular strengths of key Ministers. In retrospect, I think it was a mistake for Michael [Wilson] and me to act as your "spokesmen" at Bonn and Québec. Our particular assets are enhanced when we perform as your colleagues; diminished if we seem to be your aides. We should develop a deliberate co-ordinated strategy to showcase leading Ministers among the clienteles where we most enhance the Government.

The cynicism in the Ottawa Gallery may be irreversible, but we need a more constant strategy of contact to control the damage. Our real answer lies outside Ottawa and we are responding haphazardly. On June 2nd, I was the first Minister of our Government to visit the Editorial Board of the Edmonton Journal, since our election. That is carelessness, on my part and on the Government's. We need a small planning Committee run by someone respected, like Ian Anderson, and comprising representatives of some Ministerial offices, to plan a national Ministerial media strategy.

Collegiality

Members of Caucus, and even Cabinet, are still strangers to one another. Ottawa meetings won't break that down; events like the Mont Ste Marie Caucus can. You should consider having quarterly meetings of full Cabinet on week-ends fixed well in advance, in isolated settings where Ministers are forced to be together. The national Caucus should also meet that way at least once a year, in circumstances that encourage genuine frankness.

The Cabinet problem is most urgent, because alienation there radiates outward to Caucus and the public. Non-P&P [Non-Priorities and Planning] Ministers feel they are members of an "outer-Cabinet" with neither influence nor access. The Cabinet Committees may alleviate some of that. . . .

The other key factor is clear signals. Ministers do not function well when they're unsure of their authority, or of their standing with their Leader. Critical comments attributed to you are lethal to moral[e], and journalistic gossip about Ministers' futures does not help. In addition, your staff sometimes send confusing and contradictory signals which aggravate uncertainty.

Western Canada

There is some grumbling that our priorities (and our appointments) reflect a pre-occupation with Québec. That can be offset by a deliberate high-lighting of Western priorities, like agriculture. We should plan more "national" events in the West.

The federal party is not deeply rooted in the Prairies, or B.C. We have relied too much on provincial parties in Alberta and Saskatchewan, and may begin to pay for that. My instinct tells me that B.C. could become unstuck quickly. I think we need a thorough and professional reconnaissance of our standing there, leading to the development of a detailed strategy. I consider B.C. our most precarious province.

The danger in Manitoba is that sensitivities within the Party will diminish the all-out effort we need to beat New Democrat Premier Howard Pawley. I am convinced that a P.C. Government there will be easier to deal with than a P.C. Opposition. Sterling [Lyon, the Progressive Conservative leader from 1975-83] is symbolic in all this; his appointment to the I.J.C. [International Joint Commission] (where he would excel) would be a healing gesture. Then perhaps you could invite Filmon down privately to discuss exactly how we might help. My impression is that, right now, no one is willing to move first towards a reconciliation that is the only way to beat Pawley. Naturally, I am prepared to help in any way I can.

Public Service

Most appointments within the Service are made by Deputy Ministers, apparently under the Public Service Staff Relations Act and other legislation. The rationale is to prevent patronage. The result is to vest immense power with senior public servants, as a collectivity. . . .

As a starting point, it would be useful to have senior Ministers prepare a list of the kinds of problems on which the Public Service is not responsive. That will show us patterns where law, regulation, or attitude prevent us from filling our mandate. One example concerns the promotion of women. The system is designed by men and I am told constantly that "we have no women who are ready yet" for promotion. I can break that through perseverance—but it is an example of the system frustrating our purposes rather than serving them.

Ministerial Staffing

I think we made a mistake in limiting so severely the size of exempt staff. If we want to control policy, and run the Department, Ministers need more staff.

I also think it would be wise to encourage all Ministers to take the summer months to reflect on staffing decisions they made a year ago.

Deputy Ministers

We have discussed Deputy Ministers in External. You know my view that it would be a great loss for the system were Marcel Massé to leave. I think he would be interested in Justice or CIDA [Canadian International Development Agency]. On balance, in External I would recommend that you move de Montigny Marchand from Communications to Under-Secretary of State, and Derek Burney to Deputy Minister/Political Affairs.

Progressive Conservatism

Our electoral challenge is to hold the Centre. External Affairs will continue to be key to a "moderate" reputation. Looking ahead, I think the theme of compassion, and the issue of sovereignty, will be particularly important. Africa, the "Third Window", relations generally with "poor" countries will help demonstrate compassion. The sovereignty question will be tougher and perhaps you should request the new Committee on External and Defence to recommend affirmative actions we can take to assert Canadian sovereignty.

The South Africa paper is coming to Cabinet. We also have the issue of so-called "Arms Exports". Various Departments are working on reviews of our trade in "defence materials". You will recall the matter was raised by [New Democrat MP Nelson] Riis in the House. I expect we will have more of it, and my inclination is to tighten the rules, not widen them.

APPENDIX 3

PAYING HIS WAY

Contrary to allegations, as these documents illustrate, Brian Mulroney personally paid $211,796.18 for the furniture that he and Mila acquired for the official prime minister's residence at 24 Sussex Drive. In this exchange of letters, he was billed for the expenditure and his lawyer, Alain Paris, forwarded his cheque to the PC Canada Fund, which had originally covered the cost of interior decorations and furnishings.

PC CANADA FUND/LE FONDS PC DU CANADA

February 18, 1987

PERSONAL & CONFIDENTIAL

Rt. Hon. Brian Mulroney, P.C., M.P.
Prime Minister of Canada
24 Sussex Drive
Ottawa, Ontario
K1M 1M4

Dear Prime Minister:

I refer to your letter of March 5, 1984, a copy of which is attached.

As requested, I attach an invoice addressed to you personally representing the balance of advances made on your behalf by the Party in respect to residences.

Please arrange to forward me a cheque in the sum of $211,796.18 payable to PC Canada Fund (The Party's chief registered agent) at your convenience.

With warm regards,

Yours sincerely,
W. David Angus, Q.C.

February 18, 1987

Rt. Hon. Brian Mulroney, P.C., M.P.
Prime Minister of Canada
24 Sussex Drive
Ottawa, Ontario
K1M 1M4

INVOICE

TO reimburse the Progressive Conservative Party of Canada for the
balance of sums advanced in respect of decorating and furnishing your residences at Stornoway, 24 Sussex Drive and Harrington Lake.

<u>$211,796.18</u>

Poissant Richard Thorne Ernst & Whinney
Chartered Accountants
  2000, Ave. McGill College
      Bureau 1900
          Montréal (Québec) H3A 3H8

April 13, 1987

<u>BY COURIER</u>
<u>PERSONAL & CONFIDENTIAL</u>

Mr. W. David Angus
Stikeman Elliott
1155 Dorchester Blvd. West
Suite 3900
Montréal (Québec)
H3B 3V2

Dear David:

Find enclosed herewith a cheque of $211,796.18 payable to P.C. Canada Fund.

Brian had impressed upon me to issue this cheque as soon as possible after a meeting I had with him in Québec in the latter part of February of this year. Unfortunately, I was unable to comply with this request earlier, due to extensive travelling at the time and an unfortunate ski accident that kept me in a Vancouver hospital for 12 days in March.

Nevertheless, the first thing I am doing now that I am back at the office is forwarding to you this cheque.

I hope that this involuntary delay will not create any difficulty for you.

Best personal regards,
Alain Paris
Partner

APPENDIX 4

THE PRESIDENTIAL PMO

The presidential style of Brian Mulroney became a symbolic reference point for Canadians, who felt he became removed from their concerns; and a practical matter for his staff, who prepared minute-by-minute itineraries for the Mulroneys' every move. The following are the official schedules for a ten-minute speech by Mila Mulroney to a women's auxiliary in Montreal; a fifteen-minute drop-in by Brian Mulroney at a reception (where he never said a word) for Nobel laureate John Polanyi; and a day of political activity in British Columbia that included only a five-minute prime ministerial speech at Comox.

ITINERARY FOR MRS. MULRONEY'S VISIT TO
MONTREAL, QUEBEC
April 14, 1986 <u>FINAL</u> (Revised) 14-04/86 Time: 11:00 a.m.

EVENTS AND PARTICIPATION
MONDAY, APRIL 14, 1986

1. Reception, Salon St. Pierre, Bonaventure Hotel, Montreal
2. Speech, <u>MRS. MULRONEY</u>, Women's Auxiliary, Salon Outremont, Bonaventure Hotel
3. Lunch, Salon Outremont, Bonaventure Hotel

Dress: Cocktail Dress

DAY AT A GLANCE

MONDAY, APRIL 14, 1986

12.00 p.m.:   Depart Ritz Carlton Hotel
              Motorcade Assignment:
              L-1   <u>MRS. MULRONEY</u>
                         Bonnie Brownlee
              S-2   RCMP

12:10   Arrive Hotel Bonaventure, proceed directly to Salon St. Pierre

              (NOTE: <u>MRS. MULRONEY</u> may wish to proceed to holding room—Bonnie Brownlee to advise)

12:15   Arrive Salon St. Pierre for Main Table Reception

             (NOTE: Main Table Reception 11:45–12:25 p.m., Salon St. Pierre
                     General Reception 11:30–12:25 p.m., Salon Westmount)

             In attendance:
                 Dr. and Mrs. Phil Gold
                 Mr. Peter Black, Westmount Examiner
                 Mr. Erik Molson
                 Ms. Elsie Jean Gordon, Montreal Gazette
                 Mr. Reginald Groom, Pres., Hilton Canada
                 Mrs. Barbara Whitley
                 Mrs. Brian Gallery
                 Ms. Nancy Southam
                 Ms. Lois Hutchison
                 Ms. Sue Whittal
                 Miss Mary Whittemore
                 Dr. David Mulder
                 Dr. Arpi Hamelin, Dean of Studies, Simone de Beauvoir
                 Ms. Elisabeth Marchant, Junior League

12:20   All guests other than Main Table proceed to be seated

12:25   Main Table proceeds to Salon Outremont

         Main Table Guests:
             MRS. MULRONEY
             Miss Mary Whittemore
             Mr. Erik Molson
             Mr. Reginald Groom
             Dr. Phil Gold
             Dr. Pivnicki and Mrs. Pivnicki
             Mrs. Barbara Whitley

12:30   Mrs. Mary Maxwell introduces Main Table and then introduces
         MRS. MULRONEY

12:35   MRS. MULRONEY speaks

12:45   MRS. MULRONEY concludes

12:46   Dr. Gold thanks MRS. MULRONEY

12:50   Lunch is served

1:45   Lunch concludes

1:46   Mrs. Mary Maxwell introduces Mrs. Barbara Whitley

1:47   Mrs. Barbara Whitley speaks

2:02   Mrs. Barbara Whitley concludes

2:03   Mrs. Maxwell thanks Mrs. Barbara Whitley and guests

2:10   Mrs. Maxwell concludes

2:15   <u>MRS. MULRONEY</u> departs Salon Outremont enroute to awaiting motorcade

2:20   Depart Hotel Bonaventure

        Motorcade Assignment: AS BEFORE

2:30   Arrive Ritz Carlton Hotel

2:35   Arrive Suite
        (NOTE: Private time for balance of the day)

ITINERARY FOR THE PRIME MINISTER OF CANADA
RECEPTION IN HONOR OF PROFESSOR JOHN POLANYI, OTTAWA
THURSDAY, MARCH 5, 1987

EVENTS AND PARTICIPATION

THURSDAY, MARCH 5, 1987

(Reception, Professor John Polanyi, Capital Hall Congress Centre)

Dress: Black tie

> (NOTE: THE PRIME MINISTER will drop in on the reception
> and will be wearing a business suit)

DAY AT A GLANCE

THURSDAY, MARCH 5, 1987

6:10 pm   Depart Centre Block Office

6:15   Arrive Congress Centre

6:16   Arrive holding room

6:22   Arrive foyer, Capital Hall

6:45   Arrive room 1-B

7:00   Depart room 1-B

7:02   Depart Congress Centre

7:12   Arrive 24 Sussex Drive

DETAILED ITINERARY

THURSDAY, MARCH 5, 1987

(NOTE: Reception starts at 6:00 pm)

(NOTE: Approximately 250 to 300 guests)

6:10 pm   THE PRIME MINISTER departs Centre Block office enroute to motorcade

          MOTORCADE ASSIGNMENT: S-1 RCMP
                                       L-1 THE PRIME MINISTER
                                              Richard Morgan
                                       S-2 RCMP

6:15   THE PRIME MINISTER'S motorcade arrives at the Congress Centre (Colonel By entrance)

        THE PRIME MINISTER will be met by Mr. George McCabe, General Manager of the Congress Centre and proceed to the holding room, led by Advance Luc Vaugeois

6:16   THE PRIME MINISTER arrives at the holding room

6:21   THE PRIME MINISTER departs holding room enroute to the foyer outside Capital Hall, led by Advance Luc Vaugeois

6:22   THE PRIME MINISTER is met outside Capital Hall foyer by The Honourale Frank Oberle

        THE PRIME MINISTER accompanied by the Honourable Frank Oberle circulates among the invited guests

6:45   THE PRIME MINISTER and the Honourable Frank Oberle proceed towards the room 1-B, where Head Table guests have assembled

HEAD TABLE GUESTS INCLUDING WIVES
Dr. Stuart Smith, Science Council
Professor Polanyi
The Honoruable Frank Oberle
Mr. Bruce Howe, M.O.S.S.T.
Dr. Art May, N.S.E.R.C.
Dr. Larkin Kerwin, N.R.C.
Dr. Bill McGowan, N.M.S.T.
Dr. Alexander McKay, Royal Society
Dr. Gerhard Herzberg, Nobel prize winner

7:00   THE PRIME MINISTER departs 1B enroute to awaiting motor-
        cade, led by Advance Luc Vaugeois

7:02   THE PRIME MINISTER'S motorcade departs Congress Centre
        enroute to 24 Sussex Drive

        Motorcade assignment: S-1   RCMP
                                 L-1   THE PRIME MINISTER
                                        Richard Morgan
                                 S-2   RCMP

7:12   THE PRIME MINISTER'S motorcade arrives at 24 Sussex
        Drive

ITINERARY FOR THE PRIME MINISTER OF CANADA,
MRS. MULRONEY AND FAMILY
VISIT TO COMOX AND CHEMAINUS
August 1, 1988

DETAILED ITINERARY

MONDAY, AUGUST 1, 1988

(NOTE: Luggage call at: 10:30 a.m.
Advance to coordinate)

10:00 a.m. Private meeting with Jim McCaughley

10:25 a.m. THE PRIME MINISTER, Mrs. Mulroney and family depart
suite and proceed to awaiting elevator, led by Advance
Rex Rexon

ELEVATOR MANIFEST: THE PRIME MINISTER
Mrs. Mulroney
Caroline Mulroney
Mark Mulroney
Ben Mulroney
Nicholas Mulroney
Cathy Auchinleck
Advance Rex Rexon
Insp. Dion
Elevator Operator

(NOTE: There will be a second elevator for staff)

10:30 a.m. THE PRIME MINISTER'S motorcade departs the Westerly
Hotel enroute to Comox Nautical Days Parade Reviewing
Stand (Comox Avenue)

MOTORCADE ASSIGNMENT: A-1   RCMP
S-1   RCMP
L-1   THE PRIME
MINISTER
Mrs. Mulroney
S-2   RCMP
L-2   Caroline Mulroney

(van)	Mark Mulroney
	Ben Mulroney
	Nicholas Mulroney
	Cathy Auchinleck
S-3	RCMP
PMO-1	M. Lortie
	R. Morgan
	B. Brownlee
	B. McCarthy
	S. Murray

10:45 a.m. THE PRIME MINISTER'S motorcade arrives Comox Nautical Days Reviewing Stand

Met on arrival by Advance Barbara Barry

(NOTE: Advance Barbara Barry to coordinate umbrellas if necessary)

(NOTE: Advance Rex Rexon and Robbie Robertson available for crowd control if necessary)

THE PRIME MINISTER, Mrs. Mulroney and family proceed to Reviewing Stand, led by Advance Barbara Barry

11:00 a.m. THE PRIME MINISTER, Mrs. Mulroney and family review Comox Nautical Days Parade

(NOTE: Parade will last for 25 minutes)

(NOTE: Darlene Weir, Comox Alberni PC Candidate will be in the parade in a pick-up truck with banner)

11:30 a.m. THE PRIME MINISTER, Mrs. Mulroney and family depart Reviewing Stand and proceed to Comox Town Hall (holding room), led by Advance Barbara Barry and Dave Durrant

11:35 a.m. THE PRIME MINISTER, Mrs. Mulroney and family arrive holding room

Met on arrival by Advance Robbie Robertson

(NOTE: Private time: 11:35–11:45 10 minutes)

(NOTE: Advance Robbie Robertson to coordinate holding room)

11:50 a.m.   THE PRIME MINISTER, Mrs. Mulroney and family, accompanied by Darlene Weir, depart Town Hall and proceed to Foreshore Marine Park stage, led by Advance Barbara Barry and Ray Castelli

            (NOTE: Dignitaries may include:
                – Mayor George Piercy
                – Mayor George Cochrane
                – Mayor Bronco Moncrieff
                – Minister Stan Hagen, Provincial MLA and Minister of Advance Education, Job Training and Science and Technology
                – Mr. Ray Skelly, Federal NDP MP
                – Mr. Bob Skelly (former BC NDP leader who is running against PC Candidate Darlene Weir)

11:55 a.m.   THE PRIME MINISTER, Mrs. Mulroney and family, accompanied by Darlene Weir, arrive Foreshore Marina Park

            Met on arrival by Advance Rex Rexon

11:57 a.m.   Mayor George Piercy introduces THE PRIME MINISTER

12:00 p.m.   THE PRIME MINISTER brings greetings for BC Day

            (NOTE: OPEN MEDIA COVERAGE)

12:05 p.m.   THE PRIME MINISTER concludes

            Dennis Durrant thanks THE PRIME MINISTER

            (NOTE: Mayor George Piercy will present t-shirts to the family)

12:10 p.m.   THE PRIME MINISTER, Mrs. Mulroney and family proceed on tour of Foreshore Marina Park, accompanied by Darlene Weir, and led by Advance Barbara Barry, Ray Castelli and Robbie Robertson

12:40 p.m.   Tour concludes

            THE PRIME MINISTER, Mrs. Mulroney and family proceed to awaiting motorcade, led by Advance Barbara Barry

12:45 p.m.   THE PRIME MINISTER'S motorcade departs Foreshore
             Marina Park enroute to the Filberg Festival

MOTORCADE ASSIGNMENT: AS BEFORE

1:00 p.m.   THE PRIME MINISTER'S motorcade arrives Filbert Festival

             Met on arrival by Advance Dave Durrant

             THE PRIME MINISTER, Mrs. Mulroney and family proceed
             on tour of grounds and displays at Filbert House, led by
             Advance Barbara Barry and Dave Durrant

             Tour includes:
             – Animal petting farm
             – Craft exhibits
             – Entertainment

             (NOTE: PHOTO OPPORTUNITIES requested with:
                     – group of exchange students from Japan
                     – PC Candidate from North Island
                     – three significant local fundraisers)

             (NOTE: Advance .... to coordinate Filberg
             House as a holding area)

1:30 p.m.   THE PRIME MINISTER, Mrs. Mulroney and family proceed
             to awaiting motorcade, led by Advance Barbara Barry

             THE PRIME MINISTER'S motorcade departs Filberg
             Festival enroute to CFB Comox

             MOTORCADE ASSIGNMENT: AS BEFORE

1:55 p.m.   THE PRIME MINISTER'S motorcade arrives CFB Comox

             Met on arrival by Advance Margaret Grant

             THE PRIME MINISTER, Mrs. Mulroney and family proceed
             to board awaiting Challenger, led by Advance Margaret Grant

2:00 p.m.   DND Challenger departs CFB Comox enroute to Cassidy
             Airport, Nanaimo

MANIFEST: THE PRIME MINISTER
Mrs. Mulroney
Caroline Mulroney
Ben Mulroney
Mark Mulroney
Nicholas Mulroney
Cathy Auchinleck
Rick Morgan
Bonnie Brownlee
Insp. H. Dion

Type of aircraft: DND Challenger (12 seats)
Flight time: 35 minutes
Time change: none
Food on board: Coffee, tea, soft drinks, biscuits

2:35 p.m.   DND Challenger arrives Cassidy Airport

Met on arrival by:
– Mr. Ted Schellenberg (Nanaimo Alberni)
– Kate and Meghan and Simon Schellenberg
– Advance Diana Buric

THE PRIME MINISTER, accompanied by Mr. Schellenberg, proceeds to 2nd floor boardroom of Cassidy Flight Services Centre, led by Advance Stuart Murray

(NOTE: PHOTO OPPORTUNITY)

2:40 p.m.   Meeting commences

Participants:
– Mr. Ted Schellenberg
– Mr. Frank Naye, Mayor
– Mr. Geoff Matthews, Chairman, Gas Committee
– Mr. Dean Finlayson, Vice Chairman, Gas Committee
– Mr. Larry Hume, President, Chamber of Commerce

3:00 p.m.   Meeting concludes

2:40 p.m.   Mrs. Mulroney and family, accompanied by Mrs. Schellenberg and family, proceed to awaiting motorcade, led by Advance Diana Buric

Mrs. Mulroney's motorcade departs Cassidy Airport enroute to Transfer Beach, Ladysmith

MOTORCADE ASSIGNMENT: A-1   RCMP

                                                L-2   Mrs. Mulroney

                                                        Mrs. Schellenberg

                                              S-2   RCMP

                                              L-2   Caroline Mulroney

                                        (van) Mark Mulroney

                                                         Ben Mulroney

                                                         Nicholas Mulroney

                                                         Cathy Auchinleck

                                                         Kate Schellenberg

                                                         Meghan Schellenberg

                                                         Simon Schellenberg

                                            S-3   RCMP

                                                         Bonnie Brownlee

2:50 p.m.   Mrs. Mulroney's motorcade arrives Transfer Beach

Met on arrival by Advance Jackie Townsend and Kevin Warn

(NOTE: Ladysmith, Dogwood Festival will be in progress)

<u>THE PRIME MINISTER</u> departs 2nd floor boardroom of Cassidy Flight Services Centre and proceeds to awaiting bus, led by Advance Diana Buric

3:00 p.m.   <u>THE PRIME MINISTER'S</u> bus departs Cassidy Airport enroute to Transfer Beach, Ladysmith

MOTORCADE ASSIGNMENT: A-1   RCMP

                                              S-1   RCMP

                                              B-1   <u>THE PRIME</u>

                                                         <u>MINISTER</u>

                                                         Mr. Schellenberg

                                                         M. Lortie

                                                         R. Morgan

                                                         B. McCarthy

                                                         S. Murray

                                            S-2   RCMP

3:15 p.m.   <u>THE PRIME MINISTER'S</u> bus arrives Transfer Beach

Mrs. Mulroney, the family, Mrs. Schellenberg and her children board <u>THE PRIME MINISTER'S</u> bus and depart for Chemainus

(NOTE: Advance Jackie Thompson and Kevin Warn to coordinate)

(NOTE: THE PRIME MINISTER and Mr. Schellenberg remain on bus)

BUS MANIFEST: THE PRIME MINISTER
                 Mrs. Mulroney
                 Caroline Mulroney
                 Ben Mulroney
                 Mark Mulroney
                 Nicholas Mulroney
                 Ted Schellenberg
                 Kate Schellenberg
                 Simon Schellenberg
                 Meghan Schellenberg
                 Rick Morgan
                 Bonnie Brownlee
                 Marc Lortie
                 S. Murray
                 B. McCarthy
                 Insp. Dion

                 S-2   RCMP

3:30 p.m.   THE PRIME MINISTER'S bus arrives Chemainus (intersection Cyprus and Willow)

Met on arrival by:
– Mr. Rex Hollett, Mayor
– Mr. Stefan Bugil, Managing Director
– Advance Barbara Barry and Jane Burnes

THE PRIME MINISTER, Mrs. Mulroney and family, accompanied by Ted and Kate Schellenberg and family, proceed on tour of murals, accompanied by Mr. Stefan Bugil and led by Advance Barbara Barry and Jane Burnes

(NOTE: PHOTO OPPORTUNITIES at two murals)

(NOTE: At the conclusion of the tour, Mr. Stefan Bugil will present T-shirts to the children)

4:10 p.m.   Tour concludes
THE PRIME MINISTER, Mrs. Mulroney and family, accompanied by the Schellenberg family, proceed to awaiting bus, led by Advance Barbara Barry and Jane Burnes

4:15 p.m.   THE PRIME MINISTER'S bus departs Chemainus enroute to Duncan Forestry Museum

BUS MANIFEST: AS BEFORE

4:30 p.m.   THE PRIME MINISTER'S bus arrives Duncan Forestry Museum

Met on arrival by:
– Mr. Michael Osborn, Museum Manager
– Advance Ron Shore and Kevin Warn

THE PRIME MINISTER, Mrs. Mulroney and family and accompanying party proceed to board steam train (Samson #25) at Alderlea station for ride to picnic area, led by Advance Ron Shore and Kevin Warn

(NOTE: THE PRIME MINISTER, Mr. Schellenberg and Nicholas Mulroney will ride with Mr. Ralph Davies, the Head Engineer

Mrs. Mulroney and family as well as Kate Schellenberg and family will ride in the third car

Staff will ride in subsequent cars

The Media will be in the second open car)

5:00 p.m.   Steam train arrives picnic area (North Cowichan Station)

THE PRIME MINISTER, Mrs. Mulroney and family are met on arrival by Advance Ray Castelli

THE PRIME MINISTER, Mrs. Mulroney and family circulate through crowd in picnic area, led by Advance Ray Castelli

(NOTE: In attendance will be members of the Nanaimo Alberni PC Association)

THE PRIME MINISTER, Mrs. Mulroney and family proceed to board steam train, led by Advance Ray Castelli

5:35 p.m.   Steam train arrives Alderlea Station

5:40 p.m.   THE PRIME MINISTER, Mrs. Mulroney and family, accompanied by the Schellenberg family, proceed to awaiting bus, led by Advance Ray Castelli

5:45 p.m.   THE PRIME MINISTER'S bus departs Forestry Museum enroute to Cassidy Airport

BUS MANIFEST: AS BEFORE

6:15 p.m.   THE PRIME MINISTER'S bus arrives Cassidy Airport

Met on arrival by Advance Diana Buric

THE PRIME MINISTER, Mrs. Mulroney and family bid farewell to Mr. Schellenberg and his family then proceed to board awaiting DND Challenger, led by Advance Diana Buric

6:20 p.m.   DND Challenger departs Cassidy Airport enroute to Kelowna Airport, Flightcraft Hangar

MANIFEST: THE PRIME MINISTER
                 Mrs. Mulroney
                 Ben Mulroney
                 Mark Mulroney
                 Caroline Mulroney
                 Nicholas Mulroney
                 Cathy Auchinleck
                 Bonnie Brownlee
                 Rick Morgan
                 Insp. H. Dion

Type of aircraft: DND Challenger (12 seats)
Flight time: 55 minutes
Time change: none
Food on board: Sandwiches, vegetable tray

7:15 p.m.   DND Challenger arrives Kelowna Airport, Flightcraft Hangar

Met on arrival by:
– Mr. Al Horning (Okanagan Centre PC Candidate)
– Mayor Jim Stuart
– Mr. Cliff Serwa, MLA
– Mr. Larry Chalmers, MLA
– Mr. Barry Lapointe and Jim Rogers of Flightcraft
– Advance Duncan Burnham

7:20 p.m. THE PRIME MINISTER, Mrs. Mulroney and family, proceed
to PC Reception in boardroom of Flightcraft, accompanied by
Mr. Horning, Mayor Stuart, Mr. Serwa and Mr. Chalmers, led
by Advance Duncan Burnham

THE PRIME MINISTER, Mrs. Mulroney and family, and
accompanying party, arrive boardroom

Met on arrival by Mr. Jim Doak

(NOTE: There will be coffee, soft drinks and donuts available)

(NOTE: Advance Dunc Burnham to arrange for private
holding room in Flightcraft)

THE PRIME MINISTER, Mrs. Mulroney and family circulate
amongst guests

(NOTE: CLOSED TO THE MEDIA)

(NOTE: Option: The children may proceed ahead to Vernon)

7:40 p.m. THE PRIME MINISTER, Mrs. Mulroney and family depart
boardroom and proceed to awaiting motorcade, led by
Advance Dunc Burnham

7:45 p.m. THE PRIME MINISTER'S motorcade departs Kelowna
Airport enroute to the Village Green Hotel Inn, Vernon

MOTORCADE ASSIGNMENT:
	A-1	RCMP
	S-1	RCMP
	L-1	THE PRIME MINISTER
		Mrs. Mulroney
	S-2	RCMP
	L-2	Caroline Mulroney
	(van)	Mark Mulroney
		Ben Mulroney
		Nicholas Mulroney
		Cathy Auchinleck
	S-3	RCMP
	PMO-1	R. Morgan
		B. Brownlee
		S. Murray

(NOTE: luggage can proceed motorcade to Village Green Inn
Advance .... responsible for
luggage)

8:30 p.m.   THE PRIME MINISTER'S motorcade arrives Village Green
Inn

Met on arrival by:
– Mr. Jake Spoor, Okanagan Shuswap PC Candidate
– Mr. John Williams, Hotel Manager
– Advance John Aisenstate

THE PRIME MINISTER, Mrs. Mulroney and family proceed
through lobby to awaiting elevator, led by Advance John
Aisenstate

ELEVATOR MANIFEST: THE PRIME MINISTER
                            Mrs. Mulroney
                            Caroline Mulroney
                            Mark Mulroney
                            Ben Mulroney
                            Nicholas Mulroney
                            Cathy Auchinleck
                            Advance John Aisenstat
                            Insp. Dion
                            Mr. John Williams

(NOTE: There is only one elevator)

8:35 p.m.   THE PRIME MINISTER, Mrs. Mulroney and family arrive
suite

Met on arrival by Advance Dennis Sorenson

(NOTE: Private time for balance of evening)

(NOTE: Staff meeting at 9:00 p.m.
          Stuart Murray to advise)

OVERNIGHT VILLAGE GREEN INN

APPENDIX 5

GENTLEMEN, THAT REMINDS ME . . .

The following is the text of a speech delivered by Mila Mulroney to the annual meeting of the highly informal Gatineau Hills Gentlemen's Club, a private gathering of Conservatives, which was delivered on February 14, 1993. The date is significant because there was much speculation in the air about Brian Mulroney's impending departure from office.

I was really stunned when I received the invitation to be the "Mystery Speaker" for tonight's dinner. My initial reaction was to beg off. Then I thought to myself, what the heck, I'll borrow a pair of earrings from Allan Gregg and do it.

I know we're low in the polls, but surely we're not down to this—Saturday night with *this* mob; even Mel Hurtig wouldn't do this event. I enjoy being with alert, exciting, upwardly-mobile people. Don't get me wrong. I enjoy these Dinners as well.

What a crowd tonight! It never dawned on me when I accepted that there would be so many people in Ottawa interested in leadership review. I don't know what *he's* doing, but I'm here tonight to tell you: *I'm staying.*

It was so nice of several of Brian's colleagues to come out this evening to support me—Kim [Campbell] and Michael [Wilson] and Barbara [McDougall] and Perrin [Beatty] . . . all at the front door to meet us and shake our hands and hand out those cute little buttons.

Don't be misled by people who are reading tea leaves and chicken entrails regarding our future plans. You'll know for sure if Holt Renfrew ever has a grand clearance sale. . . .

Some of the stuff you read is just preposterous: can you imagine me living in Hudson, Quebec? Hudson, Quebec—for Gawd's sake!! There's not even a Polo shop there! There was the time I lost my platinum American Express card; Brian didn't report it for a year. Fact is, he said, the thief was spending less than I do!

Actually, the only time I was ever really angry with Brian was when he turned down the UN job. [Mulroney had been in the running for Secretary-

General.] If he had been smart, he could have jetted around the world, hob-nobbed with beautiful people, kissed Question Period goodbye, enjoyed a life of luxury—just like the rest of his ministers.

Apparently some of the media took exception to the hard-hitting, take no prisoners exposé written about me last year by Sally Armstrong. [The editor of *Homemaker's Magazine* had written a biography sympathetic to her friend Mila.] I'm told that, in the interest of balance, [*Toronto Sun* reporters] Bob Fife and Tim Naumetz are digging through garbage cans trying to prove that my hair, which is naturally blond, is died gray every three weeks by Rinaldo at a secret meeting of the Federal Business Development Bank at *Le Jardin*. [Rinaldo, Mila's hairdresser, had been appointed by Mulroney as a bank director.]

Combining politics with a young family is not easy. Feeding, hugging, counselling, wiping away tears, cleaning up the messes—and then you have to leave the PMO staff behind, come home and start all over with the children . . . And have you noticed the new svelte Hugh Segal? He's on a crash diet. This new diet allows him to eat all he wants—but he can't inhale.

But I hear that a lot of you were impressed by how well organized I am. Last week, in the middle of the night, Brian got up to get a glass of water and when he came back, the bed was made! Recently, I asked Brian what our most important domestic issue was. He said: "The economy . . . (Pause) . . . Darling! We need to kick start the recovery by restoring consumer confidence." So, I said, "Brian, this is your lucky day. Where is my purse—call Stats Canada!" I mean, who in this country knows more about department store sales and commodities than I do?" I support NAFTA. I've always been a free trader—I trade freely on Bond Street, Rodeo Drive, Fifth Avenue, Worth Avenue.

As people look around for the leaders of the future—I notice that people keep talking about a candidate X—a candidate not in the Caucus or Cabinet but who meets all the genuine criteria. Bright, affable, bilingual, young, perhaps female—unsullied by political office. A family person. Perhaps a warm and supportive spouse. Maybe even an ethnic, with real life parental responsibilities. To quote Bill Davis—"I have no plans to have any plans."

But, of course . . . if there's a draft . . . if my nation calls . . . if Brian will stay home with the kids—well, there may yet be a further service I can render the country. And, I would be prepared to ask my spouse to walk three paces behind and perhaps chair a taskforce on my behalf—perhaps on the future of Prime Time News in Canada. Don't forget, Bonnie [Brownlee, Mila's personal assistant] is already at the National Defence College studying military strategy. So, don't rule out a coup, either!

So let us move forward with confidence—with the future ahead of us, the past behind us, the present underfoot—and the good will of St. Valentine's Day in our hearts! And, as I have said on many occasions—to my husband and to the press—political spouses don't announce that they are staying— only that they are leaving. And I have no announcement to make here tonight, at this time, with you, on this occasion.

But to quote a great Canadian—stay tuned!!

Ask not what you can do for your party; ask what the party can do for me.

APPENDIX 6

"YOU HAD AN OPTION..."

Others practised it, the Mulroney Conservatives perfected it to the level of a science. The following is a secret internal PMO progress report to the prime minister of patronage appointments made within eleven months of Mulroney's election on an anti-patronage mandate.

<u>Patronage Tally</u>
<u>Aug 29, 1985</u>

From September 17, 1984 to Aug 14, 1985, the government made 1,337 Governor-In-Council appointments. Of this total of 1337 appointments, 326 (24 per cent) were routine or administrative appointments. This category included judges made acting administrators for Lieutenant-Governors; RCMP promotions; regular consular postings for career diplomats and commissioners empowered to take oaths.

The remaining 1,011 (76 per cent) appointments made by the government were political.

– 550 appointments to various agencies, boards and commissions.

– Forty-one appointments of Parliamentary Secretaries, House of Commons Commissioners, and the Speaker of the Senate.

– Eight Honourary Consuls abroad.

– Twelve staff members of the Prime Minister's residences.

– Twenty-six appointments of Queen's Counsel.

– Fifty-four Judicial appointments.

– Forty-five appointments of Senior Public Servants—DM [Deputy Minister] level.

– Forty appointments of Public Servants to directorships of Crown Corporations.

– Twelve appointments of auditors.

– Four appointments to Royal Commissions or Commissions of Inquiry.

– Two appointments of Lieutenant-Governors.

– 217 Reappointments of incumbents.

Using the 550 *very political discretionary appointments* [emphasis added] as a base, the appointments broke down as follows:

Male:	73.7%
Female:	25.4%
Anglophone:	76.7%
Francophone:	22.5%
Ethnic:	10.2%

	Percent of Discretionary Appointments	Percent of the Canadian Population
Yukon	.08	.08
NWT	.02	.01
B.C.	11.20	11.40
Alberta	5.70	9.30
Sask.	2.50	4.00
Manitoba	3.60	4.20
Ontario	36.60	35.50
Quebec	20.10	26.00
PEI	1.90	.40
N.B.	5.10	2.80
N.S.	6.10	3.40
Nfld.	6.10	2.30

APPENDIX 7

SINCERELY, ERIK

Three months before the Conservatives won the 1984 election, partly on the promise of Brian Mulroney to end the Liberal abuse of patronage, the party had well-advanced plans for their own purge of top appointmentees and their replacement with Tory loyalists. In these secret memos, deputy leader Erik Nielsen informed the prime minister of the coup to take effect within sixty days of taking office; the addenda provided an intimate glimpse of the party dividing the spoils. Nielsen presented a different version in his 1989 autobiography, The House Is Not a Home: *"I had thought that we were going to clean up politics once and for all," he wrote, "but for some people it was clear that the intention was simply to clean up."*

PROGRESSIVE CONSERVATIVE PARTY OF CANADA
PARTI PROGRESSISTE-CONSERVATEUR DU CANADA

FOR THE LEADER'S EYES ONLY

May 25, 1984.

MEMORANDUM TO: Hon. Brian Mulroney, P.C., M.P.
FROM: Hon. Erik Nielsen, P.C., M.P.

Unless otherwise directed by you, it is my intention to proceed immediately with the Appointments process as herein outlined.

Throughout, I am assuming certain priority objectives that you wish to achieve and be perceived as characterizing your administration in the first stage.

1. Economic management and Parliamentary accountability
2. Industrial revival–jobs
3. Trade expansion
4. Technological opportunities
5. The resurrection of cooperative federalism
6. External affairs

There would, of course, be subsequent objectives which you will wish to pursue which would be reflected by later changes.

APPOINTMENTS ADVISORY COMMITTEE

To plan the process for change I intend to implement with one or two minor exceptions the "Nomination Model" presented to you for approval by Finlay MacDonald and Peter Harder. This includes the establishment of a small Appointments Advisory Committee composed of Finlay MacDonald, Guy Charbonneau and Janis Johnson. You would probably want to add Norm Atkins and perhaps others post election day.

SECRETARIAT TO ADVISORY COMMITTEE

This committee is to be assisted by a small secretariat of five persons. David Dyer will propose the names of these persons who would be drawn from existing Ottawa resources so that, when selected, they could carry on their work, in training, in addition to their regular jobs. The Secretariat would eventually be located in the P.M.O. to maintain liaison with the Chairmen of Provincial Advisory Committees. The five regional groupings in the Secretariat will be Atlantic, Quebec, Ontario, Prairies and British Columbia. Dyer will provide job description and suggested compensation prior to recommendation.

PROVINCIAL CHAIRMEN

I believe we should now, in the utmost confidence, identify the Provincial Chairmen so that they can be in place and prepared to function on day one. We would make them aware now of what as expected of them as to methodology and the qualifications and balance we expect from their provincial committee members. They would come to Ottawa immediately following the election for extensive briefings. They would bring with them their recommendations, for your approval, of those persons they would like to see serving on their respective provincial committees. Under no circumstances would they discuss the matter with anyone prior to your approval of their nominees. There should be a member from each provincial caucus on the provincial committee.

GOVERNOR-IN-COUNCIL APPOINTMENTS

(a)   Deputy Ministers

Changes or reassignments in certain key departments would follow immediately the swearing in of your Cabinet. I have in mind the following for the first stage—others would follow:

(i)   Finance
(ii)   Treasury Board
(iii) External Affairs (Under-Secretary)
(iv)   Energy
(v)   Revenue (Income Tax and Customs and Excise)

(vi)   DRIE (Industry and Commerce)
(vii) Agriculture
(viii) International Trade
(ix)   Science and Technology
(x)   Employment and Immigration
(xi)   Transport

The new Deputy Minister would come from the existing public service, or very highly recommended <u>senior</u> provincial bureaucrats and possibly the private sector. I believe that it is necessary to proceed as far as we possibly can now to identify these persons. In this regard, I have commenced a collation of the recommendations of our caucus critics. In addition, I propose to put in place a small committee of three professionals to commence this urgent work.

Included in the first stage changes would be certain A.D.M.s [Assistant Deputy Ministers] in the foregoing key departments. These are as follows:

(i)   Finance—Associate Deputy Minister
(ii)   Treasury Board – Deputy Secretary Personnel and
                        Collective Bargaining
(iii) External Affairs – Deputy Minister (Marchand)
                        – Ambassador to Washington
                        – Ambassador to the United Nations
(iv)   DRIE – Associate Deputy Minister

I will be suggesting others after my review of critic reports has been completed.

In addition to the two HOP [Head of Post] changes suggested in External, which will signal the importance of changes in policy direction you will be making, I would also plan now for the replacement of Jamieson in London, Dupuy in Paris, Benson in Dublin, Béchard in New Orleans, Danson in Boston and Steers in Japan.

Unless you direct me otherwise, I will assume you approve and will proceed with planning for the identification of potential nominees.

(b)   "Other" G.I.C. Appointments

Here the question arises as to what appointments should be planned to be made within the first sixty days with or without the benefit of input from the provincial committees. The assumption has been that it would take approximately 60 days for provincial committees to be in operation. I believe that by identifying the provincial chairmen now, this time lag can be substantially shortened.

I would suggest that no announcements of any changes be made in this category within the first week. Needless to say, if you announce the changes I have already suggested, it will take a week or two for the tremors to subside. There is one exception and that is C.D.I.C. I propose an immediate replacement of [Joel] Bell and [Maurice] Strong. It goes without saying that [Senator Jack] Austin goes. The recruitment prior to the election, of proposed heads of the remainder of the crown corporations and agencies would, in my view, be dangerous. C.D.I.C. is the obvious exception.

One other key area where change should be effected immediately is P.C.O. [Privy Council Office]. I propose that Osbaldeston remain. Both Deputy Secretaries (Operations and Planning) however, should be changed. I will proceed to identify proposed replacements unless otherwise directed by you.

I have spoken with Bill Jarvis. He has agreed to assist. I propose, initially, to have him focus on Staffing and, once that is under control he will assume direction of Appointments planning. In both cases, directly responsible to me. This should free me to concentrate on the vital work of machinery.

Erik

ADDENDUM—ONE

NAC [National Appointments Committee] Meeting #3
Friday, November 30, 1984, 8 a.m.
MINUTES

Attendance: N[orm] Atkins was unable to attend.
L. O'Connor took minutes.
D.A. [David Angus, president, PC Canada Fund.]
E.N. [Erik Nielsen, deputy national leader.]
B.R. [Bernard Roy, Quebec chair campaign committee.
Later Mulroney's chief of staff.]
P.W. [Peter White, Appointments chair.
Later Mulroney's principal secretary.]
K.S. [Kay Stanley, women's issues adviser.
Sister of Marjorie LeBreton, later Mulroney's appointments secretary.]

E.N. informs NAC that P.M. would like 50 appointments per week, until the backlog is eliminated.

Returning Officers:
General agreement was to wait for a decision on redistribution of electoral boundaries before discussing the appointment of new returning officers. Discussion of returning officers put over to first meeting in 1985.

I. PENDING BUSINESS

1) Advisory Council on the Status of Women
    D.A. suggests Denise Angers. He will provide C.V.
    B.R. brought up the sensitive nature of this appointment, and suggests that NAC 'red flag' this appointment and wait on it.

2) Standards Council of Canada
    Georges Archer appointed President (November 29, 1984).

3) Tax Court of Canada
    Donald Christie (Chief Judge) wishes to become Associate Chief Judge. B.R. suggests that Jean-Claude Couture be appointed Chief Judge. Should the Minister reduce the powers of the Tax Court, B.R. indicates the possible necessity of finding something else for Couture. NAC acknowledges this as a potential problem, but suggests we go ahead on Couture nonetheless.

4) Comptroller General
    Name of Lawrence Hanigan was raised. Jean Lanctôt suggested by the Québec PAC. E.N. suggests that the Canadian Organization of Management Consultants be approached for names. P.W. suggests Gordon Riehl, a senior C.A. who writes a column for *The Globe and Mail*. E.N. suggests Richard Geren, former president of IOC now living in Oromucto (P.M. thinks highly of his management ability). NAC suggests the desirability of a female. E.N. to send some information to P.W. regarding a French Businesswoman from Toronto; Lise Chartrand was also mentioned.

5) Canadian Commercial Corporation
    B.R. mentions Guy D'Avignon, but P.M. may have something else in mind. D.A. to look into a few names, including Mr. Tooley. NAC discussed the difficulty of persuading successful business people to take this position. The name of Fred McCaffrey was also suggested.

6) Canadian Security Intelligence Service
    D.A. suggests Cliff Kennedy, but he is not experienced in security.

E.N. suggests Bill Palk, a retired, fit, active Winnipeg lawyer experienced in security. E.N. also suggests Richard Rohmer. P.W. to check with Hon. Elmer MacKay, and have him contact Mr. Barr regarding candidates with a background in military intelligence. K.S. to check High Flyer's list.

7) Cape Breton Development Corporation
Appointment of Dr. William Shaw has been put on hold as the Chairmanship is not vacant.

8) International Joint Commission
NAC agrees to send the name of Hon. Davie Fulton as a formal recommendation to P.M. Since the present vacancy was held by a francophone, NAC agrees to propose a francophone to replace Blair Seaborn in December, 1985.

9) Public Archives
P.W. to get suggestions from Quebec Archivists Association.

10) Petro Canada
Recognize the need for high profile people to fill these prestigious positions. NAC suggests soliciting firm recommendations from PACs [Provincial Appointment Committees]. P.W. will check the possibility of reducing the number of Public Service positions (Remove Tellier and Stewart, not Cohen). (Handwritten note: [Pat] Carney says keep both. But remove Cohen). D.A. and J.L. suggest Chester Johnson. Possibly add a Yukon Director. E.N. suggests Art Collin.

11) Supreme Court of Canada
Registrar (B. Hofley—$63 to $75K) is sick, but is to resume work in January, 1985. Note that Deputy Registrar may become Registrar. NAC suggests a lawyer from the Ottawa region, as salary is not too high (currently $58K). B.R. and D.A. to check with Bar Association and report back.

12) War Veterans Allowance Board
K.S. will check for possible women from High Flyers list. Norma Walmsley was suggested.

13) Canadian Livestock Feed Board
Hon. John Wise to send names. B.R. suggests P.W. consult with Clement Vincent. J.C. Pelletier should contact U.P.A. and Coop. Fed.

14) Chief Pensions Advocate
NAC agrees with name of André Lemieux suggested by Hon. George Hees.

15) National Arts Centre Corporation
Pierre Boutin appointed as Chairman (November 29, 1984).

16) Canadian Livestock Feed Board Advisory Committee
P.W. to consult Hon. John Wise. Ask U.P.A. (Clement Vincent).

17) Canadian Centre for Occupational Health and Safety
NAC suggests consultation with PACs. K.S. suggests Ann Elizabeth (Betty) Smith (Toronto) and Karen Goldenberg.

18) Canada Ports Corporation
Hon. Ron Huntington appointed Chairman (November 29, 1984).

19) Economic Council of Canada
Name of Galynn Bennett (Toronto) was suggested. B.R. to get P.M.'s views.

20) Restrictive Trade Practices Commission
Richard Holden appointed Vice-Chairman and member (November 29, 1984). E.N. points out that it is bad for morale in Ministry and in Caucus to be uninformed regarding an appointment. PACs will still continue to report directly to P.W., but PACs must inform their caucus member of all recommendations.

21) Canada-United States Permanent Joint Board on Defence
Hon. Allan Lawrence appointed Canadian representative (November 29, 1984).

22) Export Development Corporation
Put over. (Handwritten note: Clark's office—separate Chm & Pres.)

23) Canadian Security Intelligence Review Committee
Review Committee appointed (November 29, 1984).

24) National Capital Commission
Jean Pigott appointed member and Chairman (Nov. 29, 1984).

25) World Bank
P.W. reported the Hon. Michael Wilson is prepared to: (a) ignore Search Committee that has been set up, (b) move Inter-American Bank individual to the World Bank vacancy or, (c) take NAC suggestions. P.W. will consult him concerning Alain Gersten-Briand. E.N. suggests Pierre Lassande, an engineer and economic consultant to Hon. David Crombie.

II. NEW BUSINESS

26) Auditors
Put over.

27) PACs Status Report
L.O'Connor to provide accurate information.

28) Atomic Energy Control Board
K.S. suggested Dr. Nancy Elgie from Ontario, where there will be a vacancy in February 1985. For present Quebec vacancy, B.R. to report back.

29) C.B.C.
K.S. suggested Nancy Kent (Prince Albert), Suzanne Olaski (Saskatoon), Margaret Strongitharm (B.C.). D.A. suggested Bruce Ledain (Montreal). P.W. to consult with Edward DesRosiers, M.P. Hochelaga, as well as P.M. and Hon. Marcel Masse. D.A. questioned Archambault. Names of Roger Régimbal and Georges Valade were also suggested. E.N. reported that the Responsible Minister is to inform Caucus Representative on PAC of every appointment. Regional Secretary is to inform PACs of selected vacancies being considered by NAC.

30) Immigration Appeal Board
NAC agrees with John Weisdorf.

31) International Development Research Centre
Check Wardlaw as possible Chairman. K.S. to recommend possible females. Chairman should be appointed first.

32) National Parole Board
P.W. to report with additional vacancies sent to PACs. E.N. suggested Guy Marcous (54); but may replace Simmons (will not know for 6

months) P.W. to ask P.M. D.A. suggested Judy Hendin (to get C.V.).
J.L. suggested we consider unsuccessful candidates.

33) <u>Teleglobe Canada</u>
Suggestion was made to send this to BC and NS PACs. P.W. to check
with Hon. Sinclair Stevens and P.M. regarding need for Public
Servants. Names of Bob Lloyd and Peter Pocklington were suggested.

34) <u>National Farm Products Marketing Council</u>
P.W. to check with Hon. John Wise.

35) <u>Tariff Board</u>
Traditionally used to place a senior Public Servant. Put over.

36) <u>Tax Court of Canada</u>
Marcel Lambert was suggested by E.N.

37) <u>Federal Court of Canada</u>
P.W. to check with Hon. John Crosbie and with James Jerome.

38) <u>Canada Labour Relations Board</u>
Marie Marchand (Northern Ontario) was suggested by K.S.
P.W. to check with Hon. William McKnight.

ADDENDUM—TWO
[Sample letter sent to Chairs of Provincial Appointments Committees]

PROGRESSIVE CONSERVATIVE PARTY OF CANADA
PARTI PROGRESSISTE-CONSERVATEUR DU CANADA

CONFIDENTIAL

July 13, 1984

Dear

Brian Mulroney is as delighted as I that you will accept the responsibilities of which we spoke.

In the utmost confidence we are selecting those people in each province who will chair the Provincial Committees, which will consider and recommend the course of action we will take on a range of matters, particularly on the selection of capable people to serve a Mulroney Government.
I refer to Governor-in-Council appointments and your role as Chairman of the   Advisory Committee.

Immediately following the general election we will convene a meeting in Ottawa of provincial chairmen who, in company with members of the National Advisory Committee, will consider matters before us and the procedures we intend to follow.

So that you might have some advance knowledge, I attach, for your eyes only, a description of the "Appointments Process". It is the result of months of planning and it has met with the approval of the Leader, our Caucus and Party officials. It seeks to encourage the widest possible consultation while attempting to make decisions expeditiously.

You will likely have questions. Rather than telephone, I would ask that you write the Chairman of our Appointments Committee, Finlay MacDonald, P.C. Party Headquarters, 161 Laurier Avenue West, Ottawa, Ontario K1P 5J2. In this way we can benefit from the records of questions and answers so that we have as much prior clarification and understanding before we convene the all important first meeting.

I cannot over-emphasize the need for confidentiality. For instance, your first priority is the consideration you will give to the members you will recommend to serve on your committee, yet—you must not discuss this matter with them in advance because the final selection will be the Leader's. You are looking for outstanding people with good reputations, fair-minded, with time to devote to their responsibilities, and a knowledge of the human resources available in your province for these important positions. You will be in the best position to determine the size of your committee but as you will see from the briefing document they must be representative of all segments of the Party.

I send you my thanks and warm personal regards.

Sincerely,

Erik Nielsen

ADDENDUM

[Text of briefing document, "Appointments Process," referred to in above letter.]

June 1, 1984.

CHAIRPERSON—PROVINCIAL ADVISORY COMMITTEE

We seek, in the strictest confidence, a short list of nominations to take on this most important task:

1. The Leader—Prime Minister Designate—will establish for each province an Advisory Committee to recommend, advise and counsel him on an important range of subjects, not the least of which will be the nomination of capable people to participate in the affairs of the Government of Canada by accepting Governor-in-Council or Ministerial appointments.

2. The Provincial Advisory Committees will be comprised of highly respected men and women chosen for their understanding of the political process; their knowledge of the human resources in their province; the thoroughness and fair-mindedness of their considerations and the expeditious manner in which they deal with the tasks required of them.

3. The composition of these committees must command the respect of all elements of the Party and they must be prepared to devote, certainly initially, a great deal of time in the administration of the committees' affairs.

4. The process and methodology would be fully explained in a Briefing Manual and the work of the committees will be assisted and coordinated by a small secretariat in Ottawa.

5. The immediate objective is to identify those people who would accept the task of Chairperson. Immediately following the General Election they will meet in Ottawa for briefing meetings and submit their nominations for members of their committees. Under no circumstances would they discuss their future roles nor carry on any discussions relating to this matter until they meet as a group in Ottawa.

APPENDIX 8

THOU SWELL...

The following letters were written to Brian Mulroney by Gerald Doucet, an
Ottawa lobbyist and the brother of senior Mulroney staffer Fred Doucet.
Doucet was a partner of Government Consultants International, which was
active at the time in six controversial lobbying efforts involving offshore oil
firms and defence and transportation contracts.

August 25, 1987

CONFIDENTIAL

Dear Brian:

Re: Improving the Media's Coverage of You and the Government

Not many governments are re-elected in Canada, against an adversarially
hostile media, even when it's a government which has been as productive
as yours.

More and more I am convinced bold affirmative steps must be taken to
eradicate the media's hostility,—especially towards you.

Last Friday's outstanding editorial in the Globe provides a real timely
opportunity to launch such an effort during its afterlife, I think, and coinci-
dent with the start of the fourth year of your mandate.

The effort should be launched on several fronts.

First, via visits with publishers, editorial boards, and media managements.
Some of your most respected ministers such as Maz, [Don Mazankowski],
[Michael] Wilson, [Joe] Clark, [Perrin] Beatty, [Benoît] Bouchard,
[Lowell] Murray and [Bill] McKnight can handle a lot of this while empha-
sizing the effectiveness of the Mulroney leadership with specific catchy,
but real, illustrations. (Only yesterday, for example, the Saskatchewan
NDP were calling on you to use your conciliation skills to personally try to
settle the railway dispute). This would avoid any self-praise perception of
you by these media audiences. (I saw and heard Joe Clark in Halifax on
Sunday with several hundred people,—it was very effective.)

Second, ministers and MP's must spend much more time co-opting regional media. This is painfully obvious but is not generally being done.

Third, the _single_ most important aching requirement is for YOU, on a one-on-one basis, and in small groups, to spend time with the national "working" media, including with some of your perceived enemies. Remind them, firsthand, about the specific achievements of your government during this short three year period, and ask them (with the hurt and the injustice you sincerely feel) why they are so cynical and so hostile. "Is it because of something my Ministers or I have done to you personally?" Tell them you feel a great need "to get to the bottom of it."

Brian, you have huge personal charm; they could not leave unaffected other than in a positive way. And, at the very least, they would be greatly flattered.

The effort would be time consuming but it could make the difference in the re-election of the government. The media power in 1987 Canada is as infuriating as it is real. Acquiring their affection is probably not in the cards, but acquiring their respect, is. Excepting in 1968 the media had no affection throughout for Trudeau, but they had respect. That respect came through consistently in their reporting, etc.

Canadian media respect, plus your government's record, almost assures re-election.

The lack of media respect, despite your government's record, puts the government's re-election in serious question.

NOW may be the opportune time to initiate the Media Effort.

Sincerely,

Gerry

October 20, 1987

<u>CONFIDENTIAL</u>

Dear Brian:

The Government's communication program is the pits!

We have tremendous opportunities for strong perceptual positioning on issues of concern to voters.

So far, we are missing out on effectively telling the people of Canada what we have done for them on:

(a) the NDP's NATO position;
(b) the refugee legislation;
(c) the postal progress;
(d) Meech Lake; and
(e) the economy.

And, more seriously, we have lost most of the early rounds on Free Trade. We cannot stand another week on Free Trade like the last one.

Can we not now move to adding a more descriptive name other than "free trade", such as "Canada's Massively Bigger Marketplace"? And, can we not employ Canada's top-notch professional communications people and firms to advise how the Government can sell its popular achievements?

Sincerely,
Gerry

October 27, 1987

Dear Brian:

RE: Feedback from last Friday's address
<u>by the P.M. to the PC 500 Club</u>

1. "Gerry, how do we get the rest of the country to see what I saw today? If that could be made to happen he would be re-elected convincingly."

2. "This isn't the same guy I've been reading and hearing about during the last two years,—it can't be!"

3. "He's done so much for Canada but it's been so poorly told. Why can't the story get told?!"

4. "No one could speak like that without notes and not mean it."

5. "I had no idea that Mulroney was this good,—he's great."

6. "I have never felt as good about my country and party as I do today."

and

7. "This was the closest to Martin Luther King's <u>I Have a Vision</u> address which I have ever heard".

Congratulations.

Sincerely,
Gerry

December 7, 1987

Dear Brian:

I saw last Friday's Question Period on television. Your performance was absolutely masterful. Its context, delivery and tone were flawless. Ten out of ten on a very tough subject!

Not only was it totally Prime Ministerial but I know of no past Prime Minister who could have equalled it.

Warm congratulations.

Sincerely,
Gerry

APPENDIX 9

SINCERELY, BRIAN

Prime Minister Brian Mulroney maintained a lively and often contentious correspondence with media baron Conrad Black during his time in office; the exchange of views seemed to provide both men with an opportunity to defend their record and clarify their thinking, while enjoying a spirited debate. In this letter to Black, the prime minister set out what was perhaps the most comprehensive version extant of his reasons for launching the Meech Lake constitutional process.

PRIME MINISTER—PREMIER MINISTRE

<u>Personal</u>

July 9, 1991

Mr. Conrad M. Black
Chairman and Chief Executive Officer
Argus Corporation Ltd.
10 Toronto Street
Toronto, Ontario
M5C 2B7

Dear Conrad,

I had intended to respond to an article you wrote in the *Financial Post*, dated February 6, 1991, in which you predict the imminent demise of Canada. I resisted the impulse until recently when I happened to see you on television repeating the substance of your earlier comments.

You blame our difficulties on: Meech Lake, Bill 178, and inadequate leadership by me.

I. An appropriate question is why was Meech Lake necessary in the first place?

Because the decision to proceed with patriation over the opposition of the Quebec National Assembly in 1981 was ominous. In the words of Senator Ernest Manning, "the feeling of betrayal would be a ticking time bomb" that would one day badly damage Canada, unless it were corrected in time.

In a recent analysis *The Economist* observes:

"the upshot [of the decision to proceed without Quebec] was that, by the mid-1980s, Canada had a constitution that was neither fish nor fowl in terms of political philosophy. Parliament was sovereign, and Canadians' rights were supposedly protected by a Charter of Rights; yet that Charter could be overridden by a simple declaration of a provincial legislature. The price of this dubious advance was disaffection in Quebec on a grand scale: the feeling there was not just that Quebec had lost powers but that the new constitution had been imposed on it by English-speaking Canada without its consent."

In 1985, a federalist party was elected in Quebec, in part on a platform of endorsing the Canadian constitution, if five conditions could be negotiated.

To this end, the Premiers met in Edmonton in 1986 and unanimously agreed to launch a 'Quebec Round' to ensure Quebec's signature on the Constitution, followed by negotiations to deal with other outstanding issues.

The federal government responded to this wish by initiating discussions, meetings and, ultimately, negotiations that resulted in the Meech Lake Accord in 1987.

The federal government did not arbitrarily begin a constitutional debate. When faced with a request from Quebec seeking to join willingly the constitutional family, the Government of Canada was honor-bound to ascertain whether this objective was achievable and, if so, remedy the serious flaw of 1982.

Meech Lake was designed to correct this feeling of injustice, which is perhaps why you were one of its early and enthusiastic supporters. In August 1988, while addressing the annual Fraser Institute forum you stated:

"I am in favour of it [Meech Lake Accord], although it has imperfections as many have commented on. I think it would be a very great plus if Quebec would subscribe to the Constitution."

Only much later did you appear to change your mind.

Each provision of Meech had, at one time or another, in some similar form, been offered to the provinces by my predecessor. Indeed, in some instances he had offered much more; in others, less.

Meech Lake therefore brought the nation together in unity. It was overwhelmingly supported by all three political parties in the House of Commons and endorsed unanimously by the ten Premiers. As the Honourable J.W. Pickersgill, one of Canada's most distinguished statesmen and Liberals, wrote:

"The miracle of Meech Lake is that it protected completely the national interest while accommodating some legitimate concerns in regard to the Province of Quebec. This was the agreement P.E. Trudeau worked so recklessly to undermine."

When, at the urging of Premier Wells, the Newfoundland legislature revoked support for Meech Lake granted by the previous legislature, I worked with all the premiers and got unanimity again. That night—June 9, 1990—Premier Bourassa made the following statement:

"Since 1981 when Quebec was excluded from the Canadian Constitution, Canada was only a country in law. From now on, with ratification of the Meech Lake Accord, for all Quebecers, Canada will be a country in fact—a real country."

Clearly, this was a most encouraging commitment to a new degree of unity for Canada. Quebec was being bound irrevocably to Canada by freely and formally signing the Canadian Constitution.

Little wonder Jacques Parizeau and the separatists were outraged. Their worst nightmare had just occurred—Canada *had* accommodated Quebec on reasonable terms and French Canadians were pleased the matter was finally resolved.

Twelve days later, the Premier of Newfoundland repudiated his signed undertaking and cancelled an historic vote scheduled that afternoon in the Newfoundland Legislature. Because all three Manitoba leaders had, earlier, publicly signalled their intention to pass Meech, that decision in Newfoundland sabotaged a genuine attempt to achieve durable constitutional unity for Canada.

In a recent profile on the Newfoundland Premier in one of your magazines, *Saturday Night*, Richard Gwyn reveals that the Premier unilaterally cancelled the historic vote of the legislature at the last moment because, contrary to his wishes, it would have carried. How inconvenient democratically elected legislatures can be!

It is quite remarkable that you could have written such a piece with no direct reference to either Messrs. Trudeau, Chrétien or Wells. They deserve appropriate mention for the destruction of Meech. Indeed, they argued it could be rejected with no consequences for Canada.

My perception was quite different. I stated it clearly on June 21, 1990 in my extemporaneous remarks to the Newfoundland and Labrador House of Assembly:

"Nobody can predict the future, but I know this: that if Mr. Parizeau gets a chance to have a referendum, that on referendum night, as you, every one of the Members of this House of Assembly right here and all the rest of us too, on that night when you're sitting there with your families and your children, one thought is going to go through your mind, and that thought is, when you're looking at your kids, is: Do you mean to tell me that we could have avoided all of this through Meech Lake? And I can also tell you that night, if that night were ever to come, the terms of Meech Lake are going to look very, very reasonable indeed to every Member of this House of Assembly and every House of Assembly across Canada."

One of Canada's most senior journalists, W.A. Wilson, recently noted that:

[Prime Minister Mulroney] "fought tooth and nail to secure constitutional amendments designed to end the constitutional isolation of Quebec arising from the 1981-82 changes when the Liberal government had mistakenly assumed that overwhelming support from the large and powerful bloc of French Canadian politicians in Ottawa would offset the opposition of René Lévesque's separatist government."

Gordon Robertson, Mr. Trudeau's Secretary to the Cabinet for Federal-Provincial Relations said that the decision to reject Meech Lake was a tragedy:

"It was seen in Quebec as a rejection of very reasonable proposals advanced by a federalist government in Quebec to repair the open wound of 1982. Almost no one in Quebec had believed, until that last week in June, 1990, that their proposals would not be accepted. The collapse of the accord fuelled the fires of resentment and of separatism. It made inevitable the crisis we see today."

II. In 1977, the Parti Québécois government of Mr. Lévesque enacted Bill 101, which included a provision regarding language of signage. This provision was challenged and, ultimately, struck down by the Supreme Court of Canada. In response to this decision, Premier Bourassa enacted Bill 178, which loosened the restrictions that had been enacted in 1977 by the Parti Québécois.

When Bill 178 was introduced, Premier Bourassa invoked the notwithstanding clause, a pernicious provision of the 1982 Constitution accepted and introduced by Prime Minister Trudeau.

This provision unique in constitutions of the world—has been branded as "evil" and "iniquitous" by scholars to the point that Mr. Trudeau himself has acknowledged his grave error in consenting to its inclusion in a document designed to protect individual rights and freedoms.

(In fact, an American analogy to Canada's 1982 result would be a constitution actively opposed by the states of New York, Texas, Florida and California—the rough population equivalent of Quebec vis-à-vis Canada—and which contained a provision authorizing the legislature of Mississippi, among others, to override the U.S. Supreme Court decisions on civil rights.

You can safely conclude that an American President who accepted such a bizarre constitutional arrangement would have swiftly been driven from office in a wave of derision and contumely.)*

---

* Contumely: Rude language or treatment arising from haughtiness or contempt. — Ed.

Incidentally, it is important to note that Premier Bourassa came under enormous public pressure to invoke the notwithstanding clause following the Supreme Court decision on Quebec's sign law. Of all the Quebec media, none urged he follow that course with greater stridency that the influential Quebec daily *Le Soleil*, which I believe you own.

III. You say I bear a "heavy responsibility for the impending collapse of the federal state".

I do not share your extreme pessimism about the future of Canada but I did inherit a festering constitutional situation and sought to solidify Canadian unity by ensuring Quebec's support of the Constitution, (the "very great plus" you mentioned, above) by the modest amendments of Meech Lake.

Exercising political leadership actually requires some degree of vision and courage—which help both to understand the unfolding of history and to withstand the criticism of contemporaries until that verdict is rendered.

I have sought to provide strong and beneficial leadership to Canada. Our initiatives to strengthen the economy, mismanaged and abused for two decades by the previous government, have been met with unremitting hostility by opposition parties, interest groups and much of the Canadian media. We have had to fight for every inch to advance the cause of Free Trade, Tax Reform, GST, Deficit reduction, Privatization and Deregulation.

Our international initiatives designed to strengthen the Canada-US relationship, enhance the Commonwealth, support NATO, help create La Francophonie and enter the war to resist aggression in the Persian Gulf were achieved because of our beliefs and our resolve to defend them, often in the face of ferocious opposition in the House of Commons and elsewhere.

Our constitutional policies were, on two separate occasions, crowned with unanimous consent by all eleven governments of Canada only to founder, at the last moment, because a Premier broke his word and refused to bring the agreement forward for a vote of his legislature.

For these efforts and results you seem to think I am blameworthy. So be it.

But I was elected to lead. That is what I have done and will continue to do.

As the *Montreal Gazette* pointed out in a major editorial a few weeks ago:

" . . . this is the Prime Minister who has brought us the Canada-U.S. free trade deal, a complete reversal of one of the fundamental elements of Canadian politics for more than a century. This is the Prime Minister who very nearly won passage of the Meech Lake accord, which in many ways was another reversal of widespread basic assumptions. This is the Prime Minister who has presided over a truly dramatic shift in the federal government's philosophy, as expressed in its tax policies and its social spending. And this is the Prime Minister who persuaded Quebec to reverse completely its century-old boycott of the Conservative party. One does not have to agree with all or indeed any of these policies to note that they all represent bold and often controversial change in the fundamental nature and structure of the country. If a leader is one who tackles sacred cows and charts new directions, Mr. Mulroney qualifies." So much for the past. Much more important, is the future of Canada.

For my part, I remain confident we can still achieve unity and constitutional agreement. My every effort is committed to this objective.

It will not be easy and the opposition will be great. I would, of course, be grateful for any support you can give us at this crucial moment in our history.

With best personal regards,
Brian Mulroney

Conrad Black's response to the Mulroney letter of July 9, 1991 provided a deeper insight into the animated and complex relationship between the two men. The verbal thrust and parry shows that neither was able to resist defending against the perceived slights of the other, while Black demonstrated in this correspondence his role of devil's advocate to Mulroney.

Hollinger Inc.
10 Toronto Street
Toronto, Canada
M5C 2B7

July 15, 1991.

The Rt. Hon. M. Brian Mulroney, P.C., M.P.,
House of Commons,
OTTAWA, Ontario
K1A 0A2.

Dear Brian:

Thank you for your formidable letter of July 9. Particularly given the heavy preoccupations of your office, it was flattering to hear from you so comprehensively.

You will appreciate that I have a number of comments, which I hope will clarify my views satisfactorily on the important matters that we are discussing.

I do not believe that it is a fair comment on my article of February 6 in The Financial Post that I "predict the imminent demise of Canada." I stated clearly that, "my own preference remains . . . . for a bicultural federal state guaranteed by an adequately endowed federal jurisdiction and based on the principle of reciprocal respect for sufficiently numerous minorities, and not on coercion." I know that you would not take issue with that.

I did not see my own appearance on the television programme that you refer to, but I recall going to some lengths to express my high regard for you personally and my reluctance to criticize in any way your performance in these difficult times. I assume that those remarks, in the midst of which the comments that you objected to were inserted, were not omitted from the telecast. The only significant criticism I expressed of you on television was that the federal government had not so far succeeded in explaining to English Canada that Bill 178 was prompted by demographic fears and was not intended to be the insult to English-speaking Canadians that millions of them thought it was, and that the federal government had also been unsuc-cessful in explaining to French-speaking Quebeckers that the failure to adopt the Meech Lake Accord was not intended to be a rejection of French Canadians but was largely prompted by a misunderstanding of the Government of Quebec's motive in invoking the notwithstanding clause and adopting Bill 178 in respect of bilingual external commercial signs.*

Maurice Duplessis said in 1957 that the only circumstances in which Quebec would be tempted to secede would be if it felt itself rejected by the rest of Canada. In the aftermath of the non-adoption of Meech Lake, there was a good deal of that sentiment which, I believe, would have been miti-gated by a more effective programme of the federal government to explain the concerns of English- and French-Canadians to each other. That remains my view.

In addition to expressing my constitutional preferences in The Financial Post on February 6, I also expressed a slight degree of hopefulness that the "demise of Canada" could be avoided, as well as my view that if it could

---

* This sentence has 137 words. One summer when David Peterson, the Ontario premier, was trying to brush up on his French, he went for a holiday to Quebec and took with him the French edition of Conrad Black's book on Maurice Duplessis. "There were so many compli-cated words in it that I had to have a French dictionary constantly at my side," he recalled. "But then I discovered that I couldn't under-stand the words in English either, so I ended up reading Conrad's book between two dictionaries — French *and* English."—Ed.

not be avoided, Canada's future could still be more politically satisfactory than the recent past.

It has seemed to me for many years that Canada has two possible political futures that are vested with any grandeur or any possibility of achieving our national potential. The one that you and I have always believed in is the preference I stated on February 6 and quoted above. Failing that, better than muddling along with what I described on February 6 as, "this degrading, excruciating, hopeless constitutional minuet," gradually approaching Yvon Deschamps's famous one-time joke of, "an independent Quebec in a strong Canada," would be for Canada, apart from Quebec, to consider how it can best help to assure that English-speaking North American democratic capitalism continues to be, without imperialism or oppression, the foremost political and economic influence in the world. The whole question of our status vis-a-vis the United States will become a matter of more and more public attention in this country as Canadians contemplate the disparity of taxation levels, cost of living and standard of living between this country and the United States.

On the questions that you put and answered in your letter, I agree that some arrangement by which Quebec would subscribe to the Constitution of Canada was and is desirable, as I said at The Fraser Institute in May 1988. I do not agree that any injustice was done to Quebec by the federal government and the other nine provinces making an arrangement among themselves, because I do not accept that Levesque's government was negotiating in good faith towards an agreement in 1982. I have written on several occasions, including in Saturday Night in September 1990, that I shared a good many of your reservations about the arrangement that was made on that occasion.

It is not the case that I was ever an "enthusiastic" supporter of Meech Lake. I was a wary supporter as long as I thought it was a solution and a definitive adherence by Quebec to some recognizable version of federalism. When Bill 178 came down, I changed my views in a manner that, I believe, Peter White explained to you and Mila, and my change of opinion on the subject was indicated in a series of articles in the Financial Post later in 1989. So your assertion, "Only much later did you appear to change your mind," is rather incomplete.

I will not be portrayed as defending the conduct of Premier Wells. I have condemned his performance in terms much more robust than you implied in your letter of July 9, especially in my lengthy article in Saturday Night in September 1990. In the same article and on other occasions, I have expressed substantial criticism of Trudeau's performance in 1982. It is inaccurate for you to express astonishment that I "could have written such a piece" (as that of February 6) "with no direct reference to . . . . . .

Chretien," since in that piece I described him as sufficiently "fatuous" that he is now "unfit for return to high public office." I know and have a high regard for Jack Pickersgill, Bill Wilson and Gordon Robertson and have discussed this subject at length with Gordon, but I happen, in this case, not to agree with them.

On your second numbered point concerning Bill 178, my condemnation of the notwithstanding clause has been at least as violent as yours, and my view that it should be repealed "in matters of defined fundamental human rights" was re-stated in the February 6 article. I am especially interested that, "Mr. Trudeau himself has acknowledged his grave error in consenting" to the notwithstanding clause in 1982. He has always told me that he had no choice in the matter, as he was going to be deserted by Bill Davis and Richard Hatfield, the only premiers who were then supporting him on the amending formula. Whether we would have been better at that stage to have abandoned the whole process of constitutional reform, considering the promises that the federal government had made in the referendum campaign in Quebec, is not as clear to me as it appears to be to you. My own view, which I have published on several occasions, is that we should endeavour to trade a scaling back of the notwithstanding clause for a greater provincial input in the composition and jurisdiction of the Senate. In any case, I am no defender of the 1982 arrangement and agree now, and have done so publicly, with most of what you wrote about it in your letter.

I am afraid we part company on the last paragraph of that section, at the top of your sixth page. It is no excuse that Robert Bourassa "came under enormous public pressure to invoke the notwithstanding clause following the Supreme Court decision on Quebec's sign law." On your second page, you record that, "In 1985, a federalist party was elected in Quebec." You know better than I how ambiguous a federalist Robert Bourassa is, but he was also elected on a platform pledged to the repeal of the existing signage legislation and the restoration of officially tolerated bilingualism. He has principally himself to blame for the accumulation of the pressure you refer to, and as you state elsewhere in your letter, "exercising political leadership actually requires some degree of vision and courage." Bill 178 effectively sunk the Meech Lake Accord, which makes your letter expressing sympathy for the Premier of Quebec, in these circumstances, especially implausible. The implications of such a curtailment of freedom of expression as Bill 178 constitutes are very serious and I don't think you adequately addressed them, in 1989 or in your letter of July 9.

You correctly describe the editorial stance of Le Soleil, under the leadership of a man whom you congratulated me on hiring, whom you named to the Spicer Commission and, I believe, considered for a high judicial appointment. He is, of course, entitled to his views, as are all our publishers, but because I dissented so strenuously from this particular opinion, I took the unusual step of publishing two signed dissenting views of my own in Le Soleil and was widely pilloried in nationalist circles in Quebec for my trouble. Without being self-righteous, I believe I discharged my responsibility as a proprietor without any damage to my good relationship with the publisher in question.

On your third and last numbered point, you appear to believe that I am opposed to "vision and courage," referred to above, and to your concept that you "were elected to lead." Nothing could be further from the truth. You cannot possibly have forgotten the extensive financial and editorial support that I have given and generated for you over many years. I have not wavered in my positive personal and political opinion of you, although I have never considered our friendship as requiring me to dissemble on the rare occasions of important principle such as this one, where I disagree with you.

I think that a huge number of non-Quebeckers will support a solution that is durable and retains a functioning federal state. The early parts of the Allaire Report confirm that Quebec did not consider the Meech Lake Accord such a solution, but only an important step towards the achievement of Quebec aspirations. If these aspirations and those of non-Quebeckers are reconcilable in a workable federal framework, I will rejoice in that fact as much as anyone and do anything I can to help it come to pass. If not, there are survivable destinies available to all sections of the country, preferable, in my view, to a continuation into absurdity of the contemporary constitutional wrangling. The Economist, from which you approvingly quoted in your letter, concluded its Canadian summary: "Sooner or later Canadians are going to become Americans. Too bad." It need not be bad nor inevitable, but that fate, properly negotiated, would be preferable to emasculating the federal government and carrying on with a ludicrous imposture of a country.

Few of our countrymen would have greater sympathy for the difficulties of the position that you occupy than I do. We do not entirely agree, but you would not suggest that my views on the Canadian situation were formulated flippantly or in any absence of good will or serious research. In all cases short of my conscientious inability to do so, you will have my "support . . . at this crucial moment in our history."

My very best wishes.

Yours sincerely,
Conrad

CMB/jea

INDEX